"And I looked, and, behold, a whirlwind came out of the north, a great cloud, and a fire infolding itself, and a brightness was about it, and out of the midst thereof came the likeness of four living creatures. And this was their appearance: they had the likeness of a man."

Ezekiel 1:3—7

2500 years ago, Ezekiel may have seen a flying saucer; 20 years ago, a boatman in Puget Sound swore that he did. Today there are hundreds of sightings on record and there seems little doubt that some otherwordly phenomenon—whatever its exact nature—does occasionally stray into our part of the universe.

Noted UFO expert Paris Flammonde has amassed a wealth of documented material, and the result is the most impressive and authoritative history and analysis of Unidentified Flying Objects to date!

"If few things are demonstrated in the apparently perceivable universe, one is that UFO exist!"

Paris Flammonde

UFO
EXIST!

Paris Flammonde

BALLANTINE BOOKS • NEW YORK

Copyright © 1976 by Paris Flammonde

All rights reserved under International and Pan-American Copyright Conventions. Published in the United States by Ballantine Books, a division of Random House, Inc., New York, and simultaneously in Canada by Random House of Canada Limited, Toronto.

This book, or parts thereof, may not be reproduced in any form without permission.

Library of Congress Catalog Card Number: 75-42925

ISBN 0-345-33951-7

This edition published by arrangement with G. P. Putnam's Sons

Printed in Canada

First Ballantine Books Edition: June 1977
Eighth Printing: May 1993

How often have I said to you that when you have eliminated the impossible, whatever remains, *however improbable*, must be the truth.
—SHERLOCK HOLMES
The Sign of the Four

Contents

Acknowledgments

THE AUTHOR WISHES to express his gratitude to Jim and Coral Lorenzen, of the Aerial Phenomena Research Organization (APRO), and to Dick Ruhl, an investigator for the group, for data and the use of illustrative material and additionally to Mr. Lorenzen for valuable consultive contributions.

Assisting greatly in the preparation of this work, especially with respect to recent sightings, has been longtime ufologist Ted Bloecher. Indebtedness to Sylvia Meagher is noted for having put me in contact with him and for a stimulating exchange we had on the subject of this book.

Recognition is extended to Judy-Lynn del Rey for providing access to a number of informative volumes; to Dr. Eden Gray, again, for making available pertinent material from her extensive files; to W. E. Moser, FRAS, of Sydney, Australia, for his aid regarding the persistent and dedicated investigations of those "down under"; to Eileen Buckle, of the *Flying Saucer Review,* of England, for swift replies to relevant queries; and to F. G. Stoddard, PhD, for time taken to verify and clarify points relating to the Bonham, Texas, sighting.

Also, permission to reprint an article, given by the Washington *Star,* was very helpful.

The answering of certain questions and the supplying of specific information by H. Walsh, of the National Investigations Committee on Aerial Phenomena (NICAP), by Dr. J. Allen Hynek and Margo Metegrano, of the Center for UFO Studies, and the cooperation of Gene Moore and the Newspaper Department of the San Francisco Public Library, of the Reference Department of the Sacramento Library, of the General Services Department of the Tacoma Library, of William Donovan, head of the Newspaper Department of the Chicago Public Library, of most of the staff of the Newspaper Annex of the New York Public Library and of many persons in the Reference Department of its Forty-second Street branch, are deeply appreciated.

The assembling of illustrative material for a work of this magnitude was a long and arduous task; among those consulted were the Aerial Phenomena Research Organization (APRO), the University of Arizona, Gray Barker, Edward U. Condon, Bernard O'Connor, George W. Earley, George D. Fawcett, Daniel W. Fry, Gabriel Green, Richard H. Hall, Harcourt Brace Jovanovich, Inc., Fred Keziah, Paul Massa and the Columbus *Dispatch,* Donald H. Menzel, James W. Moseley, the National Aeronautics and Space Administration (NASA), Charles Shaughnessy, William Cunliffe, and John Taylor, of the National Archives (Modern Military Division, repository of all of the Project Blue Book files), Ray Palmer, August C. Roberts, the Seattle *Times,* Mrs. Ivan Sanderson and Adolph Heuer, Jr., of the Society for the Investigation of the Unexplained (SITU), the Smithsonian Institution, Lyle Stuart, United Press International (UPI), the United States Air Force, the Office of the Secretary of the Air Force, the United States Army Museum, Sam Vandivert, Karl L. Veit, of *Deutschen UFO/IFO Studiengesellschaft* (DUIST), Germany, and many other individuals, institutions, and organizations.

Lastly, it should be emphasized that while she makes unique contributions to all my books, in this particular instance they extend to editorial suggestions and advice regarding every phase of the manuscript's evolution, as well as to many other details too complicated and personal to mention. In any event, there is no way adequately to measure the encouragement, the patience, and the labor invested in this book by my beloved Marcia.

—PARIS FLAMMONDE

Introduction

UFO Exist! is a companion volume to its predecessor, *The Age of Flying Saucers*. It is hoped that it partially fulfills the promise of the subtitle of that book: "Notes on a Projected History of Unidentified Flying Objects." The earlier effort was the initial comprehensive, chronological exposition of the "modern age" of Undefined Sensory Experience (USE)—which, for the sake of convenience, is regarded as having begun on June 24, 1947, with the Kenneth Arnold sighting, and necessarily included not only detailed treatment of Unidentified Flying Objects (UFO) and "flying saucers" (FS), the distinction between which will be found in both books, but a great many of the earlier derivative expressions and repercussions. The first work was intended to convey the facts and fancies, the flavor and embellishments, of an extraordinary phase in the evolution of the mid-twentieth century, here and abroad.

In contradistinction, *UFO Exist!* is intended to accomplish four major purposes:

1. To offer for the first time a concise, sequential, consistently relevant history of Unidentified Atmospheric Phenomena (UAP), Unexplained Aerial Objects (UAO), and related Undefined Sensory Experience (USE) enigmas, which seems to have a logical correlation with what came to be known as Unidentified Flying Objects (UFO), beginning with the earliest pertinent records and continuing to the present date as achievement of this survey demanded that it be based upon original, and frequently unconsidered, sources, and, of singular

importance, that it be free of the incessant and
arbitrary allusions to artifacts, architecture, and
other remnants of previous stages of civilizations
scattered throughout the world, patently devoid of
any determinable connection with the subject under
examination;

2. To take the opening of the "modern age" and, by
cautious and thorough analysis of several of the
"classic" cases, weighing the contributions of various official and independent investigators, depict
the original incidents as explicitly as possible, and
offer the reader the most accurate data and the
widest range of hypotheses from which he might
draw his own inferences and conclusions;

3. To make inescapably evident that the contention
that "the age of flying saucers" or, more accurately,
of UFO, has diminished and dissolved into oblivion
is wholly false, despite the announced cessation of
all military and governmental interest in, and
activity regarding, UFO, which was a concerted
effort to promulgate such an impression;

4. To leave no doubt that the American citizenry has
been intentionally and deliberately deceived about
virtually every aspect of the most impenetrable
mystery of our time. From the day "the modern
age" commenced, it has been insulted and as-
saulted by an incredible indifference and/or ineptitude, even when many highly placed authorities
seriously suspected the unknowns to be interplanetary spacecraft. This attitude has been ubiquitously
and continuously demonstrated by a perpetual lack
of staff, technical equipment, general facilities, in-
teragency, interservice, and intragovernmental communication, as well as by programs designed to
avoid conscientious inquiry, to corrupt any objective
study, and to impugn the professional qualifications
and personal reputations of individuals—especially
ones employed in responsible or vulnerable positions—who reported sightings of unidentified flying, hovering, or grounded phenomena.

UFO Exist! is divided into three parts. By necessity,

being devoted to historical analysis, the opening is subjected to less demanding reportorial and scientific criteria than the following chapters. The nature of the original source material relating to events that ostensibly occurred hundreds, or thousands, of years ago makes such flexibility essential. On the other hand, the two succeeding sections concentrate on the experiences of exceptionally qualified observers—pilots, radar experts, aviation ground crews, and scientists.

The source notes with each chapter and three appendixes supply the reader with direct channels of immediate reference to data of special interest to him.

It is the author's anticipation that both the novice and the scholar will find this work stimulating, for if few things are demonstrable in the apparently perceivable universe, one is that *UFO exist!*

BOOK I

The Origin of UFO

1

The Renaissance

I can assure you that flying saucers, given that they exist, are not constructed by any power on earth.

> —President Harry S Truman press conference, April 4, 1950

"THE FLYING SAUCERS are back! They were all around Saylors Lake last night!" exclaimed the voice of a local acquaintance, almost before I got the telephone receiver to my ear. The caller was virtually shouting in the kitchen of her home, which was only a few miles from the semi-secluded colony that circled the eastern Pennsylvania pond.

"Did you see them?" I asked doubtfully, having heard every possible claim before. Besides, I had done a well-received book on Unidentified Atmospheric Phenomena earlier and had no intention of being caught up in that puzzle again.

"No, but lots of other people did. It wasn't over our house. It was at Saylors Lake," my informant emphasized.

"How many is lots?" I inquired. "A couple of persons who still cover their houses with hex signs and have no idea of how many worn-out satellites are still floating around the earth?"

"This is serious," insisted my caller. "About a dozen people really saw UFOs. You should look into it. These are responsible citizens."

"Very well, I will," I agreed, and rang off.

For me that March 1973, was the beginning of "the renaissance" of UFO activity in this country. Not that it had ever actually stopped, it had merely slackened.

And with the public's growing interest in several newer fields, attention had been diverted from the enigmas in the sky.

Initially, the world was stunned by Man's leap into space when Sputnik I hurtled toward the stars on October 4, 1957, followed by the first satellite inhabited by an Earthian, even if it was a dog named Laika, a month later in Sputnik II. On January 31, 1958, the United States joined the exercise, sending up the Explorer probe.[1]

Reality replaced the possible. The continuing space achievements completely fascinated the population; it was all of the science fiction and comic books turned into real life. It was on television every night with Walter Cronkite, Chet Huntley, and Howard K. Smith telling audiences of millions that this time they *could* believe their eyes. No one called this nonsense.

Yes, despite a number of years of constant sightings, the space sprint between the U.S.S.R. and the U.S.A., bringing us nearer and nearer to sustained orbiting, sky stations, and even possible trips to the moon, pushed reports of UFO encounters farther toward the media entirely. The *need*[2] of society, which helped in the creation of "the modern age of flying saucers," had slowly, but effectively, been filled—perhaps, for a time, erased—by the extraordinary achievements of Man and his machinery. Each year was a rung in the lunar ladder, and Man climbed straight to the moon. Even where there was a great question in the minds of many about UFO—if they did exist they were "out there"—but Apollos and Vostoks, astronauts and cosmonauts, were right here. And humans always root for the home team.

Only when walking on the moon became almost commonplace in the mind of the average man, about as exciting as a replay of last week's football game, did he renew his realization that the heavens were still filled with strange things. Things that weren't birds, planes, satellites, clouds, planets, or stars. That is, UFO.

Then came the renaissance, and my telephone call. "UFO Sighted in Area—Saylors Lake," read the heading of the center column of the local newspaper, which I purchased on the following day, Friday, March 2, 1973. The front-page story was a routine statement describing the episode of the previous evening. The tone of the piece suggested it had been written by someone lacking any familiarity with the subject, but the basic facts were presented.

Alan Pfeiffer, a young man, seems to have been the first to notice the aerial objects. They caught his eye at about seven-thirty in the evening, as he was walking home. Reaching there, he called them to the attention of his mother, Mrs. Shirley Pfeiffer, and the two sat and watched the UFO for a while before it was decided that the law should be notified.

The police were contacted at nine-thirty and told that "40 unknown circular objects"[3] (other sources quoted the witnesses as having counted thirty-four,[4] thirty-nine,[5] forty-two,[6] etc.), some red, some white, and "the rest were a configuration [sic],"[7] were wheeling around at approximately two thousand feet above the resort community.

"I was there for about thirty minutes and saw four objects passing from west to east," testified State Trooper Jeffrey Hontz. "My first assumption was that they were airplanes, but I didn't hear any noise coming from them. And they were so close to the ground that we should have been able to hear something if they'd been conventional aircraft.

"Some had white lights, some had blue, and some both," he recalled. "They looked like flying Christmas trees."[8]

"Each one had four very bright lights, with another light in the center of the saucer-shaped, silver bottoms," ran the account of thirty-eight-year-old Shirley Pfeiffer. "They didn't even make a whisper. We estimated their height [sic] at about 1,500 feet."[9] The number of objects was later corrected to thirty-four, and, additionally, she confirmed Officer Hontz's observation of blue lights on the UFO and that after a considerable period they "picked up a tremendous speed and went like the dickens until they were out of sight."[10]

It was quickly established that more than a dozen individuals witnessed the remarkable occurrence, and there was general agreement regarding the nature of the UFO and their activity. No one suggested that they might have been planes, as they were silent, they hovered, and otherwise performed contrary to normal aircraft.

Among the later viewers was Mrs. Jan Young, who counted twenty-five of the unknowns. "The first I saw appeared to be totally red until it got really close," she explained. "Then we saw it had four lights forming a circle with a blue light in the middle that was blinking on and off." [11]

Carlo Uccio also observed the UFO. "I saw five of the objects that night," he remembered. "They had bright lights at each corner and appeared to stand for a while and then they disappeared into the distance, some flying slowly and some traveling at tremendous speeds.

"I was just one of the gang of people who came out to watch when the commotion was going on and Trooper Hontz arrived. None of us had ever seen anything like that before," the fifty-six-year-old resident remarked.[12]

"We got a call that people were seeing these things and I drove over to check them out. As I scrambled out of my car, I saw this object right above me. I couldn't make out its shape, but I could quite easily see that it had four lights in the shape of a cross. I'm sure that the things were not airplanes. If they were, you would expect the colors to be normal red and green running lights. It was a very clear night and we had a good view," described Paul Flores, a member of the staff of a radio station in nearby Stroudsburg, Pennsylvania.[13]

Trooper Hontz summed up the unanimous "conclusion" of the sighters: "Don't ask me what they were."[14]

Bruce P. Frassinelli, an editor on a newspaper in Easton, who lives in Stroud Township, which is ten miles from the lake, offered an account of his own experience that night. Leaving home at eight in the evening, he noted an echelon of "rounded masses, maybe 10 times the size of . . . Venus on a bright, cloudless night." The UFO appeared to radiate "a bluish-white light with a pinkish glow."[15] The reporter said that they occasionally stopped and hovered, indicating the possibility of surveillance, and then moved along. His sighting lasted ten minutes.

The local Allentown-Bethlehem Airport representative, John Doster, chief of the Federal Aviation Agency's district office, suggested the objects might have been military planes. Yet, the Defense Department dismissed the possibility, supporting the unanimous opinion of the actual viewers.

Yet it wasn't that the government had changed its approach to UFO after a quarter of a century, as was evident immediately.

" 'I'm sure there's a simple answer to what you saw,' " the traditionally anonymous Air Force spokesman told Mr. Frassinelli, " 'there usually is, you know.' "[16]

As I sat at my desk staring at the local newspapers folded to the recent UFO stories, I recalled a World War II Air Force slogan I had once read: "The difficult we do immediately, the impossible takes a little longer." It certainly seemed to apply to the riddle of the "flying saucers," except that reaching a solution to them had taken a *lot* longer. In fact, it hadn't been found yet.

Twenty-six years had passed and UFO were still a mystery.

The Air Force, fully supported by the press, had taken a variety of positions during that period. It had ignored the problem, taken it very seriously at high levels, pushed it into a small corner under the name of some "project" with a staff of two or three very low-ranked personnel; it had gathered together scientific committees to study the subject and thrown out their recommendations on how the programs could be improved; it had finally found a university and a few technologists to conduct the ultimate investigation and issue the concluding whitewash report; and it had completely closed down all of its UFO efforts and flown away from the strangest situation to arise in the twentieth century.

Outside the service, and the unseen influences in government interested in how the situation was being handled, there were an amazing number of independent groups inquiring into sightings and attempting to establish the nature and origin of UFO. The Aerial Phenomena Research Organization (APRO), founded by Mr. and Mrs. L. James (Jim and Coral) Lorenzen, of Tucson, Arizona, in January 1952, was among the original efforts of this kind in the United States[17] and, as it is still very active, ranks as the longest continuously functioning one. Despite the fact that there were private investigations begun before it, most of which have been dissolved by now, because of its impact on the public and the pressure it has applied to the military and to Congress for information as to what was being done about UFO, the National Investigations Committee on Aerial Phenomena (NICAP), of Kensington, Maryland (formerly Washington, D.C.), founded in 1956 by Townsend Brown, and directed and made famous from shortly thereafter by Maj. Donald E. Keyhoe, must be regarded as the other of the two most important UFO groups still operating.[18]

Excitement over UFO has never been confined to this country, and the oldest group in the world, especially among those still viable, is the Australian Flying Saucer Bureau, of Sydney, begun about 1950–51, and now renamed the Unidentified Fyling Object Investigation Centre (UFOIC). Second position is probably held by Ouranos-France, which was established in 1951.

Unfortunately, considering that at one time there were at least three hundred investigation groups throughout a large number of countries, no interrelationship, not even channels for the exchange of information, was ever developed by the Air Force. Such productive collaboration was explicitly forbidden in the service, as a matter of fact.

Still, in spite of the collapse of many organizations and the abandonment of UFO research by certain valuable investigators, there are numerous active groups, and much research is being conducted.

Full credit for the decline of interest in "flying saucers" cannot be given to the military and other government agencies. There was a series of apparently quite unrelated events which aided in drawing the public's attention from the unknowns in the sky.

Now, according to my caller, according to a couple of smalltown gazettes, according to a handful of people—flying saucers were back! But, as the second day passed into a third, I received no further reports and saw no fresh stories of peculiar sightings. Then, on March 5, I picked up a small community newspaper— "UFOs Appear Again—but not just locally," it announced.[19] Saylors Lake had been revisited by the disks on the previous evening, according to resident Carlo Uccio, who had summoned the state police. He had seen four more unknowns, Mrs. Pfeiffer a dozen, and several other persons varying numbers of the objects. This time the UFO were gone when the law arrived, and Sgt. Emil Weber and Troopers Dennis McMahon and Robert Werts missed seeing them.

The pattern had begun to spread. Even to Africa, where President Idi Amin, of Uganda, claimed to have watched a UFO skim across Lake Victoria, pause, and then depart. His Excellency had the supporting testimony of several companions who viewed the "spectacular object covered with something like smoke"[20] glide down from the noonday sky onto the blue waters. "After some seven minutes," continued the report, "the object was seen lifting off like a rocket being fired but moving gently. When disappearing into the sky, the last portion of it was seen like the tail of a big snake."[21]

The final segment of this account is reminiscent of reports recorded in Texas and Kansas on successive days in July 1873, which are detailed later.* In any event, the incident occurred almost simultaneously to the Saylorsburg one, and also over a lake.

On March 21 the UFO returned to Pennsylvania, with the accounts becoming even more widespread,

---

* See Chapter 4.

and Stroudsburg, about a dozen miles north of Saylors Lake, was visited for the second time. The local press, in another brief front-page story, quoted the late Richard Wolbert, assistant chief of police, as having said he had watched a " 'teardrop-shaped' "[22] object cruising across the sky, visible between the " 'moon and the mountain going down toward Shawnee,' "[23] immediately before nine-thirty on the prior evening.

Southward, the Blue Mountain Control Center listed over two dozen telephone calls testifying to the presence of objects, "with different color lights,"[24] hovering above Bushkill Township. The chief of police there, Howard Kostenbader, told of seeing three UFO, over Route 512, a few minutes before his colleague in Stroudsburg had made his observation. The objects were silent, as usual, and the Bushkill officer estimated them to be operating at an altitude of approximately five thousand feet. Nearby, a couple of hours later, the Wind Gap Control Center, and the town's police, monitored UFO which swiftly altered their courses and speeds and flashed lights of various colors. Some witnesses saw the object in groups, especially of four, and others reported only one.

In addition to the communities mentioned, UFO were also watched in the skies of Easton, Nazareth, the townships of Palmer and Williams, and across the state line above Stewartsville, New Jersey, and surrounding villages.

The number of sightings increased and it became clear that at least certain sections of America were moving into a new age of flying saucers. This was especially confirmed when the rising interest began being turned to commercial use, as in the case of the restaurant near Saylors Lake which promised "NEW UFO'S" in its newspaper advertising.

The concentration* of observations in middle eastern Pennsylvania, and spilling into New Jersey, was unquestioned. "UFO researchers said March had turned into a 'flak' period—a time of numerous sightings,"

---

* *Concentration:* an unusually high number of sightings in one location, or over a larger geographical area in a very short period of time.

reported one journalist. It was obvious that he meant to suggest a large number of local accounts, that is, a "concentration," or that the press was giving far greater coverage than usual to the sightings, in which case the word he should have used was "flap," meaning above normal media attention. The importance of knowing the difference between "concentration" and "flap" lies in the fact that often a *single* peculiar sighting or alleged landing may stir up the reporters, who rush off, write their stories, and create a "flap," while a considerable number of less sensational sightings may occur in a given region, creating a "concentration," but be almost wholly ignored by the press. In any event, there were a lot of UFO around.

A dozen, or more, residents of Belfast, Pennsylvania, gave accounts of seven unknowns on Friday, March 23. "Six of them came together and formed a V. The other one was like a leader and was at the head of the formation,"[25] explained Denis deNardo, who had worked with planes during service in the Marine Corps. Responding to comments by an official at the Allentown-Bethlehem Airport that aircraft were circling the field that night, the witness' wife said that they "saw the planes, but these weren't planes. Whenever the planes came close to an object [UFO] it would zoom away."[26] In spite of police personnel speculating that local helicopters might have been misidentified, there was unanimous agreement among the spectators that they knew what they hadn't seen, even if they were mystified by what did fly over. Further, Floyd Stem, of Forks Township, stated that about fifty citizens in this area spotted the UFO and that what he and his neighbors saw "didn't act anything like planes or helicopters. They could say what they like, but they weren't helicopters," [27] he emphasized. His position was supported by local farmer David Davidson, who watched the glowing objects with several friends and agreed that they were not aircraft.

The county newspaper ran an editorial—"UFOs Return"—on March 26.*

---

* Unfortunately such coverage perpetuated the misunderstanding of the subject, leaving people still arguing whether

If the impression has been given that this was a geographically limited phenomenon, excepting the Ugandan account, this is far from the case. Reports were pouring into the offices of various police organizations and newspapers throughout the nation. The events north of Philadelphia were interesting, but they may not have compared with the activity in the Ozarks, where most of the two thousand citizens of Piedmont, Missouri, sighted unidentifiable pulsating lights at considerable altitudes, near rooftops, and skimming along Clearwater Lake. The similarity to the behavior of the Saylors Lake object is evident, and the physical descriptions recorded are even more so. For example: ". . . the light is red, then turns multicolored while spinning white, green, red and amber lights. It moves without a sound and is very fast."[28]

Perennial ufologist Hayden C. Hewes, director of the International UFO Bureau, of Oklahoma City, Oklahoma, took a field trip to Piedmont, accompanied by two associates, and investigated the case and interviewed the witnesses. One of the results of his visit was an account of the town's high school basketball coach, Reggie Bone, who told of observing a bright light that followed his automobile as he drove from the hamlet of Ellsinore on the way to Piedmont. He explained how the object moved along about three hundred feet from the road, hovered above a pasture for a while, and then abruptly hurtled away. At the time, Coach Bone was accompanied by five athletes from the school where he taught.

Beyond such verbal testimony, Hewes was shown a picture taken by Clearwater High School photography teacher Maude Jefferis, on March 14, of "an object shaped like a child's top or gyroscope hanging in the night sky."[29]

The new sightings revived certain features of the earlier period. One was a developing curiosity about the purpose of the UFO. A simple example of such speculation arose during the Ozark sightings when

---

UFO exist or not. Of course, we know that *unidentified* flying objects, and other aerial mysteries, *exist*; the problem is to discover what they are and where they originate.

Hewes commented that the region was "noted for its rich lead fields,"[30] and suggested that the unknowns were extraterrestrial craft conducting a mineralogical survey. The newspaper story was headlined: "Are UFOs Outer Space Miners?" [31]

Meanwhile, the activity on the border of New Jersey and Pennsylvania continued. Two, among many, UFO appearances occurred on the evening of Tuesday, March 27. A sighting of unknowns over Stroudsburg took place at seven o'clock, and others were witnessed in the skies of Marshalls Creek, a couple of miles away, an hour and a half later. In each case, the record indicates the presence of "round objects which were spinning in a circle, with a white light in the center flashing on and off and red and blue flashing lights around the outer edges."[32]

Another element of the "classic" pattern soon emerged: the alleged landing of a UFO. And the sighting of alien occupants!

Mr. and Mrs. Clyde O. Donahower and their family told local authorities that they saw a *manned* vessel descend to earth in a pasture on their farm, at Robesonia, Pennsylvania, and stay for nearly thirty minutes. They claimed that "stick figures"[33] were visible moving about within the craft, which had settled no more than a thousand feet from their house. Finally, the Donahowers called the police, but the UFO had gone before the law arrived.

Now, it was no longer a telephone call from an excited acquaintance, or vague reports drifting in from technically untrained people. It was not merely a minor concentration, or a small flap created by a few rural publications. It was these in part, certainly, but it was also clearly something more.

A genuine revival of ufologism, sightings of and fascination with UFO, was sweeping across the country, and, as was soon to be evident, around the world. As in the early days, in a great many instances the reports were of more than one object, observed by a few to a few hundred people. And there was a striking consistency in the accounts.

Countless characteristics peculiar to earlier UFO

performances filled the new descriptions—the maneuvers, the sudden changes of speed and course, the blinking lights, a general glow or a pulsating radiance at the center of the objects, the noiselessness, and their attraction to relatively small bodies of water.

There simply was no question: "flying saucers" were back.

Summer was filled with sightings and by October 1973 reports of them, appearing in newspapers and detailed by television commentators, were encouraging the more hesitant witnesses to reveal their experiences. Early in the month United Press International put the story of Sheriff Nathan Cunningham, of Obion County, Tennessee, on the wire. The officer admitted that he had decided to tell of his sighting because of the increasing number of calls being received by his staff from people who had seen UFO themselves. Cunningham described how he had viewed three unknowns, one of which buzzed his house at about one hundred miles an hour.

Officer Flanning Glover, of Colier, told of seeing alternating orange-to-white-to-orange lights, apparently while with companions. "I know it sounds fantastic, but it's true. If I was by myself, I'd say I was nuts," he remarked.[34]

In another incident, two boys, thirteen-year-old Jerry Smith and his nine-year-old brother Barry, were startled into taking refuge in a chicken house on their parents' farm, located in Tennessee's southwest Chester County, when a green UFO, flashing red lights, swooped down past them.

A few days later the public began to realize that the sightings in the border state only reflected an image of what was happening throughout the entire South. Mississippi, North and South Carolina, Georgia, and other areas were being inundated by UFO and tales of sightings. Among the many accounts coming from substantial and responsible individuals was a report of National Park Service Ranger Thomas E. Westmoreland, who studied a "large unidentified flying object hovering north of Tupelo [Mississippi] for 15 minutes."[35]

Meanwhile, the revival of interest in "flying saucers" rapidly revealed itself in other ways. A typical example of this enthusiasm was the New York Channel 9 presentation of the British-made series *UFO* every evening at five o'clock. Segments of many productions from London developed ufological themes, e.g., *Dr. Who, The Avengers,* etc., and home-flown varieties, such as Rod Sterling's *Twilight Zone, Outer Limits,* and, often in near-prime time, *Star Trek,* as well as other once-weekly programs, were being scheduled on stations throughout the country on a daily basis. Many independent outlets began featuring several such shows every evening.

Responding to the lure were the three commercial networks. They devoted thousands of late-night hours to presenting every motion picture with an extraterrestrial theme they could find. Scores of these films were to reappear during late 1973, and continue to be shown up to this time. The very best of them were often scheduled during maximum viewer periods, after the seven o'clock news and in the eleven-thirty slot, with the "classics" appearing in the middle of the evening.

The actual news attention accorded the phenomena was of even greater importance. In a single week all three advertising networks—ABC, CBS, and NBC—carried feature stories about individual sightings on both their national morning and evening news shows. Each did direct interviews with Charles Hickson and Calvin Parker, shipyard workers who were allegedly abducted by aliens, taken into a spacecraft from another planet, examined, and then released. The account represented the more extreme type of report and the media coverage proved such claims were being regarded as genuine news.

On October 16 the unknowns seemed to be concentrated in the Southeast. Among the states filing reports were Arkansas, Indiana, Louisiana, Mississippi, Ohio, the Carolinas, Virginia, West Virginia, and Georgia. In one of the Ohio stories reported to the Associated Press, an apparently hysterical woman had telephoned the authorities claiming that an oblong

UFO had killed a pair of cows when it landed in a country pasture.

If nothing else would serve to convince the habitual doubter, the many articles on UFO or UFO-related subjects by Walter Sullivan, the astronomical specialist of the New York *Times,* might suffice.[36]

Now, UFO were blanketing the sky. Echelons of lights startled the citizenry of Rochester, New York. A Hoosier was followed home by a strange light. Several deputy sheriffs in Louisiana pursued five orange globes along frosted rural roads for a dozen miles before the things disappeared.

In Dover, Delaware, a trio of ladies spent forty-five minutes on Sunday evening, October 14, watching a brilliant object overhead. The police were summoned after a while and they sent up a helicopter, stationed at the Dover Air Force Base, where the radiant UFO was being viewed from the control tower. As usual, the conventional aircraft was outpaced by the unknown, which vanished down the dark sky.

Of special interest to the technically minded were two instances—October 11 and October 17—of objects traversing the northern United States at supersonic velocities, leaving concomitant "boom" wake. Seismographs indicated the effects at Pennsylvania State University, the first at 8:53 P.M. and the second at 1:26 P.M. Equipment at the State University of New York, in Binghamton, and at Virginia Polytechnic Institute, in Blacksburg, also registered the phenomena. In Michigan, the overflight elicited a reaction on an air-pressure graph.

Dr. Edward U. Condon, who had been the director of the Air Force-sponsored anti-UFO study[37] specifically designed to end all investigations of the subject, could not refrain from commenting on the resurgence. Had he spent more than half the time for which he was contracted on the project he nominally headed,[38] and had he not announced his conclusions regarding "flying saucers" before embarking upon the purportedly objective analysis,[39] more attention might have been accorded his opinions.

He observed in the autumn of 1973 that, as he

didn't believe in UFO (although, in context, it was clear he referred to "flying saucers"), "my own study of UFO's was a waste of Government money."[40] Aside from the fact that the project was not Dr. Condon's personal program, and the fact that the $313,000 assigned to it belonged to the *people* and not an autocratic "government," few would argue with his assessment. If ever an official undertaking was a waste of money, from the viewpoint of the public, scientists, historians, and nearly anyone else, it was the Scientific Study of Unidentified Flying Objects.

Countless other stories about, or relating to, the new era of UFO were appearing in the newspapers, and they were extremely varied.

Professor Samuel Kaplan of Gorky University, in Moscow, noting that Mars was closer to Earth than it had been for two years, claimed that he had isolated astronomical "radio signals that may have originated from another civilization" somewhere in deep space. The signals had been monitored by a network of four receivers operating under the supervision of the respected Soviet astrophysicist Dr. Vsevlod Troitsky, and the official position was that the daily pulsations were definitely not caused by a man-made satellite or any equipment contained in such a device.[41]

In Texas, a group attempted to signal, and entice into camera range, one of the elusive UFO. Their method was to arrange a pattern of lights intended to represent the universal hydrogen atom—and wait.

Mayor W. C. Jackson, of Palacios, Texas, told United Press International that "it just occurred to me that no one has ever made those fellas welcome,"[42] and so he published a proclamation of greeting to "flying saucers" by a town council vote. Actually, his accusation was not quite accurate. A number of "contactees"* made a career of inviting aliens to visit them. Many claim to have enjoyed a response to their hospitality. Yet, other announcements have been less friendly or suspiciously commercial. The mayor of

---

* Individuals who claim to have had personal, except in the rarest of cases physical (there are a few psychical contactees), encounters with extraterrestrial occupants of "flying saucers."

Châteauneuf-du-Pape, in France, issued a proclamation on October 27, 1954, forbidding the landing of spacecraft within his jurisdiction. He ordered the impoundment of any vessels ignoring his directive.

In Brittany, France, an innkeeper offered $35,000 reward to anyone who could capture a live Martian.

In terms of more serious receptivity to UFO, special landing pads were prepared by the Defence Ministry of the Canadian government at Port McNeill, British Columbia, and St. Paul, Alberta, in the late 1960s, although the effort was hardly comparable to our northern neighbor's enticement of 1954, when a thousand-square-mile compound was designated as a UFO landing area, over which no military or commercial aircraft were permitted to fly without explicit permission. Unfortunately, while considerably more imaginative and farsighted than most nations of the world, the Canadian government never saw its hopes fulfilled.

A remark attributed to Dr. Edward Ney, professor of astrophysics at the University of Michigan, a few years earlier, reflected the seemingly unanimous attitude of the scientific community. "Respectable scientists don't even discuss UFO's in serious terms,"[43] he said.

Nevertheless, there have always been important members of its many disciplines who were convinced of the extraterrestriality of the unknown phenomena, or at least that intelligence demanded that they maintain an open mind on the subject. As a matter of fact, to some of the young physicists, astronomers, and aerodynamicists, it was almost fashionable to assume at least a slightly "controversial" attitude.

The late Dr. James E. McDonald, professor of meteorology and senior physicist at the Institute of Atmospheric Physics at the University of Arizona, was among the most productive and promising analysts to emerge. His recent death was a severe blow to the scientists who were beginning to coordinate their various skills to the end of solving the mystery of UFO. Fortunately, many others, old-timers and ufological novices, were prepared to continue his efforts.

One of the johnnies-come-lately, who quickly gained recognition as an advocate of the plan to revive serious investigation in the field of Unidentified Flying Objects, was Stanton Friedman, holder of a master's degree in physics from the University of Chicago. In addition to his theoretical speculations he was a sometime worker in the more pragmatic areas of science, having been with Westinghouse, General Electric, and Aerojet General Nucleonics at various points in his career, before he began devoting much of his time to lecturing on "flying saucers." While he introduced little new, he made himself heard on the standard, but nonetheless valid, arguments.

"I believe it's time we mustered the top scientific talents in this country, spent some money and began a hard scientific study to prove the existence of UFO's as extraterrestrial vehicles and obtain information of real use in the development of advanced propulsion systems for use on this planet."[44]

Of course, that was what Jim and Coral Lorenzen, Maj. Donald E. Keyhoe, James Moseley, Ivan T. Sanderson, Dr. Morris K. Jessup, Ted Bloecher, Frank Edwards, John Keel, John Fuller, and many others across the country, including this author, had been saying for years. And the same position had been taken by a number of prominent scientists apart from McDonald and Friedman; they included Dr. Hermann Oberth, one of the founders of modern rocketry; Dr. Maurice A. Biot, noted aerodynamicist and mathematician; Dr. Charles Harvard Gibbs-Smith, aeronautical historian for London's Victoria and Albert Museum; Dr. Walter Reidel, another of the world's handful of rocket experts; and many internationally recognized figures within and beyond the sciences.

Eventually, the Air Force's own leading, and often only, scientific consultant, well-known astronomer Dr. J. Allen Hynek, added his nearly unique authority to the argument.

Happily, even among those who had been convinced by the evidence that UFO were extraterrestrial and quite possibly, or even definitely, intelligently operated, the desire was for a thorough and open study and analysis. Therefore, while Friedman's fifteen years' labor in the technology of the space effort and other related enterprises was a welcome contribution, some found it a little distressing to hear him offer a mirror argument of the traditional Air Force policy. The vast majority of scientists, authors, political figures, etc., who wished to see the matter penetratingly reviewed sought an objective, comprehensive program intended to determine precisely, or to whatever degree possible, what UFO are, not a typically official, prejudgmental "hard scientific *study to prove the existence of UFO's as extraterrestrial vehicles.*"[45] (Emphasis added.)

A 1971 poll conducted by *Industrial Research* indicated that 54 percent of the twenty-seven hundred professional scientists and engineers included in the sampling were convinced that UFO "definitely or probably" exist.[46]

If there remained the slightest doubt in 1973 that the cycle had swung UFO into the public's consciousness again, on November 28 a Gallup survey was published revealing that 51 percent of Americans believed that they were real, a rise of 5 percent over the pollster's figures for the same question posed in the mid-sixties. The number of persons who contended that they had personally viewed such phenomena had more than doubled, and stood at over one-tenth of the population. The new inquiry showed that the segment of the public accepting the proposition of intelligent life on other planets had gone up twelve points, to 46 percent.

Yet, it was the sober voice of confirmed skeptic Walter Sullivan, science editor for the New York *Times,* that concisely reported the situation: "Rarely, if ever, since Kenneth Arnold reported in 1947 seeing what came to be known as 'flying saucers' during a flight near Mount Rainier in Washington State, have there been such widespread reports of unidentified flying objects, or UFO's, as in recent days."[47]

As my neighbor had shouted wildly over the telephone more than six months earlier: "The flying saucers are back!"

Notes

1. Yuri A. Gagarin in Vostok I, on April 12, 1961, the first manned orbital flight, followed by the second with Gherman S. Titov in Vostok II, on August 6–7; two suborbital flights by this country's Alan B. Shepard, Jr., and Virgil Grissom on May 5 and June 21, 1961, respectively, with John H. Glenn's orbital trip in February of the following year. (These three astronauts piloted Mercury-Redstone 3 and 4, and Mercury-Atlas 6.) Valentina V. Tereshkova, in Vostok VI was the first woman to circle the planet; on June 14, 1963, and Alexei A. Lenov, in Voshkod II, to "walk in space." On June 16, 1969, in Apollo II, Man, in the person of Neil A. Armstrong, reached and stood upon the moon.

2. For an analysis of this socio-psychological condition, see Paris Flammonde, *The Age of Flying Saucers* (New York: Hawthorn Books, 1971), Chapter I and pp. 222–225.

3. *Pocono Record* (Stroudsburg, Pa.), March 2, 1973.

4. *Express* (Easton, Pa.), March 2, 1973.

5. *Morning Call* (Allentown, Pa.), March 5, 1973.

6. *National Enquirer,* May 13, 1973.

7. *Pocono Record,* op. cit.

8. *National Enquirer,* op. cit.

9. Ibid.

10. *Express,* op. cit.

11. *National Enquirer,* op. cit.

12. Ibid.

13. Ibid.

14. *Express,* op. cit.

15. *Express,* op. cit.

16. Ibid.

17. The Grand Rapids Flying Saucer Club, organized in 1951, but no longer in existence, *may* have been the earliest such group.

18. Sixty-nine active and former UFO and "flying saucer" societies, with relevant data, may be found in Paris Flammonde, *The Age of Flying Saucers,* Appendix III. The same source provides a similar number of catalogued and described UFO and "flying saucer" periodicals (see Appendix IV).

19. *Pocono Record,* March 5, 1973.

20. Ibid.

21. Ibid.

22. Ibid., March 21, 1973.

23. Ibid.

24. Ibid.

25. *Express,* March 26, 1973.

26. Ibid.

27. Ibid.

28. Ibid.

29. Ibid.

30. Ibid.

31. Ibid.

32. *Pocono Record,* March 28, 1973.

33. *Express,* March 29, 1973.

34. United Press International, October 2, 1973.

35. Ibid., October 5, 1973.

36. Mr. Sullivan was responsible for the Introduction to Edward U. Condon, ed., *Scientific Study of Unidentified Flying Objects,* commonly called the "Condon Report."

37. Condon, *Scientific Study.* Conducted by the University of Colorado, under contract to the United States Air Force No. F44620–67–C–0035.

38. David R. Saunders and R. Roger Harkins, *UFOs? Yes!* (New York: New American Library/Signet, 1968), p. 21.

39. John Fuller, "Flying Saucer Fiasco," *Look,* May 14, 1968, p. 58.

40. New York *Times,* October 21, 1973.

41. Ibid., October 17, 1973.

42. Ibid.

43. *Saucer News,* Spring 1967, p. 15.

44. United Press International, October 25, 1973.

45. Ibid.

46. Ibid.

47. New York *Times,* October 21, 1973.

2

The Mystery of the UFO

Of course the flying saucers are real—and they are interplanetary.

> —Air Chief Marshal Lord Dowding, commanding officer of the Royal Air Force of Great Britain, during World War II. Reuters, August 1954

THE TERM "Unidentified Flying Object (UFO)," used when a phenomenon is neither "flying" nor proved to be an "object," but is merely unidentified, is simply inaccurate.

"Flying saucer," the term that is most frequently used to describe the *appearance* of an unknown, although it was originated to indicate flight characteristics of something seen in the air, is another inescapable example of inappropriate definition.

Allusions to purported aliens as "spacemen," when openmindedness should recognize that, if UFO exist, we have no proof that they come from the sky, and the constant use of the word "flap" to describe a concentration of sightings, are equally misleading.

And these faults are not confined to the public and the press.

A prevailing belief is reflected in the opening sentence of Aimé Michel's internationally known work *The Truth About Flying Saucers,* which reads: "As far as I know, the expression 'flying saucers' was invented by Kenneth Arnold, an American business man."[1]

There are two errors here. The first is the incorrect supposition that the expression had not been used prior to the Arnold incident* of June 24, 1947. The Denison[2] (Texas) *Daily News* of January 25, 1878, republished a story carried in a Dallas newspaper on the previous day, with the lead "A Strange Phenomenon."

> Mr. John Martin, a farmer who lives some six miles north of this city [Dallas], while out hunting, had his attention directed to a dark object high in the northern sky.
>
> The peculiar shape and the velocity with which the object seemed to approach, riveted his attention, and he strained his eyes to discover its character. When first noticed it appeared to be about the size of an orange, after which it continued to grow in size.
>
> After gazing at it for some time, Mr. Martin became blind from long looking and left off viewing to rest his eyes. On resuming his view, the object was almost overhead and had increased considerably in size and appeared to be going through space at a wonderful speed. When directly over him it was about the size of *a large saucer* and was evidently at a great height. [Emphasis added.]

It is likely that the expression was used elsewhere before the Arnold case, but here we have a specific instance dated almost seventy years earlier. Interestingly, in that sighting the intention *was* to indicate the shape of the enigma, contrary to the initial usage in our time.

The second misconception is that Arnold "invented" the term. Writing in 1952, the pilot used the phrase "they flew like a saucer would if you skipped it across the water."[3] Four years later, Capt. Edward J. Ruppelt, drawing from the report originally sent to the Air Force, quotes him as saying they behaved like a "saucer skipping across water."[4] The expression "fly-

---

* See Chapter 9.

ing saucer" was created by some enterprising, and now anonymous, journalist.

Although an indication of shape was never intended in the use of the phrase to depict the Arnold experience, it became the only meaning of "flying saucer," regardless of the size or flight pattern of an aerial observation. The false became the fact, and thousands of Undefined Sensory Experiences (USE), the manifestations of which varied enormously, as far as the best records can determine, were arbitrarily labeled with the expression.

The elaboration on Arnold's allusion to a "saucer" was employed almost exclusively until Captain Ruppelt was assigned to direct Project Blue Book, the small United States Air Force unit responsible for monitoring, investigating, and evaluating the aerial phenomena. He "coined the phrase 'Unidentified Flying Object' [frequently acronymically condensed to U-F-O, or, less often, 'you-foe'] to distinguish what appeared to be rational sighting reports from ones sounding like excerpts from fairy tales or nightmares."[5]

Ruppelt's expression was not the only, or even the first, alternative to "flying saucer." The unusual Charles Fort, who devoted a lifetime to the collection of stories of unexplained, inexplicable, and abnormal incidents and phenomena, reported from around the world, thought that "Objects Seen Floating"[6] might serve the purpose UFO was intended to fill. Still, it is obviously even less useful than Ruppelt's phrase.

The late noted botanist, geologist, zoologist, and ufologist Ivan T. Sanderson preferred more specialized designations: Unexplained Aerial Object (UAO), when solidity was an evident characteristic, and Unidentified Atmospheric Phenomenon (UAP),[7] when that observed appeared less tangible. The magazine *Flying Saucers* introduced a term for the rarer aquatic and/or amphibious type of Undefined Sensory Experience: Underwater Unidentified Objects (UUO), while longtime researcher John Keel opted for the simple umbrella word "Anomalies."

All the proposed expressions I have encountered have struck me as inadequate, primarily because they fail to be sufficiently comprehensive to include even the majority of the interminable types of reports. The one exception is "Anomalies," and it is so general as to be applicable to virtually anything varying from one's personal concept of normality.

My preference is for a comprehensive term covering all orders of sightings, regardless of their nature or that of the phenomena observed. Admittedly, I include within its meaning certain apparently undecipherable conditions and occurrences not included in this subject, but it is applicable to all we are likely to encounter, without including everything one wishes to toss into its category. The phrase is Undefined Sensory Experience (USE).

Where a sighting specifically reports the apparent nature and behavior of a phenomenon, a simple description serves perfectly well. If it seems physcial and is said to have been at rest in a pasture, it is clearly an unknown landed object. If something is seen sailing through the night sky constantly changing shape, it is an unexplained aerial phenomenon, or, perhaps, an unexplained atmospheric incident.

Still, neither this nor other responsible books will eliminate the popular terms UFO and "flying saucer" from the vocabulary of the subject.

Following the Arnold incident the reference "flying saucers" was applied to everything in space, in the atmosphere, hovering near the surface of the earth, or on the ground that the observer was unable to categorize. On some occasions it even included inexplicable lights floating about a waking person's bedroom. It was so all-encompassing a phrase as to have no meaning.

Project Blue Book's introduction of the identification Unidentified Flying Object or UFO was intended to catalogue (primarily aerial) observations which seemed to describe inexplicable phenomena. The evaluation upon which such definitions were to be decided included the atmospheric condition during the sighting, qualities of intelligence and education of the reporter, and the general nature—light, color, altitude, speed, variance in course, persistence of visibility, manner of departure, and shape—of the subject.

Convenience and clarity indicate that the use of both popular phrases, "flying saucer" and Unidentified Flying Object (UFO), should be continued throughout this book. First, because there was no designation for the various phenomena described, individually and collectively, prior to the modern era; second, because a lengthier discussion of nomenclature, and then its introduction into the text, would be cumbersome and distracting.

Near midnight on July 19, 1952, radar equipment at the Washington National Airport, in the District of Columbia, began to scan eight "blips."* Experts immediately recognized that the reception did not describe airplanes, as the speeds recorded varied from one hundred to seven thousand miles an hour. Nearby, air crews and professional personnel in the control tower also watched the extraordinary exhibition. Without warning, the UFO disappeared.

A week afterward, virtually to the hour, the episode was repeated. This time Washington National Airport opened lines to adjacent Andrews Air Force Base, which acknowledged that it, too, was monitoring unexplained registrations on its radar. The UFO were observed for over an hour before the military "scrambled" a tandem of F-94 interceptors to confirm the scope and ground-to-air observations.

On this occasion, radar lost the "blips" as the interceptors gained altitude, then the military aviators achieved visual, air-to-air contact and initiated pursuit. The attempt proved ineffectual as the F-94s were outraced as if they had been rendered motionless. The UFO catapulted to incalculable velocities, vanishing into space.

Such a report, if one has accepted the usage, is properly classified as a UFO, or Unidentified Flying Object, account.

Eight years later, on November 27, a group of seven inhabitants of a trailer camp in California main-

---

* Scope registrations indicating an electronic response.

tained a surveillance of aerial activity for more than a quarter of an hour. Among the company were two amateur astronomers, Mr. and Mrs. Lewis Hart, who subsequently submitted an excellent report to the Air Force. Amendations to that record were published by professional ufologist Lloyd Mallan. A brief portion, which was in response to a questionnaire supplied by the authorities, read:

"In your opinion what do you think the object was and what might have caused it?"

The Harts' answer: "It was unquestionably some kind of intelligently controlled air or space vehicle."[8]

That is a "flying saucer" report.

The differentiation? The phrase Unidentified Flying Object is meant to be self-explanatory. The more an observer details a sighting the less likely the term will logically apply. That is, if a viewer states flatly that what he saw was an egg-shaped craft, with fins and rocket propulsion, one can hardly define it as "unidentified."

The Hart case is an ideal illustration of where description crosses the line from UFO into another category, one where the witnesses testify to having seen "a vehicle," which, no matter what the design, is a "flying saucer," that is, a ship of some sort, remotely or directly intelligently operated.

Accounts that offer highly detailed descriptions of actual machines and their physical characteristics represent "classic" reports of "flying saucers," which reach their zenith with stories of spacecraft crews observed, engaged in conversation, or by whom the human sighters have been abducted—namely the revelations of individuals called "contactees."[9]

Unfortunately, for the rational investigator, Undefined Sensory Experiences of these and many other types relevant to this subject have been chronicled for thousands of years.

Why did awareness of this particular class of Undefined Sensory Experience (USE), or UFO and "flying saucers," suddenly erupt nearly three decades ago and persist until this day as, perhaps, the principal mystery confounding the population?

Little could be more fascinating than the "why" of UFO, the nature of their final recognition and acceptance by Americans, and soon the remainder of the world, and the incredible variety of impacts the phenomena and concomitant repercussions made on society. But that would be a book of inquiry, analyses, speculation, and tentative conclusions. This is a record of facts.

All we need to know is that by the mid-sixties 96 percent of the people had heard of "flying saucers," with one-fifth of the female population claiming they had actually seen one. Forty-six percent of the public believed they were "real," and 34 percent conceded that creatures "somewhat like ourselves" existed on remote planets. As we have mentioned earlier, within fewer than ten years these figures increased measurably.

The world was waiting for the arrival of a trans-spacial age.

Someone was not.

The population accepted the presence of Undefined Sensory Experience (USE) as an indisputable fact, which it was, in ever-increasing numbers. UFO became regarded as more and more likely, while even the segment of society believing in the existence of "flying saucers" (as well as "contactees") continued to grow, both in the United States and abroad. Yet, there were powerful elements determined to dismiss, caricature, and baselessly deny that the sky was an enormous field of unknown activity, forces dedicated to the unsupportable contention that there were no UFO, let alone "flying saucers."

The pattern of rejection and concealment ranged from incidental indications to blatant contempt for the conviction of the public and the authoritative opinion of major scholars, scientists, and political figures. Still, that leads us directly into the "why not" regarding UFO and their investigation, and face to face with the question of "why" they appeared when, and in the fashion, they did. As just noted, these more political, sociological, psychological, and philosophical contemplations must be set aside for another volume, as we concentrate, as much as possible, on data.

Accounts of Undefined Sensory Experience (USE) are the foundation of a great portion of human culture. Within the subject one encounters Ivan T. Sanderson's Unexplained Aerial Objects, to designate sightings of apparently solid things in the sky, and Unidentified Atmospheric Phenomena, for manifestations of the seemingly less tangible; or Ruppelt's Unidentified Flying Objects, for virtually anything from reports of radar blips to descriptions of what appear to be a kind of electrical plasma; or "flying saucers," indicating any of the above, through landed intergalactic spaceships with bug-eyed crews. Chronicles of whatever kind may appeal to one reach back as far as human records, and, doubtlessly, have impressed themselves upon Man's consciousness since well into prehistory.

Yet, despite the antiquity and variety of USE, it is usually difficult, often impossible, to describe its manifestations, let alone its nature. A simple, practical example of the problem lies in language again, but this time as it differs from decade, to century, to millennium. How might ancient analogies compare with contemporary descriptions of aerial unknowns? How totally incomprehensible would ordinary things of our time seem to the most sophisticated citizen of Charlemagne's court in the ninth century?

Among the primary arguments for the existence of "flying saucers"—meaning an intelligently controlled craft, generally assumed to be extraterrestrial—are the early sources of many accounts of UAO, UAP, UFO, and like curiosities. The major response of this argument is that numerous of the historical accounts appear to be fanciful rather than literal depictions. In fact, however, the ancient versions of the kind of Undefined Sensory Experience with which we are dealing are extremely close, and often nearly identical, to the descriptions accumulated in our time.

The second largest class of old accounts consists of those that seem too allegorical and of the reports of phenomena startlingly like the present idea of interplanetary vessels. The possible interpretations of the first group are intriguing, and one is amazed at the details of the second. Today we take "miracles" for granted, but a moment's thought will remind us that Abraham Lincoln would have been stunned by the radio, Thomas Edison said airplanes would never be more than "toys," no radar, sonar, or television existed when Hitler began to take over Germany, and the eminent English astronomer Richard van der Riet Wooley saw the concept of space travel as "utter bilge" in 1956, one year before Sputnik I.

What would such devices and achievements have meant to a French serf a thousand years ago, or to a Montana mountainman nine hundred years later? How would these ordinary people have described their experiences? Not at all, since the essential principles of each invention would have been totally alien to them. They would not even have been able to construct a frame of reference into which they could put the picture of what they saw. The most educated people of their times would have had no understanding of the scientific and mechanical fundamentals involved, and would have lacked nine-tenths of the vocabulary to explain what they had seen, even if a flush of genius had suggested the nature of function of one of the manifestations or USE to them.

Assuming we continue at the increasingly accelerating pace of scientific development demonstrated since World War II, what would the brightest of us comprehend about a creation of the year 3000, based upon undiscovered natural laws and concepts not yet dreamed? How would we describe it? Not at all. We would merely stumble through some vague account of the sensory experience produced by the undefined phenomenon.

Still, to the extent that we can, let us consider how it all began.

Notes

1. Aimé Michel, *The Truth About Flying Saucers,* trans. Paul Selver (New York: Criterion Books, 1956), p. 15.
2. Not "Dennison," as some investigators have it: the paperback version of Jacques Vallee's *The Anatomy of a Phenomenon* (New York: Ace Books, 1966), p. 15, *but* correct in the earlier hardcover edition (Chicago: Henry Regnery, 1965), p. 1, where the reference is to the town, not the periodical.
3. Kenneth Arnold and Ray Palmer, *The Coming of the Saucers* (Amherst, Wisconsin, privately printed, 1952), p. 11.
4. Edward J. Ruppelt, *The Report on Unidentified Flying Objects* (Garden City, N.Y.: Doubleday, 1956), p. 17.
5. Paris Flammonde, *The Age of Flying Saucers* (New York: Hawthorn, 1971), p. 5.
6. Ivan T. Sanderson, *Unidentified Visitors* (New York: Cowles Education Corp., 1967), p. 8.
7. Ibid., p. 10.
8. Lloyd Mallan, *The Official Guide to UFOs* (New York: Science and Mechanics Publishing Company, 1967), p. 14.
9. As this aspect of the subject will be considered only occasionally and briefly in this work, it is suggested that a comprehensive survey of "contactees" may be found in the author's *Age of Flying Saucers*. For examples of particular ("autobiographical") accounts, recommended are: Orfeo Angelucci, *Son of the Sun* (Los Angeles: DeVorss & Company, 1959); George Adamski, *Inside the Space Ships* (New York: Abelard-Schuman, 1955); and other works cited in the comprehensive bibliography of *Age of Flying Saucers.*

3

In the Beginning

Certainly there are other civilizations, perhaps thousands of times older and wiser. And I believe intelligent beings from these civilizations are visiting us in spacecraft—and have been for some years.

—Dr. Charles Harvard Gibbs-Smith, aeronautical historian, Victoria and Albert Museum, London. Quoted in *Flying Saucer Menace* by Brad Steiger. (New York: Universal Publishing and Distributing Corporation, 1967, pp. 22–26)

A CLASSIC CHINESE cosmogony asserts that the universe, as we are becoming aware of it, began 2,269,434 years ago.[1] Before that the elements are thought to have drifted about in a state of gray neutrality, doing very little of interest. However, the cosmic antiquarians of the East have reckoned without the secret sources of author Desmond Leslie. This noted English authority on "flying saucers," drawing from some ancient texts, notably Indian, assumes the universe to have *become* several million years ago.

Leslie argues that a subhuman sort of creature emerged from a soulless darkness about eighteen and a half million years before our present age. Sadly, this race lacked all that is, or was then, spiritual, and could not evolve to a more developed stage.

It was at the time, 18,617,841 B.C., that "Sanat Kumara," otherwise known as "The Lord of the Flame," arrived on Earth from Venus, "Home of the

Gods," accompanied by Four Great Lords and an entourage of an even hundred.[2]

Atop a towering peak in South America are the foundations of a somewhat more authenticated ancient mystery civilization. Although the evidence of the prehistoric, or even the first period, of Tihuanacu is too vague for accurate astronomical calculations, one archeologist estimates that "the Second and Third Periods" date back to 15,000 B.C.,[3] which means that the beginnings of this culture are very old, indeed. Who constructed it, or how, remain unsolved questions.

The skeptics argue that if the saucer enthusiast's theories are correct, considering the wealth of religious, mythological, literary, and astronomical material available, it is amazing how few tales of extraterrestrial arrivals have descended to us. If, as the advocates claim, interplanetarians have been visiting for thousands, even millions, of years, why is there so little legitimate history containing incidents resembling USE as described in our time? The answer is that there exist far more such references than the novices might imagine. Actually, there are uncountable records that deserve the evaluation of the sincere and persistent investigator.

If the doubters are correct when they argue that whatever is seen has a simple psychological or astronomical explanation, and that Man has been responding to both stimuli since time began, then why was it not until ignorance and superstition had diminished a millionfold that he dreamed up, or translated normal happenings into, the age of "flying saucers"?

Of course, if Unidentified Flying Objects are, in truth, "flying saucers," and "flying saucers" began to appear near Earth only in this century, or around the time of Kenneth Arnold's first sighting, both questions are answered.

Let us examine some of the supporting sources regarded by many scholars as proof of earlier extraterrestrial visitations. The two most fascinating are the Bible and Eastern mystical writings. A few lines from Ezekiel are occasionally quoted, to accusations that they are offered "out of context" and therefore have no value. In truth, the *full* relevant verses, from which these phrases are often extracted, are far more persuasive and suggestive of an interplanetary episode. For example, there is this extraordinary passage:

> The word of the Lord came expressly unto Ezekiel the priest. . . . And I looked, and, behold, a whirlwind came out of the north, a great cloud, and a fire infolding itself, and a brightness was about it, and out of the midst thereof as the colour of amber, out of the midst of the fire. Also out of the midst thereof came the likeness of four living creatures. And this was their appearance: they had the likeness of a man. . . .
> And their feet were straight feet; and the sole of their feet was like the sole of a calf's foot; and they sparkled like the colour of burnished brass.[4]

See the picture. Twenty-five hundred years ago. A glaring wasteland in the Middle East. How more clearly could a highly intelligent and perceptive individual describe the swirl of sand spun up by the blinding retro-jet exhaust of a modern rocket descending to the dunes of the desert. The billow of settling, sand, pierced by the huge, ragged column of flame being squashed out beneath the pressure of the craft's contact with earth. Astronauts in glistening suits and distortingly weighted, thick-soled boots.

Now what happens?

> And they had the hands of a man under their wings on their four sides; and they four had their faces and their wings.
> Their wings were joined one to another; they turned not when they went; they went every one straight forward.[5]

What might the oxygen tanks and other life-support apparatus look like to a person raised to believe in winged angels and mythological monsters? Especially if the equipment was of an even more exaggerated design than that we use for underwater diving, let alone

floating about in outer space? Two extensions from
the shoulders to the waist, which would obviously
leave "the hands of a man under their wings," might
convincingly fit descriptions of creatures a witness had
never seen, except in an imagination stimulated by
the legends of his people. As speculation beyond the
actual text is pointless, it can only be suggested that
the "wings" seeming to be connected might refer to
interdependent or mutually shared life-support systems,
or that the visitors were trained to function closely as
teams, or that the planet from which they came was
inhabited by duo-beings, or what we call Siamese
twins. In any case, a number of reasonable explanations could apply here.

That "they went every one straight forward" seems
logical. Were they in reality astronauts, wandering in
circles around the base of their ship would serve no
productive purpose. If they saw indigenous animals
not too different from themselves they would most
likely head directly for them and attempt to establish
communication.

What were these visitors like? Ezekiel gives a
rather detailed account of their appearance. Consider
the verse most commonly ridiculed or dismissed by
doubters:

> As for the likeness of their faces, they four
> had the face of a man, and the face of a lion,
> on the right side: and they four had the face of
> an ox on the left side; they four also had the face
> of an eagle.[6]

Initially, the depictions sound unusually imaginative,
even for an allegory. Still, that may well strengthen
the case for the extraterrestrial theory, rather than
weaken it. That is, moralists have no need to com-
press all of their symbolism into a single sentence, or
onto one head—if we interpret that four visitors all
had the same appearance. And such seems to be intended.

Little effort is required to visualize what *might*
have been so described, even by more sophisticated

citizens of the time and vicinity. A space helmet, particularly if less globular and more pointed, after the style of certain medieval armor,[7] with a sweep of wires or fine tubes flared back from the face to the rear, could easily suggest a lion's head. A conic radio device or antenna on the opposite side might well bring to mind the horns of oxen to one who saw them daily. And should the profile of the headpiece arc downward to the chin in a hooklike fashion, or have a breathing line curving to the chest of the body garment—what with the "wings" and descent from the heavens—why not an eagle?

"As for the likeness of the living creatures, their appearance was like burning coals of fire, and like the appearance of lamps . . . and out of the first went forth lightning," the narrator soon explains.

"And the living creatures ran and returned as the appearance of a flash of lightning." [8]

One need not dwell upon the fact that any space traveler would be sufficiently technically advanced to have a flashlight, panels on his suit which blinked on and off to indicate changes in atmospheric conditions or the proximity of various kinds of sought minerals, or, perhaps, which served as simple warning signals of some problem. Were the gravity of his planet much less than that to which the proposed astronauts were accustomed and their garments and equipment far lighter and more efficient than ours, they might well move several times faster than Man. Iridescent clothing, or metallic space suits glistening in the brilliant desert sun, could easily give "the appearance of a flash of lightning."

Ezekiel continues with more details:

> Now as I behold the living creatures, behold one wheel upon the earth by the living creatures, with his four faces.
> The appearance of the wheels and their work was like unto the colour of beryl: and they four had one likeness: * and their appearance and

---

* A conclusion inferred from an earlier portion of the report.

their work was as it were a wheel in the middle of a wheel. . . . As for their rings, they were so high that they were dreadful; and their rings were full of eyes round about them four.

And when the living creatures went, the wheels went by them: and when the living creatures were lifted up from the earth, the wheels were lifted up. . . . And when they went, I heard the noise of their wings, like the noise of great waters, as the voice of the Almighty. . . . And there was a voice from the firmament that was over their heads, when they stood, and had let down their wings.[9]

Is this as incomprehensible as it may sound at first? Certainly "the wheels" and "their work was as it were a wheel in the middle of a wheel" is identical to thousands of descriptions of "flying saucers" in our own time. The same may be said of the "eye" in the "rings," which are like the accounts of lights around the center rim of a craft or, more rarely, upon the belts of alien occupants.

The creatures being "lifted up" could be explained by an elevator operated from a telescoping crane, if the ship was large, or jets fixed to the backs of the crewmen by which they could make short flights or return to the craft door. Even the most skeptical individual will grant that almost any of the visualized apparatus might make a variety of sounds and that the simplest loudspeaker, employed by an officer who had remained aboard the vessel, certainly would give the impression of a voice from on high.

And above the firmament that was over their heads was the likeness of a throne, as the appearance of a sapphire stone: and upon the likeness of the throne was the likeness as the appearance of a man above it.[10]

"Above the firmament that was over their heads was the likeness of a throne" certainly is speaking of a seat in the heavens since "firmament" means "sky." But, of course, one may be reminded that it derives from the Greek word expressing "firm or solid" and/or from a Hebraic word that probably merely means "expanse." [11] Far less elastic than a mystical explanation is that a man appeared, or even sat, on a small platform, of bluish (or red, or white, etc.) metal or other substance, extending just beyond the door.

Then the chapter concludes:

> And I saw as the colour of amber, as the appearance of fire round about within it, from the appearance of his loins even upward, and from the appearance of his loins even downward, I saw as it were the appearance of fire, and it had a brightness round it.
>
> As the appearance of the bow that is in the cloud in the day or rain, so was the appearance of the brightness roundabout. This was the appearance of the likeness of the glory of the LORD. And when I saw it, I fell upon my face, and I heard a voice of the one that spake. [12]

The not at all unusual reflection of sunlight on highly polished metal, whether of the ship, space suits, helmets, or equipment, can readily account for virtually all of the radiance and color described, and the rocket exhausts for the remainder. Without getting into mineralogy, there is still another solution for the presence of many of the tints pictured. Taking the easiest example, i.e., "the color of beryl," we find beryllium aluminum silicate, which is a very hard, lustrous substance, present on earth in a number of shades including blue, green, pink, and yellow.

Although some of the repetition of the original text has been retained so that the charge of taking the material "out of context" cannot be lodged, in review the entire episode related in the book of Ezekiel can perfectly reasonably be attributed to the report of a contemporary-type ufonaut landing in the Sinai desert. The rocket arrives in our atmosphere, orbits, selects a landing site that is free of obstructions and as

smooth as possible, and sets down, tail first with its
retro-jets blazing away. Occupants, looking something
like humans, completely covered by environment-self-
containing space clothing, exit. Each is adorned with
various components of his life-support system and
other scientific gadgetry. They communicate, work in
teams, and get orders from the ship's commander
through a system which, at least in part, can be heard
by the nomadic people who are naturally attracted by
this incredible event. Soon, in flaming glory, the visitors depart, and the witnesses rush to tell their comrades and neighbors about the incident. Eventually
it is written down, probably long after the actual occurrence; most likely by someone who heard the story
second-, third-, or fourth-hand.

It is the kind of report that has created the legends
and the history of the world, depending on who wrote
it and who believed what he wrote. Unfortunately,
there are probably no records available of the first
description of an "iron horse," miles long, as related
by a Dakota Sioux, or of the first aircraft even seen
by a Bantu chief in southern Africa, perhaps before
the First World War. And, as there appear to be none,
we will never know what a Moonman would have
thought, and how he would have subsequently described to his fellows the arrival of Apollo 11 and its
crew.

The report of Elijah's experience seems very slightly
removed from one that might have crossed the desk
of Project Blue Book: "And it came to pass, as they
still went on, and talked, that, behold, there appeared
a chariot of fire, and horses of fire, and parted them
both asunder; and Elijah went up by a whirlwind into
heaven." [13] Note the reappearance of the translation
of "whirlwind" and "fire."

Curiously, I have rarely heard anyone allude to a
passage from Zechariah which sounds even more like
a modern sighting:

Then I turned, and lifted up mine eyes, and
looked, and behold a flying roll. And he said
unto me, What seest thou? And I answered, I see

a flying roll; the length thereof is twenty cubits [thirty to thirty-six feet] and the breadth thereof ten cubits.[14]

In the present era this might easily have fitted into any of three groups of thousands of accounts: flattened spheres, elliptical forms, and, obviously cylindrical shapes. For those interested in pursuing this comparison, examples may be seen in the Chiles case (July 23, 1948), the Gorman case (October 1, 1948), and the Levelland case (November 2, 1957), three of the most famous and best-documented sightings in modern history.

Another few verses of the Old Testament that fascinate "flying saucer" devotees are found at its beginning.

And it came to pass, when men began to multiply on the face of the earth, and daughters were born unto them, that the sons of God saw the daughters of men that they were fair; and they took them wives of all which they chose. . . . There were giants in the earth in those days; and also after that, when the sons of God came in unto the daughters of men. . . .[15]

One can hardly fail to perceive the distinction made between the children of *God* and those of *men*, the former being male and *giants*, and from some removed region. Where?

"The powers of Ourania [heavens] shall be shaken: And then shall appear the sign of the Son of man in heaven," says St. Matthew. If, as scholar of prophecy Stewart Robb suggests, Ourania (of the earlier Greek script) implies uranium force, then the motive power of an interplanetary craft might be inferred as effortlessly as his more religious interpretation.[16]

To this list of saucerological biblical citations we may add almost the entire book of Revelations.[17]

Related to these scriptures, but not directly of them is the Book of Enoch, in which we are told that angels, led by Samjaza (usually: Azazel), descended to earth, took mortal wives, and bred a race of giants.[18] Enoch himself was noteworthy. Ecclesiasticus states that "no man was born upon earth like Henoch" [19] and the new Testament records that "Enoch was translated that he should not see death. . . ." [20] Translated to what? Or teleported to where? Did he rise bodily into heaven like Christ and, in revised versions of the Bible, Mary—but without dying—or did he simply rocket away?

However, even with the frequent arguments for dismissing such tales as allegories or entertainments, none are so blind as those who believe that in seeing nothing they see it all.

Nearby Egypt had its aerial vehicles and strange visitations, but, although often quite descriptively specific, they are less persuasive. Late in its history the culture finally abandoned the idea that the heavens were the underside of a gigantic cow or the arc of a female body. It had evolved into an oceanic sky. This revised religious approach accounted for the movement of the sun, moon, and planets, for if heaven was an infinite sea, then it was natural that the astronomical bodies should follow their routes in boats. Not surprisingly, the origin of these vessels was never considered, but Egypt accepted their existence until about a thousand years before the birth of Christ.

The tomb of Seti (c. 1350 B.C.) carries the heiroglyphic inscription "The god rests in the boat . . ." and is accompanied by an illustration of a sky ship. Such craft are common in the religions of resurrection, but their symbolic meaning is usually clear, and difficult to interpret as having anything to do with "flying saucers." [21]

Yet, there is at least one UFO riddle from what may be the oldest continuous culture in the world.

The papers of the controversial Egyptologist Professor Alberto Tulli are reputed to contain references to a sighting at the court of Thutmose III (c. 1504–1450 B.C.). According to the Prince de Rachewiltz translation of the account of the purportedly 18th Dynasty episode:

In the year 22, third month of winter, sixth hour of the day . . . it was found a circle of fire that was coming from the sky . . . it had no head, the breath of its mouth had a foul odor. Its body was one rod long and one rod wide. It had no voice. . . . Now after some days had passed, these things became more numerous in the sky than ever. They shone more in the sky than the brightness of the sun, and extended to the limits of the four supports of the heavens. . . . Powerful was the position of the fire circles . . . after supper, these fire circles ascended higher in the sky to the south . . . and what happened was ordered to be written in the annals of the House of Life . . . so that it would be remembered forever.[22]

This reflects the content and tone of a contemporary observation of Unidentified Flying Objects, possibly of the fireball type, more than most other aerial allusions found among Egyptian myths or historical material.

The Condon Report assembled an argument for a similarity between this record and the passages in the Book of the Prophet Ezekiel.[23] The comparisons are forced and often false, and the citations drawn from a dozen points, not sequential in the Bible, despite the writer saying they are. In fact, the resemblances claimed are strained, arbitrary, or unrecognizable. The proposition has absolutely no value and is, in reality, far less useful for the Report's purposes than an accurate and honest analysis would have been.

In an attempt to make a case for plagiarism, the "Condon" thesis suggests that the verses from Ezekiel derive from the ancient Egyptian manuscript; or, alternatively, that Tulli, Rachewiltz, or some anonymous source was responsible for a fraudulent papyrus based upon a biblical passage. Should the sole evidence for hoaxing, in either direction, be the material in the Condon Report, it may be dismissed. Of course, such does not prove that the Egyptologist's work is valid, only that the "Condon" examination is not.

Other arguments contesting the authenticity or, in any event, the veracity and value of the Tulli manuscript are more reasonable, although not convincing. Apparently, inquiries to the Vatican, which allegedly had possession of the papyrus, received the following response from Gianfeanco Nolli, "the Inspector to Egyptian Vatican Museum"; "Papyrus Tulli not propriety [sic] of Vatican Museum. Now it dispersed and no more traceable." [24]

Pursuing the matter with a diligence accorded few, if any of the "classic" UFO sightings of the twenty years prior to its establishment, the Colorado University panel received the following comment from Dr. Walter Ramberg, scientific attaché to the U.S. embassy in Rome:

. . . the current Director of the Egyptian Section of the Vatican Museum, Dr. Nolli, said that . . . Prof. Tulli had left all his belongings to a brother of his who was a priest in the Lateran Palace. Presumably the famous papyrus went to this priest. Unfortunately the priest died also in the meantime and his belongings were dispersed among heirs, who may have disposed of the papyrus as something of little value.

Dr. Nolli intimated that Prof. Tulli was only an amateur "Egyptologist" and that Prince de Rachewiltz is no expert either. He suspects that Tulli was taken in and that the papyrus is a fake. . . .[25]

It is likely that the Greeks treated the relationships between celestial beings and Earthians more explicitly than most cultures. Commuting between the valleys of mortality and the Olympus of immortality was an ordinary activity for most gods and goddesses, and not a few heroes. Yet, the interplay among terrestrials and sky people was, for the most part, specifically defined in Greek mythology. We may attribute a variety of explanations to the symbolism of a given story, but it is difficult to relate most to a modern "flying saucer" report, however bizarre.

Consider the aerial adventure of Phaëton.

Phoebus drove the chariot of the sun. When his mortal son attempted to duplicate the feat he lost control of the unearthly power. Pierced by a lance of lightning from the hand of Jupiter, he plummeted into the river Eridanus.

Now, the saucer enthusiast might read considerable significance into this tale. An Earthian presumes to pilot a scout ship from another planet, but, being the product of an inferior technology, lacks the skill and understanding necessary to the task. As he careens dangerously about the sky, the commander of the mother ship erases him from the air with an atomic ray.

All of which might have happened a couple of thousand years ago, but probably didn't.

The case of Ganymede, the Trojan boy abducted by an eagle sent by Jove, could be offered as an analogy representing the kidnapping of a human by a spaceman, an occurrence which some saucerologists do not regard as unusual.[26] Nonetheless, as with the Phaëton myth, the meaning is far more likely psychological than interplanetary.

What has been said of Greek lore with regard to "flying saucers" is even more apparent in Roman literature.

Although Origen was uncertain whether "the sun, moon and stars . . . are living beings or without life," and he speaks in terms of other worlds, successive spheres of existence, and the wanderings of souls, it is difficult to doubt that his references are to the spiritual realms, not the spacial ones.[27]

"It was three thousand furlongs, then, from the earth to the moon, my first stage; and from there up to the sun perhaps five hundred leagues; and from the sun to Heaven itself and the citadel of Zeus would be also a day's ascent for an eagle traveling light," relates Menippus in the opening passage of Lucian's tale of one of the original imaginary astronauts. And before the expedition ends the hero is chatting with the deities and is finally thrust back to earth by the god Hermes, stripped of his hawk and eagle wings "so that he may never come [to the heights of the gods] again." [28]

Plutarch is even more allegorical.[29]

Scandinavia has nothing better to offer than the Aurora Borealis, which was supposed to be the flashing of heavenly light from the armor of the Valkyrior, militant Nordic virgins who galloped about the night sky. Little of greater interest is found in the tales of North Americans, where "among the Dacotahs," the same phenomenon was regarded as indicating the presence of Wa-hun-de-dan, the goddess of war.[30]

The Unkatahe accepted the idea of travel to another planet, at least for their souls, if they dreamed of such an adventure and then proceeded to die in their sleep [31]—a typical belief of a disciple of one of the resurrection religions.

In early Mexico, Yoallichecatl, a night spirit, was said to have descended from the sky on the back, or down the web, of a great spider to present Quetzalcoatl with the gift of immortality. On another occasion, a divine stone fell to earth, split apart, and from it paraded sixteen hundred immortals who established an earthly civilization.[32]

The Greeks, the Romans, the Scandinavians, and the North Americans seem to reveal nothing in their religions and literature that argues very effectively for the arrival of early astronauts in their areas of the planet. Why, then, have a couple of pages been devoted to demonstrating that point? The answer has two parts and both are simple. The history of no culture or country that *might* contribute to our knowledge of the history of UFO should be ignored, and the negative results of exhaustive research should be presented to the reader, as well as the promising or intriguing. Such awareness allows comparisons to be made, contrasts to be judged, and these evaluations are important in the study of "flying saucers." At least it warns the reader where *not* to waste his time if he is interested in pursuing their history.

The early Eastern writings have numerous reports of extraterrestrial beings. The most valuable are those of China and India, although the scholar must always

46   UFO EXIST!

anticipate somewhat more delicate or, in the case of much Indian material, more dramatic imagery than common to Western works, even the Bible. Still, in spite of these oriental characteristics, the resemblance to countless modern episodes is, occasionally, impossible to explain.

It is difficult to view the catastrophe of Phaëton as anything other than an allegory, but considered in terms of "flying saucers" and the great passage of time, one might wonder if something more concrete motivated the creation of several ancient Chinese tales.

One of these tells us that long ago, to the north, beyond the Plain of Joy, lay the Land of the Flying Carts. It was inhabited by one-armed, three-eyed people who rode in remarkable vehicles featuring wings and gilded wheels. These amazing chariots or coaches did not travel on the ground, but swooped and sailed the air most of the time, with their drivers talking and laughing.[33] It takes little effort to relate this description to a "contactee" story, and none to recognize its likeness to some of the reports of the Sacramento-San Francisco airship of 1896.*

The legend of Heng O and her husband Shen I actually parallels portions of the experiences reported by Orfeo Angelucci, one of the most famous figures in saucerology.

Heng O, we are told, lay alone in her bed one night. Her spouse, it seems, was amusing himself elsewhere. Suddenly, a white light appeared near the roof, and the little house was clouded with the perfume of flowers. Finding a small ladder, Heng O placed it against the wall and began to ascend to the hovering brilliance. There she found, and ate, a pill of immortality.

Immediately, weightless as the wind, she began floating toward the moon. Soon she reached the ivory satellite and found that it was huge, glowing, and icy. It had no living creatures and was barren of all life except for cinnamon trees. Nevertheless, whether by choice or because she was unable to return, she made her home there. Given an option, it is not a decision any contemporary astronaut would make.

Later, Shen I visited her, arriving on the back of a great bird. Yet, subsequent stories picture him as a solar figure, in contradistinction to her being a lunar one. This, of course, reflects the *yang* and *yin* principle of oriental philosophy.[34]

It is interesting to compare the glowing globe encountered by Heng O with the "thought disk" through which Angelucci established his initial contact with the space people, and her pill of immortality with the "nectar pellet" he received from an alien, which, incidentally, exuded an "exhilarating aroma." [35] And the Shen I identification with the sun reminds one of Orfeo's description of being hurtled into the center of that flaming mass and out again, to return to Earth, purified.

Yet, if his wife's adventures are reminiscent of accounts revealed by "contactees," Shen I is not outdone. On one occasion, as he was traveling with a group of companions, this warrior observed nine shining birds. They breathed jets of fire and drifted above three mountain peaks. Growing increasingly brighter, soon they appeared like small suns. Shen I then directed an arrow into each and, as the missiles struck, the unknowns softened into crimson clouds and vanished.[36]

The nearness of the essential theme of this story to that which inaugurated the modern age of "flying saucers," as well as to other cases, is an extraordinary coincidence. Kenneth Arnold, in his report of his historic sighting, comments on three mountains—Adams, Baker, and Rainier—and the sighting which has been said to have begun it all was of nine bright discs.[37]

The arrows hurled at the "suns" bring to mind a number of attacks by Earth planes, including shooting, made on UFO, and the seemingly "plasmic" alteration of shape is consistent with a great many accounts.

Chinese myths are more easily interpreted as symbolic distortions of possible "flying saucer" sightings of a couple of thousand years ago than much similar literature in the West, but they do not begin to compare with the astonishing material contained in ancient Indian manuscripts.

The *Ramayana,* at one point, deals with the abduction of the Earth girl Sita, by the powerful prince Ravan. The event translates as if it was a Greer [38] (1959), Hill [39] (1961), or Hickson-Parker (1973) [40] "spacenapping," heightened by touches from the adventures of George Adamski. [41]

> Unseen dwellers of the woodlands watched the dismal deed of shame, Marked the mighty-armed Raksha lift the poor and helpless dame, Seat her on his car celestial yoked with asses winged with speed, Golden in its shape and radiance, fleet as Indra's heavenly steed! . . . Then rose the car celestial o'er the hill and wooded vale. [42]

Subsequently, in preparation to do battle with Ravan, Rama borrows "steeds celestial," equipped with a "heavenly car," from Indra. Ravan goes down in defeat, Sita is freed, and the hero of this epic delivers her home in the aerial chariot. "Sailing o'er the cloudless ether Rama's Pushpa chariot came . . . and on earth the chariot landed." [43]

All the reported cases of abduction by aliens in our time have happy endings, as well—except for instances where total disappearances are attributed to "flying saucer" crews, and the victims were never seen or heard from again.

Celestial weapons, vessels, and messengers are quite common to the *Mahabharata.* [44] While less literal than certain verses in the Bible, these records are much more specific than many other Indian sources. And they are only the beginning of examples of material which might be thought to have a relationship with the "flying saucers" of the mid-twentieth-century.

In the *Rig Veda Samhita* we are told that Asvins rescues Bhujya in a "winged" vessel, and the heavenly ship Agnihortra is mentioned in one of the *Brahmanas.* [45]

The *Samaràngana Sùtradhàra* devotes 230 stanzas

to glorifying descriptions of numerous extraordinary
aircraft and military machines. Aerial maneuvers are
detailed, and the ships are credited with cruising ranges
of thousands of miles. It is further revealed that space
cars can fly not only through the earthly atmosphere,
but into the solar regions, or even the Naksatra
mandala, that is, the stars.[46]

It would be difficult to come closer to the Adamski
and Angelucci adventures of our time without simply
presenting records of this sort as "flying saucer" accounts, and designating them as such.

Yet, in spite of the intriguing parallels between
some modern saucerology and ancient Indian writings,
there are still many skeptics unconvinced that they
indicate the possibility of early visits from extraterrestrials. There are several reasons for their doubts.
The craft are often pictured as of a construction we
would regard as aerodynamically impractical and are
identified as beasts and birds. The chronocentric debunker completely ignores the fact that we in the
Western world call nearly every mode of transportation by unrelated or symbolic names, whether the
subject is a horse or a submarine, an aircraft or a
bicycle.[47] In mechanical designs, attempts are often
made to create the actual characteristics of animals.
We even paint an image of the dog on the sides of
public vehicles, or weld a crude sculpture of a cat to
the front of a convertible.

It is also true that immediately prior to present
space technology it was assumed that all interplanetary
craft would have to be streamlined, have Earth, or at
most the moon, as a home port, and, in general, be
rather basic examples of mechanical force.

Today, some of the objects plummeting through
the skies or creeping across the lunar surface look
like many-legged insects; soon they will be constructed
on, and operated from, platforms orbiting this world,
and their energy may well be drawn from the sun.
It is almost inevitable that stations and personnel in
space will become wholly independent of us, and
could conceivably survive if we blow this sphere apart
or contaminate it so that it will no longer sustain life.

If almost that great a disaster occurred, and merely
the remnants of civilization survived in a primitive
state, the inhabitants of the spaceports might move
on to another planet, or create one of their own. A
couple of thousand years pass, and the ex-terrestrials,
for whatever reasons, send expeditions back to Earth,
but find it much as it is today. Perhaps they would
only watch for a while, conceivably make a few contacts, and decide that we had nothing to offer their
vastly advanced culture, and fly home.

It could happen. Since it could, maybe once it did.

After the long period of myths finally faded before
increased sophistication, the ufological historian dis-
covers that material which reinforces his theories is
increasingly more difficult to find. The succeeding era
was dominated by Church imagery, on one hand, and
semi-deified military and political figures on the other.
This left little space for additional alternatives in the
hierarchy of superbeings.

Even after a thousand years had gone by, and the
Romantic Age was emerging, the sky seemed to attract little interest, except for an occasional meteorite
being interpreted as an omen. However, incidents of
possible value are recorded.

Around the middle of the twelfth century, during
the reign of either Stephen of England (1135–1154)*
or his successor Henry II (1154–1189)† a pair of
remarkable children appeared in a

> place called Wolpittes ** after the ancient cavities
> or pits for wolves near it. The boy and girl were
> completely green in their persons, and wore
> garments of strange colour and unknown ma-
> terials when they emerged from the pits. They
> wandered through the fields in astonishment, and
> were seized by the reapers who took them to the

* William (Pettit) of Newburgh citation in *Historia Rerum Anglicarum.*

† Abbot Ralph of Coggeshall citation in *Chronicon Anglicarum.*

** Various other spellings are found, e.g. Woolpit, Wulpets, and Wulfpetes.

village. Here they were for some days kept without food and gaped at by persons from far and
near. By degrees, after many months of food and
bread, they gradually changed their colour and
became like ourselves and learnt our language.
The boy was the younger of the two and died
first. They said they had lived in a twilight land,
not warmed by the beams of the sun.[48]

One noted chronicler of saucerology quotes an "old
manuscript discovered at Ampleforth Abbey . . .
which gives a very clear account of a flying saucer
passing over the startled community of Byland Abbey
in Yorkshire." Although I was unable to trace the
description to its original source, the essential information is that, in the year 1290, several monks were
summoned from their indoor quarters by an agitated
brother and "a large round silver thing like a disk
flew slowly over them and excited the greatest terror."[49]*

A century and a half later Cardinal Cusanus wrote:

It may be conjectured that in the area of the
sun there exist solar beings, bright and enlight-
ened intellectual denizens, and by nature more
spiritual than such as may inhabit the moon—
who are possibly lunatics—whilst those on earth
are more gross and material. It may be supposed
that solar intelligences are highly actualized and
little in potency, while the earth-denizens are
much in potency and little in act, and the moon
dwellers betwixt and between. . . .
Rather than think that so many stars and parts
of the heavens are uninhabited and that this earth

---

* Samuel Rosenberg writing the chapter on "UFOs in
History" for the "Condon Report" dismisses the Byland Abbey
case on the basis of a friend's dispatch from London that
the "Ampleforth document" is a hoax devised by two school-
boys (p. 494). As versions of the alleged incident vary considerably (e.g., it even has reappeared as a distinctly separate
case. Cf. *The Age of Flying Saucers*, p. 197), it has always
been unsubstantial evidence, despite its popularity.

of ours alone is peopled—and that with beings, perhaps, of an inferior type—we will suppose that in every region there are inhabitants, differing in nature by rank and allowing their origin to God.[50]

Pictorial evidence has been far scantier than literary. Witchcraft, demonology, and the occult, for example, which might well have been expected to introduce some supporting data, offer virtually nothing to the researcher. Still, an especially receptive mind might find a few works suggestive. Joseph Ulm produced an illustration in 1404 which depicts a saucer-shaped moon hovering above various persons, including apparently itinerant conjurors.[51] A woodcut, circa 1470, presents a similar composition.[52] A 1726 translation of Bishop Francis Hutchinson's *Historical Essay Concerning Witchcraft* (1718) boasts a frontispiece of a saucerlike symbol in the sky, representing *enlightenment,* presumably.[53] But such examples are atypical and rare.

Nostradamus, the sixteenth-century seer, drew from space for one of his most intriguing prophecies, saying—

A great king of terror will descend from the skies,
The year 1999, seventh month,
To resuscitate the great king of Anglomois,
Around this time Mars will reign for a good cause.[54]

The Last Judgment, a title used around that time by both Brueghel, the Elder (c. 1525–1569),[55] and Hieronymus Bosch (1460–1518)[56] pictured (in both instances) Christ floating above mankind in a circle of half-light. Both pictures are reminiscent of saucerology's well-known "balls of fire" and of the claims of many "contactees" that they have encountered Jesus in a flying saucer, or, at least, that he originally arrived on Earth in one.

A map of the Brocken Mountains,[57] by L.S. Brestehorn, designed in 1732 and published in 1749, records the flight of witches, to the Sabbath. It might call to mind long-distance photographs of UFO groups or

Kenneth Arnold's description of his experience. Rembrandt's etching *Dr. Faustus*[58] depicts a glowing circle of light similar to those described by Orfeo Angelucci.

Those works of graphic art have been mentioned merely to point out the dearth of saucer sources in two areas of creative imagination—visual art and the study of various supernatural crafts. In looking through literally thousands of paintings, drawings, engravings, and woodcuts, nothing more persuasive was found.

"Flying saucer" people support their assertions with myths, religious tales, occasional graphic antiques, and assorted esoterica. Ufologists usually concentrate their research on early astronomical phenomena. This suggests a more scientific approach to the investigation, but how much more impressive the results may be is questionable. Certainly, the speculations of astronomers were not always to be taken seriously. A notable example is the fascinating conception of lunar geography and topography, inhabited by curious people, conceived by Johannes Kepler.[59]

Later, the real Cyrano de Bergerac regaled his readers with his attempts to visit the celestial bodies. "I fasten all about me a number of little bottles filled with dew," he relates, "and the heat of the Sun drawing them up carried me so high that at last I found myself above the loftiest clouds." Unfortunately, this initial effort in astronautics was aborted by mechanical failures, although a rocket machine eventually permitted him to visit the moon and sun, upon which he had many glorious adventures.[60]

Notes

1. Herbert A. Giles, *A History of Chinese Literature* (New York: Grove Press, n.d.), p. 3.
2. Desmond Leslie and George Adamski, *Flying Saucers Have Landed* (London: Werner Laurie, 1953). (Attributed by Leslie "to the Brahmin Tables.")
3. Arthur Posnansky, F.R.A.I., *Tihuanacu, La Cumadel Hombre Americano* (J. Agustin, 1945).

4. Ezekiel 1:3-7.

5. Ibid. 1:8-9.

6. Ibid. 1:10.

7. See *armet* types, of A.D. 1475-1525.

8. Ezekiel 1:13-14.

9. Ibid. 1:15-25.

10. Ibid. 1:26.

11. *The Oxford Universal Dictionary on Historical Principles,* third edition (London: Oxford University Press, 1953).

12. Ezekiel 1:27-28.

13. The Second Book of Kings 2:11.

14. Zechariah 5:1-2.

15. The First Book of Moses, Called Genesis 6:1-4.

16. Stewart Robb, *Prophecies on World Events by Nostradamus* (New York: Oracle Press, 1961), p. 141.

17. The Revelations of St. John the Divine.

18. The Book of Enoch. Same being apocryphal, but not of The Apocrypha.

19. Ecclesiasticus, of The Apocrypha 49:10. (Douay Version)

20. The Epistle of St. Paul to the Hebrews 11:5.

21. *The Book of the Dead,* translated and edited by E. A. Wallis Budge (Hyde Park, N.Y.: University Books, 1960).

22. Leslie and Adamski, *Flying Saucers Have Landed,* p. 46. Reprinted from *Doubt* (magazine), Tiffany Thayer, ed.

23. Condon, *Scientific Study,* p. 499.

24. Ibid., p. 500.

25. Ibid.

26. John Fuller, "Aboard a Flying Saucer," *Look,* October 4, 1966.

27. G. W. Butterworth, ed., *Origin on First Principles.* London: Society for Promoting Christian Knowledge, 1936), p. 6.

28. Lucian, "Icaromenippus, or the Sky-Man," in *The Works of Lucian,* Vol. II, translated by A. M. Harmon (New York: Macmillan, 1960), pp. 269 and 323.

29. Plutarch, "Moralia," from *Concerning the Face Which Appears in the Orb of the Moon,* translated by A. M. Harmon (London: William Heineman, 1913).

30. Ellen Russell Emerson, *Indian Myths* (Minneapolis: Ross & Haines, 1965), p. 7.

31. Ibid., p. 203.

32. Ibid., pp. 109 and 367.

33. Edward Theodore Chalmers Werner, ed., *Myths and*

Legends of China (London: G. G. Harrap & Co., 1922), p. 396.

34. Ibid., pp. 182–188.

35. Orfeo Angelucci, Son of the Sun (Amherst, Wis.: Amherst Press, 1959), p. 19.

36. Myths of China, pp. 181–182.

37. Arnold and Palmer, Coming of the Saucers, p. 10.

38. Flammonde, Age of Flying Saucers, p. 61.

39. John Fuller, The Interrupted Journey (New York: Dial Press, 1966).

40. Ralph and Judy Blum, Beyond Earth (New York: Bantam Books, 1974).

41. George Adamski, Inside the Space Ships (New York: Abelard-Schuman, 1955).

42. The Ramayana, translated in verse by Romesh C. Dutt (London: J. M. Dent, 1910).

43. Ibid.

44. The Mahabharata, Vol. 1, translated by Pratap Chandra Roy (Oriental Publishing Company: Calcutta, no date in copy consulted).

45. V. R. Ramachandra Dikshitar, War in Ancient India (Bombay: Macmillan, 1944), p. 276.

46. Ibid., pp. 276–277.

47. Considering only a few automobiles: Apollo, Charger, Colt, Cougar, Cutlass, Electra, Firebird, Fury, Jaguar, Galaxy, Gullwing, LeSabré, Mustang, Nova, Silver Ghost, Silver Wraith, Skylark, Spider, Tiger, Thunderbird, etc., with no illustrations or mere sketchy descriptions, what would an infinitely more advanced researcher in the year A.D. 5000 think they were?

48. Historia Rerum Anglicarum. William (Pettit) of Newburgh (12th Century). Quoted in Harold T. Wilkins, Strange Mysteries of Time and Space (New York: Citadel, 1959), p. 188.

49. Leslie and Adamski, Flying Saucers Have Landed, p. 22.

50. Nicolas Cardinal Cusanus, Of Learned Ignorance, W. Stark, ed., Germain Heron, trans. (London: Routledge & Kegan Paul, 1954), pp. 114–116.

51. Milbourne Christopher, Panorama of Magic (New York: Dover, 1962), p. 3.

52. Ibid., p. 5.

53. Rossell Hope Robbins, The Encyclopedia of Witchcraft and Demonology (New York: Crown, 1960), p. 253.

54. Nostradamus, *The True Centuries*, translated and inter-
    preted by Stewart Robb: *Prophecies on World Events by
    Nostradamus* (New York: Oracle, 1961), p. 132.

55. Emile Grillot DeGivry, *Picture Museum of Sorcery, Magic
    and Alchemy* (New York: University Books, 1963), p. 33.

56. Ibid., p. 32.

57. Ibid., p. 73.

58. Ibid., p. 111.

59. Johannes Kepler, "The Dream," from John Lear, ed.,
    Kepler's Dream (Berkeley, Calif.: University of California
    Press, 1965), pp. 118–163.

60. Cyrano de Bergerac, *Voyages and the Moon and the
    Sun*, translated by Richard Aldington (London: George
    Routledge & Son, 1922), p. 53.

4

The Sky of the Beholder

**These objects [UFO] are conceived and directed by
intelligent beings of a very high order. They probably
do not originate in our solar system, perhaps not even
in our galaxy.**

> —Dr. Hermann Oberth, interna-
> tionally renowned rocket and
> space travel authority, and of-
> ten called the father of the V–1
> and V–2 weaponry of World
> War II. Press conference, in
> Innsbruck, Austria, June 1954

MAN HAS REACHED for other worlds and dreamed of
the arrival of representatives of spacial civilizations
for as long as he has kept records. Undoubtedly, such
fantasies reach far, far back into prehistory. Of course,
it is testimony of alleged extraterrestrial travelers that

is of interest to the students of "flying saucers." Early in the seventeenth century, there was a strong revival of curiosity about the possibility of other life in "our" universe. While often fanciful, many of the theories were concocted by prominent men of science, the arts, and religion. Ideas of alien existences were often presented as deduction and fact.

However, *reason* was not the basis of most belief in extra-Earthians. The Right Reverend John Wilkins subtitled the first of two volumes *That the Moon May Be a World* (1638),[1] that is to say, populated. In the thirteenth "proposition" of this argument the author contends that "it is probable there may be inhabitants on this other world; but of what kind they are, is uncertain." Then he quotes Cusanus:

> We may conjecture (saith he) the inhabitants of the sun are like to the nature of that planet, more clear and bright, more intellectual than those in the moon, where they are nearer to the nature of that duller planet, and those of earth being more gross and material than either.

Wilkins speculates upon travel through space. He fully recognizes many of the actual obstacles to such adventures—the immeasurable distances involved, the tremendous speeds required, the necessarily long confinements, and the problems arising from these. Much of this is weighed in terms of the astronomical and mechanical knowledge of the day. The clergyman occasionally succumbs to mystical imagery; still, his practical and classical scholarship is impressive.

The possibilities of extraterrestrians was sketched out in formal astronomical terms by Christian Huygens (1629–1695).[2] The treatise included descriptions of planets "as wonderful a Variety" as may be found on our own land. "There's no doubt but that Metals, Crystals, and Jewels" are abundantly distributed in these remote places, he assures us. Erecting cities and a civilization, he populates them with inhabitants who have "Reason there not different from what it is here."

"That there is some such Species of rational creature

in the other Planets, which is the head and Sovereign of the rest is very reasonable to believe," he notes, anticipating Adamski, Angelucci, King,. Menger, and most "contactees" who left no doubt that humans were very inferior fellows compared to citizens of many other worlds.

Huygens claims for his space people talents in astronomy, from which he deduces that "all its subservient Arts" have been discovered, as well. Although the aliens "have Hands . . . and Feet . . . and that they are upright," he concedes that "it follows not therefore that they have the same Shape with us." Later the great majority of "contactees" followed the ancient tradition of describing their demigods in Man's own image.

"We have allow'd," concludes the philosopher, "that they may have rational Creatures among them, and Geometricians, and Musicians: We have prov'd that they live in Societies, have Hands and Feet, are guarded with Houses and Walls: Wherefore if a Man could be carried thither by some powerful Genius, some Mercury [Hermes], I don't doubt 'twould be a very curious sight, curious beyond all imagination, to see the odd ways, and the unusual manner of their setting about anything, and their strange methods of living. But since there's no hopes of our going such a Journey, we must be contented with what's in our Power."

The scholar details most levels of culture to be expected on universal worlds, including the character of buildings, the arrangement of cities, and the structure of their societies. Ultimately, Huygens creates a civilization nearly indistinguishable from the one in which he lived, with the possible exception of the inhabitants' appearance and the implication that they are somewhat more responsible and less violent than Man.

A fantasy on the possibility of life elsewhere in this solar system, and beyond, was published around the same period by Bernard Bouvier de Fontenelle.[3] This work, while neither serious scientific nor religious speculation, caused quite a stir and attracted several literary replies.

Jonathan Swift (1667–1745) came even closer to the modern kind of account, telling of "the flying or floating island" which was "exactly circular, its diameter 7837 . . . [and] . . . three hundred feet thick" —specifications not unlike descriptions of large *mother ship* types of "flying saucers." Although detailed as a natural formation, Swift makes much of "the great curiosity, upon which the fate of the island depends." This "loadstone of prodigious size in shape resembling a weaver's shuttle,"* is the motivating force of the phenomenon.

Significantly, the late Morris K. Jessup, among the more prominent of the serious researchers into Undefined Sensory Experience, offered a thesis that is not inconsistent with the ideas presented by Dean Swift more than two centuries earlier.

> Suppose that some intelligent entity was directing a concentration of potential which could make small volumes of rarified air rigid, could get up a sort of island in the gravitational or magnetic fields, moving the island about as the *spot* of a searchlight is moved on thin clouds . . . in moving the *island* would simply "freeze" on the advancing edge and "thaw" the trailing edge . . . it could have almost infinite velocity, and also acceleration . . . only the force beam would move, not the air.[4]

However, Swift's anticipation of modern astronomy, with extraterrestrial overtones, is even more astounding.

> They have likewise discovered two lesser stars, or satellites, which revolved about Mars; whereof the innermost is distant from the centre of the primary planet exactly three of his diameter, and the outermost, five; the former, revolves in a space of ten hours, and the latter in twenty-one

* A word recurring in modern descriptions of USE and UFO.

and a half; so that the square of the periodical times are very near in the same proportion with the cubes of their distance, from the centre of Mars.[5]

One hundred and fifty years afterward, in 1877, Asaph Hall, an American astronomer, "discovered" what came to be known as Phobos and Deimos—the "moons" of Mars. How did Jonathan Swift know their orbital periods were calculable in hours, rather than days, months, or years? How did he arrive at the conclusion that Deimos whirled about Mars in less than a third of the time it takes the planet to revolve on its own axis? Especially when it was considered impossible for any satellite body, which had originally derived from a major one, to have a greater orbital velocity than the rotation speed of the planet. What was the impetus for his calculations, or the source of his information? "Flying saucer" scholars have claimed that he had access to ancient and esoteric manuscripts, descended along a secret line of sages, from a super-civilization of the past. These, it is argued, revealed that the moons of Mars were artificial creations, hurled into space by an advanced technology of another age and a lost culture. Today there are an increasing number of sober scientists who regard the speculation that these satellites are not natural phenomena within the realm of reasonable conjecture.

Certainly, no one has ever offered any feasible explanation for the astronomical anticipation by one of the giants of English literature.

Perhaps the record of Undefined Sensory Experiences of purported phenomena, mystical occurrences, and other inexplicable happenings is more provocative than any of the material drawn from more popular sources. An interesting example of such a sighting took place on June 22, 1744, when twenty-six individuals observed troops of aerial soldiers high over a Scottish mountain. The phantoms passed along for two hours, but were finally obscured by darkness. A chronicler called the spectacle a mirage; a "contactee" would be inclined to suspect it was a company of space people.[6]

Across the Channel the brilliant Voltaire produced *Micromégas* (1725). The subtitle describes it as "a voyage to the planet Saturn, by a native of Sirius," who stands "eight leagues in height" and actually comes from "one of the planets that revolve round that star." [7] The moral commentary is found on the pages of the book the hero leaves when he departs the Earth. They are blank.

However, if the French ironist provides crumbs for the "flying saucer" party, Emanuel Swedenborg (1688–1772), the Swedish philosopher, theologian, and mystic, left them a piece of cake. He did not merely speculate upon the possibility of extraterrestrial life, he described it in considerable detail.[8] Certainly few "contactees" have been more unequivocal in their portrayal of other-planetarians. Since a number concede that their relationships with space people have been more spiritual than tangible, Swedenborg may be placed in the center of their claim. He is among the earliest writers to argue for the physical reality of inhabitants of other worlds. One should know what he "knew" about them.

Swedenborg recalls that "on a time some spirits came to me . . . they were from the earth which is nearest the sun. . . ." The Mercurians are wanderers, whose "sole study is to acquire themselves knowledge. These spirits are permitted to wander at large, and even to pass out of this solar system into others . . ."

"Long and frequent conversations" with the "inexpressibly gentle and sweet" people of Jupiter reveals "the education of their children" is their prime concern. Tranquil of nature, they delight in long meals, which are most often taken in the low, wooden, usually blue-interiored buildings they call home.

"The spirits of Mars are amongst the best of all," says the "contactee." He recalls that their faces "resembled the faces of the inhabitants of our earth, but the lower region of his face was black, not owing to his beard: this blackness extended itself underneath his ears on both sides, the upper part of the face was yellowish."

Saturnians are "exceedingly humble," they "feed

on fruit," and "do not bury the bodies of their dead, but cast them forth and cover them with branches of forest trees."

The Venusians, somewhat more interestingly, are divided into two orders, one "mild and humane, the other savage and almost brutal." The eighteenth-century "contactee" did not have an opportunity to converse with the less savory of these races, Still, he was informed that "they are exceedingly delighted with rapine and more especially with eating their booty." At least, this gives us a broader picture of the people of the second planet, since the modern reports of Adamski, Menger, and others usually have them radiating Christian, or godlike, virtues. Doubtless these later evaluations are of these *other Venusians* who may have somewhat prejudiciously described the "evil" tenants of their planet to Swedenborg.

The self-appointed ambassador of spacians does not confine himself to the planets proper. He tells us that Moon People appear as "children of seven years old, but more robust." They are, in fact, "dwarfs." Beyond our own solar system, we are promised, there are populated "earths" in immense numbers throughout the universe. It need not be emphasized that this opinion coincides with that of most contemporary astronomers.

Extraordinary heavenly fireworks have been observed and recorded for a couple of thousand years. By the eighteenth century they were more and more frequently noted and catalogued. The company of prominent persons convinced of extraterrestrial life was growing. Thomas Paine wrote, ". . . to believe that God created a plurality of worlds, at least as numerous as what we call stars, renders the Christian system of faith at once little and ridiculous, and scatters it in the mind like feathers in the air. The two beliefs cannot be held together in the same mind; and he who thinks he believes in both has thought but little of either." [9]

Although the opening years of the nineteenth century found many laymen intrigued by the skies, it was the astronomers who opened the new era.

"Octagonal"* stars in the London sky, great fiery bodies over Switzerland, hurtling globes of light above Florence, an immense luminescent form sighted by the inhabitants of Portugal, a satellite-appearing object in the vicinity of Venus, spherical unknowns crossing the face of the moon—all found their way into the astronomical archives of the 1800s.†

Increased consciousness of other worlds, possibly supporting races either akin or totally alien to us, laid the foundation for the execution by Richard Adams Locke of one of the cleverest "scientific" deceptions of all time. His newspaper articles claimed that "A discovery that the Moon Has a Vast Population of Human Beings" had been determined by the remarkable telescope of Sir John Herschel, located at the Cape of Good Hope (1834–1838), and convinced large portions of the public.[10]

Edgar Allan Poe based "The Unparalleled Adventures of One Hans Pfaall" upon this fraud. His hero journeys to the moon, tumbling "headlong into the very heart of a fantastical-looking city, and into the middle of a vast crowd of ugly little people, who none of them uttered a single syllable, or gave themselves the least trouble to render me assistance, but stood like a parcel of idiots, with their arms set akimbo."[11]

The trip, from Rotterdam to the lunar community, takes nineteen days and 90 percent of Poe's story. A three-and-a-half-page Note appended to the Poe tale speaks exhaustively about the Locke hoax, the general practicality of aerial commuting, and various other subjects.

Still, sightings of serious interest continued. An object, classified as a meteor, was witnessed above Malta, on June 18, 1845.[12] It was seen as "5 moons" (five times the size of the moon), its duration, which was unusually long, was recorded as "streak 60" (one

---

* Hundreds of such angular shapes have been recorded.

† Further description in *The Book of The Damned*, Charles Fort, pp. 240–41. Similar phenomena often reported in recent years.

hour). The source records the UFO as "slow, indistinctly seen; two very large together, nearly joined."*

This sighting was of an object more massive than the usual meteor, but many of considerable size were seen during the mid-century period. Ones the size of the moon, or the sun, or "1600 lbs.," or a number of times the measurements of Jupiter, or twelve times the size of Sirius, were not uncommon.

The century passed into the second half, and volumes on polluted planets continued to appear. Some were derived from contemporary works; most drew both their titles and inspiration from the earlier book by Bernard de Fontenelle.

Among the more important contributions was Sir David Brewster's *More Worlds Than One*.[13] This treatise, admittedly written in response to the Frenchman's *Conversations on the Plurality of Worlds,* comments on its predecessor and its author: "This singular work, written by a man of great genius. . . ."

It then proceeds to observe that Giordano Bruno of Nola (in *Universo Mondi innumerabili*), Kepler, Tycho, Cardinal Cusa, Newton, Dr. Bentley, the Marquis De Laplace, Sir William and Sir John Herschel, and other major intellectual figures believed in extraterrestrial life. "The arguments for a plurality of worlds. . . are so rare, and have such different degrees of force," notes Brewster in a *General Summary,* that "when the mind is once alive to this great truth, it cannot fail to realize the grand combination of infinity of life with infinity of matter."

Over a hundred years later Harlow Shapley, the noted American astronomer and director of the Harvard Observatory, would support some of the conclusions of the nineteenth-century commentators Robert Knight and Frederick William Cronhelm. He stated, in the early 1960s: "We must now accept it as

---

* Among modern USE, size, duration, and coupling are individually common, and collectively not rare; e.g., pair "nearly joined," see Tremonton, Utah, case (July 2, 1952), English Channel case (October 18, 1953), Chalmette, Louisiana, case (August 21, 1954), and others.

inevitable— there are other worlds with thinking beings." [14] However, they viewed the possibility of alien life forms rather pessimistically.

It is unreasonable to believe in the existence in this world of intelligent, and progressive, and multiplying races, who can "inhabit the water, or the dark masses of the earth, or be at home in the fire," [15] not because such things are impossible, for who can tell the variety of forms, or the compensating material elements which almighty power has at its command; but simply because such races would be able to dispute, if not destroy, man's dominancy over the earth, or even exterminate him. The highest ascendency in civilization and in the arts of war, can give but a faint impression of the superiority which such races would possess over man. His fleets would be the sport of the one, and all his terrestrial labors would be at the mercy of the other. But the most complete renunciation of the belief of such races in our history is perfectly consistent with a retention of the belief of the existence, in other worlds, of beings who enjoy compensating elements of which we are entirely ignorant. [16]

Concurrently, the religious commentaries continued to appear.

On October 21, 1866, an unusual meteor was observed by Ernest Turner, and recorded in more colorful terms than science ordinarily employs: "A curious circumstance was its stationary appearance at first, and its rapidly increasing velocity afterwards; the brilliant emerald colour of the meteor, and of its fragments." Subsequently, this fireball, which was seen over Hoboken, New Jersey, disappeared by breaking into "a perfect rain of emerald-green-coloured fragments." [17]

Another report, of an object sighted over the United States, told that "something was seen that looked like a ship's red light, as seen at a distance of 200 yards. [It] floated away steadily for three minutes . . . disappeared behind houses. The sky was cloudy and the night dark, but the light could not have had any artificial origin." [18]

The century approached its final quarter. Reports of improbable things sighted in the skies became increasingly frequent. This was a fruitful period for astronomers.

Amateur ufologists rely heavily on the miscellaneous material collected by Charles Fort, and such disciples tend to accept his notes unquestioningly. Such confidence is no more justified in this instance than in most. To induce students to seek out *original* material, one example of Fort's reliance on erroneous secondary sources is cited. [19] The inaccurate version of the Bonham, Texas, incident has appeared in so many articles and books it is regarded as the original by many scholars. Yet, it is third-hand misinformation.

On July 1 or 2, 1873, workers on a farm about a half dozen miles from Bonham reported seeing a great, serpentine shape sailing above them. Fort repeats the story with reasonable accuracy, citing as his source the New York *Times*. [20] He explains the newspaper had "copied it from the *Bonham* (Texas) *Enterprise*" of a few days earlier.

Regrettably, an original copy of the issue was not obtainable, and is very unlikely to exist. However, with that information, locating it would have been difficult. Clarification would result from unearthing a copy of the century-old newspaper, but not of Fort's (and the New York *Times*') imaginary *"Bonham Enterprise."* What must be retrieved is a copy of the *Honey-Grove Enerprise* (sic) founded by Tom R. Burnett, probably in 1870. It was published in a small community* sixteen miles east of Bonham—from which it took its name. Bonham had no newspaper of its own in those days.

A day or two later, other witnesses to the north reported a similar spectacle:

---

* Honey-Grove appears to have been christened by the great frontiersman James Bowie, who found the village rife with beehives.

And now Fort Scott, Kansas has been seeing a snake in the sky. The *Monitor* says: "The sky was clear and the sun rose entirely unobscured. When the disk of the sun was about halfway above the horizon the form of a huge serpent, apparently perfect in form, was plainly seen encircling it, and was visible for some moments."

The Editor declares that he has the statement from two reliable witnesses, who are willing to make affidavit to the above. It will soon be time for a national prohibitionary liquor law, if this sort of thing is to continue.[21]

James Nasmyth and James Carpenter published a substantial book,[22] with extremely interesting plates, in 1874. It dealt with various aspects of the moon, including its life-supporting possibilities, but concluded there was no likelihood of inhabitants.

A fascinating article by the great French astronomer Camille Flammarion appeared. In it he commented on lunar life:

Several observers have seen on the moon enigmatical lights that they have attributed to *aurorae boreales*. Thus, for example, on the 20th of October, 1824, at 5 o'clock in the morning, Gruythuisen perceived in the dark portion of the moon, while it was night on the *Sea of Clouds,* a brightness which extended as far as *Mount Copernicus,* and having a length of nearly 250 miles, and a breadth of 125. In a few minutes it disappeared; then electrical pulsations succeeded each other from half past 5 in the morning until daybreak, which put an end to the observations. The observer attributed these vacillating lights to a lunar *aurora borealis*.[23]

Charles Fort, in reporting on Gruythuisen's lights, makes the display sound like a glittering lunar skyscraper. Still, his artfully selected quotes are less provocative than Flammarion's own speculations. For example:

Lunar beings and things necessarily differ from
beings and things terrestrial.

. . . without having the idea occur to us that
such objects were the work of the Lunarian's
hands—if, indeed, they have hands.*

The famous astronomer does include a few mild
disclaimers, but concludes:

Who knows? Even while I am discussing this
question, it may be that some of the inhabitants
of the moon are up there in the valleys, and on
the velvety plain of *Plato,* gazing down upon us
from their distant abode. And perhaps they have
been prepared for a long time past to open correspondence with us.[24]

The Italian astronomer Schiaparelli produced the
first detailed study of Mars. "A highly competent observer, he had an excellent telescope, good conditions
for observing, and Mars was unusually close to the
earth." [25] Dusky patterns, interpreted to be seas, were
distinct against the ruddy dry land. In 1877, Schiaparelli identified streaks connecting the "seas" with one
another. He called them *canali,* which means channels.
Regrettably, the similarity to the English word "canal"
resulted in a narrower interpretation than intended.
This led to a good deal of misinterpretation.

Schiaparelli added [to his initial report] "their
singular aspect, and their being drawn with absolute geometric precision as if they were the
work of rule or compass, has led some to see in
them the work of intelligent beings, inhabitants
of the planet." [26]

The Italian's *canali* and the ensuing controversy
peaked with the intervention of astronomers Lowell
and Pickering, which will be described later.

An 1879† report from Henry Harrison tells of an

* A question upon which Huygens also pondered.
† April 13, 1879.

object, which he "supposed to be a planetary nebula," sighted at "about 8:30 o'clock in the evening." Its behavior was so extraordinary, he brought a friend to verify his telescopic observations. Establishing that it was not a meteorite, comet, star, or cloud, from "its shape, diameter and density . . . also for its luminosity" and pattern of activity, he pursued his study for some time. He made careful notations and calculations for three and a half hours, until it was midnight, and he retired. At 2:10 A.M. he awoke, still curious, and found the object proceeding toward the southeast. Eventually it disappeared beyond the horizon, more brilliant than ever before.[27]

A more curious report tells of witnesses watching a sudden darkening of the sun during the late afternoon. Simultaneously, there appeared a great number of round, blackish objects on the western horizon. They passed overhead in a long procession, vanishing to the east. The UFO were no more than a foot, or two, across. Occasionally, one would apparently drop to earth. Where they fell only a slimy substance was discovered. This swiftly dried and was no longer visible.* [28]

"An enormous number of luminous bodies rose from the horizon, and passed in a horizontal direction from east to west," as dawn broke over Kattenau, Germany, on March 22, 1880.[29] A glowing object was seen by hundreds of persons, from Virginia to South Carolina, on December 20, 1893. During its flight it paused at about 15 degrees above the eastern horizon for a quarter of an hour. Then it disappeared in the distance.[30] Two years later, on August 12, the Observatory of Zacatecas, Mexico, noted a large number of luminous objects passing across the sun.[31] They were reputed to be "relatively near the earth," and it was reported that a photograph was taken of the phenomena.[32]

For the special five hundredth issue of *The Observatory,* of which he had been editor for some years,

---

* Such material, called angel's hair by some researchers, is common in our time.

E. W. Maunder wrote: "I have tried to recall my most striking experiences during the past 43 years, and my memory has gone back to one that stands out from its unlikeness to any other."

The occasion was a clear evening in late autumn, some thirty-five years earlier.* It was two hours after sunset and Maunder was at the Royal Observatory, in Greenwich, England. He remembers that he "had a view uninterrupted in all directions, except for a great dome towards the S.E.," as he stood watching an auroral display, which he had anticipated, for some time. As it "seemed to be quieting down, a great circular disc of greenish light suddenly appeared low in the E.N.E., as though it had just risen. It moved across the sky, as smoothly and as steadily as the sun, moon, stars, and planets move, but nearly a thousand times as quickly." [33] Its roundness was evidently merely an effect of angle. As it moved it lengthened. "When it crossed the meridian and passed just above the moon its form was that almost of a very elongated ellipse. . . . Various observers spoke of it as 'cigar-shaped,' 'like a torpedo,' or 'spindle,' or 'shuttle.' " † [34] A third of a century later, certainly most people would have said it looked just like a Zeppelin. The object's passing took "less than two minutes to complete."

"It appeared to be a definite body," Maunder noted, adding that "nothing could well be more unlike the rush of a great meteor or fire-ball . . . than the steady —though fairly swift—advance of the 'torpedo.' " [35]

Although associating the extraordinary incident "with the great magnetic storm of 1882," the astronomer continued to regard the phenomenon as "unlike any other celestial object that I have ever seen" and a "celestial object unique in my experience." [36]

An extremely odd incident, which had originally occurred three and a half years earlier, reached public print in 1883.

On board the British India Company's steamer

---

* November 17, 1882. Maunder's original account appeared in *The Observatory*, No. 6–192.

† The recurrence of these descriptions will be noted.

Patna while on a voyage up the Persian Gulf [the writer begins] in May, 1880, on a dark, calm night, about 11:30 P.M., there suddenly appeared on each side of the ship an enormous luminous wheel, whirling round, the spokes of which seemed to brush the ship along. The spokes would be 200 or 300 yards long, and resembled the birch rods of the dames' schools. [A peculiar reference. 'Dames' schools' were classes held in the homes of the instructresses.] Each wheel contained about sixteen spokes, and made the revolution in about twelve seconds. One could almost fancy one heard the swish as the spokes whizzed past [as with the birch rods in the dames' schools?] the ship, and, although the wheels must have been some 500 or 600 yards in diameter, the spokes could be distinctly seen all the way round. The phosphorescent gleam seemed to glide along flat on the surface of the sea, no light being visible in the air above the water. The appearance of the spokes could be almost exactly represented by standing in a boat and flashing a bull's-eye lantern horizontally along the surface of the water round and round. I may mention the phenomenon was also seen by Capt. Avern, commander of the *Patna,* and Mr. Manning, the third officer.

(signed) Lee Fore Brace

A postscript was added: "P.S. The 'wheels' advanced along with the ship for about twenty minutes. —lfb." [37]

The growing number of inexplicable sightings prompted more evaluations, although some had less substance than title. In 1892, *Wonder of the Lunar World, or a Trip to the Moon* was published. Disappointingly, it proved to be nothing more than a course in basic astronomy.[38] Yet, on May 25, 1893, halfway around the world from the adventure in the Persian Gulf, another remarkable occurrence at sea was recorded.

"During the recent wintery cruise in H.M.S. *Caroline* in the North China Sea . . . on 24th February, at

10:00 P.M. . . . some unusual lights were reported by
the officer of the watch," writes Captain J. N. Nor-
cross, adding that the phenomenon was before and
above the ship. "To the naked eye they appeared
sometimes as a mass; at others, spread out in an irregular line, and, being globular in form they resembled Chinese lanterns festooned between the masts
of a lofty vessel."

The shining objects reappeared

on the following night, February 25, about the
same time . . . it was a clear, still, moonlight
night, and cold . . . the lights maintained a constant bearing (magnetic) of N.2°W, as if carried
by some vessel traveling in the same direction
and at the same speed. The globes of fire altered in their formation as on the previous night,
now in a massed group, with an out-flying light
away to the right, then the isolated one would disappear, and the others would take the form of a
crescent or a diamond, or hang festoon-fashion
in a curved line. A clear reflection or glare would
be seen on the horizon water beneath the lights.
Through a telescope the globes appeared to be of
a reddish colour, and to emit a thin smoke.

I watched them for several hours, and could
distinguish no perceptible alteration in their bearing or altitude, the changes occurring only in their
relative formation, but each light maintained its
oval, globular form.[39]

The master of the *Caroline* then provides full lo-
cational, navigational, and time data. He subsequently
read in the Kobe daily newspaper that the "unknown
light of Japan, had, as was customary at this season
of the year . . ." been observed by fishermen, in the
Shinbara Gulf, but he was unable to obtain any more
specific information regarding the incident.

In England, in 1895, a J. A. H. Murray, of Oxford,
sent a letter to the *Times* telling of having sighted a
"brilliant luminous body" low in the sky, moving eastward. "It sailed or floated majestically . . . as if driven

by a strong wind." The object grew dimmer as it approached the horizon, finally disappearing behind a treetop. The writer notes that it moved "many times slower than any meteor" and was "considerably larger than Venus." He concludes by describing the missile's course as "from near Alioth, on the top of the Bear's tail, close to the Pole Star, through Cassiopeia, towards Andromeda." [40]

Fictional fantasies, as differentiated from the spacial adventures of Verne and Wells, appeared in the mid-nineties. Two were *Daybreak* [41] by James Cowan and *The Martian* [42] by George du Maurier. The former, "a romance of an old world," deals with the moon plummeting to earth and becoming embedded in its side. It is visited by a pair of heroes who explore, have adventures, and encounter a beautiful woman, Mona.* The most fascinating passage is about "The Picture Telegraph." It functions exactly as does the contemporary television set, offering both interior and exterior views of things far removed.

Du Maurier describes the Martians as having "webbed fingers and toes . . . exquisite fur" and "telepathic powers." The story is quaint, but dated with all of the turn-of-the-century limitations.

It was not the romancers on extraterrestriality, or the science fiction giants, who were to lay the foundation of ufology. No, it was not even the astronomers, graphing the course of the remote heavenly phenomena.

The stories were written, the sightings recorded, the catalogues were compiled, and many were justifiably subjects for speculation. Yet, it was the man in the fields, the housewife shopping along Main Street, it was tens of thousands of American citizens who witnessed and reported the greatest ufological observation complex up to that time.

In 1896 truly extraordinary and inexplicable phenomena of the air began to occur. They wrote the

---

* The lively alien female is common to many "contactee" stories, with Truman Bethurum's space commander "Aura Rhanes," from the planet Clarion, a classic example.

first line of the preface to the modern age of "flying
saucers."

Notes

1. Right Rev. John Wilkins, *The Mathematical and Philosophical Works* (London: Vernor & Hood, 1802), pp.
   100–108; Cusanus quote p. 103.
2. Christianus Huygens, *The Celestial Worlds Discover'd, or
   Conjectures Concerning the Inhabitants, Plants and Productions of the Worlds in the Planets* (in Latin) (James
   Knapton, 1722).
3. Bernard Bouvier de Fontenelle, *Conversations on the
   Plurality of Worlds* (London: Lackington Allen & Co.,
   1809).
4. Morris K. Jessup, *The Case for the UFO* (New York:
   Bantam Books, 1955), p. 20. (Original hardcover, New
   York: Citadel, 1955).
5. Jonathan Swift, *Travels into Several Remote Nations of
   the World. By Lemuel Gulliver* (London: Heyward and
   Moore, c. 1840), p. 281.
6. Sir David Brewster, *Letters on Natural Magic* (London,
   1842), p. 125.
7. F. M. A. Voltaire, *Micromégas*, pp. 390–397.
8. Emanuel Swedenborg, *The Earths in the Universe* (London: Swedenborg Society, 1875), and *The Earths in our
   solar system which are called Planets* (Boston: B. A.
   Whittemore, 1928).
9. Thomas Paine, *The Life and Works of Thomas Paine*,
   Vol. III, The Age of Reason (New York: Thomas Paine
   National Historical Association, 1925), p. 74.
10. *"Great Astronomical Discoveries—lately made by Sir
    John Herschel."* New York *Sun*, August 25 through Sep-
    tember, 1835. Also see *The Moon Hoax or a Discovery
    that the Moon Has a Vast Population of Human Beings*,
    booklet published by William Gowans, 1859. For further
    information see note material on Richard Adams Locke
    hoax, at conclusion to "The Unparalleled Adventures of
    One Hans Pfaall," pp. 38–41.
11. Edgar Allan Poe, "The Unparalleled Adventures of One
    Hans Pfaall" (New York: Random House, 1939), pp. 3–41.

12. *Report of the British Association for the Advancement of Science*, No. 30, 1860, p. 83.

13. Sir David Brewster, *More Worlds Than One* (London: John Murray, 1854).

14. *Flying Saucers*, September 1961, p. 57.

15. Robert Knight, *The Plurality of Worlds* (Samuel Bagster & Sons, 1855).

16. Frederick William Cronhelm, *Thoughts on the Controversy as to a Plurality of Worlds* (London: Rivingtons, 1858).

17. R. P. Gregg, *A Catalogue of Observations of Luminous Meteors*, Supplement. *Report of the British Association for the Advancement of Science* (London: John Murray, 1867), p. 294.

18. Ibid. See also *Scientific American*, Vol. XV, No. 21 (November 17, 1867).

19. Charles Fort, *The Books of Charles Fort* (New York: Henry Holt, 1941), p. 638.

20. New York *Times*, July 6, 1873.

21. New York *Times*, July 7, 1873.

22. James Nasmyth and James Carpenter, *The Moon* (London: John Murray, 1874).

23. *Scientific American* (April 5, 1897). Article by Camille Flammarion.

24. Ibid.

25. *Scientific American* (July 16, 1910), p. 42.

26. Ibid.

27. "A Curious Astronomical Phenomenon," *Scientific American*, Vol. XL, No. 19 (May 10, 1879), p. 294.

28. *North American Review*, No. 3–319. Item by M. Acharius. Reprinted in part in *The Books of Charles Fort* (New York: Henry Holt, 1941), p. 283.

29. *Nature*, No. 22–64. Reprinted in part in *The Books of Charles Fort*, p. 222.

30. *L'Astronomie*, 1894–157. Reprinted in part in *The Books of Charles Fort*, p. 275.

31. *L'Astronomie*, 1885–347. Reprinted in part in *The Books of Charles Fort*, p. 223.

32. Ibid., 1885–349. Reprinted in part in *The Books of Charles Fort*, p. 224.

33. E. W. Maunder, *The Observatory* (39–214), Vol. XXXIX, No. 500 (May, 1916). Reprinted in part in *The Books of Charles Fort*, pp. 293–294.

34. Ibid.

35. Ibid.
36. Ibid.
37. *Knowledge,* No. 113 (December, 1883). Reprinted in part in *The Books of Charles Fort,* pp. 270–271.
38. Garrett P. Serviss, *Wonders of the Lunar World or A Trip to the Moon* (Morris Reno, 1892).
39. *Nature,* Vol. 48, No. 1230 (May 25, 1893).
40. London *Times,* Letters to the Editor, September 4, 1895.
41. James Cowan, *Daybreak* (New York: George H. Richmond & Co., 1896).
42. George du Maurier, *The Martian* (New York: Harper and Brothers, 1897).

5

The Great Airship

The least improbable explanation is that these things [UFO] are artificial and controlled. . . . My opinion for some time has been that they have an extraterrestrial origin.

—Dr. Maurice A. Biot, one of the world's leading aerodynamicists and mathematical physicists. *Life,* April 7, 1952, p. 96.

"THE GREAT AIRSHIP" first appeared over southern California in the autumn of 1896. The amusing and fascinating case remains inexplicable to this day.

Within a few weeks, as the accounts accumulated, all the characteristics of the modern era become evident. Brilliant and erratic lights were seen in the night heavens, followed by assertions that their paths had been deliberate and controlled. Craft of many and different designs, from which movable lamps glowed, were described. The scientific community flared forth with explanations that the turmoil was being caused by meteors, planets, or atmospheric conditions. Thousands of believers responded with rebuttals. A variety of unknown persons pushed into the limelight claiming to be the creator of the remarkable invention. Landings, "contactees," and most other features of the mid-twentieth-century period of ufology developed. In their own time the phenomena were described as Unidentified Flying Objects by an uncountable number of direct witnesses. Most of these testified that the sightings were distinguishable and manned craft. The case may be unique.

Among the most astonishing aspects of the great airship sightings of 1896 is that the tale remains untold to this day, except for occasional references of a few lines. From the original sources, here is that incredible record.

If delayed testimony is considered acceptable, the earliest appearance of the California UFO occurred in late October. Returning home in San Francisco, around dusk, a young lady named Hegstrom caught sight of a glowing light in the sky. It was quite unrecognizable to her. Upon her arrival she told her family of the experience. Rejected as the product of her imagination, this testimony was not revealed until the furor caused by the airship was well under way.

The first immediate account was reported to a journalist on the first of November. It was given by a mountainman and hunter named Brown who related his observation of—not a light, not at night—but an "airship," in the morning sky. He estimated it to have been no more than a hundred yards off, above some trees of Bolinas Ridge, near the city. The rising dawn mist somewhat obscured the vessel, and the apparition caused him to doubt his sanity, for a moment, but he firmly maintained that what he "saw was an airship."

Brown, a recluse by choice, as were most mountainmen, had no reason for lying. He immediately returned to his remote haunts, never to be heard again, at least in connection with this affair.

The sighting was described to a professional newsman the day after it took place. That date preceded any other substantiated record of the enigmatic craft. It is extremely likely that this was the initial report of the great airship of 1896.

Not until three weeks later did other appearances begin the general excitement. At first the glimpses were brief and the testimony frail, but the observations and accounts rapidly increased in frequency, definition, and enthusiasm. Before two more weeks had passed the phenomenon(a) was (were) the most discussed subject along the West Coast.

On the evening of November 17, 1896, a brilliant light moved over Sacramento, California. It was witnessed by hundreds of people. Unfortunately, the mayor, preoccupied with official business, had to be satisfied with the account of his daughter, who had personally observed the aerial mystery.

The assistant superintendent of the streetcar company was also forced to rely on others for *details*. Yet, he did watch the radiant globe as it sailed, in an undulating course, toward the southwest, and disappeared.

T. P. de Long perceived only a little more. He was unable to determine that the dark shadow was an actual craft, but clearly saw it progressing *against* the wind, at an altitude of three or four hundred feet.

The foreman of the trolley barn had no doubt about the overflight of a machine, of some description, at around dinnertime. Too distant for its specific shape to be distinguishable in the twilight, it carried controlled illumination, and drove straight into the strong breeze. As the foreman put it, the UFO moved like a seagoing craft plowing rough water.

Countless other witnesses saw the glowing light. Many described the ship upon which it was mounted, and, according to most, the lamp was manipulated to sweep both land and air. Such visual aid permitted the vessel to avoid collisions with high buildings, mountains, and, perhaps, other airships.

The consensus was that the object was large, had an oblong shape, with flattened ends, or was ovoid. It featured propellers or fan wheels, which pushed through opposing winds, and carried a small cockpit

above the main body or supported a cabin underneath. Reports varied regarding the last point. Numerous estimates indicated that the craft cruised the
heavens for nearly thirty minutes.

Still, such adventures were only part of the evening's entertainment. A number of persons were prepared to swear that they saw members of the incredible craft's crew. Other witnesses *heard voices*
drifting down from the vessel!

A horse trainer may have been the first Sacramento
inhabitant to glimpse the UFO, and it was low when
he initially spied it. He said that an operator was
clearly audible as he directed that the course be raised
when the ship came dangerously close to earth. As
the altitude was increased the voices became fainter.
The last remarks heard concerned not sailing too high,
as that might delay the flight schedule.

The trainer was convinced that a minimum of two
fliers were sailing the craft; some persons estimated
a complement of at least four. Most of these observers agreed that the aerial voices could be clearly
distinguished. One witness asserted that he had shouted
at the crew, asking where they were bound. He received the reply that they were expecting to be above
San Francisco by midnight.

A brewery employee confirmed the most colorful
stories, adding that he was audience to cheerful carol-
ing and airborne laughter. The gaiety was abruptly
suspended when one of the pilots snapped: "Lift her
up, quick; you are making directly for that steeple."
Then the jolliness returned as the airship sailed up
into the invisibility of the night.

Naturally, these extraordinary events gave rise to
rumors almost as improbable as some of the descriptions of the great airship. Reflecting the creativity of
some suggestions was one that the UFO had been
constructed by Thomas Alva Edison. Having perfected it, his intention was to offer it to the United
States government to facilitate its handling of problems with Venezuela and Spain. The improbability of
the New Jersey inventor's sending the craft across the

continent to be tested disturbed none of the advocates of this theory.

More practical speculators thought the craft had been constructed in the vicinity, a short distance from either Sacramento or San Francisco. The secrecy with which the alleged inventor worked seemed reasonable to them. It was assumed that he conducted experimental flights in the dark and kept his, and his machine's, whereabouts unknown so that his rights might be protected until navigational perfection was achieved and patents were procured.

Two days had not passed before a former member of a local employment agency announced he had spoken with one of the vessel's crew. The airman revealed that, during trial ascents, the ship had been restricted by a ground cable, and that it had been difficult to control. Additional tests were to be conducted farther away from the city.

None of these analyses was adopted by a very large segment of the citizenry.

Yet, regardless of what testimony now sounds valid and what exaggerated, thousands of individuals were positive that they had seen an intelligently directed light in the sky. Hundreds were prepared to take an oath that it was an aerial vessel, and scores that its pilots had been seen or heard, or both. Moreover, the press was publishing a strange assortment of attitudes. It titillated, encouraged credulous consideration, attempted, with widely varying success, humorous skepticism, and then immersed itself in sarcasm, deliberate confusion, and concentrated efforts to discredit any intelligent inquiry into the affair. That is, it foreshadowed the faults of the media of the midcentury age of UFO down to the most unrefined detail. Similarly, all levels of government ignored the phenomena as much as they could without appearing more derelict in their responsibilities than was unavoidable. What attention they were forced to devote to the business was focused on making the less supported aspects seem nonexistent and the inescapable ones absurd. In that respect they anticipated the be-

havior of officialdom during the modern era of UFO
to an amazing degree.

Nevertheless, nothing could alter the fact that the
"flap" was flourishing, and that it was solidly based
upon an incalculable number of direct sightings, in a
broad spectrum of communities, over a substantial
geographical area, including offshore water.

The debunkers were having their problems. One
journal opened a major article by calling the mystery
"one of the greatest hoaxes that has ever been sprung
on any community." But it concluded the first paragraph with the admission that if it had not called it
a fraud, "there would be the very best of reasons for
believing it true."

The great airship was moving southward. It soared
above Oakland, California, on the evening of November 20, 1896, and produced responses ranging from
delight to fright in the thousands of persons who
watched it.

A motorman had his attention called to the craft
overhead by a passenger. He stopped public transportation on its tracks, and all observed the "moving
object" for at least five minutes. One rider, an armorer
by profession, clearly noted the large lamp, the wings
or winglike propellers, and that it was heading across
the bay.

Later, inhabitants of the Mission area, in San Francisco, had their attention attracted by a strangely be-
having luminescence moving across the Twin Peaks.
The light was observed again the following evening.
Between the two sightings, during the middle of the
afternoon, an enormous flying device passed through
the sky, moving southward.

An interesting account was registered on earlier
evenings by a hotel clerk and fifty people who shared
his experience. He told of monitoring three aerial
lights, or a single horizontal one giving a multiple
appearance. In any event, the center one, or the center
of the effect, was bright red. This may have been the
first report, in this complex, to introduce color.

Inevitably, tales reflecting uncontrolled imaginations
and deliberate attempts to spoof the mysterious events

were fanciful and frequent. R. L. Lowry offered a highly detailed description of the vessel. It was an oblong "mass," motivated by vast fans on axles which were connected to a bicyclelike apparatus. Four men, stated the witness, sat astride this subsection and peddled the machine against a noticeable wind. Viewed through the chronoscope of history, two characteristics are exceptionally striking.

The more apparent is the fabulous Swiftian or Baumian nature of the vessel, its crew's alleged merriment, and the whimsicality that permeates the entire odyssey. Still, one must not lose sight of the fact that virtually every story was repeatedly slanted. The "pure," that is, the immediate and direct, observation was influenced by the personality of the viewer, his commercial or official position, the anticipated reaction of his family and friends, and was modified accordingly. It might be presented uncertainly or contemptuously. Or the witness might overstate and elaborate, submitting his report as outright facts, to be accepted by any but those who would call the teller an outright liar.

The variables increased as the witness related his adventure to a newspaperman. A version for the press, to be read by thousands of strangers—that is, the ubiquitous "them" who influence nearly every move made by the average individual anyway—would assume quite a different tone.

His interview completed, the journalist could interpret and present the material in almost any fashion suiting his purpose. The serious could be made to sound ridiculous, the improbable persuasive.

The second most intriguing face in this multifaceted gem of ufology is the amazing consistency of innumerable recollections. Regardless of how unlikely a few of the stories were, certain features constantly recurred in the reports: the egg, cigar, or ovoid shape; the hill-and-dale or "wavy" flight pattern, the low cruising survey of the communities over which the airship(s) sailed, and the continuous progress from the north or northeast to the south or southwest; the upper cockpit, cabin above or below, or the suspended gondola; the brilliant light, repeatedly compared to an arc lamp, which could be operated to scan land or sky; and the virtually unanimous opinion of witnesses that the craft was intelligently controlled. All these features of the vessel and its operation were testified to by thousands of viewers immediately after its first major appearance over Sacramento.

The machine was sighted over various towns during the days that followed, but the "huge airship" soaring about the heavens of San Francisco elicited the most intense response. Little else was discussed. Then came a new development.

A man of some substance in the city, an attorney named George D. Collins, leaped into the limelight and revealed that he was the personal representative of the "inventor of the remarkable airship."

The lawyer from Alameda assured the public that the extraordinary device existed and was the creation of a prosperous client of his. It had been constructed in Oroville, California, to the northeast, from sections and material imported from the East, for the sake of secrecy. Collins said that he had been contracted to go to the nation's capital personally to obtain patent protection. His client distrusted the United States mails.

According to Collins, negotiations entrusting him with the secret and the mission took some time. The designer appeared at his office, rambled about other subjects, and avoided the purpose of his visit several times before he took the attorney into his confidence.

The curious client was said to be in his middle years, and of some wealth, and Collins conjectured that "people [would] call him a genius." Emphasizing that he must censor his revelations, the agent said work on the vessel had been in progress for several years. Collins also reported that its range far exceeded sixty miles, a distance it could navigate in an hour or less. The only remaining problem, said the lawyer, was that the ship tended to be "a little wavy" in its flight, which might disturb those inclined toward seasickness. He concluded these comments by advising the newsmen that "if the night is at all pleasant" his client was most likely to fly "his machine about half a mile over the earth startling some of the inhabitants of this State."

Soon Collins announced that he had visited the designer and received a demonstration of the craft. It had taken off, circled up and then down, finally landing "as lightly as a leaf."

Despite being unable to clarify his earlier statement that the vessel was propelled, in some fashion, by compressed air, Collins assured the reporters that it was 150 feet long, and capable of accommodating more than a dozen people. Further, its two sweeping wings were eighteen feet wide, constructed of canvas over a frame, and the main guidance system was a rudder.

The attorney provided little information regarding the anonymous "inventor," revealing only that he was from Maine, had been a student, and then a scholar, of aerial navigation for about fifteen years, and had relocated on the Pacific coast about halfway through that period of research.

One notable characteristic of the airship was its attraction to the capital city. Regardless of how often it wandered elsewhere, even to San Francisco, it was repeatedly observed above Sacramento. On November 22, a weatherman, along with thousands of other citizens, witnessed the clear, white light. Occasionally, it dimmed to a hazy glow with a halo, but each time it resumed its usual definition and intensity. As was often the case, the UFO traveled in a rising and falling flight path.

The city editor of the *Record-Union,* Nick White, watched the activity for a while. He was convinced that not only was the light carried by an airship, but that he had seen several lights rather than one. This was the first multiple-light pattern reported, unless the previously described white-red-white phenomenon was not a single unit.

The apparition was seen constantly in the skies of San Francisco, adjacent areas, and over the bay. Journalists rarely let George Collins out of sight, peppering him with questions whenever the chance arose. The attorney occasionally avoided reporters, but for the most part gloried in the attention.

Emerging from his office late one afternoon he acknowledged that, although undetected by the reporters, his client had delivered fresh information to him that morning. The vessel had successfully been flown during the storm of the previous evening, meeting the conditions without stress. The run had begun from a hidden field, where its hangar was situated, and passed over the island of Alcatraz. It hovered for fifteen minutes above the seal rocks in the bay, shining light upon the sleek brown creatures moving about below. Overflying Sacramento, it finally returned to where it was hidden, near Berkeley.

Understandably, newsmen were anxious to determine the identity of the supposed designer. Repeating that he was tallish, in his early forties, with no financial worries, Collins added that he had roomed for two years with a family. The private house was located on the south side of a particular thoroughfare, between two streets which he named. He then expressed regrets that he was not free to furnish the inquirers with any additional information.

It was clear that Collins—short of providing a specific address—had left the amateur detectives with nothing to do. Immediately the press announced that the only resident living in any of the twenty-odd possible places fitting the description provided by the lawyer was Dr. E. H. Benjamin. The lodger was characterized by his landlord as an accredited dentist who did little or no work in his profession, although he thought he occasionally sold pianos. The major portion of his time seemed to be devoted to "experimenting" or brief journeys. The gentleman had not bothered to enter his name in the local medical directory, and certainly had no proper office in the city. At the time the press discovered his residence, the mysterious "inventor" was still on one of his frequent trips.

The general excitement continued, encouraged by countless sightings from the previous evening, delivered by hundreds of reputable people. Witnesses included patrolmen, mountain deputies, streetcar operators, shopkeepers, and housewives.

One week after the aerial affair began in the Sacramento heavens, events took a new twist. Collins had not claimed merely to be the personal agent of the inventor of the airship, or simply to have seen the craft and watched it fly. According to him, his client had promised to fly back and forth along the length of Market Street for all the citizens to see. The city and the state were to be identified as the birthplace of a new aeronautical age.

Now, that changed. The bearded young lawyer emphatically denied ever claiming the actual existence of an "airship." Interviews containing such remarks by him he dismissed as preposterous. By extension, any allegations that he had reported seeing such a mechanism in flight were absurd to the boundaries of libel. Collins granted mentioning that a client of his was interested in aerial navigation, and may have worked on a model of a device designed to achieve flight. However, said the attorney, to quote him as having said he was associated with a concept so "vulgarly improbable" as a flying machine could only come from a "liar and a son of a liar."

While a strange element in a complicated episode, the Collins business was actually an incidental issue. The subject was the "great airship." The accounts continued to pour in to the press, to various police departments, and to many governmental offices. "I saw the light, and am satisfied it was attached to an airship," commented Police Officer Clarence Coogan; the light "seemed to be attached to some dark object," observed attorney James A. Hall; "I am satisfied that the mysterious light was attached to an airship," asserted Police Captain Wittman; "I am inclined to believe that the light was attached to some dark object," remarked Dr. J. H. O'Brien; and the affirmations from responsible witnesses continued.

Mayor Sutro, previously dependent upon the accounts of members of his staff, had a personal viewing of "lights carried by an airship." So did Colonel Menton, of the Southern Pacific Company; Samuel Foliz, a newspaper advertising director; and Professor C. H. Murphy of the Polytechnic High School.

Collins was totally reversing his position while initial arguments for the existence and activity of an aerial invention were simultaneously being supported by highly respected citizens. Yet, it was quickly evident that the attorney was not finished with the matter. He had begun as a proclaimer of the reality of the enigma. Then he denied its existence entirely. By November 24 the pendulum of his opinion had slowed and stopped—he claimed ignorance. "It would be presumptious [sic] for me to say the story that an airship was being worked about the bay was a fake . . . it is not for me to say that these people have not seen an airship."

Suddenly the alleged inventor for whom Collins had prepared the way renounced all claims that he was the creator of the mysterious vessel. Dr. E. H. Benjamin admitted he knew Collins, and occasionally had been his client, but insisted that he had absolutely nothing to do with any aerial experiment.

Within twenty-four hours of Benjamin's disclaimer, a fresh development occurred. It was announced that the "destinies" of the airship were in the charge of W. H. H. Hart, former attorney general of the State of California. It was explained that this action was the direct result of George D. Collins' inability to exercise discretion in his relationship with the press.

The second aspect of the new situation was headlines that announced that the craft would "PROBABLY BE USED TO DESTROY THE CITY OF HAVANA." The information amazed some people, especially as we were not at war with Cuba at the time. Obviously Hart was no more interested in such technicalities than earlier and subsequent politicians and militarists. In his words: "I believe two to three men could destroy the city of Havana within forty-eight hours." Hart rattled his new weapon so loudly that more interesting data was nearly obscured—that is, the newspaper story that the "real" inventor of the airship was a Dr. Catlin, and that Benjamin, despite his denials, was his chief assistant in its construction.

A fourth aspect of the unfolding story was that if Collins "leaked" material to journalists, Hart's mouth was a veritable floodgate. Collins had misled reporters as much as he had led them; confused them as often as he had convinced them, despite his obvious pleasure at seeing his name in print day after day. The former state attorney general had assumed authority over the airship's "destinies" allegedly because Collins talked too much to the press. Yet Hart immediately proceeded to attract much more newspaper coverage than his predecessor ever had. He told all that he knew and, quite apparently, much that he didn't.

The effect was to dilute serious inquiry, to clear the field for "official" pronouncements regarding the future of the great airship, and to distort efforts to discover the truth. Whether Hart was the blustering fool he seemed or a masterful public relations expert is another of the unavoidable questions in the investigation of the California "flap."

Whatever the truth, the politician was as talkative as ever on the afternoon following his replacement of Collins.

"I have not myself seen the machine in action or at rest," he grunted, during his second interview. Then he put it to the newsmen straight out that the device had been airborne on the previous night. As usual, there were many witnesses prepared to swear that they had sighted it sailing along. When asked to confirm that the vessel was a success he replied: "Yes. I have implicit confidence in it . . . it is very like the one I saw in New Jersey, and which I witnessed make a flight of fifteen or twenty rods." Regrettably, he would reveal nothing further about the East Coast wonder. Citizens were momentarily distracted by the puzzle of who was, and who was not, representing the designer of the flying riddle, and who had, and who had not, created it. Hundreds of sightings in various locations, a constantly increasing number of converted skeptics, and the inevitable occasional jokers and hoaxers were what really fascinated the public.

E. H. Keiser, owner of the house in which the first alleged inventor lodged, announced that Dr. E. H.

Benjamin had "gone to get his airship and take this lady to Europe, where he will marry her." In spite of the landlord's attempted humor, Dr. Benjamin had seemingly disappeared. Then his credentials as a dentist began to be confirmed. Dr. Joseph D. Hodgen, secretary of the State Board of Dental Examiners, revealed that while not practicing in the city regularly, he did handle patients in the office of a colleague occasionally. Also Benjamin had worked on several experiments relating to improving bridges.

Hart's eagerness to be interviewed by newsmen became increasingly evident after his first press conference. Collins had offered simple, if colorful, responses to queries. The former attorney general poured forth grandiose claims and breathtaking promises so swiftly reporters found it difficult to interrupt him long enough to present questions of their own.

For example, the new spokesman clarified his previous military speculations by explaining that the inventor had not suggested that the airship should blow Havana off the map in the name of the United States government. Not at all; he was prepared to do it all on his own—for ten million dollars.

Another correction was that he was not actually offering to annihilate the capital city. Certainly not for his own government. Rather, he was presenting the proposition to the Cubans. He would blow up the "Spanish stronghold of Cuba," and they would all be free. Or something to that effect.

However, despite the continuous and peculiar remarks of Hart, they were *still* not of primary importance. The fundamental question was and remained: what was flying around the skies of northern California?

One answer seemed extremely likely. The same thing, or the same sort of thing, that was invading the airspace to the south. Although passing over previously unvisited communities such as Petaluma, to the Bay City's immediate north, it was also being seen in Tulare, and much farther on, over Los Angeles.

Among the positive accounts was one contributed by Walter F. Parker, secretary to Mayor Rader.

Particularly interesting was the fact that virtually all of the reporting observers continued to give identical accounts of what they had spied. Of even greater concern to the investigator were certain characteristics credited to the phenomenon. A classic description was of "triple lights dancing in a zigzag way and moving on parallel lines." Disregarding the color consideration, this would constitute the third hard testimony of three lights. Such detail was an element of thousands of accounts during the modern era. The zigzag and parallel motions have also been constantly encountered up to this date.

Hart's next announcement was that the inventor was the cousin "of the electrician of General Antonio Marco, commander of the patriot forces in Cuba." One could hardly escape recognizing that the airship was being put to political use. Considering the international implications, the question of the federal government's interest was inevitable. On the day before, Marco had won what many analysts thought might be a decisive victory on the Caribbean island.

A major sighting was then recorded. It was made by a professional educator, Dr. H. B. Worcester, president of the Garden City Business College, who viewed an unknown for several minutes, under conditions that recall the Lubbock Lights case of August 25, 1951. It occurred during the early evening. The professor's experience was shared by a number of other individuals, including Professor M. S. Cross, dean of the University of the Pacific and a noted linguist, and other people. Another group nearby also watched the phenomenon. A curious coincidence of names is found in this and the Lubbock, Texas, business. In the Texas case Hart was the name of the young man who was able to get photographs of the objects.[1]

Also of importance was the sighting that evening of a vaguely birdlike, undulating craft. It featured, in addition to the expected white spotlight, jets of colors —red, blue, green. The UFO was seen by residents of

Tacoma, Washington,* the location of the Maury Island Mystery.

Hart swung out in an increasing circle, encompassing a growing number of believers. It seemed to him that a letter—really a proclamation—was appropriate. He proceeded to write and publish it.

In reference to the airship which has been puzzling and astonishing many of the people of California I will say this:

I have not seen it personally, but have talked with the man who claims to be the inventor. I have spent several hours with him. He has shown me drawings, and diagrams of his invention and I am convinced that they are more adapted for the purpose for which he claims them than any other invention making such claims that I have ever seen.

It seems to me that the evidence that THE CALL has been enterprising enough to collect in reference to this airship, the character of the people who have seen the same, the fact that it moves against the currents of air as well as with them, the fact that it has the power to dart from side to side or forward, ought to convince the people that there is something in the invention.

I asked the gentleman who claims to be the inventor what his desires were in regard to carrying on the business, and he stated that he did not desire any money; that he didn't ask or want anyone to invest in it; that he was not a citizen of California, and that he had come here to perfect and test his airship as the climate and currents of air were most suitable to his purpose. He further stated that he had progressed so far since coming to California that California certainly was entitled to the honor of his invention, as it was in quite a crude state when he first came here; that he had two airships already constructed. One, he said, was of large size, capable

—————
* See Chapter 10.

of carrying three persons, the machinery, the fixtures and 1000 pounds of additional weight, and another that was much smaller, capable of carrying one man, the machinery, fixtures and 500 or 600 pounds of other matter.

He also stated that he was a cousin of Mr. Linn, who was Antonio Marco's electrician, and that he is expected to take it to Cuba for the purpose of aiding in the capture of Havana as soon as he could perfect it and acquaint his associates with the handling of it.

He was a man of dark complexion, dark eyed and about 5 feet 7 inches in height and weighed about 140 pounds. He looks considerably like the gentleman playing the part of Arion, the aerial acrobat, but is a little taller.

He claims to have three assistants with him, all of whom are mechanics; that he used two kinds of power, gas and electricity; that his lights are sometimes produced by electricity and sometimes by gas, with the aid of reflectors.

He claims to have moved 120 miles at one flight and in a little less than six and a half hours, and at that time was not going wholly with the currents; that he uses electricity for propelling his vessel against the wind, and uses gas largely in going with the air currents. He does this in order to save power.

He proposes to build another airship, and in fact one of the parties interested with him has told me that they are now at work on the third airship, which is to be more commodious and more perfect than the other two, and that it would be so constructed that in the event the machinery got out of order and it should fall into the water it could be used as a boat by detaching a portion of the airship. When this is completed and ready for use the inventor intends to leave California for Cuba.

So far as the electrical power is concerned, the Fargo electric storage battery is of sufficient capacity, as to power and lightness, to furnish the requisite power for aerial navigation, and the inventor proposes to use this power in connection with the other for his operations. The battery can be stored to its full capacity, which is 20 horsepower, in 17 minutes.

I am of the opinion that this airship will be a success, and that its success is far more probable at this time than the Morse telegraphy was at the time he first offered the same to the public.

So far as the public is concerned this inventor does not ask anyone to invest in this enterprise. Perhaps this may be evidence of insanity. I will admit that this is the first time to my knowledge that anybody had anything in California in which he did not want anybody to invest money.

More and more, the two stories had separated; or so it was clearly evident seventy-four hours later. Hart, his clients, their airships, Cuba, politics, and war had completely split apart from the actual aerial phenomenon, or phenomena. In one evening Undefined Sensory Experiences (USE) were seen, as either Unidentified Atmospheric Phenomena (UAP), Unidentified Flying Objects (UFO), or specified vessels over San Francisco, Oakland, Redding, San Jose, Alameda, Tehachapi, and Los Angeles. Within forty-eight hours they had ranged from Tacoma, Washington, to southern California. Soon the sightings were as frequent and widespread in the lower portion of California as they had been for two weeks from Oroville to San Jose. More important was the fact that it, or they, had been seen beyond the borders of the single state.

The first real "contactee" story occurred on December 2, 1896. The event began early in the morning along the beach near Pacific Grove, a village north of San Francisco. There Giuseppe Valinziano and Luigi Valdivia, two local fishermen, were astonished to see a modest-sized aircraft glide down from the sky, coming to rest on a sweep of white beach. Immediately, the fishermen's conclusion that the device was intelligently directed was confirmed. Three occupants stepped out. The crew then carried the obviously light craft across the sand and into the nearby woods.

Bringing their small boat to shore through rough surf, Giuseppe and Luigi proceeded forward to the trees. One of the strangers quickly reappeared and suggested they move away. However, Valinziano, an aggressive and confident fellow, insisted upon some conversation. Then he declined to leave the area without a glimpse of the extraordinary craft. His firmness proved profitable. The aeronaut told the fishermen to wait while he consulted with his companions. A quarter of an hour later the entire crew returned. It was led by an imposing individual, whom the others merely called "Captain." He made it quite clear that any attempt to approach his invention beyond a designated point would meet with physical resistance. However, he permitted the fishermen a long-range view. Following this privilege, the villagers from Pacific Grove were invited to picnic with the airmen, and urged to wait long enough after the lunch to see the airship take to the sky. Regrettably, although Valinziano and Valdivia agreed to witness the departure, necessary repairs on the machine proved more complicated than anticipated. The ascension had to be delayed until after dark, and as dusk approached the fishermen started homeward.

Later, Valinziano speculated that the mysterious captain of the air might have delayed them deliberately, to prevent their telling of the landing, and especially of the whereabouts of the airship, before a return to the sky was achieved.

The two witnesses were never closer than fifty feet from the craft, but they agreed that it was twenty yards long, cigar-shaped, and featured great wings which could be folded against the fuselage of the ship. This description is of additional interest when one recalls that the vessel was carried by only three aeronauts. Many citizens were completely convinced by the report, but many more were not.

Events of the following night shifted the balance in favor of the likelihood of truthfulness. An airship was seen to pass over the city's Twin Peaks, ap-

parently flounder in the air, and plummet to the
ground. From it two crew members, bruised and bat-
tered, either extricated themselves, or were pulled,
according to immediate witnesses.

> The propeller was twisted and bent; one elevat-
> ing fan was ripped off and lay on the ground,
> while the other was badly twisted from the force
> of the shock.
>
> A large hole in its side permitted the escape
> of a sickish smelling gas. The steering aparatus
> [sic], rudder as it was called, which had been on
> the bow was also broken off . . . the machine . . .
> was of cylinder shape, with both ends cone-
> shaped.

Allegedly, one of the crew was J. D. de Gear and
the other the anonymous inventor. Gear made clear
that the vehicle was, indeed, an airship of his friend's
making. The excursion had been its christening flight
and, therefore, it was in no way connected with any
of the earlier sightings along the entire Pacific coast.

Yet Collins' statement, Attorney General Hart's
assumption of authority, the contact with the aeronauts
by the Pacific Grove fishermen, and the disaster of
the crashing craft did not even begin to explain anything at all about the great airship mystery. Various
of the foregoing might, in some curious and unexplained manner, have been related to the essence of
the mystery. Certainly each of these, and other, events
confused and obscured the real riddle. The possibility
of that having been their primary purpose cannot be
dismissed by the serious analyst.

A previously unmentioned factor strongly supported
the suspicion of deliberate misdirection. One of the
newspapers which most heavily covered the travels
of the vessel was William Randolph Hearst's San
Francisco *Examiner*. Invariably its terms and tones
ranged from complete skepticism to scathing sarcasm.
A simple example of its restrained reporting of the
affair was headlined: PROBABLY DUE TO LIQUOR,
another THE RESULT OF BEER.[2]

Meanwhile, across the continent, the New York *Morning Journal* was assuming a completely opposing position. A typical positive assertion is found in the opening of a late November story. "The biggest problem of the age has been solved. Man has won what seemed to be his hardest battle with nature. A successful airship has been built." [3] The New York *Morning Journal* was also owned by William Randolph Hearst.

Who was William Randolph Hearst? Among many fascinating things, a man who desperately wished to be President of the United States.[4] Also one who is held by many to be a, if not the, primary catalyst which sent this country into the Spanish-American War. The prelude to that conflict was being vigorously developed by the publisher in flamboyantly headlined columns, side by side with the coverage of the great airship.

Unavoidable is the query: why was Hearst, a brilliant newspaperman and financier, deeply involved in America's international and military affairs, directing his editors on each coast to present the business of the aerial phenomenon in contradictory reportage? It seems additionally peculiar when the attacks came from the periodical published in the *very locale of the events* and the assurances of authenticity appeared in his newspaper *on the other side of the country.* Hearst was a man of singular ability, sweeping imagination, and a gambler for the highest stakes. He did nothing without a reason. Discarding an obvious program to stimulate the circulation of both newspapers by direct competition, the riddle remains. What did America's most aggressive newspaperman know about the great airship that he wished to have obscured. If nothing, what purpose was the elaborate and seemingly illogical misdirection intended to achieve?

The opinion of other journals were emphatic and prominent: HEARST'S AIRY CHAMELEON, AN OSTRICH-LIKE ATTEMPT TO DELUDE THE PEOPLE, and CONFLICTING STORIES PRINTED BY THE SIAMESE-TWIN FAKER [Hearst] SHOW THE UNRELIABILITY OF THE TWO SHAMELESS PAPERS.

That was how "the great airship mystery" began.

In the fashion briefly described it developed and fragmented into barely related stories. There was the scrambling opportunism, the indiscriminate exploitation, the pure fictionalizing, and the blatantly intentional deceit. Despite all of the errors deriving from intent, ignorance, and overexcitement, nothing altered the fact that tens of thousands of people had viewed the light or the lamp and the object, or, even, specific craft. Most relevant was that a considerable percentage of the often detailed accounts originated with highly reputable and responsible individuals. Something began happening in the skies of the Pacific Coast of the United States in November 1896. Before it ended few Americans would remain untouched. The opening of this extraordinary drama has been presented.

How did it continue? How did it end?

Notes

1. Flammonde, *Age of Saucers,* pp. 34–36.
2. San Francisco *Examiner,* November 28, 1896.
3. New York *Morning Journal,* November 28, 1896.
4. A member of the House of Representatives from 1903 to 1907; unsuccessful candidate for mayor of New York City in 1905 and 1909, and for governor in 1906, he openly bid for the Democratic presidential nomination while in Congress.

6

Americana: April 1897

Flying saucers—unidentified flying objects—or whatever you call them are real.

> —Senator Barry Goldwater, brig-
> adier general, United States
> Air Force Reserves

THE EXTRAORDINARY SIGHTING complex of the turn
of the century is often referred to as the great airship
mystery of 1897. During April what had commenced
in California in November 1896 swept across the
entire nation. It disappeared as suddenly and inexplicably as it had begun six months before on the Pacific
shore. Yet, disregarding the case's lack of resolution,
the conclusion that emerged was nearly unique. Rarely
were sightings so frequent, widespread, and different
as those of what must properly be designated as the
great airship mystery of 1896–1897.

Its appearance over Tacoma, Washington, on
November 24, 1896, seemed to have signaled the
craft's geographical liberation. Thereafter, it began
venturing eastward. It was seen in a wide variety of
places, across the West and Midwest, throughout the
next several months. The activities of the airship (or
airships) produced the most extraordinary journalistic
records of an era when extravagance in the press was
commonplace.

April Fool's Day, 1897, found the wandering radiance in the skies of Kansas City, Missouri. The performance started at about eight o'clock in the evening,
as a huge lamp swept the air, and the streets, house-

tops, and bluffs upon which the public gathered to observe the wonder. It moved at considerable speed, crossing the city at 45 degrees above the horizon, and continued northward, roller-coasting an easy, wavy course. Sometimes the intensity of the light dimmed. Then "falling or stationary or sweeping along horizontally it blazed out brilliantly again." [1]

An hour after its arrival the UFO ascended high into the darkness. Its radiance decreased, and it grew smaller as it moved away. Finally, it evolved into a definitely reddish color and vanished to the northwest.

Shortly after its disappearance, Everest, sixty miles away in the neighboring state of Kansas, reported the light had passed overhead.

The Kansas City witnesses numbered in the thousands, and included the governor. A variety of other officials and professional people, and countless ordinary citizens, agreed that the unknown swept one way and then another in abrupt changes of course. It demonstrated strange and acrobatic maneuvers, hovered motionlessly, and once extinguished its lights and hung as a vast black mass. Finally it was gone. It remained for ninety minutes, during which time "the powerful lights on board were reflected on the cloud[s] and the outlines of a ship about thirty feet long apparently were clearly distinguished." [2]

Testimony to most of these observations was presented to the press in the form of an affidavit. It was signed by the owner of the major hotel, an officer of a local mill, a gentleman merely described as "a capitalist," an entrepreneur, and others, "all men of high repute." [3]

The phenomenon, which the local press claimed had been overflying the state for the preceding four months, floated above Omaha, Nebraska, on the next night. It was broadly recognized as a very real airship, and the majority of viewers agreed that it was deliberately directed. Many persons were convinced that it had been invented locally. While such assumptions conflicted with similar ones held by residents of various California communities, it is entirely possible that the

Middle Americans were unaware of the West Coast origin of the airship.

One popular story declared that John Preast,* a well-educated semirecluse of German background who had resided on the outskirts of Omaha for a score of years, was the creator of the astonishing vessel. Although some citizens of the town viewed the loner as an eccentric, many regarded him as an individual of marked intelligence and creativity. Two additional points supported the argument. Preast made no secret of his interest in aerial navigation or of his craft models intended to demonstrate some of his theories. Second, a group of his neighbors insisted that every time the UFO appeared it eventually vanished in the vicinity of the scholar's home. But even in light of the popular suspicion, Preast flatly denied responsibility for the machine.[4]

Actually, as the newsmen had reported, the mystery craft had already made a visit to the area. Less than three weeks earlier a local compositor, residing in South Omaha, reported watching it for more than thirty minutes. As he was returning home from church, "a bright light, about a foot in diameter" caught his attention. "We could distinguish some dark body below the light," he remembered. The printer granted that he and his companions were less able to detail the form they thought they perceived below the brilliant disk. A considerable number of other persons were comparing their observations the next day. Within two weeks, thousands of people around Omaha testified to such experiences.

The flow of reports was so constant and originated in such separated places that crediting all of the activity to a single craft was a problem.

Needless to say, there were always experts anxious to provide full solutions for the cryptic phenomena which had yet to be identified. The self-anointed authorities dismissed the entire business of airborne lights, objects, and craft. They were all atmospheric

---

* Elsewhere (cf. *Detroit Free Press,* April 1, 1897, p. 9) Pries.

activities, planets, stars, and frauds. Even our old friend the second planet from the sun, so constantly juggled about by Air Force spokesmen and occasional observatory technicians throughout the "modern age," was among the more popular explanations offered at that time. Yet, then as now, it could almost always be clearly demonstrated that the pale blue orb of Venus had nothing whatever to do with what was seen.

The great airship was not finished with the Sunflower State. A night later it reached Topeka, and reappeared on several consecutive evenings, and quite a few other communities registered their accounts of visits from the aerial wanderer.

On the fifth the rover returned to Omaha. Ridicule of those who thought they had observed a flying machine was lessened by the newspaper accounts. One story stated that "it was the first time the outline of the vessel could be clearly seen." [5]

A hundred of the city's most prominent citizens were prepared to testify that they had monitored more than a mere light, however brilliant and fanciful in its flight. They had seen an *airship*.

Many brothers of the fraternal organization Ak Sar Ben ("Nebraska" spelled backwards) supported testimony that the inexplicable incident had occurred. Spokesmen said a few of the society had glimpsed the radiant object above one of their homes, as its brilliance flooded windows on its west side. Leaping up to get a look, they saw what "appeared to be a steel body, the length of which could only be estimated at thirty feet." [6]

Racing from the building, the group watched the object, for a number of minutes, from a distance of a quarter mile. After pursuing a course along an arc of about 180 degrees above South Omaha, it changed direction again and was lost behind a cloudbank. Later, a few brothers saw the craft reappear, driving into the wind and vanishing to the north.

Following its nights above Kansas City, Missouri, with much activity over Kansas and Nebraska, the phenomenon resumed its easterly momentum. On the evening of April 7, it was exciting inhabitants of Sioux City, Iowa. Especially interesting was the boast of a fellow named Butler who said that he had seen the craft landed—in his driveway—shortly after midnight. He "took the object for a big cigar-shaped balloon. It was about 35 feet long, 10 or 12 thick and lay on its side. Underneath it was a car . . . it had a row of windows along the side and the light shone through them." [7]

He approached the vessel. It was his impression that this startled the occupants, for it swiftly took to the air and was soon lost in the night sky. The theory of friends was that Butler might have had his imagination heightened by some earlier refreshments. Nevertheless, the incident is almost identical to hundreds of observations of grounded UFO to be found in recent records.

Continuing eastward, the voyagers of the heavens proceeded to entertain the citizens of Cedar Rapids, Burlington, and other Iowa towns. In numerous cases it was lost to sight as it moved in a northwesterly direction, in one instance over the Minnesota line. Regardless of digressions, the general, and seemingly determined, path of the UFO was across the continent toward the Atlantic seaboard.

The rapidly growing catalogue of sightings makes it extremely difficult to attribute all of them to a single craft. The "high speeds" described were relative, and not impressive by contemporary standards. One might infer that the machines were limited in their velocity, or that they were deliberately operated to completely disguise their actual potential. Conceding a much greater capacity for speed than seems reflected by the available data, the large number of communities reporting UFO at the same time makes the conclusion of more than one vessel reasonable.

One of the Iowa cases emphasized sound, but it was not a return of the aerial minstrels of the Pacific coast. The noise in this instance was a "hissing." It was heard as the device glided overhead, although it was silent when altering its course or hovering. This recollection also deviated from the norm in another way. The craft was seen at an altitude of about one thousand feet, a great deal higher than usually cited.

On April 9 one of the St. Louis periodicals gave the Preast story a full treatment. In Omaha, a couple of men sent up a large balloon, with burning wood shavings, one evening. The hoax fooled few people.

If one accepts the theory that all the sightings were of a single vessel, then two-thirds of the continent had been traversed by April 10 when it appears to have arrived over Chicago.

People stared at it from the top of a skyscraper in the Loop. It was the object of attention throughout the south, west, and north sides. Students in Evanston testified they saw rotating green and red lights. THAT AIRSHIP NOW IN CHICAGO and ASTRONOMERS INCREDULOUS were among the headlines the next morning.

The vast majority of the population accepted the fact that an actual flying vessel had finally made its way to the lakeside city. The segment of the community that regarded itself as representing the "scientific" viewpoint asserted that the remarkable phenomenon was a star. This stand was voiced by Professor George W. Hough, of the Dearborn Observatory at Northwestern University, and astronomy Professor Sherbourne W. Burnham. Both stated that the brilliant visitor was no more than a misinterpretation of Alpha Orionis, a first-magnitude member of the constellation of Orion. The green and red alterations of the color were attributed to variations in the conditions of the atmosphere.

Nonetheless, enormous numbers of people, including countless individuals of high station and education, argued that "the moving object was an airship." Multitudes stated outright that they had perceived *two* cigar-shaped craft. Most observers described the UFO as having wings, a directable searchlight, and smaller green, white, and red lamps.

Max I. Harmar,* secretary of the Chicago Aeronautical Association, responded to skeptics by pro-

---

* Elsewhere "Max L. Kasmar, Max L. Hosmar."

claiming that he and his colleagues had anticipated the arrival of the device. The only surprise was that it had reached the city a couple of days before it had been expected. Harmar freely claimed secret knowledge of the vessel's existence and origin, stating that it had a crew of three and that he was acquainted with one of them. He explained to journalists that the ship had left the San Francisco area a month earlier * and had Washington, D.C., as its ultimate destination. In the capital, he said, inspection of the machine would be permitted.

Harmar dismissed the idea that the ship was constructed of steel, or any other such substantial material. It was made of paper. He explained it employed gas, but that the creators of the craft had discovered a new method of propulsion, and that the entire operation was fully controlled. Reporters were informed that the president of his organization, Octave Chanute, was even more informed as to the details of the marvelous experiment, its origin, and its personnel. Allegedly, Chanute, who was then in California, and some associates interested in the problem of air travel had financed the entire project.

Suddenly, the story—but not the airship—was jerked back to Omaha. A letter had been received by Secretary Walisfield,† representing the management of the Trans-Mississippi Exposition, from an unknown individual claiming to be the inventor of the great airship.** It demanded that a 870,000-square-foot area (about thirty-five acres) be placed at his disposal for the exhibition of his vessel. Identifying himself as the designer of the vessel, he revealed that it was capable

---

* This would have been four months following the initial major West Coast sighting of the craft. Also, observations in the West and Midwest much preceded such a departure date.

† Elsewhere "Wakefield."

** One "John A. Heron," of San Jose, California, simultaneously claimed authorship, contending he had flown his machine to Hawaii and back.

of ascending to an altitude approaching four miles, was built to accommodate a score of passengers and crew, and was "the greatest invention and discovery ever made." [8] It was signed "A. C. Clinton.* " [9]

In Chicago, more modest revelations were exciting the people. On April 10, photographs were obtained of the aeronautical spectacle. They were taken by Walter McCann a newsstand dealer of Rogers Park, then a village about thirty miles to the north. An abnormally early riser, because of his business, McCann observed the UFO as he stood before the door of his shop at about five thirty in the morning. Immediately, he began to suspect that the phenomenon was the much discussed "airship." Darting back into his store, he grabbed a small box camera recently acquired by his son. Returning to the pavement at a run, he swiftly snapped a shot of the thing in the sky. As he was doing so a neighbor arrived and urged that another picture be taken if possible. Trotting along in the direction the strange craft was moving, McCann was able to procure a second photograph, which, fortunately, produced a more clearly defined image. Upon examination by experts both negatives were declared absolutely authentic and free from the least indications of tampering.

The upper portion of the vessel was an elongated ovoid. As described by the alert newsdealer, his friend, and scores of other witnesses, it had the appearance of a large silk envelope, below which was a cabin of light construction, giving the appearance of white metal.

One inhabitant of the Windy City announced that while not the inventor of *the* airship, he was in the final stages of completing one of his own. He modestly characterized the result of his creativity as a small vehicle.

Suddenly, from even farther east—Kalamazoo, Michigan—came the devastating rhetorical question and ominous reply:

---

* Almost certainly Clinton A. Case, a local violin maker.

AIR SHIP BLOWS UP?

The Strange Wanderer of the Western Sky
Passes Away with a Dull Thud

The article then stated that "the air ship, that ghost-like and meteoric wanderer through the realms of the Western sky which has startled and awed the mighty West for several months, is now a thing of the glorious past. The dull thud did it. It came, it was seen, and it blew up—so the report says." [10]

Two old soldiers were sitting up with a sick friend, a horse. They unexpectedly glimpsed the craft, and almost instantly heard a report reminding them of a firing cannon, but more muffled. This sound was followed by the whistling hiss of things thrown through the air. Then all was silence and darkness.

On the next morning, corroboration came from a Mrs. Wallace, who said her family had been aware of the thunderlike noise. It was asserted that elements of the machine were discovered scattered about the vicinity, although some of the alleged parts were as much as two miles from one another.

Nevertheless, all was not lost. From Oklahoma, several towns in Illinois, other locations in Michigan, and Kansas and Indiana came accounts. The seemingly omnipresent airship, or fleet of them, soared on unimpaired.

Obviously, by this time, the mysterious machine was a cause célèbre throughout much of the country. It had been seen in dozens of states, scores of major cities, hundreds of towns, and by thousands of witnesses. Its fame was national. No, it was international.

The Parisian newspaper *Figaro* revealed its fascination with the legend from the other side of the Atlantic on April 14. "The news seems to be more than a canard," it remarked, noting that the inexplicable voyager "has traveled over the new world at an average height of from five to six hundred metres [far below many of the estimates], and is stated to have been seen by thousands, and, what is more, photographed." [11]

The European periodical then cited Omaha as its point of origin, and described it as sailless, wingless, and formed after the fashion of a spindle. The writer conceded that "no machine in France can lift its weight by screws or any other system by one-third, without counting engines and passengers or provisions or fuel." [12] He then modified his report by stating that "Americans are no further advanced in the science of aerostatics than the French." [13] Acceptance of the speed and other attributes credited to the airship, he concluded, would require a complete revision of prevailing scientific knowledge and the admission that a new power, or a different use of understood force, had been discovered.

Halfway through the month, a letter claiming to be directly from, even written on, the meandering mystery itself appeared. This story began when the population of Appleton, Wisconsin, saw the glaring lamp, surrounded by its vast, shadowy bulk, soar through the night sky. Shortly thereafter, attached to an iron rod speared into the earth on the farm of N. B. Clark, a letter was discovered. Dated "Aboard the Airship *Pegasus,* April 9th 1897," [14] it confirmed that the difficulties of skyflight had been surmounted. The correspondents had been "cruising" about the nation for four or five weeks, satisfying themselves that their craft had been refined to near-perfection. The note announced that they had exceeded 150 miles an hour and had ascended to an altitude of 2,500 feet. It was said that the propellant was steam, that the light was powered by electricity, and that it was able to transport half a ton.

Generally speaking, these figures fell well within the range of those ascribed to the performance of the great airship.

However, the ending of the letter introduced entirely different data regarding the craft's creation. The *Pegasus,* it said, "was erected at a secluded point ten miles from Lafayette, Tenn., and the various parts of the machine were carried overland from Glasgow, Ky.," after having been assembled from Pittsburgh, St. Louis, and Chicago. In an incidental footnote, the author of the letter, if not the invention, remarked that trips from Lafayette to Yankton, South Dakota, of about seventy-two hours each were part of the *Pegasus'* regular schedule.

Any doubt of the especially American flavor of this continuing aerial adventure is removed by a letter received and printed by an editor of a New York newspaper. It suggested that "the Western airship" ought to be delivered, by its creator and crew, to the city for participation in the April 27 parade to Grant's Tomb, being marched in commemoration of "the nation's hero."

Chicago was still maintaining its attraction for the device. The vessel had returned repeatedly. ALL THE WEST IN A FERMENT read one headline, and nowhere was the excitement more intense. On the evening of April 15, another vast number of people watched it as it moved about the skies. Typical of the accounts was the declaration of G. A. Overocker, who said:

> This strange invention came within six hundred feet of the earth, as near as I could estimate it. The lower portion of the airship was thin, and made of some light white metal, like aluminum. The upper portion was dark and long, like a big cigar, pointed in front and with some kind of arrangement in the rear to which cables were attached. The pilot pulled these and steered the course from south to northeast . . . I can swear that I saw the airship.[15]

Said R. A. Allen:

> I really consider myself fortunate in being permitted to see the mysterious "ship," and I am willing to take all the consequences of expressing the opinion that Professor Hough is wrong. It is not a star, and it has nothing to do with the solar system. Myself and half a dozen other men in the neighborhood took special pains to note every manifestation of this object, and certainly

no star ever acted in the manner displayed by the lights we saw.[16]

Reports were dispatched from many locations, with Ripon, Wisconsin, Elkhart, Indiana, and Lake Forest, Illinois, being added to the rapidly growing list. The machine seemed to be all places at most times. Or was more than one vessel cavorting the air lanes of America? For example, it was back in Iowa on the morning of the sixteenth; appearing above Linn Grove. This unusual daytime sighting showed the craft to move slowly overhead and, some time afterward to land briefly a few miles beyond the community. Seen from an estimated distance of about two thousand feet by local citizens, it was purported to have a twin pair of huge wings. Upon reaching a certain altitude, during its departure, it emitted "two large boulders of unknown composition." [17] As will be noted, this incident was amazingly similar to the Maury Island Mystery of 1947.*

Meanwhile, hundreds of miles away, farther along its primary course, or *their* collective flight paths, the UFO indulged in new activities. One account in particular prefigured the "modern age," as the ship passed from land over water. Of course, there were a number of reports placing it above the San Francisco Bay, and, also, the Pacific Grove episode, where the fishermen saw the airship above the coastal ocean before it landed on the beach. Still, there had emerged few, if any, accounts of the machine crossing relatively large bodies of fresh water.

This case originated in Cleveland, Ohio. A fisherman, piloting his vessel across the light waves of Lake Erie, saw an odd, forty-foot craft, with a cabin ahead. A young man, a woman, and a boy were on deck. As the sailors, including the captain, Joseph Singler, approached the strangers, an enormous, elaborately decorated cylindrical balloon, approximately fifty feet in length, inflated. Suddenly, it swept the boat and its occupants at least two hundred yards into the

---

* See Chapter 10.

sky, where it circled several times. A member of the crew claimed that a large swordfish was thrown from the flying craft, crashing onto the deck of the *Sea Wing*. Then, with considerable speed, the incredible device soared out of sight high into the clear heavens. As will be apparent later on, this incident also reflects characteristics of the Maury Island sighting. In combination the Iowa and the Lake Erie affairs emphasize the similarity to an even stronger degree.

By midmonth observations of people in, or on, flying or landed craft were becoming less rare, although not common. An inhabitant of Bloomington, Illinois, claimed to have seen a device descend and land in the field where he was engaged in his work. Abruptly, a door opened in the body of the machine and six individuals alighted. Remaining for a short time, some of the crew even chatted with him—although he failed to recall the subject of their conversation. Then they reembarked and took to the air.

Obviously, this is a typical "contactee" story, and it is not introduced as the best evidence. Nonetheless, there have been a continuously increasing number of serious investigators who do not entirely dismiss the direct confrontation accounts.

Other contact stories seem to reinforce the suggestion that the airship was of earthly origin. An example of one such case occurred on the same date as several of the foregoing episodes which focused on the landing of a craft, or the landing and the communication with citizens by the crew of a flying machine. The press tells of the daybreak landing of a UFO in Iowa. One of its operators emerged and indicated that the pause was to be brief, merely long enough to make some minor mechanical adjustments. Journalists wrote that he had parking arrangements with the farmer who owned the property upon which his craft had come to rest, and that he carried a rifle to keep everyone away from it.

The newspaper described the vessel as forty feet long, constructed of varnished canvas stretched over a cigar-shaped frame and surmounted by a cockpit. It had wings, some kind of rudder, and a tail pipe exuding steam.

A voyage around the world was the objective of his journey, the pilot revealed.

All the immediately foregoing were reports of encounters taking place on April 15, as were additional ones in St. Louis, Missouri; Birmingham, Iowa; Clarksville, Tennessee; Louisville, Kentucky; and several towns in Texas.

It is extremely easy to doubt these astonishing claims but there were countless more to come. On April 18, on a small farm a thousand yards north of Astoria, Illinois, Bert Swearing discovered a grimy envelope attached to a reed. It carried the statement that it was from the mysterious vessel, which "passed over here at half-past two P.M. . . . about 2,300 feet high, going east and north." [18] This external message was signed "Harris." The soiled envelope was opened, revealing a letter addressed to Thomas A. Edison. After being examined by the authorities, it was forwarded to the proper recipient.

One week later, a member of Edison's staff acknowledged that the letter had been received. The famous man was inspecting some of his mine holdings and was not available for immediate comment. His aide took it upon himself to make one. He described the communication as composed of indecipherable penmanship, although there was some suggestion that the text might be rendered in code. Journalists were informed that the origin noted was "Airship No. 3," and that it was signed by "L. C. Harris." No one associated with Edison had ever heard of the correspondent.

April 18 introduced the craft to Sisterville, West Virginia. During the next fifty years that area of the country was to be one of the focal points of UFO activity. First observed at nine in the evening, it moved briskly across the hilltops toward Cochransville, Ohio, where its speed diminished. Seen through field glasses it was perceived to be a sixty-yard-long cone with fins and brilliant red, green, and white lights on one end. Another of the accumulating affidavits was prepared by those who witnessed the aerial wonder and entered in the historical catalogue of that period of ufology.

The following day saw the delivery of a new message from the occupants of the, or one of the, craft. But on this occasion there was a difference. It was an SOS. How a practical response was to be effected was not explained. The occupants might be able to toss down a distress signal from their vessel. In fact, that is precisely what the note claimed. Yet, how help was to be gotten to them presented a considerable problem since they were the ones who allegedly had the power of controllable flight. In any event, the message, squeezed in a small container, was directed to the first person to come across it on the ground.

"There are three of us loose in an airship," [19] it announced, identifying the group as C. J. Pillsbury and Pierre Humbert of Boston, Massachusetts, and C. D. Novina, of Paris, France. The note said they had not touched solid earth for nearly two weeks, at which time they had descended for a short rest near Emporia, Kansas. Once they returned to the clouds again, for some unexplained reason they appeared to have lost control of the vehicle. The message bemoaned that, as they had been soaring about in undeterminable directions, they had no idea where they were. Their provisions and water were virtually exhausted. They had little hope left of surviving.

On the morning of the nineteenth, an estimated three thousand people of Cripple Creek, Kansas, saw a UFO glistening in the sunlight about a mile high. Inspection through a telescope revealed a large, slowly moving, conical object. If the UFO was as high as stated, it may have been moving faster than estimated. The sighting continued until well past noon.

Halfway across the country, Edison had returned. He responded to press inquiries regarding the letter forwarded to him from "Airship No. 3."

The inventor immediately assured the newsmen that "this is a pure fake," without clarifying whether he meant the communication or the reports of the airship. Still, it seemed consonant with his personality to infer he was indicating both. He confirmed his assistant's contention that L. C. Harris was unknown to him.

Edison proclaimed: "I am not, however, figuring on inventing an air ship. I prefer to devote my time to objects which have some commercial value. At best air ships would only be toys." [20]

Despite his prophecy, on the following day another affidavit was filed, in Le Roy, Kansas. The formalized testimony of Alexander Hamilton was that, on the previous Monday evening, he had clearly seen a large vessel glide down from the darkness. It had come to rest in a pasture about two hundred yards from his home. He approached to within 150 feet of the craft as it was settling, accompanied by his son and a hired hand. It was enormous, approximately the length of a football field, and was principally composed of a crimson substance. The design was that of a gigantic cigar. Beneath was attached a cabin designed of alternating strips of the body material and some substance as clear as glass. The Kansans easily distinguished no fewer than six occupants. They thought them to be "the strangest beings [they] ever saw." Certainly the implication is that they were not human or reminiscent of any animal with which a comparison might have been made.

A sound began and a great wheel began to spin. It was ten yards broad and located beneath the craft. In moments it had accelerated to a buzz and a blur, and the airship rose gently upward. At an altitude of about a hundred yards the vehicle paused above a calf caught in the wire of a nearby fence. Hamilton's group suddenly realized that some sort of line from it was tied to the heifer, which could not free itself from the barbs. Loosened from the fence, the calf was pulled up and disappeared, with the ship, in the darkness overhead.

On the following day, a fellow farmer, whose place was situated a few miles away, came upon the legs, head, and hide of a young cow. He brought the skin into town in an attempt to determine its owner. Hamilton encountered him and recognized his brand. His affidavit concludes with a most persuasive passage: "Every time I . . . drop to sleep I . . . see the cursed thing, with its bright lights and hideous people. I don't know whether they are angels or devils, or what; but we all saw them, and my whole family saw the ship, and I don't want any more to do with them." [21]

Hamilton, who had been a member of the House of Representatives, was popular throughout the four surrounding counties. People who knew him, some for thirty years, testified in an affidavit that they "have never heard his word questioned, and . . . do verily believe his statement to be true and correct." This much longer and emphatic amendment to the witness' account of his experience was signed by the sheriff, deputy sheriff, justice of the peace, postmaster, registrar of deeds, a banker, attorney, pharmacist, and druggist, and notarized on April 21, 1897. [22]

Only days after the filing of this extraordinary paper, a judge in Texarkana, Arkansas, testified to having discovered a landed craft and to have seen its personnel.[23] They were three in number and appeared to the legal man to be Japanese. (How many men of that nationality he had previously encountered was not stated in the press.) Nevertheless the crew was hospitable and showed him through the ship. Regrettably, either he did not reveal to the newsmen, or they did not inform their readers of, any details noted on this tour. While descriptions of extraplanetarians often picture them as having oriental features, this is likely the first such story in the chronicle of the 1896–97 series.

A new claimant for the title "inventor of the airship" appeared on April 24. A young Scot named Volney Stewart, who resided in Brule, Wisconsin, and allegedly had been aided by two brothers named Foster, was singled out as being the probable source of the mystery vehicle. The story argued that the trio had labored on the device for three years before vanishing. Evidence for the reporter's deduction included the word of a young fellow who had entered Stewart's barn uninvited and discovered before him a remarkable craft of some thirty by ten feet. It was

shaped liké a screw, with a pointed front end. Supporting the newsman's argument was the testimony of
another trespasser who told of seeing a jumbled pile
of discarded iron, bands of brass, pieces of wood, a
variety of bolts and hasps, and scraps of canvas, rope,
wire, etc., on the property. A note was found that was
highly reminiscent of earlier messages, as well as of
Collins' original explanation of why he had been selected to serve the alleged "inventor" of the West Coast
machine. It read: "Gone to Washington to get a
patent," and was signed "Volney Stewart." [24]

A new description came from a Presbyterian minister in Portland, Indiana. He had sighted an "aero-
drome" consisting of parallel fuselages, one over the
other, with movable fins, swirling fans, and the appearance of being turbine driven. In New York, the
foreign touch was added to the religious when Professor Raffaele Paroselli had his interpreter call attention
to the existence of his "motorized balloon ship, with
gondola," which he intended to launch at any moment.

Suddenly, the climax. The conclusion to the extraordinary transcontinental voyage was reached. On
April 30, 1897, the great airship was seen over
Yonkers, New York. Three local citizens were returning to their homes in the very early morning when
they spied the craft with its brilliant lamp shaded so
that it appeared as a crescent. Harry Folkersamb is
said to have seen it first, calling the attention of his
companions, Haney and Barry, to it at once. Subsequently, other witnesses came forward to admit that
they had also observed the flying machine and the
remarkable radiance directed from it.[25] Yet, the number of accounts was quite small compared to those that
had poured in by the thousands as the sky traveler
crossed the nation. This was completely understandable as the vast majority of the earlier sightings had
occurred at dusk or in midevening. Remaining ones
with few exceptions, had been experienced during the
light of day. In contrast, the Yonkers viewing took
place at 3 A.M. Few individuals were on the streets
at that hour.

The mighty age ended. The fantastic UFO sighting

complex, which seems to have begun on November 1 above the Bolinas Ridge in California, and resolved on the night of April 30, heading northward from Yonkers toward the sea, was completed. A flight across the country, or a pattern of coordinated aeronautical activity by many craft, had been witnessed by tens, perhaps, hundreds of thousands of people. It had featured nearly every form of phenomena which was to follow it more than a half-century later. It had led to explanations of practically all possibilities. While these ranged from simple single floating lights, multiple lights, and shadowy presences around these illuminations, to clearly recognizable craft of a wide variety of designs, the great majority of reports indicated the viewers had seen the same thing. Or the same sort of thing. Hoverings, landings, observations of occupants, conversations with vessel crews, friendly, taciturn, and incomprehensible, and, even, a glimpse within one of the machines—all had followed as the adventure evolved. And there had been hoaxes, but they had been unexpectedly infrequent and extremely inept.

The *Scientific American* of a month after the Yonkers finale dismissed the incredibly vast catalogue of sightings with fifty contemptuous and closed-minded words. Expectedly, it attributed everything that had occurred, each of the thousands of observations, to "creations from the brains of imaginative persons." [26] The "scientific" commentary represented an attitude that would persist to this day.

What swept the breadth of America during that six months? Undefined Sensory Experiences (USE) of many types or of one type? Unidentified Atmospheric Phenomena (UAP)? Unidentified Flying Objects? Certainly in many instances the phenomenon was never identified. An interplanetary craft? Conceivably, if one realizes that recognition of such a vessel implies a design minimally conforming to the prevailing concepts of how an aerial vessel would look. In our time, even the wildest of the "contactees" invariably describe spaceships acceptable to the layman's idea of how such a visitor might appear, as H. G. Wells, Jules

Verne, Alex Raymond (Flash Gordon), and science fiction, collectively, had foreordained. The manifestations of modern UFO have introduced only slightly updated designs, despite the evidence that actual Earth-made interplanetary craft are graceless, ovoidal cubes or truncated cylinders, and our landing vehicles apparent representations of mutant insects. That is, if extra-Earthians desired to survey this world, it is possible that their capabilities would permit them to employ flying machines harmonious with speculations already common here.

Was the vehicle, or were the vehicles, from Earth? An invention of Man? If so, the mystery fits into a recognizable pattern more conveniently. It is possible that a craft was invented, constructed, flown, and then, when the inventor suddenly died or was killed, was destroyed, along with plans for its design, leaving only an unsolvable riddle. That would answer more of the queries than any other supposition. Still, it does not feel comfortable. It seems that word of such an invention would somehow have got out. Too many people would have been required to execute such a plan for it to have remained a secret.

A creation that worked wonderfully well, and was suppressed? But why? By whom? Yet, precisely the same questions are with us today, regarding the UFO history of our age.

Curiously, when the 1896–97 complex stopped, for all practical purposes it stopped cold. Various sightings continued to be recorded through the years, but this particular phenomenon reached a dead end at the shores of the Atlantic. No byproduct reports, virtually no new sightings emerged from the areas over which it had soared. It was all over.

The country, perhaps the world, was not tuned to whatever had happened, to whatever it implied. It came, sailed to a climax, and evaporated into the atmosphere of ultra-altitude and legend.

Its like would not be seen again for fifty years.

Notes

1. New York *Sun*, April 3, 1897, front page, col. 4.
2. Ibid., April 3, 1897, p. 2, col. 1.
3. Ibid.
4. Ibid., April 10, 1897, p. 2, col. 7. Also St. Louis *Globe-Democrat*, April 9, 1897, and New York *World*, April 4, 1897, p. 7, col. 4.
5. Ibid., April 7, 1897.
6. Ibid.
7. New York *World*, April 9, 1897, p. 11, col. 3. Also, New York *Sun*, April 10, 1897.
8. New York *Herald*, April 11, 1897, p. 5, col. 1.
9. Ibid., April 13, 1897, p. 8, col. 6.
10. New York *Herald*, April 14, 1897, p. 11, col. 1.
11. Ibid., April 15, 1897, p. 8, col. 1.
12. Ibid.
13. Ibid.
14. Ibid., p. 9, col. 5.
15. Ibid.
16. Saginaw (Michigan) *Courier-Herald*, April 16, 1897.
17. New York *Sun*, April 18, 1897, p. 3, col. 4.
18. New York *Herald*, April 19, 1897.
19. New York *Sun*, April 20, 1897.
20. New York *Herald*, April 20, 1897.
21. Yates Center (Kansas) *Farmer's Advocate*, April 23, 1897. Also see New York *World*, April 27, 1897, p. 10, col. 5.
22. Ibid.
23. *Daily Texarkanian*, April 25, 1897.
24. New York *Herald*, April 26, 1897.
25. Ibid., May 1, 1897.
26. *Scientific American*, June 1897.

7

Third Planet from the Sun

> ... many professional astronomers are convinced that saucers are interplanetary machines. . . . I think they come from another solar system, but they may be using Mars as a base.
>
> —Dr. Frank Halstead, Darling Observatory, Duluth, Minnesota. *Flying Saucers*, June 1957, p. 84

UFOLOGY in the twentieth century began quietly. The first ten years were left to the professional astronomers and they were primarily concerned with the "canals" of Mars.

One of the first events of interest was the publication in 1900 of *Des Indes à la planète Mars*.[1] This work, by a former professor of psychology at the University of Geneva, was based on the purported psychic exploits of the famous English medium Hélène Smith. Miss Smith, who in previous existences had been Simandini, an Indian princess, and Marie Antoinette, was a space traveler—at least in *spirit*. The height of the clairvoyant's adventures was her visit to Mars. She described the semi-mortals and their customs. The fluency of her exchanges in the planetary native tongue remind one of her predecessor Swedenborg.

Other Worlds Than Ours emerged the following year. It was of a slightly different order. The author, while frequently referring to "the inhabitants of Mercury" or "of Venus," devotes his attention to the

habitability of these and other planets. Speaking of
Mars, he notes:

> Surely, if it is rashly speculative to say of this
> charming planet that it is the abode of life—if
> we must, indeed, limit ourselves to the considera-
> tion of what has been absoluetly seen—it is yet
> to speculate ten thousand times more rashly to
> assert, in the face of so many probable arguments
> to the contrary, that Mars is a barren waste,
> either wholly untenanted by living creatures, or
> inhabited by beings belonging to the lowest or-
> ders of animated existence.[2]

Published the same year were Garrett P. Serviss'
more conservative theories of extraterrestriality. They
offered no conclusions.[3]

In 1902, the possibility of solving the riddle of life
elsewhere was dismissed theologically *"because Revelation is silent"* on the subject. For this reason, a
writer in *The Irish Ecclesiastical Record* [4] approached
the question scientifically. However, his science proved
rather mystical. Reasonably, he concedes his argument is not very strong. The author suggests that the
conversion of the world's population to Christianity
was progressing slowly. The rate was about three-to-
one in his time. Catholicism was evolving even more
gradually. Therefore, the writer speculated on the
possibility of the existence of more redemptively
successful worlds.

The remainder of "The Comparative Insignificance
of Our Solar System Ad Gloriam Dei Creatoris"
argues for the likelihood of creatures with souls occupying other planets.[5]

One year later, Orville and Wilbur Wright just
managed to get their clumsy crate off the sovereign soil
of North Carolina for 12 seconds and 120 feet—aided
by a 27-mile-an-hour tail wind.

Meanwhile, astronomers Lowell and Pickering were
exploring the avenues they felt would prove the existence of extraterrestrial life.

In the introduction to an article by Pickering,[6] the

editor observes that, along with Professor Lowell, the author is one of the leaders of the "important group of astronomers who hold that it is extremely probable —if not absolutely proven—that Mars is inhabited by highly civilized beings."

The arguments of both of these scientists relied on the "canals" of Schiaparelli. Wrote Pickering:

> The first drawing ever made of a dark area or sea on Mars was of *Syrtis Major,* by Huygens, in 1659. The first map showing a canal and a lake was constructed by Beer and Maedler in 1870 . . . the canals were first recorded in large numbers by Schiaparelli in 1877 . . . [and] in 1882, Schiaparelli announced that the canals in Mars were sometimes double [and, also, disappearing and reappearing in habit].
>
> There is little doubt now that Mars possesses vegetable and perhaps animal life; but the question that interests humanity is, Are there intelligent beings there? The only important argument in favor of their existence is the presence of the canals.[7]

Percival Lowell, in the next couple of years, concentrated on this question. He conceived not only of an intelligent civilization, but also of its demise, the result of a planetary lack of water. Then "the planet will roll a dead world through space, its evolutionary career forever ended."[8]

Later, in discussing the intelligent creatures of Mars, Lowell notes that "we are assured to develop the theme that the probably artificially constructed webbing of canals indicate the necessarily intelligent and non-bellicose character of the community which could thus act as a unit throughout its globe."[9]

On June 30, 1908, more immediate evidence of the Lowell/Pickering thesis may have hurtled through our atmosphere. It appeared in the form of a flaming, sun-bright object, which crashed into a remote region of Siberia. The impact was heard two provinces away and was registered on the seismograph at the Irkutsk

Observatory. Reportedly, the tremendous explosion
illuminated the heavens for several minutes and more
than 1,000 miles.

Twenty years later, L. A. Kulik, a Russian meteor
expert, visited the area, near the river Tunkguska-Un-
der-the-Stones. He discovered a wasteland of 800
square miles. Even more fascinating was the total
absence of a crater and meteorite fragments.

Subsequent examination and evaluation led some
scientists to the conclusion that the explosion had
occurred as much as a mile above the earth. Certain
data indicated severe magnetic disturbance and (a
half century later) considerable radioactivity.

In recent years, Alexander Kazantsev has insisted
the incident was not one of a meteor landing, but of
an enormous spaceship—perhaps of Martian origin—
plowing like a powerful projectile into Earth. This
contention has attracted much controversy, especially
in Russia—with the dissenters in the majority. Yet,
even their explanations leave much more to be
desired.[10]

In 1909 there occurred a minor 1897 type sighting
complex. It was localized and of brief duration, but
possessed much of the flavor of the affair of a dozen
years earlier. The original reports follow.

AIRSHIP STIRS CITY

Worcester, Mass., Dec. 22nd [front page]—
Flying through the air at an average speed of
from thirty to forty miles an hour, a mysterious
airship to-night appeared over Worcester, hovered over the city a few minutes, disappeared
for about two hours and then returned to cut
four circles above the gaping city, meanwhile
sweeping the heavens with a searchlight of very
high power. The news of its presence spread like
wildfire and thousands thronged the streets to
watch the mysterious visitor.

The airship remained over the city for about
fifteen minutes, all the time at a height that most
observers set at about two thousand feet, too far

to enable even its precise shape to be seen. After a time it disappeared in the direction of Marlboro, only to return later.

Coming from the southeast, the sky voyager veered to the west, remained in sight a few moments, and then disappeared to the northwest. In five minutes the searchlight was again seen glowing in the distance like a monster star, and the ship came up, hovered over the city a short time and disappeared to the southeast.

Two hours later an eager shout from the waiting crowds announced its return. Slowly, its light sweeping the heavens, it circled four times above the city and then disappeared, finally heading first southly and then to the east.

At the time of the airship's visit Wallace E. Tillinghast, the Worcester man who recently claimed to have invented a marvellous aeroplane, in which he said he had journeyed to New York and returned by way of Boston, was absent from his home and could not be located.

Marlboro, Mass., Dec. 22nd—An airship was sighted over Marlboro early tonight, going northwest at thirty or more miles an hour. Persons in all sections of the city reported having had a glimpse of it. Its general course, they say, was in the direction of Clinton.[11]

The next day revealed it was definitely moving southward.

AIRSHIP NOW AT HUB

Pulsation of Engines Heard and Its Bulk Outlined Against the Sky

Boston, Mass., Dec. 23rd—The searchlight of what is supposed to be Wallace E. Tillinghast's mysterious aeroplane shot across the sky line, high above the city tonight. The Worcester inventor, if it was his airship that was seen, has circled the city, the harbor and the neighboring towns again and again since sundown, always flying with speed and ease, unhampered by a gale that is blowing at fifty miles an hour.

The airship passed over the city for the first time a few minutes after 6 o'clock. The visit was unexpected, and it left the streets of the city clogged with little knots of people who, staring skyward with wonder stricken eyes, nearly tied up traffic. A few minutes later it passed over Lynn, in full sight of three thousand persons in the shopping district, and swerving in its course, headed toward Marlboro.

In Marlboro the airship came so near the earth that the pulsations of its engines could be heard, and its looming bulk was clearly outlined against the sky. Back again over Lynn it flew and then across Nahant, and Revere Beach and Boston Harbor, again circling Boston and going back again over the same course. People in all parts of the city saw it, and as it flew away to the north again queries began to pour into the newspaper offices and the police stations regarding the remarkable visitations.

In passing over Boston the airship kept high in the air, but once inside the city limits it came within a thousand feet of the earth. Then, in passing over Revere Beach, the aeronaut evidently lost his bearings and dropped earthward to get them again.

As one of the local garages had an aeroplane landing station it was thought that the machine was about to alight. Alexander Rambell, proprietor of the garage and himself an aeroplane owner, saw the aeroplane distinctly. He described it as a monoplane with a 70 foot wing spread and a 40 foot tail and propeller. From the rotations of the explosions he decided that the engine was either a six or eight cylinder, probably the latter. The description fits that of the Tillinghast machine.

The operator, however, apparently got his bearings, for, rising steadily and with startling ease, he sailed out to sea, heading apparently for Nahant. The machine was seen later in Lynn and then disappeared altogether, probably having returned to the secret station established by Tillinghast somewhere in the vicinity of Worcester.[12]

These sightings evolved like a highly condensed, miniaturized version of the great airship mystery of thirteen years earlier. The East Coast was being given a fleeting glimpse of what the complex on the other side of the country had been like. Still, the emphasis on *one* "inventor" or "operator" introduced a slightly different quality.

The New York *Tribune* report continued by saying that most local businessmen accepted that Tillinghast had created a practical commercial flying machine and credited him with a flight from their city to Boston on September 8, 1909.

Tillinghast supported the claim by saying that he could and would "fly about in the air with my invention" when he felt inclined. He noted, with bloodshot eyes and windburned face, that the observed flight had been "very successful." However, "It was said here to-night that Mr. Tillinghast could not have been the navigator of the airship to-night, as he remained at his home."

Willimantic, Connecticut, was heard from immediately: "An airship was seen in the southeastern part of the city at 7:30 o'clock to-night and it is believed that the mysterious craft was that of William Tillinghast, which has startled the country with its nocturnal trips." The account then described events very similar to those reported by the people of Worcester. After hovering over the city for fifteen minutes, it sailed off into the darkness.

The story was widely covered for about a week. On December 25 one column in the New York *Times* was headed LIGHTS FLY AT NIGHT AS WITCHES FLEW.

It was all over by the end of the month. Other news—including numerous air activities, such as the attempted crossing of the English Channel by the great dirigible Clement-Bayard II—had superseded the

"flap." Since the assertion that it had been Tillinghast's can scarcely be supported, the true nature of
the mystery ship was to remain unknown forever.

The city of Chattanooga was the scene of several
days of similar sightings in 1910.

> An airship passed over Chattanooga at a great
> altitude at 9 o'clock this morning. Thousands saw
> the craft and heard the "chugging" of the engine.
> Tonight a dispatch from Huntsville, Alabama,
> announced that the airship passed over that city
> travelling at a high speed.[13]

The distance between Huntsville and Chattanooga
is about seventy-five miles, considerably beyond the
accepted range of dirigibles of the day. Prizes were
being awarded for flights of one-tenth the distance.

> A white dirigible passed over Chattanooga at
> 11 o'clock this morning. It came from the South.
> A man was discernible in the machine. A mys-
> terious airship was reported in Southern Ten-
> nessee and northern Alabama last night.[14]

And on January 15:

> For the third successive day a mysterious white
> airship passed over Chattanooga about noon to-
> day. It came from the north and was travelling
> southeast, disappearing over Missionary Ridge.
> On Wednesday it came travelling south and on
> Thursday returned north.[15]

Then, as had happened with similar occurrences in
the past, the aerial activity above Chattanooga suddenly ceased.

The *Journal of the Astronomical Society of Canada*
carried an excellent article, in 1913, on the meteoric
fireworks of February 9 of that year. Accompanying
it was a "flying saucer" type illustration—an astronomical plate—which, unfortunately, is so lacking in
graphic contrast as to make it virtually unrepro-

ducible.[16] A brilliant object with a luminous appendage is reported to have sailed across the skies of Canada, the United States, and the Caribbean. Purportedly, it grew in size. Some observers thought they saw a single body; others, a multiple structure having three or four parts, each with tail features. It moved across the zenith with "a peculiar majestic deliberation." As the object, or object-group, disappeared beyond the horizon, another one, or many, arose from the original starting point and followed a similar course. This happened several more times. Charles Fort has one viewer saying: "There were probably 30 or 32 bodies . . . moving in fours, threes, and twos, abreast of one another; and so perfect was the lining up that you would have thought it was an aerial fleet maneuvering after a rigid drilling." [17]

Yet an examination of Professor Chant's second report of the meteoric procession, published in the Society's journal at the end of 1913, while stimulating, leaves a somewhat less ufological impression.

   . . . the extraordinary flight of meteors witnessed across Canada and the United States on Feb. 9th, 1913 . . . [was] unparalleled in two respects *viz.*: (1) Its multiple nature, consisting, as it did, of a long procession of meteors. (2) The great length of its observed luminous flight extending over more than one-tenth of the earth's surface.[18]

Even this account will activate the enthusiasm of some ufologists. The remainder of the article indicates that astronomers pictured the phenomenon as unique. In the words of W. R. Winter: "This display was unlike anything we have ever seen before and is not as far as I can find accounted for in any astronomical work . . . the general behavior was more like that of semigaseous bodies than that of ordinary meteors."

Now the Victorian Era, the Gay Nineties, and the Edwardian Age were passed. Periods of security, providing time for new and fanciful revelations and adventures, were gone. The horror of modern war descended.

World War I introduced a new type of Undefined Sensory Experience (USE). Combat pilots began encountering ghost ships, phantasmal craft of no certain reality.

The world was growing smaller and grimmer.

Suddenly, it was flooded by a great, miraculous light. On October 13, 1917, at two in the afternoon,

> what appeared to be the sun [came] down through the clouds. It rotated three times for about four minutes each time, radiating various coloured lights and intense heat, although it was not too bright for the people to gaze directly at it. Some described it afterwards as a silvery disc. After about twelve minutes the disc appeared to move back to its normal place in the sky, where it resumed its usual brilliance. . . .[19]

A craft descending and ascending against the sun's molten light might have resulted in such testimony.

A further description represents the effect as giving the impression of "a pale disc, not dazzling at all . . . like stainless steel . . . [or] silver . . . [or] mother-of-pearl. . . ."[20]

The event, witnessed, according to some, by sixty thousand persons, was "the miracle of Fatima."

1918! The world thought war was over. Caring little for metaphysical wonders, it concentrated on having a good time.

Meanwhile, the search went on:

> During April, 1920, Dr. Frederick H. Miller spent weeks trying to establish communication with Mars from his giant wireless station in Omaha, Nebraska . . . but was [finally] convinced no attempt was being made by the inhabitants of other planets to communicate with the earth by wireless.[21]

The twenties began and newspapers headlined:

MARCONI BELIEVES HE RECEIVED WIRELESS MESSAGES FROM MARS

J. C. MacBeth, London manager of the Marconi Wireless Telegraph Company, Ltd., told several hundred men at a luncheon of the Rotary Club of New York yesterday that Signor Marconi believed he had intercepted messages from Mars during the recent atmospheric experiments with wireless on board his yacht *Electra* in the Mediterranean.[22]

Marconi, the article continued, made much of the fact that the signals received were 150,000 meters, since the "maximum length produced in the world today [1921] is 14,000 meters."

The scientist did not realize how close he was to the truth. At least, the truth according to Vesta La Viesta, the pseudonymous authoress of a sixty-four page revelation.[23] The quasi-occult writing suggests that he who would be "ready to join the cosmic centre" had better contact her "telepathics college where soul language is taught." There one would learn "how to send and receive mental messages," i.e., to be one's own seeress. All in all, an institution promising even higher levels of learning than George Van Tassel's Ministry of Universal Wisdom, Inc., which flourished in the fifties and early sixties.

Elaborating on magnetic auras, cosmic consciousness, the universal coil, and other essentials, this bold-staring, hard-jawed, plump lady (as revealed by the jacket photograph) gets down to fundamentals. She proceeds to describe "the inhabitants of the Sun."

They are "eight feet tall and self-illuminated; they are bald-headed, and each faculty (or organ) in the head scintillates and appears like a glistening jewel." After such imagery, it is a little disappointing to be told that "their principal occupation is to shine."

"Of all creepy hobgobblong [sic] theories that have been voiced," observes the seeress, "those regarding the moon are, perhaps, the most squirmishing and terror producing." Lunarians are six to seven feet in height, "angular, flat-chested and broad-shouldered, with an enormous growth of brownish hair." They apparently exude "an etheric cloud" when emotionally aroused and "live in one continuous round of chemical exchange," which may have been La Viesta's way of talking about sex. Their homes are rough wooden structures two stories high and fifteen hundred feet long. On the moon everyone is middle-aged—there are no children and no old people.

Jupiter is populated by creatures much like "the average civilized man." Except when angered. Then they may take "the form of a huge toad with an enormously big mouth, [and] two flat tapering rattle snake-like colored tails, some ten or twelve feet in length."

A "noble race of men" as "black as ebony" inhabits Mars; small fairies populate Venus; Saturn is the home of wild "heart wreckers," carousers, and "Socialists."

So goes the universe—Uranus, Mercury, Neptune, Heaven, and Hell. The book concludes with general observations and spiritual admonitions from one who knows the dangers of uncountable worlds.

Meanwhile, back on Earth, the less esoteric investigators pushed on.

Fascination with the idea of contacting Mars by radio continued. It intensified in 1924 as the distance between the two planets lessened. Proximity did not help. The press announced that, as far as visual indications were concerned, Mars had "cut us dead" during its nearest approach in a hundred years. Still, they did record that "from three places on the Earth's surface" came reports of strange air noises that might have been Martian messages. London, Vancouver, and Newark all "picked up" something. Whether it was an unearthly broadcaster signaling, or merely some terrestrial practical joker they could not say.

"In Newark two radio operators . . . said they heard a weird succession of sounds alternating between a low wave length of 75 meters and a high wave of 25,000 meters." They doubted the Martian communication theory, but conceded that it was possible.[24]

In England, Professor A. M. Low also monitored

some curious, musical effects, but declined to attribute them to interplanetary contact. On the other hand, Low observed that Martians might be present on Earth in "thought forms invisible to the human eye. We don't know," he declared, "that Martians are not already upon this earth, or that they are not keeping us as we'd keep horses or cows. Our eyes are only suited to vision things of a certain density and a certain size." [25]

The warning went unheeded. Later, each part of his theory reappeared in the writings of various modern saucerologists.

Simultaneously, across the Channel, the famous astronomer Camille Flammarion continued to assert that "Mars must have human life."

"Mars is a much better planet than ours," he stated, ". . . not only is the climate better but the inhabitants are much more intelligent, for they have had several million years more of life and progress is the law." He did add, however, in the true Gallic manner, that Paris undoubtedly boasted more beautiful women than the scarlet lady of the sky.[26]

The Vancouver, British Columbia, report of that time was brief but interesting. It stated that "mysterious signals picked up at a Point Grey Wireless Station here during the last week culminated today in a strange group of sounds, causing wireless experts to wonder if Mars is trying to establish communication with the earth." "The fact that I distinctly got four groups of four dashes convinced me that some intelligent communication force was at work," commented Dr. Buford, an "operator of long experience." [27]

The year and the favorable conditions for radio contact passed. And so did much of the interest in messages from outer space.

The year 1927 saw the publication of *Life in the Stars*,[28] a somewhat mystical, Swedenborgian work postulating other worlds of near-angelic beings. It featured an interesting interplay of theology and politics in the author's description of an *elected* God. In any event, a Supreme Leader with a temporary term of office. *Other Worlds*,[29] a reinterpretation of astronomical data presented a "journey" through the universe. Its main attraction is the curious coincidence of author Schuster's first two names being Otto John. A John Otto emerged three decades later as a well-known, if lesser, figure in American saucerology.

The theory of the Martian canals was reexamined in 1929 in the book *Enigmas*. The conclusions were skeptical.[30] During the same year an intriguing episode was published, although almost buried, in a travel diary by Nicholas Roerich. A journal of an expedition through India, Tibet, Sinkiang, and Mongolia, this work is of special interest to the ufologist because of the following passage:

> On August fifth—something remarkable! We were in our camp in the Kukunor district, not far from the Humboldt Chain. In the morning about half-past nine some of our caravaneers noticed a remarkably big black eagle flying above us. Seven of us began to watch this unusual bird. At the same moment another of our caravaneers remarked: "There is something far above the bird." And he shouted his astonishment. We all saw, in a direction from north to south, something big and shiny reflecting sun, like a huge oval moving at great speed. Crossing our camp this thing changed in its direction from south to southwest. And we saw how it disappeared in the intense blue sky. We even had time to take our field glasses and saw quite distinctly the oval form with the shiny surface, one side of which was brilliant from the sun.[31]

Support for life on Mars seemed to increase among astronomers. *Major Mysteries of Science* remarks: "Dr. William Pickering, director of the Harvard College branch station . . . takes the advanced view that it is almost certain that Mars is inhabited by intelligent beings and suggests that the Martians are signalling to us." [32] The book lists among astronomers believing in the possibility of intelligent beings on Mars, Dr. Henry Norris Russel, director of the Princeton Observatory;

Dr. Robert G. Aiken, director of the Lick Observatory; Dr. Clyde Fisher, curator of astronomy at the American Museum of Natural History, and others. It also includes a skillfully drawn depiction of a Martian landscape of sky, canal, and the bordering trees and vegetation, as well as a scene of a Venusian volcano and sea.

The thirties and early forties proved a poor climate for the nurturing of serious speculations regarding interplanetary travel, visitors from outer space, and life beyond this world. Times were savagely real for many; others didn't want to think about them. Everyone wanted escape material and half-minded measures were acceptable. Hollywood filled the need with an incessant stream of musicals. Extraterrestrialism in science fiction came into its own. The great, now classic, pulp magazines *Amazing Stories, Astounding Stories* (later *Astounding Science Fiction*), *Wonder Stories* (later *Thrilling Wonder Stories*), *Astonishing Stories*, and *Startling Stories* flourished. The comic-strip characters Buck Rogers, Flash Gordon and others reigned. When this golden age of space adventure ended, during World War II, for the rocket-ship knights and, by 1950, for their more serious counterparts, it ended for good. Reality had run them down, as had been the case with all the romance figures who had gone before them. No matter how hard they tried, the imitators who fell heir to the *genre* would never equal the originals. Even Hollywood, where every conceivable facility would be available, would never create another space-oriented science fiction film like *The Shape of Things to Come* or another serial like the adventures of Flash Gordon.

In 1941 another world war was underway, and in Germany the first of many subsequent "flying disks" was being conceived and designed.[33]

The year also saw the reappearance of theology in the field of extraterrestrialism. *Jesus, the Savior of the Worlds,* a religious tract, demonstrated that there are, and will continue to be, other populated planets. All of these, as with Earth, were or are destined to be spiritually serviced by Jesus Christ.[34]

A paperback appeared a few years later dealing with

the comparative similarities of craters on Mars and those in Texas.[35] Attention was also given to twin craters, canals, double canals, linear networks, and such, to the end of establishing indirect and circumstantial evidence for intelligent life on Mars.

It was also in 1944 that the *foo-fighters* appeared.

BALLS OF FIRE STALK U.S. FIGHTERS IN NIGHT ASSAULTS OVER GERMANY

The Germans have thrown something new into the night skies over Germany—the weird, mysterious *foo-fighter,* balls of fire that race alongside the wings of American *Beaufighters* flying intruder missions over the Reich.[36]

Revealing that our aviators had been harassed by the "eerie *foo-fighters*" for more than a month, during night flights, the account conceded that neither American science, nor the military had been able to determine the nature of the new "sky weapon."

The flaming globes were said to appear from nowhere and pace the planes for considerable distances, at speeds exceeding three hundred miles an hour. Intelligence suspected that the effects were remotely controlled by radio.

" 'There are three kinds of these lights we call *foo-fighters,*' Lieutenant Donald Meiers of Chicago said. 'One is red balls of fire which appear off our wing tips and [others] fly in front of us, and the third is a group of about fifteen lights which appear off in the distance—like a Christmas tree in the air—and flicker on and off.' "

The image used by the World War II fighter pilot in referring to the third type of UFO is precisely that given by State Trooper Jeffrey Hontz in his description of the Saylors Lake sightings twenty-eight years later.*

The particular squadron discussed by the press specialized in night patrols and had been operational for about sixteen months when the foo-fighters were initially encountered. Nothing up to that date com-

* See Chapter 1.

pared with them in pure strangeness. Few doubted that
the unknowns were intended to achieve psychological,
as well as military, results. Especially as "attacking"
maneuvers by the things were rare.

Lieutenant Meiers told of one instance when a foo-
fighter moved in on his ship at seven hundred feet and
pursued him for twenty miles along the Rhine Valley.
"I turned starboard and the balls of fire turned with
me," he recalled. "I turned to port side and they turned
with me. We were doing 260 miles an hour and the
balls were keeping right up with us." [37]

The aviator recounted another experience when the
UFO paced his wing tips at 360 miles an hour, and
suddenly zoomed into the highest altitudes, out of
sight. "When I first saw the things . . . I had the terrible
thought that a German . . . was ready to press a button
and explode them," Meiers said. In his case, they never
actually became belligerent, but "just seemed to follow
us like will-o'-the-wisps." [38]

Lieutenant Wallace Gould, of Silver Creek, New
York, remembered how lights raced along, feet beyond
his wing tips, and abruptly hurtled twenty thousand feet
upward and vanished.

A comrade encountered the UFO twice. To Lieutenant Edward Schlater, of Oshkosh, Wisconsin, unknowns resembled shooting stars. He thought they
were a new jet-propelled enemy fighter. Closer observation, possible when the things came in very close,
seemed to negate that conjecture. As he put it, "None
of us saw any structure on the fire balls." [39]

The disturbing sightings were by no means isolated
incidents. Their numbers grew rapidly. Pilot Henry
Giblin and his observer, Walter Cleary, were tailed at
1,000 feet by an immense crimson light traveling at
200 miles an hour. A few days before Christmas, in
1944, two spherical glows came up on a night fighter
at about 2 miles altitude. They pursued briefly, and
then wheeled away, suddenly extinguishing themselves
in the distance. On the following evening, Lieutenant
David McFalls and Ned Baker reported a "glowing
red object shooting straight up, which suddenly

changed to a view of an aircraft doing a wing-over, going into a dive and disappearing." [40]

However, not all of the *"foo-fighter* sightings" (derived from the *Smokey Stover* comic-strip philosophy that "where there's foo, there's fire" *) were nocturnal. A P-47 pilot contributed his daytime encounter with "a gold-colored ball, with a metallic finish." [41] Often the UFO were characterized as phosphorescent, silver, white, and various shades of red, sometimes a yellow, green, or blue. Usually, radar checks verified that the accompanied or pursued ships were completely alone in the sky. One of the final USAF European sightings reflected this apparent contradiction. On this occasion the pilot swore he felt prop wash rush past him and his craft.

Witnessing aerial improbabilities was not an experience confined to American personnel. The English, French, Russians, and others reported such observations. Nor was it an allied phenomenon. Japanese and German pilots saw them and thought they might be Russian or American devices.[42]

In the battle for the East, our fighters submitted accounts virtually identical to those of their comrades halfway around the world. Balls of fire, glowing spheres, phosphorescent globes; orange, white, red, yellow; pursuing, maneuvering, intelligently controlled —and all permanently, totally unexplained.

Yet, perhaps, not totally.

The German "flying disk" went airborne, in experimental flight, for the first time in 1945.[43]

Originally designed by German scientists Schriever, Habermohl, and Miethe and the Italian Bellonzo, the project to construct such a craft had been started four years earlier. A stabile, semiglobular cabin, with a flat, rotating ring, constituted the basic Habermohl-Schriever model, while Miethe developed a broad disk with adjustable jets. On February 14, 1945, the

* The argument that the term derives from the French or German word for "fire" is linguistically feasible, but, as the expression was originated by American youths and the above explanation encompasses it, such is almost certainly the derivation.

Habermohl-Schriever "flying disk" took off from
Prague and, within three minutes, is reported to have
achieved 40,000 feet and a speed of almost 1,250
miles an hour. Ultimately, the inventors expected to
double the velocity. That was more than thirty years
ago—before "flying saucers."

The elaborate and expensive experimentation was
supposedly nearing completion as hostilities concluded,
but all of the models and prototypes were destroyed
before the enemy armies could reach the plants.*
Habermohl is reputed to have been taken by the
Russians and Miethe came to work for the United
States and Canada. It may reasonably be assessed that
their talents were not permitted to go to waste any
more than were those of Von Braun and his Soviet-
situated counterparts.

Most of the results and many of the people connected with the "flying disks" have been obscured by
international manipulation and the passage of time.
Regardless, resultant riddles are minor compared to
the aerial hocus-pocus of December 5, 1945.

Throughout history there have been countless "disappearances"—things, animals, people, even entire
communities, but, although saucerologists often attempt to include them all in their potpourri of "evidence," they rarely appear to bear any relationship to
the mystery of UFO, perhaps because these instances
of sleight-of-sight seldom occur above the surface of
the earth. Still, there are vanishing acts performed in
the sky and none has remained so totally answerless
as the following event.

A flight of five TBM Avenger bombers took off
from the U.S. Naval Air Station, at Fort Lauderdale,
Florida, at two o'clock in the afternoon on December
5, 1945. The command craft carried a complement
of two, while the remaining four planes each had
three-men crews. Five large planes and fourteen men.

The day was clear, visibility considerable, and the
projected flight a simple one for the personnel whose

---

* It is a classic claim among certain more politically
oriented researchers that the Soviet Army captured one
prototype.

flight and navigation time ranged from one to six years. They were to fly east about 160 miles, north for 40 miles, and, from that point, return to base.

A couple of hours later, at about the time the flight was due back, the flight leader informed the field that his command was in an emergency state. He was unable to locate his position for the tower, nor could the other craft. The five planes and fourteen men were incapable of navigationally deducing where they were. Instructed to bear due west, the flight replied it didn't know where west was. The day was still clear, and the sun brilliant over the western horizon.

Forty minutes passed as the planes talked among themselves. The pilots voiced more and more confusion regarding their situation. Tones revealed greater and greater tension and apprehension. Suddenly, the flight leader abdicated control of the flight to his second-in-command. An extraordinary action. This was immediately followed by a final radio contact restating the fact that they were lost, but suggesting they might be about 225 miles northeast of the base.

A Martian flying boat, fully rescue-equipped, with a crew of thirteen, was dispatched at once. After checking in by radio several times, it fell into complete silence.

Subsequently, one of the most exhaustive air searches in history was conducted, employing the facilities of the aircraft carrier *Solomons,* countless other vessels, and in excess of three hundred planes.

No wreckage, debris, fragments of any order were discovered. No trace of the six planes and twenty-seven men was ever found.

The British South American Airways lost a four-engine Tudor airliner,* with forty passengers and crew, on January 29, 1948, and another, its sister ship,† headed for Kingston, Jamaica, via Kindley Field, Bermuda, carrying twenty persons on January 17, 1949. Despite each plane's disappearance being exhaustively

---

* *Star Tiger.*
† *Star Ariel.*

investigated not so much as a bolt was ever retrieved.[44]

These curious occurrences lend themselves to the
orthodox slit-in-time or dimensional space warp theories. A number of saucerologists support the abduc-
tion-by-aliens arguments, often in conjunction with the
existence of huge "mother ships" at great altitudes.

A year after the war ended, a new spate of sightings
of unknowns occurred. This time the complex was
localized, for the most part, over Sweden.

"A limited censorship has been imposed on information concerning unidentified missiles—believed to
be flying bombs or rockets—that have been sighted
over Swedish territory in recent weeks," read a July
28, 1946, article. "The authorities have banned the
publication of names of localities where the missiles
have been sighted and newspapers have been required
to use the dateline 'Somewhere in Sweden' when writing about the subject." [45]

The Swedish military issued a press release on
August 11, " 'Ghost rockets'—mysterious spool-shaped
objects with fiery tails*—have become a common sight
in Sweden," [46] it acknowledged. It proceeded to assert
that authorities were certain their country was in the
path of experimental, electronically directed missiles.
Some of the unknowns were depicted as fairly small,
squarish, and, at least partly, colored red.

Reassurances continued the next day, accompanied
by the admission that formation of "rocket bombs" had
flashed through the skies over Stockholm at ten o'clock
the previous evening. As had been true in the past,
their course was from southeast to northwest.

Washington entered the confusion without helping
to remedy it. Officials in the capital said that the
Scandinavian sightings were thought to originate in the
Soviet Union. It was argued that they might have been
launched from Peenemunde, the former center of
German rocket science.

The Swedish military was being deluged with ac-

---

* A description that has been employed, almost verbatim,
for hundreds of years, including through modern times.

counts of fire balls, with long luminous tails, and of slow-sailing, cigar-shaped bombs soaring along at fifteen hundred feet.

Testimony to crashes was also being received. All reports were investigated. Nothing was found.

One remarkable story came from the midlands of the country. A newly completed barn imploded for no apparent reason. Immediately preceding the collapse "flying bombs" had overflown the area. There was no fire; a cracking sound and the building fell.

The population was being made very uneasy by these incidents. Therefore, the authorities directed that the locations of the crashes be concealed. This practice had been established during the days of Germany's V-1 and V-2 threats.

An earlier rumor was amplified. It said that officers of Russian Air Force research had been removed for failing to keep abreast of the nuclear development of the Western powers. Replacements had been attempting to compensate for the deficiency with new experiments employing unloaded missiles.[47]

Sweden had brought the full force of her radar network to bear against the Unidentified Flying Objects. Notwithstanding this effort, the great number of unknowns filling the heavens over the center of the nation on August 13 brought concern to a feverish pitch. The press hinted that the military was arranging for the temporary use of several sophisticated radar systems from England to hasten its program to determine what was actually occurring.

One newspaper announced that long-distance bombing expert Lieutenant General James H. Doolittle, then retired from the United States Air Force, had been summoned to Sweden to inspect the existing radar defenses. Officially, it was said, the famous American flier was supposed to be visiting on business, in his capacity as an advisor to the Shell Oil Company.

Still, on the same day, the press stated:

The Swedish General Staff today described the situation as "extremely dangerous," and it is obvious that Sweden no longer is going to tolerate such violations of her integrity.

The General Staff received more than 1,000 reports on rocket bombs last night and this morning.[48]

It is likely that the concentration of UFO over Sweden was the most intense in history, from the point of view of the overall effect on a single nation. The government, the military, the scientific community, and the average citizen were stirred to confusion, apprehension, and anger.

No astronomer questioned the presence of the unknows, but none could identify them. One professional, who was a meteorologist as well, monitored a flight and produced an excellent record.

While watching some cloud formations through his telescope he suddenly found a brilliant light on his lens. It was located on the horizon. His initial response was that he had picked up an airplane and the sunlight reflecting from it. Nearly at once he discarded this notion as the object was far exceeding the speed of a conventional craft. Then, within ten seconds, he had distinguished the form of the UFO.

"I managed to get a clear view of the bomb's body and estimate that it was at least 90 feet long. The body was torpedo-shaped and shining like metal," said the astronomer, duplicating some of the description E. W. Maunder had offered regarding an episode of nearly seventy-five years earlier.* "No sound could be heard although the bomb was only two kilometers away. At the explosion, a terrific light flashed up that for a moment blinded me. No fire, no smoke or sparks were noticeable." [49]

It must be granted that a silent explosion is most unusual. Combined with the lack of fire or smoke, it suggests that the astronomer had no observational or deductive knowledge that the unknown was a "bomb." He merely accepted the military announcement. In

---

* See Chapter 4.

actuality, neither he nor the government had any idea as to the nature of the phenomena.

Accounts mounted, and most tended to agree. The primary distinction among them was that some persons saw the great fireballs and others the cigar-shaped object. There seemed to be a consensus with respect to both varieties propelling small, flaming globes in their wakes.

The public, or the press, had come to calling the things "phantom bombs" or "Russian V-4's," [50] but not always.

The major newspaper *Aftonbladet* spoke of a pair of "ghost rockets" on the following day. It was a report of one of the rare cases which came close to causing casualties. A UFO plummeted into a lake and barely missed a small boat in which a young couple were relaxing. Near Goetberg, a troop of Boy Scouts observed one of the objects sail overhead, abruptly alter the course 35 degrees, and vanish in the direction from which it had originally appeared.

The phenomena finally broke through geographical and national boundaries on August 13. Although previous testimony had placed a few unknowns above neighboring countries, the report of a "ghost rocket" from Denmark was the first strong confirmation that they were violating other sky space.

Briand Jensen, a night watchman of Struer, West Jutland, saw one of the objects approach from the northeast, racing overhead, and explode with a resounding noise. The effect created a tremendous flash and lighted the heavens for several miles in all directions.

Finally, military and government spokesmen in Sweden conceded that all of the allusions to "missiles," "rockets," and "V-type" weaponry were baseless speculation. *Aftonbladet* revealed that "authorities said today they had received no tangible proof from foreign experiments with aerial missiles." It added that "it ought to be possible to state whether they are meteors or not, and if they are rockets one should be caught." [51]

The Scandinavian critics were to discover that de-

termining the nature and origin of Unidentified Flying
Objects was a little more difficult than they imagined.
As did their colleagues in the United States—for over
a quarter of a century.

Aftonbladet suggested the possibility of two explanations of the UFO: the first was a reiteration of
the theory that they were Russian projectiles; the
second was that "Sweden is being used as an object
of demonstration, directed not to us but to the big
world." [52]

Naturally, most ufologists supported the latter argument.

Comments had not ceased to flow from Washington. One release from the State Department reported
that Under-Secretary Dean Acheson was personally interested in the matter, but had announced that the
United States government had not been officially consulted on the subject.

The New York *Times* of August 15 disclosed that
Swedish Army investigators had come upon a fragment
of metal. It was less than three inches long and letters
were found on it. The implication was that this physical
"evidence" might help solve the mystery.

Despite the hands-off policy of the United States
military, before another week passed both General
James Doolittle and General David Sarnoff were in
Stockholm. Both were repeatedly identified as authorities on aerial warfare. Nevertheless, the press emphasized that the arrivals were completely independent
of one another, and each was traveling as a private
citizen.

Immediately, the superficial pretense was abandoned. An interview with Colonel C. R. S. Kempf,
Chief of Swedish Defense, revealed that he was anxious
to consult with the two experts.

"Doolittle expressed surprise that the Swedes had
not yet found a trace of a rocket and also that no
theory had been advanced," wrote one journalist.[53]
These remarks indicated that the piece of lettered metal
had failed to yield results and that the military there
had not accepted either of *Aftonbladet*'s alternatives.

August 22 brought word that the country's Defense

Staff had told newsmen that some "results" were being gotten from radar readings. The source and nature of the UFO were to be identified shortly, it added.[54] On the following day the British government, from which special electronic equipment had been borrowed, issued a brief release. It said that English radar experts, having returned from Sweden, had "submitted secret reports to the British Government on the origin of the rockets." [55]

Two weeks passed before the USSR finally responded to the frequent speculation that it was involved in the activities of the unknowns. The Soviet *New Times* described any such assertions as slanderous.[56]

Dr. Manne Siegbahn, Nobel-Prize-winning Swedish physicist, remarked: "There is no clear evidence that any guided missiles have been flying over Sweden. I, myself, examined one reported to be such a missile and found it to be a meteorite. I am very suspicious of the existence of any such thing." [57] Obviously, Siegbahn's examination accounted for only one of hundreds of sightings and a number of "crashes."

Sarnoff was of a different opinion. He discarded the myth and meteorite theses, concluding that the UFO were "real missiles." [58]

In the autumn of 1946 the final results of the inquiry into the remarkable invasion of Scandinavian skies was delivered to the public.

Swedish military authorities said today that they had been unable to discover after four months of investigation the origin or nature of the ghost rockets that have been flying over Sweden since May.

A special communiqué declared that 80 percent of 1,000 reports on the rockets could be attributed to "celestial phenomena" but that radar equipment had detected some [200] objects "which cannot be the phenomena of nature or products of imagination, nor can be referred to as Swedish airplanes."

The reports added, however, that the objects

were not the V-type bombs used by the Germans
in the closing days of the war.[59]

Yet, the Swedish board of inquiry had nothing of
which to be ashamed. Its "non-conclusion" regarding
UFO was at least as clear and rational as that reached
by the United States Air Force during the succeeding
twenty-five years.

Notes

1. Theodore Flournoy, *Des Indes à la planète Mars Étude
   sur un cas de somnambulisme avec glassalalie* (Geneva:
   Eggiman, 1900).
2. Richard A. Proctor, *Other Worlds Than Ours* (New York:
   P. F. Collier, 1901).
3. Garrett P. Serviss, *Other Worlds* (New York: D. Appleton
   & Company, 1901), p. 127.
4. "It's Our Earth Alone Inhabited," by E. A. Shelly. O.S.A.,
   The Irish Ecclesiastical Record, Ser. 4, Vol. 12, 1902,
   pp. 416–444.
5. Ibid.
6. William Pickering, "Are There Men on Mars?", *Technical
   World Magazine*, Vol. V, No. 5 (July 1906), pp. 449–472.
7. Ibid.
8. Percival Lowell, *Mars as the Abode of Life* (New York:
   Macmillan, 1908), p. 207.
9. Percival Lowell, *Mars and Its Canals* (New York: Macmillan, no date in copy consulted), p. 377.
10. *Flying Saucers,* No. 25, May 1962, and No. 32, September
    1961, *Star Weekly Magazine,* July 1971. Donald H. Menzel
    and Lyle Boyd, *The World of Flying Saucers,* Doubleday,
    1963.
11. New York *Tribune,* December 23, 1909, also New York
    Times and New York *Sun,* same date.
12. New York *Tribune,* December 24, 1909, also New York
    Times and New York *Sun,* same date.
13. New York *Tribune,* January 13, 1910.
14. New York *Tribune,* January 14, 1910.
15. New York *Tribune,* January 15, 1910.
16. C. A. Chant, "An Extraordinary Meteoric Display,"

Journal of the Royal Astronomical Society of Canada, Vol. VII, No. 3 (May/June 1913), pp. 145–215.

17. Charles Fort, *The Book of the Damned* (New York: Henry Holt, 1941), p. 297.

18. C. A. Chant, "Further Information Regarding the Meteoric Display of February 9, 1913," *Journal of the Royal Astronomical Society of Canada*, Vol. VII, No. 6 (November/December 1913), pp. 438–447.

19. *Annals of Our Lady of the Sacred Heart* (Australian), Vol. 65, No. 10.

20. *Annals of Our Lady of the Sacred Heart* (Australian), Vol. 65, No. 11.

21. New York *Tribune*, September 2, 1921.

22. Ibid.

23. Vesta La Viesta, the cosmologist and planetary explorer, *Peoples of Other Worlds* (New York: George T. Funk Press, 1923).

24. New York *Sun*, August 23, 1924.

25. Ibid.

26. Ibid.

27. New York *Times*, August 22, 1924.

28. Sir Francis Younghusband, *Life in the Stars* (London: John Murray, 1927).

29. Otto John Schuster, *Other Worlds* (Boston: Christopher Publishing House, 1927).

30. Ruppert T. Gould, *Enigmas* (London: Philip Allan and Company, 1929).

31. Nicholas Roerich, *Altai-Himalya* (New York: Frederick A. Stokes Company, 1929), pp. 361–362.

32. Haig Gordon Garbedian, *Major Mysteries of Science* (New York: Covici-Friede, 1933), p. 255.

33. Rudolph Lusar, *German Secret Weapons of the Second World War* (New York: Philosophic Library, 1959).

34. Frank Hamilton, *Jesus, the Savior of the Worlds* (Ventnor, N.J.: L. B. Printing Company, 1941).

35. Donald Lee Cyr, *Life on Mars* (El Centro, Calif.: 1944).

36. New York *Times*, January 2, 1945.

37. Ibid.

38. Ibid.

39. Ibid.

40. Jo Chamberlin, "The Foo Fighters Mystery," *American Legion Magazine*, December 1945.

41. New York *Times*, January 2, 1945.

42. Various newspaper sources and Harold T. Wilkins, *Flying Saucers on the Attack* (New York: Citadel, 1954).

43. Lusar, *German Secret Weapons*, pp. 164–166.

44. Personal conversations with investigators of the American incident (December 5, 1945) not affiliated with a government agency. Maj. Donald E. Keyhoe, *The Flying Saucer Conspiracy* (New York: Henry Holt, 1955); *American Legion Magazine*, April 1962; James W. Moseley, *Book of Saucer News* (Clarksburg, W. Va.: Saucerian Publications, 1967).

45. New York *Times*, July 28, 1946.

46. Ibid., August 11, 1946.

47. Ibid., August 12, 1946.

48. Ibid., August 13, 1946.

49. Ibid.

50. Ibid.

51. Ibid., August 14, 1946.

52. Ibid.

53. Ibid., August 21, 1946.

54. Ibid., August 22, 1946.

55. Ibid., August 23, 1946.

56. Ibid., September 4, 1946.

57. Ibid., September 17, 1946.

58. Ibid., October 1, 1946.

59. Ibid., October 11, 1946.

BOOK II

USA, USE, and UFO

8

Modern Ufology

I've been convinced for a long time that the flying saucers are interplanetary. We are being watched by beings from outer space.

> —Albert M. Chop, deputy public relations director, National Aeronautics and Space Administration, and former United States Air Force spokesman for Project Blue Book, and on Unidentified Flying Objects, *True,* January 1965.

THE STUDY OF Unidentified Flying Objects and "flying saucers" has no experts. But some investigators are more expert than others.

Once one has recognized the difference between ufologists and saucerologists, the kinds of each seem as numerous as the phenomena reported. Countless skeptical ufologists deny any UFO was ever more than a misinterpreted object (balloon, plane, firefly), a physiological effect (reaction of an optic nerve), an illusion (psychologically based), a celestial occurrence, or a "natural" phenomenon of another kind.

These analysts themselves fall into two classes, those with good scientific or technical credentials (astronomers, meteorologists, pilots, radar operators), and those with few or none. It should be understood that professional standing guarantees no expertise in the isolation and explanation of Undefined Sensory Experience (USE). This applies whether the observer's encounter has been interpreted as an airborne craft or eerie lights hovering in a forest.

Initially one must determine if a scientist or technician examining a case personally viewed the UFO. The informed evaluation of a report of an obvious aircraft, from an individual wholly unaware of the existence of such machines, might be of far greater consequence than the actual account. Yet, a third-hand analysis of a sighting, detailed by a scientist or technician reading repeatedly interpreted notes, could be of little reliability or use.

The best descriptions of UFO usually come from an original source, whose emotional condition, immunity to religion or superstitious orientations, intuitive faculties, intelligence, education, field of specialization, and honesty combined to create a superior observer, especially where the climate, atmosphere, lighting, and other considerations are the most desirable. The value of any account diminishes in direct ratio to the decline in one, or more, of these traits and/or conditions.

Most impressive records of UFO are the result of many personal and impersonal aspects of the sighting and the report; the character of the phenomenon or phenomena noted, in conjunction with the prevailing conditions. When and where seen (dawn, afternoon, night, and geographical location), environment (skimming housetops or winding through a canyon), altitude (stratosphere or floating at 100 feet), shape (disk, globe, very elongated), appurtenances (upper cabin, wings, tail), secondary structural characteristics (rockets, vents, windows), color (silver, red, green), composition (metal, plasm, light), expulsion (exhaust, flare, "angel's hair"), speed (hovering, 5,000 miles an hour), course (approximating that of typical lighter-than-air object, resembling a conventional airplane, inconsistent with known aerodynamic principles—e.g., instantaneous reversal of flight at tremendous velocities), as well as a number of other attributes and behavioral patterns, are vital variables.

The majority of UFO reports are submitted by scientifically and technically untrained persons. An extraordinarily large number are received from individuals with desirable professional qualifications. One must not underestimate the perceptive powers of the former, nor exaggerate those of the latter. A description detailed by an astute, attentive housewife is of greater value than a vague one from a dim-visioned, forgetful geneticist.

It was not until the press created "flying saucers" that any consolidated attention was focused on undefined observations of "things" seen in the sky. In spite of individual sightings and, occasionally, continuous viewings over a period of months having been chronicled for millennia, this may be attributed to two reasons. First, the media extrapolated from a phrase the existence of "flying saucers" (intelligently controlled, extraterrestrial phenomena). Second, the confusion permeating all levels of interest—professional, military, and laic—was compounded by an enormous misuse of terminology.*

As the years progressed these problems were complicated by official deception, public bewilderment, religious fanaticism, pseudo-occult charlatanry, the ignorance of scientific commentary, the growth of the neurotic and psychotic subculture of saucerites, political manipulation of individuals, and cults devoted to various schools of interplanetary communication. Professional and popular joking and misinterpretation, misinformation, and pure fiction woven throughout the radio and television news drastically distorted attitudes about the phenomena. Further, fiction in the films, newspapers, magazines, and books of the nation, and of the world, contributed to the situation. Alleged concern was so evasive, misled, and disoriented it soon bore no relationship to what was actually happening.

There was only one credible alternative conjecture regarding the aerial unknowns for which the Establishment had no explanations. The public was victim of the inexplicable plans of a group of men who wished to camouflage true extraterrestriality in the air above America, or who successfully screened events,

* See Chapter 6.

or coming events, of a more earthly, but equally stunning purpose.

Officialdom was slow and bumbling with respect to investigating the mystery of odd things seen in the sky—at least as far as could be determined by the public or private researchers. Science appeared unconscious of the phenomena altogether, except for an occasional academician dismissing the entire matter. The federal administrations of the late 1940s and early 1950s and, subsequently, small segments of the scientific community finally did deign to comment on the rapidly increasing number of sightings. These evaluations were merely unsupported theories, contending that virtually all reports were of normal aerial craft, planets, stars, clouds, birds, and reflections of sunlight on ice crystals. Public relations of this sort, by inescapable implication, classified the observers as mental or optic incompetents, ignorant, and generally unable to perceive with average efficiency and/or evaluate with reasonable accuracy. The indifference to some accounts was justified because of the witnesses' lack of familiarity with objects or conditions that might have created the effect noted. Still, in hundreds of instances, the assaults were upon the professional education, expertise, and experience, and the intelligence and integrity, of military, professional airline, and private pilots, radar scanners, airport tower and ground personnel. Often the reports of distinguished scientific reporters, including astronomers, were treated contemptuously. With virtually no exception, the purportedly qualified debunkers had no firsthand experience with UFO monitoring. Few could claim education or knowledge in more than a small fraction of the disciplines which might contribute to an explanation of the unknowns. One characteristic problem was the inability of the career skeptics to recognize the fact that *an* explanation of a *phenomenon* did not answer the thousands of other sightings on record. Their personal theory of an isolated occurrence frequently failed to even clarify the single incident. Often several ideas might offer equally acceptable solutions. Still, this tended to make the problem more complex, rather than less. Having accepted reasonable explanations of thousands of sightings, the most inexplicable ones remaining were either cases where numerous "identifications" were possible, but none could be clearly determined, or reports where no analysis successfully incorporated all of the hard facts. In cases where different explanations might apply, the Air Force usually arbitrarily discarded all but one answer and flatly stated that it was *fact*. When confronted by a situation too complex to be covered by any available speculation, the usual approach was to select an explanation which allowed for as many of the characteristics of the UFO as could be acceptably included. Usually this required the rephrasing of the original report, including remarks never made by the observer, and dismissing or denying aspects of the firsthand account which didn't fit the chosen thesis. The result was then announced as truth.

An era of particular Undefined Sensory Experience (USE) remains a riddle. The responsibility for this lack of resolution primarily lies with the government (both as represented by succeeding administrations and the permanent company consisting of career and civil service), the scientific community, and the broadcast and printed areas of "news." Recognizing this historic foundation, an examination of the beginning of the modern era of Undefined Sensory Experience is in order.

It has become almost universal practice for ufologists, from novice to the rare scholar, to view the "modern age" as the period that began with the sighting by Idaho aviator Kenneth Arnold over the Cascade Mountains on June 24, 1947. Yet, the sole reason for denoting that episode as the inception of the "new" era is that from countless observations of confusing aerial phenomena the press of the United States selected his adventure to publicize and, ultimately, designate as "the beginning." Arnold's sighting was not unique, or even among the more enigmatic or exciting reports. A newsman snatched at his unthinking, and actually involuntarily inaccurate, description of his experience,

in which he included the word "saucer," and extrapolated it into an instant fad.

It is important to realize that the UFO continuum
was unbroken from ancient times to the day Arnold
perceived nine shining disks on the horizon dominated
by Mount Rainier. And there has been no interruption
in the sightings following that event. The pilot's case
was one of thousands and was by no means among
the most important when consideration is restricted to
the few minutes of the encounter. But that was not
Arnold's full participation in the evolution of theories
relating to UFO. He was quite active in the Maury
Island affair. The role he played in this singular bewilderment may someday be revealed as of considerably more consequence than his personal observation
as a flier. Or, at least, the sighting over Puget Sound,
several days before Arnold's experience, and the confusing circumstances under which it was eventually
buried, certainly may have been.

If one feels the need for a specific "beginning" to
the age of "flying saucers," meaning, in actuality, of
UFO, the Maury Island Mystery is as likely a starting
point as is historically available. Unfortunately, it is
not simple to determine precisely where the Maury
Island Mystery began. It is more difficult to decide
where, if ever, it ended.

9

The Arnold Archives, the Shaver Story, and the Palmer Method

Personally, I believe in the reality of the flying saucers, even if they come from another planet.

> —Admiral Gerson de Macedo
> Soares, Navy General Secre-
> tary of Brazil. *O. Globo*, Rio de
> Janeiro, February 27, 1958.

THE MAURY ISLAND affair is ignored in most serious books on Unidentified Flying Objects. And for good reason. Much of what is said to have occurred makes little or no sense, measured by usual and reasonable inductive standards. The case embraces both "hard" air-to-air and ground-to-air sightings and contentions that sound paranoid.

Attempting to offer an understandable record of these complex events presents many problems. A simple unraveling of the purported facts is a task. Ultimately, the only feasible approach is to deal with the matter in a logical and chronological way. This leads to a sequence of sightings—Bakersfield, Puget Sound, the Cascade Mountains, and then to the extraordinary investigation of the Maury Island (Puget Sound) incident—an inquiry that reached out to encompass Kenneth Arnold's experiences, and possibly much more.

A curious precursor of the imminent Arnold sighting occurred to pilot Richard Rankin. On course from

Chicago to Los Angeles, he tracked ten disks, with diameters, from thirty to thirty-five feet. They were flying at about 560 miles an hour in a triangular deployment, at two in the afternoon, on June 14, 1947, over Bakersfield, California.[1]

If the Maury Island Mystery had a beginning, Rankin's experience might be it, although it is rarely mentioned at all, and virtually never in relationship to the Puget Sound affair. Kenneth Arnold's treatment of the incident has always seemed strange. In his book he covers the puzzling series of events before and after his famous sighting. More than two pages are devoted to an autobiographical sketch of Rankin (including anecdotes regarding his remarkable psychic abilities and many extraneous reminiscences about his brother), but only two sentences were in any way pertinent. They read:

> Dick Rankin, a famous pilot, had sent word over the [United Press teletype] wires that Davidson and Brown [Air Force Intelligence "investigators," some of whose activities will be detailed later] had talked to him about his reports of flying saucers. He felt that Davidson and Brown were really hot on the trail of finding out what the saucers were.[2]

The reference would have been to August 1 or August 2. In the calendar of events, this places it barely five weeks after Arnold's encounter, six following the initiation of the core of the Maury Island business, and seven later than the actual Bakersfield sighting. Yet Arnold omits Rankin's experience when writing about him. He has him believing that official inquiries about the unknowns, which were only then being revealed to the public as a continuing and often collective phenomenon, were not only under way, but already beginning to develop into a recognizable pattern—at least to some small secret segment of the government, presumably the same clique that would direct the succeeding three decades of denials.

Nearly everything about Rankin's relationship with

UFO is peculiar. Arnold's need to allude to him, while avoiding any consequential material, is typical. The June 14 sighting of ten circular unknowns was more than an ordinary report. Considering the furor that was to fan across the country within a matter of weeks, it is odd how it was disregarded. As the Maury Island circumstances unfold, it is difficult to relate the paragraph quoted from Arnold with any of what allegedly transpired—either the episode itself or the "investigation" of the case, by several persons, which evolved from it. If Rankin and his sighting were not related to Arnold's amateur detecting, and had nothing to do with his own experience ten days afterward, why did he mention the man at all? Particularly without remarking on his sighting?

No reasonable reply suggests itself. Still, compared with countless other aspects of the Maury Island case, this question will diminish to join lesser unresolved questions. Those first exploratory probes into ufology led all to confusion, and some to death. Where the way ended, or even how it went, no one ever discovered.

The early months of 1947, although relatively quiet, produced numerous sightings. One example was a fireball seen over Puerto Rico on January 12, the residual tail of which was photographed after the main body was no longer visible.[3] In late spring activities began to increase, especially in quality. A disk-shaped unknown was followed across the skies above Richmond, Virginia, in April by a professional weatherman who was monitoring a balloon with a theodolite.[4] It was described as being flat-bottomed and domed. Reported as dirigible-shaped or as a disk viewed from a deceptive angle, another object was seen on May 18, as the sun was setting.[5] Around noon, on the following day, a silvery UFO appeared over the Colorado desert. After hovering for a while, it performed a series of highly acrobatic maneuvers before sweeping over the horizon, against the wind.[6]

Several unknowns were sighted in the first week of June, here and in many other countries. Central eastern Europe, particularly Hungary, was accorded an even greater concentration of UFO as more than fifty observations of "silvery balls" hurtling across the daytime skies were reported.[7] Half a world away in Douglas, Arizona, unusual events were in progress. Standing on her back porch one evening, scanning the heavens for meteors, the noted ufologist and cofounder of the internationally known Aerial Phenomena Research Organization Coral E. Lorenzen observed a "tiny but well-defined" ball of light rise from a range of hills and, consuming only four to six seconds, vanish upward among the stars.[8] Around the same time records have William A. Rhodes photographing a parabolic unknown over Phoenix.[9] And pilot Richard Rankin spotted between thirty and thirty-five foot-broad disks sailing along in echelon formation during the middle of the afternoon over Bakersfield, California, on June 14.

Then came Maury Island. Two sightings over Puget Sound by a pair of purported harbor patrolmen, who ultimately appear to have occupied no such positions. A request by a Chicago editor that a professional aviator who had encountered UFO himself and had been unintentionally responsible for the modern usage "flying saucers" investigate the case. Another flier, boasting a long impressive record with commercial airlines, was brought into the business. Army Intelligence in, out, then in again—and suddenly dead. Claims and counterclaims of disguise, duplicity, hoax, and murder. A quarter of a century of confusion and calculated distortion still permeates this chapter of ufology.

The first of the two actual Maury Island incidents is alleged to have occurred to Harold Dahl, his fifteen-year-old son, two crewmen, and the boy's dog shortly after noon on June 21, 1947. While Dahl's identity and occupation have never been more than vaguely defined, he is often characterized as a simple boatman, or volunteer, semi-professional, or regular member of the harbor patrol in the waters of Puget Sound, off Tacoma, Washington. Considering the craft's complement, it is not surprising that in versions claiming to quote him directly, he is frequently found describing himself as the captain of the vessel.

Apparently, the green sea was scudding into white-caps and low, dark clouds were moving along above. The boat was being kept close to the bayshore of Maury Island, some three miles from the mainland.

Something attracted Dahl's attention. He glanced up from the wheel to be startled by the presence of six unknowns shaped like inflated inner tubes.* They were hovering above the vessel at an estimated altitude of 2,000 feet. Lack of movement suggested balloons but this idea was quickly dismissed. Dahl perceived that five were moving around the sixth as it descended precipitously, seemingly due to some malfunction. Soon the center UFO stabilized above the man, boy, crew, and dog at an altitude of a couple of hundred yards, surrounded by the companion craft.

The seafaring spectators were able to discern no structural accessories—jets, rockets, motors, propellers, or any other indications of the device's operation. The objects were judged to be about 100 feet across, including the holes in their centers, which constituted a quarter of the UFO's total diameter. Described as appearing metallic, either golden or silvery, or both, they featured symmetrically placed portholes around the perimeter and a large, round, near-black observation window in the underside.

Apprehensive of a possible collision with the unstable craft, Dahl beached his boat. Taking advantage of the pause, he grabbed up his simple movie camera and, focusing on the UFO, rolled several feet of film. Meanwhile, one of the circling craft glided down and gently juxtaposed itself—surface to surface—with its handicapped companion for a number of minutes. Despite the absence of any other activity, the impression was that it had come to the assistance of the faltering vessel. A sound not unlike that of distant thunder was heard. The apparently malfunctioning UFO expelled a flurry of silver snow, aluminum-foil-weight flakes that showered over the entire area. This glittering feathery metal was followed by the dispersal

---

* A term that seems more descriptively suitable than the expression "doughnut-shaped," popularly applied to phenomena of such shape.

of a much bulkier, hot, slaglike material, which hailed down on the beach and surf. The water turned to steam where the fragments splashed into the sea.

Somewhat protected by nearby cliffs, the group continued to watch the discharge from the UFO. The defense provided by the island failed to prevent injury to the boy's arm and the death of the pet, which was buried in the sound on the trip back to the mainland. The episode was over as the center UFO appeared to have recovered, and the flight began to drift swiftly toward the horizon, gaining greater and greater altitude until they were no longer visible.

Normal conditions having returned, the crew attempted to radio the patrol base but static, attributed to the residual effects of the UFO, thwarted the effort. An examination was made of the damage to the boat caused by the dark, rocklike debris emitted by the departed unknowns. Samples of it and the lighter, whiter metallic refuse were collected, and they returned to port.

Dahl procured aid for his boy's superficially injured arm, and immediately reported to Fred L. Crisman, identified by him as his superior officer. He deposited with him the two types of specimens he had collected and the camera and film used to photograph the UFO. Crisman gave the impression of being incredulous. Nonetheless, he announced that he would personally investigate the shores of Maury Island, where Dahl estimated "at least twenty tons of the debris had fallen." [10]

This is the original version of the initial Maury Island incident, according to the writing of Kenneth Arnold. It has been repeated by the more informed ufologists—as Dahl's true version—for over a quarter of a century.

Fred L. Crisman, it is recorded, concluded the older members of the crew might have been imbibing a bit. Surveying the damage done to the boat and ordering its repair, Crisman visited the island. He found the shoreline strewn with the glassy, near-black rock and the shiny foil, according to his remarks to Arnold. Suddenly, a UFO swept down from frothy clouds and circled the sound. It fitted the description provided the previous day by Dahl. Reflecting that he held a pilot's license and had flown "over a hundred missions in a fighter over Burma" [11] during World War II, Crisman later detailed his own impressions of the physical characteristics of the unknown. "It was a brassy, almost golden, metallic aircraft, with a burled finish which showed more brilliance than a polished surface would show." [12] Shaped like an inner tube, its portholes measured no less than five feet across, and there was an observation window. The device operated in complete silence.

"I had the feeling as Crisman talked that, solid as he appeared, *he definitely wanted to domineer the conversation and trends of thought about the entire Maury Island incident*," wrote Arnold later. "Dahl in no way attempted to sell his story to me . . . he didn't try to convince me of the truth of what he had already told me." [13]

Nonetheless, the possibility that Arnold was being deceived, or actually manipulated, cannot be ignored. Precisely how the ufological detective dealt with the two saucer sighters of the Puget Sound "harbor patrol" will be pursued shortly.

The Tacoma sighters were intriguing, but they did not make the headlines. Still, lively coverage of a sighting by the press was imminent. It would scatter fascination with flying saucers throughout the West, across the nation, and, soon, around the entire world.

Three days following Harold Dahl's experience with UFO, around two o'clock in the afternoon,* Kenneth Arnold, member of the Idaho Search and Rescue Mercy Flyers, flying deputy for the Ada County Aerial Posse, acting deputy federal United States marshal, aerial salesman and originator of the Great Western Fire Control System found himself the central figure of an episode that would confound the nation. He observed a flight of nine UFO.

---

* The reader will note the compounded and statistically improbable time and geographical coincidences—the three successive sightings occurred along the Pacific coast and at approximately 2 P.M.

Arnold has remarked that both humanitarian impulses and a five-thousand-dollar reward motivated him the afternoon he was destined for Yakima. Cutting short a conversation with Herb Critzer, chief pilot for Central Air Service in Chehalis, Washington, he went in search of a downed C-46 Marine transport plane. The aircraft was believed to have force landed or crashed in an area of the Cascade Range of mountains with which he was particularly familiar. A highly experienced "mountain pilot," he was flying a craft modified for contending with the atmospheric conditions and often unexpected weather problems inherent in such aerial specialization. For rescue work, especially in land spired with peaks, in addition to the experience of the pilot and the adjustments to the plane, there is a third essential. The ship must always be thoroughly checked out before takeoff. Not simply routine things, but an inspection of functional parts of the machine the reliability of which might vary. Such care was exercised before Arnold hit the sky that Tuesday afternoon, June 24, 1947.

The speed and altitude limitations of a light plane restrict its searching scope, and Arnold decided to concentrate his attention on the Mount Rainier plateau for about an hour. Later, cruising at more than nine thousand feet, he completely reversed his course over the community of Mineral and was taken aback when a "tremendously bright flash lit up the surface" of his plane. Visual examination of the space about him revealed nothing but an ordinary DC-4 over his left shoulder. Suddenly, the radiance exploded again. Despite the unexpectedness of its appearance, Arnold was able to determine that it had originated from the north, to his left, about a hundred miles away, above Mount Rainier. The cause was a cluster of brilliant objects racing across the sky. Occasionally they flitted behind a peak for an instant—behavior that was to implement Arnold's judgment of their distance from him and, consequently, the velocity of the UFO. His observation of the objects, combined with his years of the flying which made him a more than qualified observer, established that they were "no aircraft I had ever seen before." [14]

Initially, their swiftness and the distance between him and the UFO made it difficult for the pilot to be certain of their design. It was evident to him that there were nine aerial unknowns flying in an inverted echelon pattern, with a noticeable break between the first four and the final five, at about 170 degrees across his path. They appeared to be coming from the direction of Mount Baker and heading over Mount Rainier.

Seeing the original flash, he thought of a P-51, and dismissed that explanation because the unknowns were lacking tail assemblies. Thinking that they might be some sort of jets with the rear ends skillfully camouflaged to create such an effect, he recorded the possibility. But immediately he realized that they were phenomena foreign to his experience. "I observed the objects' outline plainly as they flipped and flashed along against the snow [coating the mountain peaks] and also against the sky," [15] Arnold remembered. He was intrigued by the peculiar horizontal course of the UFO, which he compared to the erratic horizontal fluctuations of "speed boats on rough water." Regrettably, to reporters in Pendleton, Oregon, the flier was later to describe the *flight* (not the shape) of the unknowns with the words: "They flew like a saucer would if you skipped it across the water." [16]

The first three words of this sentence are of especial consequence. They clearly indicate that Arnold in no way suggested that the UFO were *shaped* like saucers but merely that *their aerodynamic behavior* was reminiscent of one skimmed along the surface of a tranquil pond.

At times their formation reminded Arnold of the flight pattern of geese. The pilot was captivated by "how they fluttered and sailed, tipping their wings alternately and emitting those very bright blue-white flashes from their surfaces." [17] These effects, he concluded, were caused by the glistening of sunlight from "the extremely polished surface of their wings."

Arnold seemingly regarded the entire fuselage of the UFO as "wings." In his pictorialization of the objects they look like very graceful, symmetrical boomerangs. The fronts constituted a third of a circle, or about 120-degree arcs making up the uninterrupted forward edge. Matching, shallow, half-width curves formed the rear of the ships, creating a cusped center tail and very pointed swept-back "wings." No other external characteristics were evident except for an apparent cockpit with a full-window canopy.

The flight of the objects was foreign to aerodynamic behavior with which Arnold was familiar.

The geographical landmarks, the state of the weather, and the relationship between the UFO and his plane were excellent for attempting a determination of the unknowns' speed. The afternoon was bright and sunny, his instrument panel included an eight-day clock, with a sweep second hand, and between the ideal points of reference of Mount Adams and Mount Rainier lay a high plateau, the rim of which was clearly discernible at its north and south ends.

He knew his own exact position, and the unknowns defined theirs by passing, for an instant, behind a familiar peak. They were approximately twenty-three miles away. Arnold noted that as the leading UFO passed beyond one edge of the plateau the last was moving over the opposite side. After personally duplicating their path he was able to deduce that the entire "chain-like formation" stretched for close to five miles. Comparing this with the time he had clocked for the UFO overflight he arrived at the figure one minute and forty-two seconds.

The aviator knew that this suggested great speed. He and some mathematically oriented friends began calculating the figures and it became obvious that the nine objects had been traveling more than seventeen hundred miles an hour. (It should not be forgotten that the incident described allegedly occurred in June 1947, almost four months before the first supersonic flight.) Swiftly, it was realized that the computations were being made on the basis of the distance from the tops of the pair of mountains. Beginning again, estimates were derived from the base-to-base measurement of barely under forty miles. Arnold wrote that this approach "was so far on the conservative side that I knew it was incorrect." Nevertheless, the UFO had sped over the Cascades at about 1,350 miles an hour.

"They were guided missiles, robotly [sic] controlled," concluded Arnold that evening. "I knew that speeds of this velocity the human body simply could not stand, particularly considering the flipping, erratic movements of these strange craft." [18]

The following days produced sightings of all kinds and Kenneth Arnold was an avid follower of the encounters of other individuals. He had been assured by an authority he respected that the United States possessed neither operational models nor even experimental prototypes of guided missiles capable of the maneuvers he had observed. When a friend suggested they fly up to Sekiu for some Chinook salmon fishing he responded readily to the chance for a brief respite. To their disappointment and amazement they found the object of their trip, an ocean inlet, crimsoned by a remarkable tide which was rapidly poisoning the fish by the thousands. The odd coloration was caused by a gelatinous red substance the villagers could not identify. "Even though the scientists had a name for it, I admitted red tides into my collection of phenomena along with flying saucers," [19] wrote Arnold of the day he turned about and flew back to his home in Boise, Idaho.[20]

Having eliminated all other options Arnold concluded that the objects must have been missiles or remotely directed experimental devices. Ultimately, these explanations were proven untenable and Arnold became a believer in UFO.

Among the most interesting aspects of this initial phase of the age of "flying saucers" were the many pilots who were reporting strong, frequently multiple, sightings. It was difficult to deny that, as a class, they were far better qualified to observe, analyze, and arrive at conclusions regarding aerial phenomena than the average citizen or even most scientific people. They might not be confronting their normal neighbors, but they were in their natural professional environment.

At 2 P.M. [21] or 3:15 P.M.,[22] on June 28, USAF aviator Lieutenant Armstrong was cruising his F-51 jet 6,000 feet over Lake Mead, Nevada, when he saw a half-dozen snowy disks. Six hours later "four Air Force officers, two pilots, and two intelligence officers from Maxwell AFB in Montgomery, Alabama, saw a bright light traveling across the sky . . . as it traveled toward the observers it 'zigzagged,' with bursts of high speed . . . overhead it made a sharp 90-degree turn and was lost from view as it traveled south." [23]

The following day's accounts included one by C. J. Zohn, a rocket expert stationed at White Sands, New Mexico. He monitored a large, silver, circular unknown moving northward at about ten thousand feet.[24]

Two weeks after the Mount Rainier incident had stimulated the curiosity of a large portion of the population, one of Arnold's acquaintances participated in an aerial encounter. Captain E. J. Smith, his co-pilot Ralph Stevens, and the rest of the United Air Lines Flight 105 crew were adjusting themselves to being airborne and abruptly found themselves involved in a UFO sighting.

To begin a practice which will be repeated elsewhere in this work, two versions of this sighting are offered. The reportorial and the official tones make the descriptions sound as if they were of two separate experiences. According to Arnold, this is what Captain E. J. Smith told him:

> We landed our DC-3 at Boise, Idaho shortly before nine last night and, afraid to be late in our schedule, we took off promptly at 9:04 P.M.*
> The weather was perfect. It was a funny thing, but just before take-off as I was climbing aboard our DC-3 someone in the crowd piped up and asked me if I had seen any flying saucers. Up to this time I not only hadn't seen any, but really didn't believe there were such things . . . and

---

* Compare with "official" version, which follows.

yelled back at him that I would believe them
when I saw them.

Brother, you could have knocked me over with
a feather when about eight minutes after takeoff, at exactly 7,100 feet over Emmett, Idaho,
we saw not one, but nine of them. At first I
thought it was a group of light planes returning
from some Fourth of July celebration, but then
I realized the things weren't aircraft, but were
flat and circular.

The first group of five appeared to open and
close in formation, then veered to the left of the
transport. At this time, I . . . called the Ontario,
Oregon, C.A.A. radio communications station
which was about 45 miles north and west from
Boise. I didn't tell them what I was seeing but said,
"Step outside and look to the southwest, about
fifteen miles, and see what you can find." The
operator came back . . . stating he saw nothing.

At this time my co-pilot informed me the first
group of disks had disappeared. It was then the
second group, three together and the fourth off
by itself, appeared. By then the transport had
reached 8,000 feet altitude and was cruising over
the rugged country leading to the Blue Mountains,
toward Pendleton, Oregon.

My co-pilot saw exactly what I did when he
stated that these objects seemed to merge, then
disappear, then come back in sight, and finally
they vanished again to the northwest. This second
group seemed to be higher than our flight path
and when they did leave, they left! Fast!

I positively know they were nothing from the
ground in the way of fireworks, reflections, or
smoke. I know they were not aircraft that I am
familiar with. I don't know how fast they were
going, but we all saw them. [Elsewhere, alluding
to the sighting, Arnold mentions that a stewardess, Martie Morrow, was called to the cockpit and seeing the phenomena through the front
window exclaimed: "Why, there's a formation of

those flying disks!"] They were bigger than our
aircraft.[25]

The "official" account was reported to the public
as follows:

Five "somethings," which were thin and
smooth on the bottom and rough-appearing on
top, were seen silhouetted against the sunset
shortly after the plane took off from Boise at
8:04 P.M. We saw them clearly. We followed
them in a northeasterly direction for about 45
miles. They finally disappeared. We were unable
to tell whether they outsped us or disintegrated.
We can't say whether they were "smearlike,"
oval, or anything else but whatever they were they
were not aircraft, clouds, or smoke.[26]

The Fourth of July was to be the date of a number
of reports, especially for less technically trained observers. A pilot, plus police and civilians, watched
from three to thirty fluttering UFO overpass Portland,
Oregon, on the holiday. In a typical crowd sighting,
at about seven o'clock on the still light summer evening, more than two hundred people of Hauser Lake,
Idaho, saw a disk circle and shoot upward, disappearing into the troposphere.[27]

Actually, beginning with the Rankin case, or the
Maury Island affair (rejected by some investigators),
or Arnold's confrontation, the modern era was initiated with what would come to be known as "flap"—
i.e., a time of concerted press coverage of UFO, although not necessarily a period of an unusually large
number of reports. The term is often employed in
contradistinction to a fairly notable general rise in
sightings, or a specific concentration of UFO accounts
emanating from a particular locale. The majority of
sightings was in the North American northwest. Almost three-quarters of the accounts were west of the
100-degree longitude line. The National Investigations Committee on Aerial Phenomena (NICAP)
analyzed late June and July 1947 some years later. It

concluded that, from 125 reports received at that time, almost a third came from Washington with 38. Quantitatively Colorado with 16, Idaho with 11, Utah with 8, and Oregon, California, New Mexico, Wyoming, and Arizona, with 6, 5, 3, 2, and 2, respectively, followed. Farther east, Oklahoma had the most with 9, and several other states had one or two reports.[28]

On July 7 the Maury Island site attracted attention once again when patrolmen Evan Davis and Stan Johnson, of Tacoma, witnessed three whirling objects, and radiating sparks, hover, move off, make precipitous maneuvers, and spin away.[29]

The Idaho *Statesman*'s aviation editor, Dave Johnson, a friend of Arnold and an expert flier, was operating his National Guard AT-6 plane at an altitude of about two and a half miles, while slightly east [30] (west) [31] of Boise, on July 9. He sighted and attempted to photograph [32] a large, round, seemingly black unknown. The observation continued for nearly a minute as

> I watched a circular object dart about in front of a cloud bank . . . over the nose of the [his] aircraft I saw the object . . . clearly and distinctly. I turned the plane broadside to it and pulled back the Plexiglas canopy so there would be no distortion. The object was still there.
>
> It was rising sharply and jerkily toward the top of the towering bank of alto-cumulus and alto-stratus clouds . . . turning so that it presented its edge to me . . . as a straight, black line. Then, with its edge still toward me, it shot straight up, rolled over at the top of the maneuver, and I lost sight of it.[33]

Acknowledging that he had not been able to estimate the distance between him and the object, he remarked that the "circular thing was maneuvering very swiftly." [34]

Dr. Clyde Tombaugh calculated the presence of a

new planet where none was thought to exist. Isolating
it in 1930, he introduced Pluto to the cosmography
of our solar system—to the consternation of many
astrologers. At 4:47, on the clear, bright afternoon
of July 10, while driving down a New Mexico highway
with his wife and two daughters, he observed a "curious shiny object, almost immobile." [35] It appeared to
have a wobbling motion. [36] The shape was elliptical,
the surface seemed polished, and the outline was defined. Shortly after it was initially noticed the unknown
moved up into a cloud cluster. Reemerging, it began
to rise at an accelerating speed, which the astronomer
estimated to be from six to nine hundred miles an
hour. Reporting to the Air Force, Professor Tombaugh
concluded: "The remarkably sudden ascent convinced
me it was an absolutely novel airborne device." [37]

Up to this point any effort being exerted by the
Army Air Force with respect to "flying saucers" was
being administered by the Technical Intelligence Division of the Air Material Command. "Administered"
because apparently there was no investigation under
way. The reasonable inference is that no serious attempt at evaluation was being made, either. Reports
came in, were deposited in some general category, and
filed. Two explanations offer themselves for such conduct: bureaucratic ineptitude or someone in government already knew the identity and character of "flying saucers." In either case, the rebuttals to accounts
of sightings by qualified observers were rarely convincing. In certain instances, sober ufologists suspected
that they were calculated to be transparently incom-
petent. If some element of power in our country was
attempting to camouflage or totally obscure the meaning of "flying saucers," it seemed likely it would have
available all the facilities to achieve the desired end.
It would not deal in clumsy subterfuge. Even had the
explanations been the product of bureaucratic bungling the unimaginative repetitions could hardly be
justified—simple atmospheric conditions, Venus, birds,
and jetcraft. One could not be oblivious to the fact
that a very high percentage of the sightings were being
made by extremely experienced commercial and pri-

vate aviators. *"Identified* flying objects" were common in their daily environment.

If the matter was being handled inefficiently, amateurish analyses were to be anticipated, but only up to a point. If deception was a programmed policy, it is possible that no one could conceive of a publicly acceptable solution. In that event, the power clique might intentionally take the path of greatest incredibility, quite reasonably assuming this would create the widest conflict of opinion and the most durable state of general confusion. Granting some validity to this speculation, it is apparent that the concept proved effective. Masses never act with *reason:* that is the prerogative of rare individuals.

Inconsistencies between sighters' conclusions regarding their experiences and the Air Force's, or other establishmentarian, assessments will be introduced from time to time. An early example is reflected in the military's appraisal of the Kenneth Arnold classic.

The flier told his story in great detail. What was the official response to the episode?

Captain Edward J. Ruppelt, who was director of the government's inquiry into the subject of UFO for some time, begins his written comments on the case by remarking that "some points in Arnold's own account . . . do not jibe with what the official files say. . . ." [38] He then explains how several years later, he went to second-, third-, and fourth-hand sources, before he was satisfied that he had compiled "what I believe is the accurate story." [39]

Ruppelt states that Arnold arrived in "the vicinity of Mount Rainier" [40] at "about 3: P.M.," [41] based upon the pilot's recollection that he took off at two "with the intention in mind of delaying my trip to Yakima for at least an hour, which I would spend on top, in and around the high plateau of" [42] the peak. Arnold spent an hour flying about 50 miles (the approximate distance from Chehalis to the mountain mesa). Ruppelt has the aviator "looking down at the ground when suddenly he noticed a series of bright flashes," [43] although the viewer's version specifies that, having been alerted by a flare about a half minute earlier, he was actually scanning the skies all around him. "Disk-shaped objects, which he estimated to be 45 to 50 feet in length," Ruppelt writes (since he describes them as being round presumably he means to indicate their diameter here).[44] As previously noted, Arnold specifically *did not* describe the UFO he saw as circular. He saw them as having a third-of-a-curve fore edge, with the fuselage sweeping back into streamlined wings, and a rear consisting of two curved cutouts meeting in the center as a cusp.[45] Ruppelt fails to mention that Arnold observed a DC-4 over his shoulder almost immediately before he caught sight of his nine unknowns. Quite important because it gave him another —this time an airborne—point of reference. The Air Force officer relates that the pilot had calculated that the UFO had been traveling at about 1,700 miles an hour. This was the original estimate. According to Arnold, he realized that he was judging the distance in question from "far too high up on both Mount Rainier and Mount Adams" [46] (the reference points of the flight path). The pilot reevaluated velocity by using the distance from base to base of the peaks. The revised estimate of the speed of the UFO was about 1,350 miles an hour, which Arnold regarded as definitely too modest a conclusion.[47]

Captain Ruppelt, with Dr. J. Allen Hynek, was probably the best and most honest man the military ever had operating in the area of Unidentified Flying Objects.* His overall coverage and final analysis conveys the impression that he believed that Arnold saw what he described. To his premature death, he appeared to remain undecided as to what had hurtled across the Washington skyscape.

The Puget Sound case began with sightings. What ensued involved Arnold, Smith, and other persons recently drawn into the aerial riddle. Further, the Maury Island mystery had some inexplicable connection with a strange subcultural "literary"/publishing event which, itself, has yet to be explained.

The age of "flying saucers" came and flourished,

---

* A phrase Ruppelt created.

absorbing a number of lesser legends, developed adjunct cults which attracted suborbits and moons of their own. Other areas of esoterica—astrology, spiritualism, extrasensory perception and similar allegedly psychic activities, and religious and political sects—overlap paths and interests with saucerology from time to time, even in symbiotic exchange, but not in relationships of dependency.

The Shaver tale is a legendary example of one of these subcultures.

One of the greatest of the science fiction pulp magazines was *Amazing Stories,* inaugurated in 1926. Among its earliest regular purchasers and would-be authors was Ray Palmer, an adolescent from Wisconsin. Twelve years later he had exceeded the role of contributor and become the managing editor for the Ziff-Davis publication. One of the most popular departments of the magazine was titled "Discussions," and included correspondence from readers. In the issue of January 1944 a letter was printed that began the Shaver Mystery, one of the primary sources of certain aspects of the age of "flying saucers." Nonetheless, within the subsequently woven web of ufology, it constitutes a strange diverting thread.

Asserting that modern English had embedded within it the residue of an incredibly early language, the correspondent seemed unclear as to whether its essence was Atlantean or Lemurian. Still, he left no doubt that the Rosetta Stone for decoding this transhistoric cipher was the "Mantong" alphabet, and the sender was the sole cryptographer capable of receiving and decoding it. The writer was a war-plant welder named Richard Sharpe Shaver, living in the town of Barto, Pennsylvania.[48]

One contention was that Shaver's memory, presumably of a previous incarnation, had been revived. He clearly recollected the days of Lemuria. Additional data was constantly provided by voices emanating from his welding equipment.

Dominic Lucchesi, a long-time saucerologist, interprets the situation differently. He relates that the messages reaching Shaver, as he labored in a Philadelphia shipyard, were not really "voices," nor did they derive directly from the machinery with which he worked. The investigator's understanding is that the communications were actually coming from "Mutan Mion," a sage of immeasurably ancient times. The means of transmission was a clairaudient (and, in some reports, clairvoyant) device called a "telaug." This instrument was replaying preservations of Mutan Mion's "thought records" from where it and they had been, and were still, secreted in subterranean caverns.

Encouraged by the publication of his initial revelations, Shaver decided to confide in the responsive editor even further. He dispatched to him a manuscript —of sorts (allegedly scrawled on the backs of envelopes, laundry bills, paper bags, and other scraps receptive to a pencil). It was titled "A Warning to Future Man" and claimed to be recovered race memories of life in the legendary civilization on the long-lost continent of Lemuria.

Conceding that "the story, as a story, was no good," [49] the skillful editor recalls he rewrote and expanded it to three times its original length (although this was subsequently denied by Shaver).[50] According to skeptic Donald H. Menzel, Palmer was promoting the material as *fact* "well in advance of publication." [51] Regardless, the March 1945 issue of *Amazing Stories* featured the beginning of Shaver's "I Remember Lemuria," as well as "Mantong, the Language of Lemuria," bylined by both the author and editor.

Shaver told his readers that English is the original and universal language, the natural speech among the billions of stars on their millions of inhabited planets. According to some of the Shaver disciples, it is also the tongue of the angels, although, in its primary dialect, it is properly called Mantong. The "old" alphabet is composed of the same twenty-six symbols as ours. All other terrestrial verbal communication derives from the basic Mantong/English.

The foundation of the Shaverian etymology is tonic-cryptic. That is, "just starting at the top and taking the letter *A* we find that 'when Adam named the animals, he was using the basic, unchanging meaning of the

sounds [letters], and he named correctly . . .' " [52]
Thus, upon the *animal* with *power* and *energy* was
bestowed the designation a + p + e = *ape*. So that
the world will not be denied access to the more than
half-million English words remaining, here is a sim-
plified outline of the key to

THE MANTONG ALPHABET [53]

A—Animal   (Use *AN* for short.)

B—Be   To exist. (Often used as a com-
                mand.)

C—Con   To see. (*C*-on; to understand.)

D—De   Detrimental, disintegrant energy.
                (The second important symbol in
                the alphabet.)

E—Energy   (An all-pervading concept including
                the idea of motion.)

F—Fecund   (Used "fe," as in fe-male—fecund
                man.)

G—Generate   (Used "gen.")

H—Human   (A very metaphysical concept here,
                not fully understood, but used in the
                sense "*H*-you-man"; a human is an
                H-man.)

I—Self, Ego   (Same as our English I.)

J—Generate   (A duplication of *G*, but with a deli-
                cate difference in shade of meaning.
                Actually *Ja*, in contrast to *Ge*, is a
                very important distinction. *G* is the
                generating energy, while *J* is animal
                generation per se.)

K—Kinetic   (The force of motion.)

L—Life

M—Man

N—Seed   Spore (Child, as "ninny.")

O—Orifice   (A source concept.)

P—Power

Q—Quest   (As "quest-ion.")

R—Horror   Danger (Used *AR*, symbol of a dangerous quantity of disintegrant force in an object.)

S—Sun   (Used "sis"; an important symbol, always referring to a "sun" whose energy is given off through atomic disintegration.)

T—Integration,
Growth   (Used *TE;* the most important symbol of the alphabet; the true origin of the cross symbol. It signifies the integrative force of growth; as, all matter is growing—the intake of gravity is the cause. The force is *T*. *TIC* means the science of growth. Integration-*I*-C*on* [understand].

U—You

V—Vital   (Use *VI*; the stuff Mesmer called "animal magnetism.")

W—Will

X—Conflict   (Force lines crossing each other.)

Y—Why

Z—Zero   Nothing. Neutralization. (A quantity of energy of *T* neutralized by an equal quantity of *D*. Futility.)

The citation of the period from which Richard Shaver was drawing his data has varied considerably. Palmer has said that Shaver puts it "many thousands of years ago," [54] despite his specifying "twelve thousand years ago" twelve years earlier,[55] and Dom Lucchesi opts for "45,000 years ago." Whichever one chooses, considering the author's complicated explanation of the astronomical confusion of the time, the lost civilization seems too recent, even in terms of science fiction—and "I Remember Lemuria" is purportedly true.

The faded manuscript, in expertly polished Palmer penmanship, tells of prehistoric Atlantis, classically located west of Gibraltar,[56] and Lemuria, which is usually misplaced in the center of the Pacific by amateur mystics,* but properly lays south of Asia, in the area of the Indian Ocean ranging from Ceylon to Madagascar, according to Rudolf Steiner.[57] As Shaver relates it, there were giants in those days known as Titans, or Atlans (the imagery of whom, he believes, produced all of Man's mythologies). These creatures had originally come to this planet from other and infinitely more magnificent worlds. Following many halcyon epochs the solar system began to die. Lucchesi's interpretation of the scriptures has the star losing its more dangerous radiation. Palmer's information is that there was an explosion on its surface. Whatever took place, a destructive radioactive solar emanation, including strontium 90, began bombarding earth,[58] soon making it virtually uninhabitable.

Those demi-deities who still retained their health banded together and fled the planet, hurtling off in their great spacecraft to sequester themselves in some safer refuge of the galaxy. They left behind all who had already begun to suffer the effects of the deadly permeation. Some who remained persevered, but were eventually reduced to a condition of pre-Neanderthalism. Others, who had hoped to escape this planet entirely, missed the evacuation for one reason or another. Finally they were forced to forsake their optimistic program and flee to some of the earth's most remote natural caverns, or to construct other vast subterranean

---

* One is inclined to wonder if the parlor occultists would be as enchanted with the imaginative mystery of Lemuria if they were aware that its name most likely derives from the monkeylike, huge-eyed mammals common to the trees of Madagascar? On the other hand, their disappointment, if any, might be mitigated by learning that the creatures' name traces back to the Latin lemures, meaning "ghosts" or "specters," which, in turn, leads to the Greek lamia, for a female vampire or a half woman, half reptile blood-sucking monster.

catacombs in which they burrowed complex communities.

Lucchesi's explanation of this aspect of Shaverian history is that the rays of the sun were still being used in a supplemental way. A screen of filters scanned out the debilitating factors, but these protective devices eventually failed and the subterraneans began to be affected. As a result, most of the cave dwellers became a colony of corrupted and distorted mini-men, dominated by morbid minds and sadistic personalities. A few racial remnants survived, remaining to defend themselves against the larger, deteriorated group.

Surviving Earthians were called *terros* in Shaverism. To some self-acclaimed scholars of Mantong, the term originated with "integrative robots," [59] while to others "terrestrial robots." The degenerated, evil inhabitants came to be known as *deros*. The meaning here is even less certain. Menzel claims it represents "detrimental robots." [60] The science-fiction writer Frederick Pohl says "deranged robots." Different sources attribute the derivation to "abandoneros," [61] the etymology of which is obvious.

The Shaver account confirms how dwellers of the deep still (as in the olden, nostalgic days) communicate telepathically and travel via light beams and pre-Arnold saucerlike devices; *stim* machines are employed for reinvigorating the sexual powers (of considerable value as the deros, according to a number of disciples of the lore, devote most of their time to open-ended orgies, many of which cause the participants to become even more physically, psychologically, and psychically distorted and corrupted than they already are). Radiation from the *ben* instrument restores the depleted and overabused. Countless additional pseudo-science-fiction wonders have been retained or developed for the benefit of deros and the endangerment of modern, surface-swarming Man, who, after diminishing to a Neanderthal state, eventually returned to his present condition. Of course, deros no longer live for a thousand years, or more, as they did; still, one can't have everything.

The Shaverians generally agree that there are several

entrances to the fathomless catacombs of the deros. Some may be reached through caves, some through especially and deceptively constructed elevators which can plummet through the lowest basements of buildings in several major cities. Palmer has asserted that he had received a "conducted tour" of the entrances of two innerearth communities, but concedes that he encountered no deros, nor saw any of the incredible machinery.[62] Still, he warns that he has known of persons who entered such avenues of descent and never were heard from again.

The full Shaver story, "with the fiction removed," was republished a few years ago by Palmer under the collective title *The Hidden World*.[63] Other writers have offered their addenda (*Etidorpha, The Smokey God,* etc.) to the tale in volumes of their own. The originator eventually retired to dairy farming in Wisconsin, not far from his mentor, but left behind him a name immortal in the outlands of saucerology.

The additional consideration—apart from Palmer's direct relationship with all aspects of the subsequent phenomena, and specifically the Maury Island mystery —is that before the contemporary era started the editor was interpreting Shaver's theses and offering conjectures of his own about "the secret of their airships that walked on beams of light,"[64] "this space travel business—about curves and angles,"[65] "a ship whose weight is reduced to a very little by reverse gravity beam can attain a great speed,"[66] and "as for space ships . . . personally we believe these ships do visit the earth."[67] One and two years before the Puget Sound sightings and before the Kenneth Arnold encounter—i.e., a long time before the age of "flying saucers" began—ufology was confined to the inquisitive minds of occultists and dabblers in the unknown.

Notes

1. Vallee, *Anatomy of a Phenomenon,* p. 50.
2. Arnold and Palmer, *Coming of the Saucers,* pp. 69–70.
3. Menzel and Boyd, *World of Flying Saucers,* p. 99.

4. Vallee, *Anatomy*, p. 49.

5. Ibid., pp. 49–50.

6. Ibid., p. 50.

7. Aerospace Technical Intelligence Center, official U.S. Air Force files.

8. Lorenzen, *Invasion from Outer Space*, p. 16.

9. Wilkins, *Saucers on Attack*, p. 57.

10. Arnold and Palmer, p. 33.

11. Ibid., p. 38.

12. Ibid., p. 39.

13. Ibid., pp. 39–40.

14. Ibid., p. 11.

15. Ibid., pp. 10–11.

16. Ibid., p. 11.

17. Ibid.

18. Ibid., p. 14.

19. Ibid., p. 16.

20. Inexplicable red substances falling from the sky have been recorded for centuries, and, perhaps, millennia. Excluding a variety of physical consistencies—hail, snow, sand, soil, resinous matter, and numerous other—which would be quite long and might not seem analogic, one may remark on the fall of thick, viscous matter which descended at Ulm, Germany, in 1812 (*Annales de Chimie*, #85:266), a red substance from the sky at Piedmont, Italy, on October 27, 1814 (Charles Fort, *The Book of the Damned*. New York: Boni and Liveright, 1919), the dropping to earth of an "eight by one inch bowl-like colour resembling blood," at Amherst, Massachusetts, on August 13, 1819 (*American Journal of Science*, #1–2:335), red matter raining on Siena, Italy, in May 1830 (Arago, *Oeuvres*, #12:468), and on other occasions, including the sequence beginning when a crimson substance poured for two early-morning hours and again later in the day on December 28, 1860, with recurrences three days afterward, and on the succeeding afternoon, and in each case on "exactly the same quarter of town" (*Year Book of Facts*, 1861, p. 273). Italy has had more than one such series of remarkable meteorological occurrences and it has not been confined to a single locale. Genoa was the recipient of material falling from the sky on February 17, 18, and 19 of 1841, which, when analyzed, was said to be red and oily (Fort, *New Lands*. New York: Boni and Liveright,

1923). Then a substance resembling coagulated blood showered Cochin, China, on December 13, 1887, while Mildenhill, England, was similarly visited by apparently organic matter—"pigeons seemed to feed on it"—early in 1901 (London *Daily Mail*, February 22, 1901). And additional examples are countless.

The examples have been limited to falls of *red* material that was also not completely unlike the Sekiu jelly in composition. Records of almost identically described aerial flotsam and/or jetsam, but not always of the same color, in fact of a great many different tints and hues, are almost commonplace to the scholar of the discards of "science."

21. Vallee, *Anatomy*, p. 50.
22. Ruppelt, *Report on Unidentified Flying Objects*, p. 19.
23. Ibid.
24. Richard Hall, ed., *The UFO Evidence* (Washington, D.C.: NICAP, 1964), p. 30.
25. Arnold and Palmer, pp. 18–19.
26. Ruppelt, p. 20.
27. *UFO Evidence* (Washington, D.C.: NICAP, 1964), p. 157.
28. Ibid.
29. Ibid., p. 64.
30. Arnold and Palmer, p. 22.
31. Ibid.
32. Associated Press, July 10, 1947.
33. Ibid.
34. Ibid.
35. *True*, January 1950.
36. *UFO Evidence*, p. 13.
37. Ibid.
38. Ruppelt, p. 16.
39. Ibid.
40. Ibid.
41. Ibid.
42. Arnold and Palmer, p. 6.
43. Ruppelt, p. 17.
44. Ibid.
45. Arnold and Palmer, p. 162 (drawing to Arnold's specifications).
46. Ibid., p. 14.
47. Ibid.

48. Richard Shaver, *Amazing Stories*, Vol. XIX, No. 1, March 1945.
49. Ray Palmer, "The Man Who Started It All," *Flying Saucers from Other Worlds*, June 1957, p. 79.
50. Ray Palmer, *Amazing Stories*, Vol. XIX, No. 4, December 1945.
51. Menzel and Boyd, p. 18.
52. Long John Nebel, *The Way Out World* (Englewood Cliffs, N.J.: Prentice-Hall, 1961), p. 137.
53. Ibid.
54. Ray Palmer, "The Man Who Started It All," p. 79.
55. Ray Palmer, *Amazing Stories*, Vol. XVIII, No. 5, December 1944.
56. Lewis Spence, *An Encyclopaedia of Occultism* (New Hyde Park, N.Y.: University Books, 1960), pp. 49–50.
57. Rudolf Steiner, *Cosmic Memory*. Rudolf Steiner Publications (Englewood Cliffs, N.J., 1959), p. 71.
58. Ray Palmer, "The Man Who Started It All."
59. Menzel and Boyd, p. 19.
60. Ibid., p. 18.
61. Nebel, p. 138.
62. Peter Kor, "From the Critic's Corner," *Flying Saucers*, July 1961, pp. 49–54.
63. Richard Shaver, *The Hidden World*, twelve vols. (Amherst, Wisc.: Ray Palmer, issued individually through the 1960s).
64. Palmer, *Amazing Stories*, Vol. XIX, No. 1, March 1945.
65. Palmer, *Amazing Stories*, Vol. XX, No. 6, September 1946.
66. Palmer, *Amazing Stories*, Vol. XIX, No. 1.
67. Palmer, *Amazing Stories*, Vol. XX, No. 6.

10

The Maury Island Mystery

I showed to Admiral [H.B.] Knowles [United States Navy, Retired] the small piece of a flying saucer which the U.S. Air Force kindly loaned [sic] to me for examination. That was July of 1952.

> —Wilbert B. Smith, head of the official Canadian Unidentified Flying Object Program. November 1, 1961

A NEW ERA began around the middle of July 1947, when Arnold received a letter from Palmer, followed by a second requesting a full report of his experience. The pilot had never heard of the inquirer, but sent him a duplicate of the account he had forwarded to the Air Force.

In response, the editor wrote of having heard of some unusual, and conceivably related, incidents which had occurred to two local "harbor patrolmen" in Tacoma, a Harold A. Dahl and a Fred L. Crisman. He asked Arnold if he would investigate the case and forward to him some of the fragments of material supposedly thrown from the aerial unknowns, offering to cover the expenses involved. The flier decided to consider the proposition for a few days.

Meanwhile, Arnold tells of having been visited by "two representatives of A-2 Military Intelligence of the Fourth Air Force," [1] Captain William Davidson and Lieutenant Frank M. Brown, who seem to have been assigned an A-26 bomber by the military for the sole purpose of coming to interview him. The officers took him to dinner, expressed interest in the details of his observations, and claimed they had no idea what the objects might have been. From Arnold's version, the only one extant, his hosts seemed oddly wide-eyed and wondrous about the whole matter for men in their profession.

The two intelligence officers were even more delighted when Arnold mentioned that Captain E. J. Smith, who had also had an excellent sighting, would have a stopover in Boise that evening as he flew east from Washington. They leapt at the opportunity of meeting him and hearing of his adventure too. At the airport was a second bonus—aviation editor for the Idaho *Statesman,* Dave Johnson, who had viewed and attempted to photograph a "disk-like object" while flying his National Guard AT-6 plane, at 14,000 feet, over the Anderson Dam, near Boise. Arnold saw that the conversation of the sighters and the investigators revealed little not known to all parties from each other or the press—or, in the case of the officers, from whatever other sources they had supplying them with relevant data.

Davidson and Brown went through the large stack of mail the aviator had received asking about the UFO, removing many inquiries from "societies or organizations." Again emphasizing that he should telephone or telegraph them at "A-2, Fourth Air Force, Hamilton Field, California," should any new information arise, the intelligence officers, who had also collected a full report of his experience from Dave Johnson, left Arnold's home to return to their base.

On July 29, Arnold had accepted Palmer's offer and was on his way to Tacoma, Washington, to check out the sighting there. He left Boise shortly after sunup and was pleased that "it was a perfect day to fly. The air was sharp, moist, clear and crystal and smooth as silk." An hour later, as Baker, Oregon, "sparkled in the sunlight" 7,000 feet below, he dipped his wings in salutation to an old Empire Airlines Boeing cruising along a few miles to his right, and began to descend for a planned refueling stop at La Grande, Oregon. Passing over the community of Union at a one-mile altitude, he suddenly saw a score of brass-looking UFO, similar in configuration to those he had encountered five weeks earlier, flashing across the length of the Mount Rainier plateau. They were traveling at tremendous speed and hurtled past his plane no more than 400 yards away. He attempted to obtain cinematic photographs and pursue them. Yet, so swift was their departure both efforts proved unrealistic.

While Arnold "realized they had the same flight characteristics of [sic] the large objects" he had monitored previously, there was one distinct difference —which, for the initial second of visual contact, caused him to think they might be ducks. He estimated *these* unknowns to be two to two and a half feet in diameter. Despite subsequent checking that indicated some farmers had told of seeing a strange cluster of birds that morning, Arnold did not have to make much of an evaluation to accept that no ducks, blackbirds, or even hawks would be able to outrace his plane as if it were hardly moving. Unfortunately, the motion pictures showed the UFO only as tiny dots.

Arnold arrived in Tacoma and made several calls for accommodations, but for some reason none was available. Then, "just for a lark," he tried the finest hotel in the city and was understandably caught unaware when he was told that it had a reservation for room and bath in his name. His curiosity motivated him to ask to speak with the clerk who had made the arrangements, but he was told that that employee was off work and no one knew where or how to contact him. Still, he was anxious to get his investigation started and upon reaching his room immediately located Harold A. Dahl's listing in the telephone book. Some hemming and hawing prefaced the boatman's agreement to come to the hotel and relate the details of his experience.

Now, in addition to the previously recounted experience, Dahl claimed that on the day following the adventure an unknown man, of medium height and undistinguished, except that he wore a black suit, appeared at his door. The stranger suggested that, as there were things they should discuss, it would be appropriate for them to breakfast together. The harborman agreed, assuming it had something to do with his activities in selling marine equipment or in salvaging. In his own automobile Dahl followed the man in black to a small waterfront café, where they sat down in a booth.

If Dahl had not yet considered the man or his behavior unexpected, he did then. The stranger instantly described the incident on Puget Sound, point by point, "as if he had been on the boat with them the entire trip." [2] Dahl quoted the man as having concluded this recitation with " 'What I have said is proof to you that I know a great deal more about this experience of yours than you will want to believe.' " [3] Finally, the man in black informed Dahl that he and the other persons on the boat had seen things which, for some unspecified and very secret reason, should not have been observed. He and his entire family would be in great jeopardy should he discuss the matter with anyone, he was told. In spite of the abrupt and ominous nature of these concluding remarks, Dahl —who is described as "over six two inches tall and well over two hundred pounds, as two-fisted a lumberjack looking fellow as I ever saw" [4]—decided that the stranger was an eccentric or a fraud, and dismissed the threats. Nevertheless, they may have had a residual subconscious effect, causing him to hesitate for thirty minutes before agreeing to be interviewed when Arnold telephoned him. Even after he arrived and the questions began to flow he remained silent. The first time he actually spoke was to suggest they forget about the conversation, and that he return home. In the face of the investigator's persistent interest he agreed to relate his story but with the warning: " 'Mr. Arnold, I still think it would be good advice to you [Dahl's leaving his report untold]. This flying saucer business is the most complicated thing you ever got mixed up in.' " [5]

Having revealed the aftermath to his sighting, the seaman offered the idea of visiting his "secretary," at whose home he had deposited a few of the unanalyzed bits of slag expelled from the floundering UFO. [6] The pair drove to a small corner house, somewhat separated from other residences, parked, and crossed a deteriorating pavement to a screenless and bare porch. Noting that the building was in need of paint and appeared to have been constructed several decades earlier, the amateur investigator stepped through the door after Dahl. The parlor's very modest dimensions were accented by the presence of a piano and an old, cumbersome radio of the 1930s. A door to a bedroom was evident to one side and the kitchen could be seen beyond a narrow arched hall, through which they passed immediately. A slightly less than middle-aged woman was immersed in a pile of paperwork with every available surface cluttered. After a cursory introduction (Arnold never could recall the "secretary's" name), Dahl led him back into the living room, handing him a piece of the jetsam collected from the Maury Island beach. It was being used as an ashtray. The pilot was disappointed. It was his impression that the mysterious alleged debris appeared to be nothing more than igneous, or volcanic, rock. Unfortunately, although stuffed in one of his pockets, he had not had an opportunity to read a certain newspaper clipping. Buried amid other sightings, it described "cinder or lava ash particles that had fallen from the sky near Mountain Home, Idaho, the twelfth day of July after a formation of flying saucers had passed over that area." [7]

The boatman offered no argument to Arnold's indifference. He admitted his geological ignorance, and merely reiterated the debris' origin and the fact that the island shore was strewn with "tons more of" whatever it was. An offer was made to escort the pilot to see his superior, who had the fragments of the other silvery metallic stuff which had been recovered. However, it was decided to pursue that aspect of the inquiry later.

Suddenly Dahl was out of his chair, into the kitchen, and back again, explaining that he had hoped to find an anonymous letter he had received shortly after the sighting. It appeared to have been misplaced, but the Tacoman reconstructed its contents. The writer had contended that the "flying disks were actually manned by beings such as we, *only less dense,* so to speak, than we are," [8] and that they had become visible to us because of radiation caused by atomic detonations. "These flying disks, which were all shapes and sizes, were vehicles which the gods of this earth used to protect this earth from outside dark influences or enemies." [9] While they had been our guardians for millennia, it was said that they were now undergoing an attack by malevolent forces intent on destroying them and us.

Arnold interviewed Crisman on the succeeding day and got his first glimpse of the second type of debris on the day after that. He asked Dahl for copies of the motion picture he had taken, regardless of its deficiencies, and requested specimens of the white, flaky substance.

While having achieved his goal of interviewing the two sighters, and although it appeared that he was going to acquire samples of each type of fragment, Arnold was beginning to feel in less than full command of the situation. He called Flight Operations of United Airlines at the Seattle Airport, where Capt. E. J. Smith was based, and suggested that, having had a UFO encounter of his own, he might like to come to Tacoma for a few days and contribute his expertise. The commercial pilot agreed and Arnold flew the roundtrip from one seaport to the other, returning with Smith. The two were soon cloistered with Crisman, who had picked them up at the airport, and Dahl in Arnold's hotel room, where the boatmen told their complete stories again. Only then did Arnold show Smith the news clipping about the other instance of a sighting accompanied by cinder or lava ash which had allegedly occurred more than two and a half weeks earlier. Smith was fascinated and expressed determination to stay as long as he could to aid in the probe of the Maury Island mystery and its related conundrums. The two novice investigators reinterrogated Crisman and Dahl and discussed every aspect of the case for a couple of hours, but the two reports seemed to hold firm and the conversation developed no fresh ideas. The session concluded around dinnertime, but Captain Smith asked Crisman to drive him back to Seattle so that he could pick up his automobile and a change of clothes. The latter agreed and by eight o'clock he had rejoined Arnold.

The two pilots analyzed everything that had been assembled about the Tacoma affair and discussed what relevance their own experiences might have to it. They weighed the broader implications of sightings being reported around the country and the emerging recollections of, and evidence for, like unknowns being common in the past. Especially curious to them was the material said to have been thrown off by UFO, as had occurred over Puget Sound. Yet, the conversation invariably led back to the accounts of Dahl and Crisman and an agreement that while cross-examination had not altered their individual and collective contentions, something about the story, them, or the entire situation seemed inconsistent.

"We both had a peculiar feeling that we were being watched or that there was something dangerous about getting involved with Crisman and Dahl," wrote Arnold later. "First was our suspicion of a hoax. Second was our suspicion that Russian espionage was baiting us on the whole affair for a very simple reason—to find out if we actually knew that these flying saucers were made in the United States and were a military secret." [10]

Their doubts were hardly diminished by information from the head of the United Press in Tacoma, Ted Morello, who informed the pair that some anonymous caller was providing the wire service with verbatim reports of the conversations and interviews taking place in Arnold's hotel room. Since each of them had flatly refused to speak with reporters, especially a very persistent local newsman, Paul Lance, of the Tacoma *Times,* they agreed that only two possibilities appeared likely. Either Dahl and/or Crisman were responsible directly, or through a third party, or "someone had planted a dictaphone in our room." [11] Reflection brought to their attention the fact that some of the material quoted to them by Morello had been excerpts of exchanges which had taken place when the two of them had been speaking alone. They decided the "bugging" explanation was the more probable answer, since it was unlikely that someone had been lurking on one knee, ear to the keyhole, in the hotel hallway outside the door. But even though they "spent the next hour tearing the room apart, from mattress to transome," [12] they were unable to discover any sort of audiosurveillance equipment. Arnold appears not to have connected the fact that when he arrived in Tacoma he could not get a room in several hotels, but found himself registered by an unknown benefactor and an unidentifiable clerk in a specific room of a preselected hotel. It would have been little problem for a professional intelligence operator, trained in electronic surveillance, to secrete a listening device in quarters into which Arnold would be channeled by a simple arrangement of circumstances.

The UFO fragments arrived on the morning of July 31, when Dahl and Crisman appeared with numerous samples of each kind of the debris. During the initial examination of the substances Crisman announced that the crew of the bombarded craft was in a waterfront café. He had decided that they all should breakfast together. Apart from "a number of references made . . . to the original sighting of Dahl on June 21 on Maury Island," [13] it is odd that "we [Arnold and Smith] did not ask them to verify the stories of Crisman and Dahl." [14] Presumably an explanation would be forthcoming. Arnold took footage of Smith, Crisman, Dahl, "and their respective automobiles" (?) [15] on the pavement and street before the restaurant * and they returned to the hotel.

---

* Despite this photographic exercise, I have never met anyone who has seen the motion picture, or heard of its whereabouts, but am fully aware that verified photographs of either of the boatmen are so rare as to be nearly impossible to obtain. Considering the subsequent melting into anonymity of the pair, both the absence of the film and any other pictures of them is worth consideration, for who more than intelligence men—especially "sleepers"—avoid leaving representations of their appearance once they have completed a task and departed. The author has seen photographs of persons identified as Dahl in two instances and Crisman in one, but they were totally unsupported assertions; he can only assume Arnold may still have the motion pictures he took in Tacoma.

Settled once again in their room, the pilots meticulously inspected each bit of the "slag" and the "flakes." The former was reminiscent of lava, deceptively weighty, apparently fused by very high temperatures, glossy and arced on one of its faces, and the color of brass. Arnold recalled that a piece no more than six by four by one inches required some effort to handle.

"Someone suggested that these fragments could have been the lining of some kind of a power tube. When we lined up all the pieces, following the curve of the smooth surface, we saw that they could have been a lining of a tube of some kind about six feet in diameter. From this speculation *everything seemed to be* shaping up in a sense that we could understand," * Arnold remarked after the fact.[16] Yet, what it was he, or they, began to comprehend was never amplified in his book. A quote or two, possibly apocryphal, attributed to him subsequently implied extraterrestriality.

In contradistinction to the "slag," the elemental confetti was concluded, by the amateur detectives, to be only aluminum chips—of the type from which certain elements of large planes are constructed.

If this was truly the light metal that Harold Dahl said was spewed from these strange aircraft we knew, or *thought we knew,* that it was a fake.† We had seen hundreds of piles of this stuff in salvage dumps many places throughout the United States where surplus Army bombers had been junked.

There was only one unusual thing about this white metal that made us stop and wonder. On one piece that Crisman handed us we could plainly see that two parts of it had been riveted. I had never seen that type of rivet used in the aircraft we manufacture and I don't think Smithy had either. *This piece of metal did not correspond with Harold Dahl's original description of the extremely light white metal.*[17] **

---

* Emphasis added.
† Emphasis added.
** Emphasis added.

Having finished the superficial examination of the substances, Arnold and Smith asked to see the film footage of the UFO taken by Dahl, but Crisman said he had not brought it with him. Still, he assured the investigators that he would produce it in a matter of hours.

Arnold was feeling increasingly less equipped to deal with what was becoming a more and more complex puzzle, particularly with the two witnesses whose behavior was unpredictable and not always mutually consistent. The arrival of Captain Smith had buttressed his sense of capability to a degree, but now the veteran of the United Airlines skyways was beginning to share Arnold's conviction that the entire problem should be in the hands of professionals. The main question at that time was—and perhaps still is—professional what? In 1947, to Arnold, the only available possibility seemed to be intelligence agents. During a session when all four men were present he suggested calling the Fourth Air Force Base at Hamilton Field to ask Brown and Davidson to come to Tacoma and assume charge of the baffling case. The responses were, and remain, interesting. Smith agreed, but with a marked lack of enthusiasm; Crisman was practically jubilant at the thought; and an apparently apprehensive Dahl announced that he would refuse to speak with the military men as he had a "peculiar feeling this whole business is going to end up in a lot of bad luck for somebody." [18] It was clear that he regretted, or wanted it to appear that he regretted, ever getting involved in the business, and was anxious to abandon the matter from that moment forward. Smith dismissed Dahl's attitude as "superstitious" and "nonsense," yet this had no impact upon the boatman's decisions to avoid any contact with the pair from Army Intelligence.

The result of the conflicting opinions was that Kenneth Arnold called Brown, person-to-person, at his office at the military installation. The lieutenant refused to accept the call there but indicated that he would return it from a public telephone off the base. Within a few minutes he did. Arnold outlined the Puget Sound events and the overall Tacoma developments.

He made it clear that neither he nor Smith could come to a determination as to the authenticity of the tale, the true mineralogical composition of the fragments, or, in broad terms, just what was really transpiring. Brown told him to suspend everything as much as possible, and that, should he not telephone again within the hour, it could be assumed that "we'll be there." [19]

The return call did not come and so it was understood that Brown, and probably Davidson, were on their way to the Maury Island mystery. During the wait, Ted Morello rang up to say that his anonymous tipster was on another line and he wanted Arnold to clarify for him exactly who was present. Since both Crisman and Dahl were there, and the United Press reporter was certain the voice speaking with him on the other telephone was the same he had heard conveying to him earlier accounts of what was happening in the hotel room, it appeared as if the two harbor patrolmen were not involved with the mysterious messages to this newsman.

Morello rang off, and another caller got through. It was newsman Paul Lance, whom the pilots had been trying to avoid for several days. They had no desire to discuss the matter. Taking the receiver, Smith politely, but pointedly, established that no one present would consider speaking with Lance regardless of the subject. Everyone was somewhat taken aback when, a few minutes later, there was a sharp knock on the door and the tenacious reporter was found standing on the threshold. Although it was not clear to Arnold why, Smith swiftly patted down the new arrival to confirm that he was carrying no handgun. Then, before Lance could begin his pitch, the tall, wide-shouldered commercial aviator gently rousted him into the corridor and closed the door. The four men sat silent for a moment, but no encore of raps resounded. Lance had apparently departed.

Dahl rose and, handing Arnold a scribbled telephone number through which he could be contacted, left. Smith suggested a private conversation with Crisman, and they exited for the hotel lobby.

Kenneth Arnold sat in his room, staring out the

window. Some of the events of the day passed across his mind, and one in particular bothered him. At one point he had asked Crisman if he knew how Ray Palmer, off in Chicago, had known of the Puget Sound affair so quickly. Crisman had somewhat switched the query around by replying that he was aware of Palmer's existence because of reading *Venture* magazine, in which the Midwesterner was presumably published or with which he was editorially involved—but Arnold knew there was no such magazine. As he had on more than a single occasion, Arnold sensed that Crisman was attempting to divert the investigation and completely becloud his own actual identity. Soon his thoughts wandered to other aspects of the case as he gazed at the low Tacoma skyline and the interminable space stretching billions of light-years above it.

Soon his introspection was interrupted. The telephone rang and Lieutenant Brown announced that he and Captain Davidson were in the city and, at that moment, on their way up.

Upon entering the room the superior officer seemed to want to offer Arnold some explanation. It was immediately apparent that he and Brown were fully assigned to the investigation of the aerial unknowns. Then Smith returned with Crisman, rechanneling the conversation into what Crisman could tell about the Maury Island incident. The two amateur detectives contributed what they could about the two sightings and the pattern of odd things which developed since they entered the case.

Davidson showed Arnold a drawing of a disk-like design, and the mountain pilot recognized that it closely resembled *one* of the nine UFO he had observed—but one which was different from its companions and which he had not bothered to differentiate from the others in his description of the craft when he gave his first interview to the press on June 24. In fact, he later asserted that he had never mentioned it to anyone before the intelligence officer handed him the picture.

"This is a drawing of one of several photographs we consider to be authentic. We just received it at Hamilton

Field," [20] explained Davidson, according to Arnold. Brown verified the statement, adding that the original negatives had been flown to Washington, D.C.

Now it was the witness' turn. Crisman detailed the Dahl story, following it with his own. He indicated an assortment of the two types of UFO debris which was lying on the floor. There were about two dozen fragments, but the military pair glanced at them only superficially. The inquiry soon progressed to Ted Morello's anonymous eavesdropper, the pertinacity of local newshawk Lance, and various other problem-related considerations. The meeting concluded around twelve o'clock with Crisman offering to race home— the location of which Arnold and Smith never discovered—to prepare a box of the slag and flakes so that the officers might take samples back to the Army base. Curiously, Davidson and Brown abruptly became bored with the entire affair, both information and the allegedly foreign substances, and rose to leave. In a matter of moments they simply dismissed the whole business without explanation, announcing that they were flying back to Hamilton immediately—considerably past twelve o'clock. Remaining for the night seemed the practical thing to do. Nonetheless, Brown insisted that the B-25 which had been assigned to them had been completely updated with all the latest Air Force equipment, including two new engines, and was required for a morning test flight.

Arnold and Smith agreed that the officers' excuse for not staying until the next day was transparently thin. It was also opaque; they could not perceive what was behind the reluctance.

". . . they gave me the impression they thought Smith and I were the victims of some silly hoax. When we offered them pieces of the fragments . . . they were just not interested." [21]

The intelligence men had ordered a military vehicle from McChord Field to come to the hotel, pick them up, and deliver them to their plane. As they were about to depart, Crisman raced up in his automobile with a box everyone assumed contained the UFO material he had sped home to get. The carton was placed in the trunk of the car. When it was being stowed away, Arnold was able to see some of the contents under the streetlamp. The material "looked similar to the fragments we had in our room. Somehow, though, they looked more rocky and less metallic." [22] Taking a closer look he discovered that the segments "were much thicker than any of the pieces" [23] Dahl and Crisman had given Smith and him.

When the weary detectives returned to the hotel room, Ted Morello called again. He reported that the voice he had come to recognize had called once more. It had detailed all that had been discussed throughout the examination of the Maury Island case which had been conducted by the military intelligence officers. Arnold declined to make any comment, but did sense more concern than reportorial zeal in the wire service man's voice. The question of how the monitoring was being achieved was revived, but the two pilots became convinced that such surveillance was difficult, perhaps to the degree of being impossible. They were unconscious of the variety of ways it might have been accomplished, with or without the participation of one or more of the prime subjects of the eavesdropping. Having taken the probably useless precautions of securing windows, doors, and even the transom, the pair retired in preparation for a boat ride to Maury Island early the following day which had been promised them by Fred Crisman.

Yet, the unexpected erupted again. This time more strikingly and more ominously than at any previous stage of the case. The accidental roommates were up before nine, and about a half hour later the telephone rang. When Arnold answered, the voice of Crisman exploded into his ear.:

" 'Did you hear over the radio this morning that a B-25 exploded and crashed some twenty minutes after taking off from McChord Field about 1:30 this morning? I think you and I know who was aboard that plane!' " [24]

Stunned, Arnold collapsed into a chair as he shouted for Smith, who was bathing. The latter raced in soaking wet, whipped across the room, and snatched the receiver. His face was already blenched, as if anticipating something disastrous. Hearing a repeat of the two-sentence message, he broke off the call and dialed the airport, which confirmed the crash of the B-25. Morello was contacted, and from him or the earlier call, it was determined that there were four men on the craft when it took off: Technician Fourth Grade Woodrow D. Mathews, who was merely cadging a lift—a not uncommon practice when an Army plane was flying with empty space—to California, Master Sergeant Elmer L. Taff, Brown, and Davidson. The two enlisted men had parachuted to safety. Both officers died. Why is not known to the public, or anyone, to this day. Except possibly to a small, unseen, sect buried deep in the body of governmental bureaucracy.

Neither of the men had fully collected himself when, having dressed, they decided to leave the room and almost collided with Crisman, who was racing down the hall toward their door. The three converged uncertainly, and then returned to the room. Once there, no one could find anything to say. Unlike the amazing incident on Puget Sound, or any of the labyrinthine paths down which they had been led or had led, or the assortment of inexplicable events which had occurred or which were claimed, the traumatic effect of the deaths appeared to be too appalling for discussion or speculation. The trio sat about, nearly transfixed by the news.

Then Arnold, responding to the kind of conditioned pragmatism necessary to a successful mountain and rescue pilot, began to reevaluate his situation. It was not back to his own sighting that his thoughts went, but to the beginning of his involvement in the Tacoma tragedy —specifically to when he had been contacted by an unknown man named Palmer in Chicago. Then to his undertaking the assignment suggested by the editor to conduct a private inquiry of the Maury Island sightings. He deeply regretted having ever gotten involved and decided to disengage himself from the entire obligation. He would telephone Palmer, tell him that he was returning the two hundred dollars expense advance, confess that the situation had gotten out of

control and that he did not feel trained or equipped
to pursue the investigation. In fact, he would be
submitting no report of his efforts at all. And he did.

Palmer took the resignation calmly. He suggested
that Arnold not take any of the fragments he still had
aboard his plane. Mailing the samples to himself would
be a wiser plan if he wished to keep some for whatever
reason. The editor also advised the flier not to let
Smith retain any of the substances. A peculiar attitude,
as Palmer presumably knew little of the United Airlines man. Still, it was not as odd as Arnold's response:
"I felt the advice was good." [25] In his account, written
about five years later in collaboration with Palmer,
Arnold constantly reiterates his faith in, and reliance
on, "Big Smithy," whom he brought into the affair
because he felt a great need for assistance.

Before the call was concluded, Crisman and Palmer
spoke for a few minutes. Much later the editor was
to tell Arnold that he recognized the voice as belong-
ing to someone who had telephoned him, on various
occasions, from different areas in the United States.
Arnold failed to explain what these other calls were
about, if he ever discovered, or even if Palmer's saying he "recognized" the voice indicated that Crisman's
earlier communications had been under another name
or anonymous. Clearly, if he had called using his own
name, Palmer's remark would have made no sense.
Another of the ever-mounting curiosities which were
starting to seem like the total substance of the in-
tangible Crisman.

The point had been reached when Arnold had little
idea of whom he should trust—if anyone. He had become more and more dubious of Crisman, and these
doubts were in no way diminished by the "harborman's" remark of the previous day that he knew
Palmer through having bought a copy of the magazine
Venture, a periodical the pilot knew was not to be
found among the publisher's efforts. Despite wanting
to rid himself of the entire business, Arnold could not
decline Morello's suggestion that he and Smith listen
to a recorded interview conducted with one of the
survivors of the death plane. It seemed apparent that

the presence of Master Sergeant Elmer L. Taff on the ship was happenstance. He was merely an Army man who had been given a free lift in the direction of his home in California. Taff remarked that he knew neither the pilot, co-pilot, nor Technician Fourth Grade Woodrow D. Mathews, but he did recall that the first two had loaded an obviously weighty carton aboard the B-25 immediately before takeoff. Fifteen or twenty minutes following the departure the left engine burst into flame. When Mathews attempted to activate the emergency fire-fighting system it was discovered to be inoperative.

Suddenly Lieutenant Brown appeared from the front of the plane and ordered the two enlisted men to slip into their parachutes and jump. According to the sergeant, he was actually pushed from the craft. A few minutes later he landed, hurting his leg, but otherwise in good condition.

Davidson and Brown had not followed the same course of action. They had stayed with the ship, and were killed when it crashed.

The tragedy was followed by Crisman finally taking Arnold and Smith to view the "harbor patrol" boat from which the sightings had been observed. The Idaho investigator found the vessel to be no more than a rather decrepit, semi-enclosed, coastal-type fishing boat. Both pilots were of the opinion that it was, at best, of unlikely seaworthiness, in addition to quite apparently not having been subjected to the ravages of the aerial barrage reported by Crisman and Dahl. Regardless, they took a few feet of film of the small inboard boat.

Before leaving they asked Crisman, once more, about the photographs Dahl was supposed to have taken of the inner-tube-shaped aircraft. The question was clumsily evaded. They departed, as far as Arnold was concerned, never to see the strange man again.

Local newsmen were somewhat more tenacious. Paul Lance caught up with the investigators on their way back to the hotel. After but a short time in the room, Morello called to say that his seemingly ubiquitous, but always anonymous, tipster had telephoned. His newest report was that on August 5, Smith would be summoned to Wright-Patterson Air Field to be interrogated by military intelligence, particularly about an airliner the captain had been flying recently, at which shots had been fired. The caller claimed that Arnold had also been the recipient of such ballistic attention on several occasions. Further, the informer revealed that the B-25 carrying Davidson and Brown had been struck from the sky by a 20mm artillery shell. None of the statements by Morello's anonymous source was ever proved to be true, and the Air Force explanation of the disaster was that the craft had plummeted to earth because of a mechanical defect in the left engine. This completely dismissed two points: Brown had full opportunity to make certain that the two passengers got into their parachutes, opened the door, and jumped free, but neither he nor Davidson had the time to radio a "Mayday" call or to leap to safety themselves. The Army man who had cadged the lift reported, when interviewed, that at least ten minutes passed between the time he was helped from the B-25 and the time the plane began its dive to earth from its 10,000-foot altitude. No explanation of their failure to save themselves—if they could—has ever been offered.

The Tacoma *Times* issues of August 1 featured an article by Paul Lance topped by the provocative heading:

SABOTAGE HINTED IN CRASH OF ARMY BOMBER AT KELSO

Plane May Hold Flying Disk Secret

Asserting that the newspaper had been told by an unnamed informant that the B-25 disaster had been caused by deliberate tampering with the ship, or that it had gone down after being shot, the article contended that the tragedy was the result of efforts to determine that "the disk parts . . . which plunged to earth on Maury Island recently" [26] never reach Hamilton Field, California, or be subjected to any serious scien-

tific analysis. While the piece seemed somewhat specu-
lative, it was a fact that the names of the dead officers
were identified a half day before the Army released
that information to the press.

Of considerable interest was Lance's verification that
"at McChord field an intelligence officer confirmed the
mystery caller's report that the ill-fated craft had been
carrying 'classified material.' " [27] This was amplified
with a direct quote from a Major George Sander:
" 'Classified material means that there was a somewhat
secret cargo aboard the plane. No one was allowed to
take pictures of the wreckage until the material was removed and returned to McChord Field.' " [28] No clarification of what the "secret cargo" was has ever been
offered. Nothing has ever suggested that it was other
than the alleged "flying saucer" refuse collected by
Dahl and ultimately delivered to the intelligence officers. Regardless of the cause of the B-25 crash,
Brown and Davidson certainly seem to have died while
attempting to transport it to Hamilton Field, or some
unknown destination, for analysis or some different
purpose. Simply, despite the arguments that arose
over the sighting and the sequence of events that followed, it remains the "Maury Island mystery."

In spite of that, it will continue to be examined as
much as is practical, and the opinion of other investigators weighed, for the case has developed into
one of the most acrimonious and multifaceted debates
in modern ufology.

Arnold and Smith were ready to abandon the inquiry. Before doing so, the former made every attempt
to arrange one last exchange with Crisman. All of his
efforts were in vain. The man had disappeared.

Morello relayed information from his telephone
voice that Crisman had been whisked off to an unknown location in Alaska via an Army bomber. While
no passenger list could be obtained from official
sources at McChord, it was conceded that such a
plane, with a specific destination, had departed at the
time given.

Two or three days of waiting ensued. Hourly the
pilots expected to be contacted by a new representative

of military intelligence. It began to seem as if it too had disappeared. Or, perhaps, was also off watching films—but of what?

Finally impatience overcame Captain Smith and he accosted the agency's nearest representative, Major Sander, of S-2 Army Intelligence, stationed at McChord Field—in Arnold's words, a middle-aged man, just under six feet, with blue eyes set in a pleasant face, and a very soft voice. Smith told the officer his own version of all that had occurred throughout the bizarre business. Then he got Sander to accompany him to the hotel room, where Arnold gave his independent testimony of the series of events, without knowing precisely what his companion had already reported.

The completion of the recital to the military man elicited a reaction reminiscent of the attitudes of Davidson and Brown, a sense that his attention was tangential, or that their account was incidental to some more encompassing interest. Arnold later wrote that, while separately told, his account and that of his friend were virtually identical and thus mutually verified each other. The major suggested that both had succumbed to some pattern of deliberate deceit. He failed to explain what the purpose of involving the two men in a highly complex and extremely prolonged fraud might be. Actually, the improbability that Army investigators really viewed the affair as a fraud was reinforced by the officer's request that neither of the pilots discuss the matter with anyone. He left assuring them that the "office of A-2 Military Intelligence of the Fourth Air Force" [29] would provide them with a full, private explanation of the entire matter within less than a month.

The major from McChord reduced Arnold's hopes for some kind of reassurance. It was plain that Sander wished to leave the impression that officialdom regarded the puzzle of Puget Sound as a hoax, pure and simple. He discounted the "slag" and "white metal" as of no consequence. Nonetheless, he delayed his departure long enough to gather every piece—large, small, or fragmentary—in the room. Tying these up in a

towel he had every sample, except for one each in the
personal possession of the mystified Arnold and Smith.
The collection was climaxed by the officer insisting
that these two final mementos be deposited with the
rest of the bits and chips of evidence. "We don't want
to overlook even one piece," Arnold quoted the major
as having explained. "I would like to have them all." [30]

The performance was hardly convincing—even to
the Idaho pilot who had originated the Tacoma inquiry,
at the request of the midwest publisher. "This Major
Sander is a pretty smooth guy," he recalls thinking at
the time, "but he's not smooth enough at this point to
convince me that these fragments aren't pretty important in some way." [31] The charade theory being
advanced had already faded, as far as Arnold was concerned: "I suddenly felt that no one had played a
hoax on anybody!" [32]

Obviously, he had not yet had the opportunity to
weigh the new development in which he was immersed
that very moment.

Arnold's evaluation that the officer was probably
"a phony dressed up in a lot of sheer intelligence as
to how to psychologically to handle men [sic]" [33] did
not prevent him from falling under the spell of the
explanation the strange fellow then offered.

Sander asked that the aviators accompany him for
a brief drive, after the purportedly fraudulent non-
evidence had been carefully stored away in the trunk
of Sander's vehicle. The destination was identified by
a sign with the lettering TACOMA SMELTING COMPANY
or something similar. A number of mounds of slag
resembling the dark stuff expelled from the "flying
saucer" were visible. Again the pendulum swung and
Arnold decided that he might have been deceived,
earlier on, after all. However, apparently the Army
man erred at that point. Both Smith and Arnold were
satisfied, and had the car simply carried them by and
back to their hotel they almost certainly would have
left town and gone home. Instead, Sander stopped the
automobile and urged the two passengers to make a
closer examination of the dark piles of material. Despite the resemblance of the company slag in weight

and general appearance to the original aerial refuse, both discerned a distinctly different "feel" about it. Their tactile sense did not confirm its sameness; rather, the contrary. Arnold's words sum up their attitude, as they drove back to the hotel, quite explicitly:

> At this point, if there is such a thing as hypnosis or hallucination that could have affected us in this evaluation, we would certainly have been affected to believe conclusively that all the fragments were smelter slag from this very smelter. This dump was handy to town. The stories of Crisman and Dahl did not ring completely true. And Captain Smith and I, if we had a desire at all, wanted to believe that the whole thing was a hoax. For some reason we couldn't convince ourselves it was all as simple as the Major put it.[34]

By then the pair of amateur investigators anticipated nothing with greater pleasure than getting out and away from the entire Maury Island mystery. They packed and were in Smith's automobile heading for the airport when—remembering that Dahl had said that he would be working on some books at his secretary's house that afternoon—they decided to look in for a moment and say goodbye. Taking the identical course Arnold had followed on his first visit, his friend drew up before the small corner house. To his astonishment, the house was quite clearly unoccupied. Still, there was absolutely no question in Arnold's mind that it was the very one to which he had been brought less than four days earlier.

He left the car, walked up the short walk, and stepped on the porch, where a board squeaked, as he recalled it having done on the previous occasion. There were cobwebs on the front door, next to a frosted window he remembered well. The house gave him the impression of complete abandonment, as if many months had passed since anyone had lived there. He wandered about peering through dusty windows, finding the distribution and structural appearance of the rooms, of the entire house, precisely as it had been preserved by his memory. Yet, it was a hollow house, devoid of the life which turns buildings into homes. An extensive search, commencing with driving along all of the streets within a considerable distance, located no place that vaguely resembled the ghost cottage.

Arnold eventually forsook his search, went to the airport, and prepared to fly home. Subsequently he attempted to trace Harold Dahl numerous times, with no success. Less than a month after leaving the city he put through a call to him, only to be informed by the telephone company that they had no record for any such individual. He asked that older books and newer books be consulted; none, it was reported, carried the name. Yet, when in Tacoma, Arnold had seen his name in the directory and had even telephoned him at the number listed. At last he disassociated himself—physically and mentally—from the matter, resigned that the solution of the case would probably never be known to him. As he concluded in his notes on his efforts: "Today [in early 1952] it is still as big a mystery as to what actually took place in Tacoma as it was on August 3, 1947." [35]

Arriving at the airfield he personally checked out his plane, as he had done on thousands of other occasions—magnetos, gas lines, fuel valves, etc. He found everything functioning maximally. It was a bit late in the day for the trip to Boise, but he wished to get away from the tragic maze into which he had inadvertently wandered, and return to the calm and normality of home and family.

Refueling in Pendleton, Oregon, he took off again for the final segment of his journey. Suddenly, at no more than fifty feet his motor went dead. No cough, no sputter—the power simply ceased. At that altitude, the only possibility was to descend again, although the low speed made this extremely risky. But, for Arnold, it was the only plane in town. Fortunately, his considerable skill and experience served him extremely well. He accomplished the emergency landing without injuring himself, but his landing gear and a spar suffered damage.

Few of the elements of the business following the

sighting were stranger than this incident. As a matter of fact, it was not until Arnold wrote his account of the entire affair—to the extent he knew it—that he revealed this finale to his role in the Maury Island mystery.

As the craft came to a stop Arnold leapt out and tested the movement of the propeller. It was perfectly normal. Immediately he returned to the cockpit, where he hoped to determine the cause of the engine failure. His fuel valve was shut off. Adjusting it, he found that his motor turned over exactly as it should. The summation of this singular recollection is found among the final lines of his personal account. The sole explanation of a man with thousands of hours of airtime, a pilot who knew many planes inside and out, a specialist in a particular field of hazardous flying. With respect to the cut-off fuel valve which nearly cost him his life, Arnold wrote five years afterwards:

". . . there was only one person who could have shut that fuel valve off—and that was myself." [36]

Notes

1. Arnold and Palmer, *Coming of the Saucers*, p. 21.
2. Ibid., p. 34.
3. Ibid., p. 35.
4. Ibid., p. 29.
5. Ibid., p. 30.
6. Records of slag falling from the sky are not extremely rare; see Charles Fort, *Book of the Damned*, pp. 30, 70, 71, 128. For instances of "cinder" falls, see pp. 73, 112.
7. Arnold and Palmer, p. 40.
8. Ibid., p. 55.
9. Ibid.
10. Ibid., p. 44.
11. Ibid., p. 45.
12. Ibid.
13. Ibid., p. 46.
14. Ibid.
15. Ibid.

16. Ibid., p. 47.
17. Ibid.
18. Ibid., p. 48.
19. Ibid., p. 49.
20. Ibid., p. 52.
21. Ibid., p. 54.
22. Ibid., p. 56.
23. Ibid.
24. Ibid., p. 58.
25. Ibid., p. 59.
26. Ibid., p. 66.
27. Ibid., p. 67.
28. Ibid.
29. Ibid., p. 75.
30. Ibid., p. 77.
31. Ibid.
32. Ibid.
33. Ibid.
34. Ibid., p. 79.
35. Ibid., p. 82.
36. Ibid., p. 84.

The Age and the Authorities

I have absolutely no idea where the [UFO] come from or how they are operated, but after ten years of research, I know they are something from outside our atmosphere.

> —Dr. James E. McDonald, Professor of Atmospheric Physics and Senior Physicist at the Institute for Atmospheric Physics, University of Arizona. *Saucer News,* Spring 1967, p. 15.

THE PEOPLE of a country rarely move as one. Only when a condition becomes stunningly obvious, overbearingly burdensome, and *persists* for a long time is the public motivated to demand the elimination of incompetence or the excision of corruption. All polls can indicate majority support for a given action, reach two-thirds, even three-quarters, but if *power* decides to ignore the electorate, that is precisely what it does. UFO are among the most startling examples of this indifference. A number of fairly early national surveys established that more than half those interviewed believed that "flying saucers" were "something real," [1] an increase of almost 400 percent in a decade. Numerous members of the United States Congress, about twenty Senators and fifty Representatives, expressed public support of an inquiry into UFO.[2]

Officialdom declined to institute any genuine investigation of the unknowns when they first appeared. Fourteen years later its tactics had not changed. The public was told again that "no House investigation of the Unidentified Flying Objects would be held this session. The Air Force * is understood to have succeeded in blocking it." [3] Once more the Air Force appeared apprehensive that there might arise dispassionate inquiry, while it repeated for the unnumbered time that "all the sightings can be explained away as familiar objects." [4] Of course, no serious investigator doubted the Air Force † could "explain them *away*"— the problem was that there were many incidents the obstructionists *could not explain*.

The military kept a very low profile for the first few months of the new era. Most of its personnel were highly skeptical of the existence of UFO—except the pilots who had encountered them. Then an episode arose to confound the Technical Intelligence Division of the Air Material Command. It is usually catalogued as the Muroc case.

The official account indicates that the unusual series of events of July 8, 1947, which comprise this report commenced with a group of officers and airmen at Muroc Air Base ** in California viewing a formation of three silver circular aerial unknowns moving westerly. This observation was followed ten minutes later, at 10 A.M., with a sighting of a single UFO by a test pilot. He was conducting a trial run of a craft with a new XP-84 engine. Glancing upward, the aviator thought he perceived a balloon, but realized that the object was progressing in opposition to the wind. Basing his estimate of the UFO on its being the approximate dimensions of "a normal aircraft," he deduced that the yellowish globe was traveling at more than 200 miles an hour, about 2 miles above the surface of the earth.

It wasn't until shortly afterward, at 11:50 A.M., that a group of base technicians, located at nearby Rogers Dry Lake, had the opportunity of seeing the climax of this sighting complex. The crew was staring into the sky at a pair of P-82s and an A-26, which were

---

* Probably read Central Intelligence Agency (CIA).

† Emphasis added.

** Subsequently Edwards Air Force Base.

maneuvering at an altitude of about twenty thousand feet in preparation for a pilot emergency ejection test, when they "observed a round object, white aluminum color, which . . . resembled a parachute canopy." [5] Initially, everyone thought that the test had occurred before they had anticipated it would, but it was quickly agreed that this was not what had happened. "The object was lower than 20,000 feet, and was falling at three times the rate we observed for the test parachute, which ejected thirty seconds *after we first saw the object.** As the object fell it drifted slightly north of due west *against the prevailing wind.*"* [6] While the technicians were unable to make any accurate determination regarding the speed of the UFO, they agreed that it was less than that of an F-80 traveling its fastest.

"As this object descended through a low enough level to permit observation of its lateral silhouette," continued the account, "it presented a distinct oval-shaped outline, with two projections on the upper surface which might have been thick fins or nobs [sic]. These crossed each other at intervals, suggesting either slow rotation or oscillation.

"No smoke, flames, propeller arcs, engine noise, or other plausible or visible means of propulsion were noted." [7]

The UFO was silver, said the men, suggestive of a painted cloth, but not the least interesting observation was that it "did not appear as dense as a parachute canopy." [8] Does this indicate some degree of translucency? If so, it tends to show that the theories of semitangible intelligence, perhaps an organism, that became popular many years later had an early beginning and a long gestation period, in terms of modern ufology.

The object was calculated to have been in full sight for a minute and a half before it vanished behind some mountains. Regarding its visibility another curious aspect of the sighting arises. Of the five men composing the crew, only four are said to have seen the object.

---

* Emphasis added.

The report does not state whether this is because the
fifth technician was napping under the observation
truck, whether he was so phlegmatic he did not bother
to look up, or if the unknown was not apparent to
him for physical, psychological, or psychical reasons.
Or, perhaps, because some characteristic of the UFO
made it invisible to 20 percent of the viewers. Nevertheless, the conclusion of the remaining men was that
"it was man-made, as evidenced by the outline and
functional appearance. Seeing it was not an hallucina-
tion or other fancies of sense." [9]

Yet that was not the end of the matter.

Minutes preceding four o'clock on the afternoon of
the same day, an F-51 pilot, operating at 20,000 feet,
about 40 miles south of Muroc Air Base, encountered
a "flat object of a light-reflecting nature." He saw no
appendages such as fins, wings, tail or canopy. Despite
the aviator's efforts to achieve the altitude of the unknown above him as it ascended, the fighter plane
could not function at that height or velocity. When
the pilot landed and entered his report it was quickly
determined that no airfield in the area had any craft
aloft by which the F-51 flyer might have been confused.

The Air Force had declined to come to investigate
the unknowns. Had *they* come to investigate *it*? An
increasing number of officials became more and more
nervous and

> by the end of July 1947 the UFO security lid was
> down tight. The few members of the press who
> did inquire about what the Air Force was doing
> got the same treatment that you would get today
> [circa 1955] if you inquired about the number of
> thermonuclear weapons stock-piled in the U.S.'s
> atomic arsenal. No one, outside of a few high-
> ranking officers in the Pentagon, knew what the
> people in . . . the Air Technical Intelligence Cen-
> ter were thinking or doing. [10]

The military was less imaginative than the interested
public. Early on it arrived at the conclusion that UFO

fell, or flew, into one of a pair of categories: they were mundane or extraterrestrial. With respect to the first possibility, the suspicions had the USSR the odds-on favorite, with the U.S. Navy's experimental aircraft the XF-5-U-1 an outside possibility—at least until the admirals assured the Technical Intelligence Division that work on it had been abandoned. The other category, for the most part, revolved about the interplanetary spacecraft thesis, with an occasional semifrivolous speculation about etheric organisms. The noted scientific scholar Ivan Sanderson made an intriguing case for this argument a score of years later. [11]

The usual human "logic" was followed. Man is the center of the universe (things have changed little since the Inquisition terrified Galileo into recanting his philosophy*). The greatest threat to the world is the Communists. Therefore, officialdom decided that Russians had been, and still were, responsible for the cryptic phenomena.

The Pentagon much preferred to believe that such technical advances had been achieved by the military weapon experts of Germany than that they were the product of the despised Red scientists.† Therefore, intelligence officers began recalling the foo-fighters of the recent war. High Army officers ignored the fact that UFO had been seen in virtually every quarter of the world, including far outside the range of even extranormal Nazi air capability. It researched, investigated, and discovered that Germany had some sort of "flying disk" before the conflict concluded. These, and other similar craft—which have been described in Chapter 7—caught the fascination of the Technical Intelligence Division. It was simply a matter of whether *their* German scientists (captured at the end of the war) had known more and been able to achieve greater results than *our* German scientists

---

* *E pur si muove*, attributed to the post-recantation period, is regarded as an apocryphal reaffirmation by many, perhaps most, scholars.

† Despite the fact that modern concepts of rocket propulsion probably originated with Konstantin E. Tsiolkovsky (1857–1935).

(captured at the end of the war). We had enlisted the talents of the enemy's greatest rocket expert, Dr. Hermann Oberth,* often designated the father of Germany's V rockets. Additionally, we had von Braun. Technical Intelligence Division knew of no one of their stature, in the potential extraterrestrial aircraft field, caught up in the Soviet net. Still, that did not prove a German scientist of such aeronautical brilliance had not been ensnared, and there was always the possibility (as USSR space accomplishments were soon to prove) that the Communists did not have to acquire all of their successes through abduction and espionage. They might have some extraordinary space theoreticians themselves.

In spite of such speculation, plus the deluge of sighting reports coming in from throughout the country (there appeared to be a concentration of such accounts from the Pacific coast, especially in the north), formal action was not initiated. No specific project was established to really determine what the rash of phenomena sparkling above America actually was. Even the great many observations made by members of the Air Force did little to energize officialdom and many went wholly uninvestigated. Where units throughout the military did undertake some sort of probe, they did so autonomously. Neither higher levels of their service, nor the government itself, provided incentive or aid, and no program for exchanging information between such was effected. To paraphrase Stephen Butler Leacock: the Air Force flung itself into its plane and flew madly off in all directions.

Finally, the accumulation of accounts of "flying saucers," the number of professional flyers who had encountered the unknowns, and then multiple sightings as exemplified by the Muroc incident caused the military to reverse itself as completely as UFO which assertedly spun around 180 degrees while hurling along at thousands of miles an hour. By the end of July "classified orders came down to investigate *all*

---

* One of the trio, including Tsiolkovsky and Goddard, whose research created the conceptual launching pad for interplanetary travel.

UFO sightings ... the order carried no explanation ... this ... and the fact that the information was to be sent directly to a high-powered intelligence group within Air Force Headquarters stirred the imagination of every cloak-and-dagger man in the military system." [12] It took another couple of months before a project was created for the specific purpose of collecting, collating, investigating, analyzing, and drawing conclusions regarding the phenomena. Several such units were created, one after another, in the succeeding quarter of a century. All were subminimally (or, perhaps, subliminally) staffed, most were consistently enept, and misdirection and deceit were frequently discernible. At one time it would have verged on the impossible to convince any average citizen of the United States that his government was capable of such extremes. However, with the assassination of John F. Kennedy producing a summation which more than two-thirds of the public found unacceptable,* through the following decade culminating in the Watergate events, the cover-up, the indictment and resignation of the Vice President of the country, the indictment and conviction of federal cabinet officers, and the eventual resignation of the President in disgrace, reasonable individuals had less of a problem in recognizing symptoms common to governmental inefficiency, political intrigue, or condescending parentalism.

The beginning stages of the official investigation of UFO were placed within the jurisdiction of the Technical Intelligence Division of Air Materiel Command,† among the most specialized branches in the United States military. During the three months—nearly to the day—following the Arnold adventure, the highest

---

* The "Warren Commission" judgment that Lee Harvey Oswald was a *lone* assassin. Statistic from Gallup polls following November 22, 1963.

† Despite Captain Ruppelt's referring to the command authority over such inquiries as Air Technical Intelligence Center from its inception, the author's correspondence with the office of the Department of the Air Force (Colonel L. J. Churchville, chief, Public Information Division) indicates that this responsibility was not assigned to the ATIC until 1951.

levels of Air Materiel Command, under which the Technical Intelligence Division functioned, attempted to deal with questions for which there were no replies, silence in responses to requests for data, unsought accounts of irrelevant observations, and limitless speculation. The only consensus seemed to be that this country had no aircraft even approaching the alleged aerodynamic characteristics of at least some UFO. This stand was consolidated when not merely the head of the TID, but Lieutenant General Nathan Twining, of the Air Materiel Command, replied to a verbal request from the commanding general of the Army Air Force with a letter, dated September 23, 1947, saying that preliminary efforts of his group led to the conclusion that " 'the reported phenomena were real.' "[13] This communication also advised that a permanent unit for the purpose of a concentrated study of the aerial mystery be created immediately. After the fact, an official press release, still being used in 1969, reduced the impact of the directive by simply saying that it "expressed the opinion that there was sufficient substance in the reports to warrant a detailed study [of UFO]." [14] Twining also recommended priority for the proposed new project and suggested that it be assigned a code name and be accorded a high security classification. The result was that the Air Materiel Command's advice was taken and, on February 11, 1948, Headquarters AMC Technical Instruction No. 2185 was issued through its Technical Intelligence Division. It was cryptically designated "Project Sign," given the second highest priority rating (2-A) dispensable by the Air Force, and enveloped in as tangled a security web as they could weave when first they started.

The practices and pronouncements of the Air Force confused the public. Logical analyses of its behavior was put beyond the independent investigator. One could, and can, depend fully on no source. Whether discrepancies are the result of deliberate deception or typically amateurish writing and/or editing is sometimes nearly impossible to ascertain. A simple pair of examples may be found within fewer than the first thirty pages of Edward J. Ruppelt's volume on the subject, despite his being the best of all early "official" sources (or perhaps merely the most proficient at the task assigned him) and head of the Air Force UFO project for two of the early, vital years. He assigns authority over the UFO problem to the Air Technical Intelligence Center from the inception of the military probe, but the Secretary of the Air Force representative stipulates that the ATIC (or the ATIC nominal designation) was not inaugurated until about four years afterward. UFO from then back to Arnold were under the administration of the TID of the Air Materiel Command. Soon after, Ruppelt has "Project Sign" functioning in the autumn of 1947, e.g., "Project Sign" ended 1947 with a new problem." [15] Official records have the unit commencing months later, in the following year, on February 11, 1948. Ruppelt ran the Air Force operations on the phenomena for two years and wrote what was the only, and decidedly most rational, brief for the administration position on the enigma.* Unfortunately, his work contains these, and other fundamental errors. Once more the puzzle looms before us—ineptitude (difficult to believe in Ruppelt's case) or intent.

The sighting of Kenneth Arnold is often classified by serious ufologists as the first "classic" UFO incident, if only for chronological reasons. Many dismiss the Maury Island episode with a variety of excuses, not the least being that the Air Force, in general, and Ruppelt, in detail, flatly declared it was a hoax. Granting the Idaho aviator the primary position in the historical annals, it would be difficult to contest that the "second classic" was the case of Capt. Thomas F. Mantell, Jr., and, in two respects, it was to introduce to ufometrics new dimensions. One: it was the first death directly attributable to a contact with a UFO in the modern era. The plane crash killing Brown and Davidson was

---

* The sole other government-approved, publicly distributed books on the subject were the flimsy *Flying Saucers and the U.S. Air Force*, by official UFO spokesman (1958–1961) for the service Lieutenant Colonel Lawrence J. Tacker, and the ill-informed and misinforming Condon Report.

within the UFO gestalt, but there was no testimony
that an unknown ever approached the ship in which
they went down. The pursuit of an ascending "light-
reflecting" object by the F-51 pilot on the day of the
Muroc complex, at four in the afternoon, south of the
air base, the pattern of which was very similar to
Mantell's actions, did not result in a fatality. Second:
it hurled the conjecture of alien hostility into a great
debate which more and more absorbed everything related to the subject. It will be suspected that an event
involving such serious aspects was, and remains, highly
controversial, and such an inference will be justified.
Few agree as to what happened in fact, particularly
with respect to the final phase of communication with
Captain Mantell. Even more theorists diverge in their
conclusions as to what ultimately occurred.

For the American public the story began in 1948
with an Associated Press release, which was carried in
the New York *Times*.

FLIER DIES CHASING A 'FLYING SAUCER'

Plane Exploded Over Kentucky as That and Near States Report Strange Object

Louisville, Ky. Jan. 8 (AP)—Several areas of
Kentucky and adjoining states were excited today
over reports of a "flying saucer" which led to the
death of one National Guard flier and fruitless
chases by several other pilots.

The National Guard headquarters at Louisville
said Capt. Thomas F. Mantell, Jr., 25 years old,
was killed while chasing what was reported as a
"flying saucer" near Franklin, Ky.

Other Kentucky National Guard fliers looked for the
unknown, as well. James Garret and William Cren-
shaw, a pair of Hopkinsville pilots, reported pursuing
a flying object which they believed to be a balloon.
Astronomers at Vanderbilt University, Nashville,
Tennessee, monitored an unknown at the same time
and came to the same conclusion. However, the Nash-

ville Weather Bureau said none were in the area at the specified hour.

A flaming red cone was observed in southern Ohio, near the Army Air Base at Wilmington, Army spokesmen were unable to provide information on the UFO or its origin.

Col. Guy F. Hix, commanding officer at Godman field, adjoining Fort Knox, said he observed the "flying saucer" for some time. He said contact was made by radio with three * National Guard planes and the pilots were asked to investigate.

"We lost contact in about twenty minutes," Col. Hix said. "Two of the planes later called back and reported no success."

Captain Mantell, an air hero during the allied invasion of Normandy [and other European action], was the third pilot. His mother, Mrs. Thomas Mantell, said in Louisville she was informed her son flew too high in his pursuit of the object and lost consciousness.

Glen Mays, who lives near Franklin, said he saw the Mantell plane flying at an extremely high altitude just before it seemed to *explode in the air*.†

"The plane circled three times, like the pilot didn't know where he was going," Mr. Mays said, "and then started down into a dive from about 20,000 feet. About halfway down there was a terrific explosion." [16]

Much of the general picture is conceded, but the discrepancies are sufficiently great to give the impression that various individuals are dealing with different episodes. One could easily conclude that the primary file did not contain, or that Ruppelt never read, the original news story. The following is based upon his official (i.e., amended) account.

---

* This newspaper description is inaccurate. Four planes were in the flight contacted.

† Emphasis added.

One week after New Year's Day, on January 7, 1948, several groups of citizens in Maysville, Kentucky, a little community less than a hundred miles east of Louisville, called the state police barracks to say that they had seen some curious object pass over the town. By a quarter past one the highway patrol was in communication with the nearby Godman Air Force Base to discover whether it had anything in the sky that might have attracted and confused the witnesses; if not, whether it was in ground-to-air visual contact with such an object. Control tower personnel at Godman assured the telephone officer that they had no knowledge of such a UFO, and proceeded to check with Wright-Patterson Air Force Base. The command at the Ohio installation could contribute nothing.

The switchboard at Godman AFB lighted up again and the highway patrol reported that the single sighting had evolved into a complex. They had received accounts from additional towns, including Owensboro and Irvington, which were located in northwest Kentucky, on the other side of Louisville, and some distance removed from the initial observations. The cumulative viewings produced a clarification of the description of the UFO. There appeared to be broad agreement, according to police records, that it was "circular, about 250 to 300 feet in diameter" [17] and was continuing to fly westward quite swiftly.

Among the persons said to have been interviewed subsequently were "Red" Honnacker, George Towles, Al Deyarmond, Nick Post, and other citizens of the communities over which the UFO had flown. The immediate and later additional descriptions of the object varied,[18] as would be expected from observations made at different altitudes, horizontal distances, angles of perception, atmospheric conditions, and visual acuity, but included "like an ice cream cone [a long cone topped by a semisphere] tipped with red." [19] "a parachute" [20] (viewed in its entirety from canopy to harness very similar in configuration to the foregoing), "round and white" [21] (as the cupola part of such an object would appear if seen from one end as it was traveling horizontally), "a small white object" [22] (which same

might appear from almost any angle at a greater distance), and "one fourth the size of the full moon." [23] *
One observer reported the UFO as "huge and silver or metallic," [24] reflecting Mantell's final radio transmission, according to most approximated transcripts. Initially, the accounts do not seem excessively alike. Arranged in a logical sequence, and subjected to merely a few of the conditions that might have obtained when many of the witnesses saw the UFO, the astonishing fact is not their variety but their similarity. Ruppelt, in reevaluating the case several years later, did not seem conscious of this consideration.

For no reason he cared to, or could, explain, Ruppelt later wrote that Godman "theorized that since the UFO had had to pass north of Godman to get from Maysville to Owensboro [although they had still seen absolutely nothing of it] it might come back." [25] In spite of this speculation reflecting nothing logically deducible from the known behavioral characteristics of the phenomena, the Air Force writer accepts this odd anticipation by Godman's command without comment. More improbable was that the object did seem to follow the prognosis. A half hour [26] after the original call had been put through the assistant tower operator at Godman sighted the object. Compounding the strangeness of the beginning of this episode—for the account becomes "curiouser and curiouser!" as it develops—is the information that he *failed to notify anyone, including the chief officer of the tower, of his monitoring of the UFO for "several minutes."* [27] †
When this omission was corrected, and he and his superior had thoroughly satisfied themselves that the object was neither plane nor balloon, nor anything else they recognized, they decided to inform Flight Opera-

---

* Virtually all of these descriptions might apply to a single phenomenon being viewed from a wide variety of angles and heights, through different atmospheric conditions, by witnesses whose vision, perception, knowledgeability, and psychological attitudes were unique to each.

† Emphasis added.

tions * wanting the officer in charge to observe and support their conclusions as to what the phenomenon was not. Little time had passed before the tower staff, the operations officer, the intelligence officer, and a few additional ranking personnel had watched the UFO with unimplemented vision and through the 6 x 50 binoculars with which the control facility was equipped. Not one could identify it. Nor could Colonel Guy F. Hix, base commander, or his executive officer, Lieutenant Colonel Garrison Wood, when they arrived and viewed the aerial enigma.[28] Ruppelt's summation of the situation is more than adequate—the complement of Air Force witnesses was "baffled." [29]

Forty-five minutes, according to the official report, was consumed in attempting to define a course of action. Forty-five minutes? Finally, the necessity of making a decision, particularly a command decision, was obviated by the appearance of a flight of four F-51 fighter planes spearing through the sky from the south. A solution had presented itself, one that created a permanent precedent most aptly called "pass the UFO." The matter was flung up from the tower into the lap of the flight leader, Captain Thomas F. Mantell, Jr., who was asked to investigate the thing flying around the Kentucky skies and, perhaps, examining a United States Air Force Base, and try to determine what it was. As the fuel supply of one of the quartet was low he was instructed to continue to their destination, Standiford Field, Kentucky, while the remaining aircraft undertook the assignment.† The pilots were not yet in visual contact with the unknown and so, in the beginning stage of the pursuit, were being directed from the Godman control tower, the occupants of which saw the planes disappear along the southward course of the UFO.

---

* Regarding UFO, the Air Force, in terms of particular personnel and the service collectively, was to become infamous in succeeding years for indecision or deliberate delay.

† "Psychoanalyzing the Flying Saucers," *Science Digest*, May 1950, from condensation of article in *Air Force*, The Official Journal of the Air Force Association, February 1950, erroneously has *four* planes pursuing the UFO.

Outracing his wingman, by the time they reached 10,000 feet Mantell was far ahead and above them, and barely visible. Only fifteen minutes had passed since the chase request had been issued when the captain radioed the field saying, "I see something above and ahead of me," [30] while one of his trailing companions was heard to ask, quite understandably, "What the hell are we looking for?" [31] Certainly, at the time, there was little doubt that no one at Godman knew.

In effect, the question was put to Mantell; he was asked to detail what he was pursuing. This brings us to another of the catalogue of oddities regarding this case, for, as Ruppelt puts it, "no one can remember exactly what he answered." [32] As if such bungling were not sufficient, the onetime head of the United States' investigation and analysis of phenomena resorts not to Godman AFB citations, either records or personnel. Nor does he rely on any military, or even semiofficial, sources, but continues his narrative with: "saucer historians [to whom he refers he does not explain] have credited him with saying. . . ." Elsewhere throughout his book Ruppelt, at best, only glances askance at "saucer historians." Purportedly he had full access to all of the Air Force's material on UFO before, during, and after his incumbency as the head of its unit responsible for their explanation. How is it he can do no better in the extremely important case of Captain Thomas F. Mantell's death, while tailing a UFO, than paraphrase some unspecified "saucer historian"?

This is what Ruppelt and his source have the aviator saying. It must be kept in mind that those in the tower were the only auditory witnesses, excepting possibly his wingmen, and so a consensus regarding the main portion is to be expected.

"I've sighted the thing. It looks metallic and it's tremendous in size. . . .[33] Now it's starting to climb." [34] A brief pause is said to have followed before he spoke again. "It's above me and I'm gaining on it. I'm going to 20,000 feet." [35]

Ruppelt contends that all of the personnel in the tower that afternoon agree on the last sentence, but says there was not complete unanimity with respect to whether the flier described the UFO as metallic and/or tremendous. The opinions of other ufologists cover the range of obvious possibilities * and will be considered shortly.

Meanwhile the two other pilots had attained 15,000 feet and were vainly attempting to make radio contact with the flight leader. None of their aircraft was equipped with oxygen and Mantell was certainly approaching the maximum altitude for his F-51 lacking an additional support system. Leveling off, the two other pilots found that repeated transmissions elicited no reply. They began their descent, passing over Godman on their way to their ordered destination at Standiford Field. Landing and refueling, one of the two fliers went up again to search further for his comrade, but with no success. At Godman visual contact with the UFO had been lost at ten minutes to four. The report of Mantell's crash and death reached there very shortly after that.

Apparently the immediate reaction of the Air Force was to steamroller out any kind of explanation and "so almost before the rescue crews had reached the crash, the word . . . went out . . . Mantell had been killed trying to reach the planet Venus." [36] This, not surprisingly, satisfied newsmen—who were as alienated by the idea of extra-Earthian visitors as most humans were. The explanation simply lay there and took a year to die. A little later officials attempted to bury it with an equally arbitrary and, to many, wholly untenable solution. Nevertheless the concept of an experienced fighter pilot trying to pace the blue planet was still being propounded to writers for the *Saturday Evening Post* the next spring and appeared in a two-part piece "What You Can Believe About Flying Saucers." Written with official cooperation, the feature had the Air Force representative insist, without reservation, that "they checked again and it was Venus." [37]

It came as a bit of a shock to the authors of the article when, within weeks, an official Air Force re-

---

* There are many rarely or never considered lines of speculation in this case and countless other UFO reports.

lease completely contradicted the adamant assertion, in "a masterpiece in the art of 'weasel wording,'"[38] saying that the UFO responsible for the death of Captain Thomas F. Mantell, Jr. *"might* have been Venus or it could have been a balloon. Maybe two balloons [but that] it probably was Venus *except* that this is doubtful because *Venus was too dim to be seen* in the afternoon."[39] *

Not surprisingly, the flight leader's mysterious demise continued to be widely discussed within officialdom, by serious independent investigators, † and among professional and objective newsmen. Ominous rumors pulsated along the network of interest including suggestions that the plane simply disintegrated in midair, that only fragments were ever retrieved, that the pilot's remains revealed inexplicable injuries—often said to be indicative of "ray" burns, that the officer's remains were never recovered, at all. The continuance of such stimuli being fed into the Office of Public Information, over a period of three years, motivated the Director of Intelligence to contact Captain Ruppelt in 1952 requesting that he reinvestigate the matter and arrive at some reasonable—or, at least, less than laughable—conclusion, which might be delivered to interested and justly skeptical individuals and groups.

It might be appropriate to note that Ruppelt participated in World War II as a B-29 bombardier and radar operator, later flew and accumulated some medals in the Pacific theater, and maintained his peacetime reserve status by serving as a navigator. During this period he earned his degree in aeronautical engineering. Recalled to action for the so-called Korean War, he was assigned to the Air Technical Intelligence Center, which was responsible for monitoring all foreign aircraft and remotely controlled missiles. He was placed in charge of this new Project Grudge, another reorganization of the UFO unit, which subsequently became more famous under a later designation, Project Blue Book, established in March 1952.

---

* Emphasis added.

† Yes, there were some of us even back then; perhaps the majority still in their minority.

Notes

1. George Gallup, *The True Report on Flying Saucers*, No. 1 (New York: Fawcett, 1967), pp. 52–53.
2. *UFO Evidence* (Richard Hall, ed.), pp. 172–177.
3. Waterbury *Republican*, Bulkley Griffin. (Waterbury, Conn.), August 6, 1961.
4. Ibid.
5. Ruppelt, *Report on Unidentified Flying Objects*, p. 21.
6. Ibid.
7. Ibid.
8. Ibid., p. 22.
9. Ibid., p. 22.
10. Ibid. (actually Technical Intelligence Division of the Air Materiel Command).
11. Ivan T. Sanderson, *Uninvited Visitors* (New York: Cowles Education Corp., 1967).
12. Ruppelt, p. 23.
13. Ibid., p. 16.
14. Press release sent from the Department of the Air Force on December 23, 1968.
15. Ruppelt, p. 28.
16. New York *Times*, January 9, 1948, p. 11.
17. Ruppelt, p. 31.
18. A few sources falsely state that "all reports agreed as to the color and general appearance of the object." "Psychoanalyzing the Flying Saucers," *Science Digest*, May 1950, condensed from *Air Force*, The Official Journal of the Air Force Association, February 1950.
19. Ruppelt, p. 36.
20. Ibid.
21. Ibid.
22. Ibid.
23. Ibid.
24. Ibid.
25. Ibid., p. 32.
26. "Psychoanalyzing the Flying Saucers" has the Godman sighting, which commenced at 1:45 P.M., "beginning at 1445," an inaccuracy of an hour.
27. Ibid.
28. "Psychoanalyzing the Flying Saucers" contends that Hix watched the UAO "for 1-½ hours . . . it seemingly re-

mained stationary." This does not conform, in either
point, to most accounts, including "official" ones.

29. Ruppelt, p. 32.
30. Ibid.
31. Ibid.
32. Ibid.
33. *Saturday Evening Post*, April 30, 1949; *New Yorker*, September 6, 1952; *UFO Evidence*, p. 34.
34. Ruppelt, p. 32.
35. Ibid.
36. Ibid., p. 33.
37. Ibid., p. 34.
38. Ibid.
39. Ibid.

12

Disaster and Deceit

During the ensuing year there will be authenticated
sightings of roughly 200 Unidentified Flying Objects,
of which the Pentagon will be able to disprove 210.

—*Life*, January 6, 1958, p. 16

CAPTAIN EDWARD J. RUPPELT, director of the new
Project Grudge, a unit within Air Technical Intelligence Center replacing Project Sign, which had functioned out of the Technical Intelligence Division of the
Air Materiel Command began to reconstruct the
Thomas F. Mantell case.

Step by step Ruppelt discovered difficulties which
one might, at best, attribute to negligence. The original
material had been microfilmed, "but something had
been spilled on it" [1] so that some segments were value-

less. Then he found that "many sections were so badly faded they were illegible." [2] He was able to reestablish contact with but a few of the civilian citizens who had witnessed the events; regrettably he fails to mention, or never knew, how many were interviewed by Air Force Intelligence in the first instance. Apparently practically none of the military personnel who had been stationed at Godman were available—they had all been transferred elsewhere. The file he was given *did not even contain the names of Mantell's wingmen!* Ruppelt either did not, or could not, discover the new stations of any of the field personnel. If he did, no effort was made to communicate with them to get their accounts freshly, or where such no longer were to be found in the file, to acquire them initially. Cuttings from the press were far from comprehensive, let alone complete. A few mentioned that the unspecified (by Ruppelt) major who had been offered as the Air Force expert on UFO had alluded to concrete proof that the "accident" had been caused by an unrecognizable Venus—but the file contained nothing resembling support for that thesis, certainly no solid evidence. Additionally, Ruppelt quickly found that the government's "expert" was a Pentagon desk man who had once been responsible for a single brief intelligence summary on "flying saucers," and knew little about the subject. The man had never even been attached to the Technical Intelligence Division, which was responsible for the service's activities in this area at the time of the Mantell fatality. *He was simply the best the Air Force could produce as an authority on "flying saucers"* almost seven months after the Arnold case, and years after unknowns had been recorded over America. Ruppelt evaluated the unsupported pronouncement by concluding that the major "had evidently conjured up alleged expert testimony to support his [reaffirmation of the] Venus answer because the writers at the press conference had him in a corner." [3]

Eventually, seemingly realizing that the Air Force "file" on the Mantell case was worthless from an objective point of view, Ruppelt resorted to the remaining hope for some pertinent—if only secondary—information. The earliest, and almost sole, scientific consultant to the service on the subject of unknown aerial phenomena was Dr. J. Allen Hynek, director of the department of astronomy at Ohio State University. When the captain was appointed to head the revised unit, it is possible that only one somewhat qualified individual had ever been associated with official UFO research—i.e., Hynek—notwithstanding his concession that "he had been responsible for the weasel-worded report" [4] about which Ruppelt was quoted a bit earlier. Discounting his previous speculations, Hynek, after a discussion with Ruppelt, stipulated that he seriously doubted that the mystery object was the second planet from the sun. He declined to follow the pattern of contemporary and continuing allegedly scientific opinion by confining his comments to his area of expertise, specifically astrophysics, and offered no opinion of the canopy reflection, sundog, and the eventually substituted balloon theories.

Ruppelt became convinced that most of these alternatives were no more reasonable. He knew of two occasions when sundogs had disappeared when "pursued" briefly by aviators because the increased altitude or change of horizontal position by a couple of thousand feet had placed the pilots out of position to perceive the reflection of the parhelia. He was also aware that these atmospheric phenomena rarely, if ever, projected impressions with hard outlines. To the contrary, their diffusion of light caused them to appear to have distinctly "fuzzy edges." [5] He dismissed canopy reflection because it was unbelievable that a highly experienced pilot—or even a relative neophyte—could be deceived by one for more than a few seconds, and *certainly not for over a quarter of an hour*—particularly when the ship was in a constant high-speed change of altitude and angle to *everything* on earth, in space, or between the two.

Ruppelt whittled away all useful (to the Air Force) explanations but balloons, and only one type of balloon even approaches having sufficient physical and behavioral characteristics to be considered—an experimental, hundred-foot-diameter design called a Skyhook.

It was possible, by allowing the imagination a degree
of flexibility, to apply the descriptions supplied by
civilian and military witnesses to such an object—providing the acceptance that it had been viewed at different times, in numerous places, from many aspects,
under various optimum (for the argument) conditions.
The probability factor was immediately diminished by
the consideration that only after a search of the complete Air Force "file" on the Mantell incident could
the captain unearth anything to support this lingering
thesis. Still, his industry was rewarded. He retrieved
all of *two* allusions to balloons which he had not found
earlier, although he almost pointedly does not specify
that they referred to the large Skyhook type. His readers are simply led to infer, from his several interwoven
mentions of them, that whenever he uses the word
"balloon" the prefatory Skyhook is to be understood.
In his final report to his superiors—at least as drawn
from his records—Ruppelt was too honest to offer
more than the most tiny and tentative "out" for the
Establishment propagandists.

Now, with his old pair of references to balloons,
what sort of story was Ruppelt able to compose? It
was a fragile one. Soon after the UFO could no longer
be seen by anyone at Godman Air Force Base—probably between 2:35 P.M. and 2:40 P.M.—a man in
Madisonville, Kentucky, called in a report of an unknown which, with the aid of a telescope, he had
identified as a balloon. The time element is not given,
except that Ruppelt says it was "not long" after it
could not be seen by personnel at Godman, about 125
miles away. The sighter is left anonymous, and so we
know nothing of his qualifications as a competent observer and whether his telescope was something picked
up in a novelty shop or a strong-lensed semi-professional model.* Clarification of those points might have
meant nothing if the viewer had reported no more

---

* See Chapter 9. Ruppelt gives no reason to believe either of
these were the "Vanderbilt University" astronomers, and even
less that they had any connection with the "Hopkinsville
pilots."

than Ruppelt did about the object, i.e., that what he
saw "was a balloon." [6] Obviously this could be anything from a toy to a globular device within or without man's potentials of speculation. In conclusion, no
description of the balloon, estimates as to its altitude,
distance from the recorder, color, or any other data
was supplied.

The UFO, as determined by the chronology of the
reports from Maysville, passed Godman AFB and
Owensboro and traveled a fairly straight southwestern
course. If you try to squeeze in the first of Ruppelt's
"balloon" reports from Madisonville, the course is
maintained, and the distance covered, in less than an
hour and a half, is about 200 miles. Attempting to tie
in his second and last vaporous sighting means that
from Madisonville the object abruptly shot off in an
entirely new direction, southeast.

If anyone offered the Air Force such material as
evidence that any *particular* thing flew across a section of sky he happened to be observing, even a
balloon, it would have been one of the briefest interviews and swiftest entries in the wastepaper basket
file in history. Not having anything of substance with
which to replace the Venusian tale of the Air Force,
Ruppelt injected this tidbit. He was beginning to function as if the service's public relations department
"had *him* in a corner."

The notation of the second "sighting" consisted of
two sentences. It contributed little. This "balloon"
had been perceived by an astronomer—name and
qualifications also omitted, who happened to have a
telescope handy. Once more Ruppelt, who, when he
desired to be, was very specific, said nothing more.
It can only be assumed that he had no more to say
as he summed up the two sightings with the remark
that *"in the thousands of words of testimony* and evidence taken on the Mantell Incident this [these] *were
the only* references to balloons." [7] *

Having set aside a balloon as about the only possible
explanation, the head of Project Grudge acknowledges

---

* Emphasis added.

—even more, emphasizes—that it is inconceivable that as highly trained an aviator as Mantell, fully schooled in high-altitude flying and the capabilities of his craft, could have deliberately ventured above fifteen thousand feet without a supportive oxygen system. It was Ruppelt's notation that achieving that great a height without succumbing to minimal stages of anoxia was restricted to a "few of the more hardy souls," [8] adding that, in his experience, "nobody ever got over 17,000." [9]

Agreeing fully with this assumption was a flying friend of Mantell who was very familiar with the pilot's professional habits, attitude, and philosophy. He stated that " 'The only thing I can think was that he was after something that he believed to be more important than his life or his family.' " [10]

Again, what was Ruppelt able to construct from these two anonymous and descriptionless balloon reports? Certainly his best. Nevertheless, what he offered was a conjuration of supposition wrapped in imagination inside amnesia.

Contacting the individuals responsible "for all sky-hook research flights for the Air Force . . . at Wright Field," [11] he discovered that "they had no records on flights in 1948," [12] but, in response to his continued probing, some "did think that big [as remarked earlier on, Ruppelt presents material not citing Skyhook in a manner easily permitting the careless reader to infer that he has] balloons were being launched from Clinton County AFB in southern Ohio at the time." [13]

Forging ahead on the basis of this extremely misty remembrance, he proceeds to, in his phrase for other Air Force spokesmen, "weasel-word," remarking that in spite of the fact that the sighting times recorded in his non-file "were not exact . . . it was possible to partially reconstruct the sequence of events." [14] He has fragmentary notes on unnamed viewers of alleged balloons, assurance from the original keepers of the accounts of Skyhook balloon experiments that no records existed for the day, the week, the month, or, even, the year in question. Still, he launches forth with the vague recollection of some other anonymities that

some "big balloons" *may* have been dispatched "at that
time." "That time," within the framework of his reference, being almost 1,500 times larger than the specific
period with which he is supposedly concerned, i.e.,
the couple of hours covering the complete Mantell-
related UFO episode. Ruppelt's third piece of con-
jectural evidence is that an unconfirmed balloon, which
may or may not have been a Skyhook, may or may
not have been sent aloft on January 7, 1948. No
records are extant or even recollected, suggesting that
this actually occurred. Someone merely told Ruppelt
that there was a possibility that a device might have
been dispatched *in that year*. No one recalls even that
clearly, which the investigator admits: "Somewhere in
the archives of the Air Force or the Navy there are
records that will show whether or not a balloon was
launched from Clinton County AFB, Ohio, on January
7, 1948. . . ." [15] Having discovered an amateurishly
assembled and mostly destroyed or vanished official
"file" on the first Air Force death related to a UFO
pursuit, Ruppelt makes a wholly groundless assumption
with respect to the existence of an account of a dispatched balloon. Even if one was sent up. Even if it
was January 7. Even if it was a Skyhook, etc., "I could
never find those records," [16] he frankly admits.

All Ruppelt was able to obtain from Wright Field
was "a record [or was it an example] of the winds," [17]
and this was partial. Allowing himself every conceivable liberty with his speculations as to the conditions
of the air currents, the behavior of any lighter-than-air
object subjected to their scripted activity, and then
assuming that the hundred-foot-diameter Skyhook
would have conformed to the path pattern presupposed,
Ruppelt creates a page of was-possibles, could-bes, be-
ables, could-haves, presuming so-and-so would-haves,
strong-indications, it-seems, with several of the phrases
of hypothesis reappearing frequently, only to conclude
—"It *could* have been a balloon. This is the answer
I phoned back to the Pentagon." [18] *

After what was quite apparently an intense, lengthy,

----

* Emphasis by Ruppelt.

and serious effort to find some sort of palatable, if not convincing, explanation, Ruppelt decided that "whatever the UFO was, it was slowly moving away," [19] and that it *could* have been a balloon.

Yet, what was the response of other researchers in ufology?

Major Donald E. Keyhoe was one of the earliest responsible and certainly among the best-known investigators the field had produced. A couple of years after the sighting by hundreds, probably thousands, of Kentuckians he offered his first analysis of the general situation.[20] This was followed in 1954 with his well-known *Flying Saucers from Outer Space*,[21] which he introduced with a Foreword crediting the Air Force with having provided its complete cooperation to the end. In his terms, his "book reveals, I believe, all that the Air Force has learned about flying saucers." [22] In it he tends to accept a simple service position and supports its dismissal of any of the more unorthodox allegations about the incident, the death, or the condition of the ship or pilot's body in the ensuing examination of the episode and the site of the crash.

The retired Marine Corps officer and future director of the National Investigations Committee on Aerial Phenomena, based in Washington (which was the second important research group to be formed in the United States, preceded by only the Aerial Phenomena Research Organization, of Phoenix, Arizona, founded by Mr. and Mrs. L. J. Lorenzen in 1952), was later to split drastically with the Air Force. The confidence he had that they had been completely candid with him during the composition of his second book was destroyed.

Shortly after the Mantell tragedy, in 1949, Keyhoe conducted an investigation in response to a magazine editor's request. It was followed by publication of an article on the subject. Pro-UFO, it indirectly elicited a response from the Air Force. The service told the public that there were no such things as "flying saucers." The Mantell fatality was the result of his scouting Venus, assured spokesman Major Jere Boggs, an intelligence representative. There seems little doubt that this was the officer alluded to by Ruppelt in his later book.[23] *

The aggressive Keyhoe sloughed off excuses that Boggs was too busy to see him and eventually was accorded an interview, which was also attended by General Sory Smith (deputy, and later full, director of Air Information) and other press officers. Replying to Keyhoe's query, Boggs reaffirmed that " 'Mantell was chasing the planet Venus when he was killed.'

" 'But Venus was practically invisible that day.' I said. 'And that's a flat contradiction of the April Project report. After checking for fifteen months, they said it was *not* Venus—that the object was still unidentified.'

" 'They rechecked after that,' Boggs said calmly." [24]

The interrogator could not budge them from the assumption. Considering the method from which it derived it could hardly have been regarded as a conclusion. Boggs having departed, Keyhoe asked General Smith if he could view the original file on the case and was told there was no reason why he shouldn't. Not unexpectedly, even after he repeated the request twice at later dates, it was never shown to him. Was it then in the vandalized state that made it so useless to Ruppelt a couple of years later, *when the Pentagon asked him to do a total reevaluation of the case?*

The general was somewhat taken aback when Keyhoe inquired whether he believed the Venus explanation, remarking that " 'if Wright Field says that's the answer, it must be right.' " [25] Soon, the ex-Marine flyer found that no such report had been issued; he could draw only a single inference, Boggs had simply ad-libbed whatever came into his mind when he found himself, in Ruppelt's phrase, "in a corner." [26] Then circumstances placed the Project Sign account of the Mantell tragedy in Keyhoe's hands. It was in absolute contradiction—as Ruppelt would later write—to the inventions of the major and many other professional defenders of the government explanations of the rapidly growing mystery. Keyhoe quotes a section of the Mantell material, which fills in regrettable omissions

* See Chapter 11.

by Ruppelt in his subsequent "official" analysis. The
head of the new Project Grudge and the Project Blue
Book must have found some or all of it missing when
he conducted his reevaluation. Or, for some reason—
perhaps because it tends to rebut the already feeble
solution he prepared as a substitute for preceding
versions—he decided not to include it. Regardless, this
is that excerpt from the official segment, as offered by
Major Keyhoe.

"Under exceptionally good atmospheric conditions, and with the eyes shielded from direct
rays of the sun, Venus might be seen as an exceedingly tiny bright point of light. However, the
chances of looking at just the right spot are very
few.

"It has been unofficially reported that the object was a Navy cosmic-ray research balloon. If
this can be established, it is to be preferred
as an explanation. [This was later proved
false.*] However, if one accepts the assumption that reports from various other localities refer to the same object, any such device must
have been a good many miles high in order to
have been seen clearly, almost simultaneously,
from places 175 miles apart . . . no man-made
object could have been large enough and far
enough away for the approximate simultaneous
sightings.†

"It is most unlikely, however, that so many

_____

* The interpolation is Major Keyhoe's, and it should be
remarked that it seriously diminished Ruppelt's interpretation
offered three years after this book was written. The main
text of this Project Sign report goes even further in antici-
patorily diminishing the believability of the substitute explanation the Project Grudge and Blue Book director submitted to
the Pentagon, at its request.
† Here, it should be noted, the calculations of Harold T.
Wilkins, whose analysis of this case follows, contend that the
probable object exceeded five hundred feet in diameter and,
including the tail, or conic portion, might have approximated
fifteen thousand feet in length.

separated persons should at that time have
chanced on Venus in the daylight sky . . . the
sighting might have included two or more balloons (or aircraft) or they might have included
Venus (in the fatal chase) and balloons. . . .
Such hypotheses, however, does still necessitate
the inclusion of at least two other objects than
Venus, and it certainly is coincidental that so
many people would have chosen this one day to
be confused (to the extent of reporting the matter)
by normal airborne objects." [27]

Harold T. Wilkins, noted for his advocacy of the
some-UFO-are-hostile thesis, also wrote on the subject [28] before Ruppelt's book emerged. He quoted base
commander Colonel Hix on the appearance of the
UFO: "It was umbrella-shaped, half the apparent
size of the moon, and white in color, except for a
streamer of red which seemed to be rotating." [29] He
asserts that one of the wingmen radioed that the object "looked like a teardrop and at times seemed
almost fluid!" [30] Then he offers his version of the
Mantell transmission:

"The object is traveling at half my speed, and
at 12 o'clock high. I'm going to close in right
now, for a good look. It's directly ahead of me.
The thing looks metallic and of *tremendous size.*
It's going up now and forward as fast as I am.
That's 360 miles an hour. I'm going up to 20,000
feet, and if I'm no closer, I'll abandon chase." [31]

Wilkins then contends that the two other pilots
reported that they, too, had reached 20,000 feet, and
that the flight leader was considerably ahead of them,
adding: " 'this strange object is too high for us to catch.
It's going too fast.' " [32] Further, he asserts that portions of the messages were never revealed (seemingly
not even to project director Ruppelt), including a
final Mantell comment: " 'Am not gaining on it. I
shall have to break off the chase soon.' " [33] At this
point it is stated that he must have been very much

over twenty thousand feet, as his considerably outpaced comrades had attained that altitude themselves.

Wilkins, as well as writing that there are even more
unrevealed portions of the final communication from
Mantell, contends that a witness who saw the conclusion of this extraordinary episode—Glen Moyes,
address not cited—maintained that the aviator's "machine was seen to explode in mid-air . . . that Mantell's
plane . . . went into a dive, at 20,000 feet, and began
to disintegrate when about half that height above the
ground." [34] On the other hand, Wilkins claims a woman
viewed the crash and said that his ship roared above
her home and fell apart along the tops of the trees.

Unlike many ufologists, Wilkins has little, if any,
doubt about what happened. He addresses himself to
the explanation for several pages, but a brief excerpt
gives one an excellent idea of his candidly exotic approach:

> Some may say—and the present author is im-
> penitently among them!—that some lethal ray of
> immense power and unknown type had been di-
> rected at Mantell and his plane by the entities in
> the weird and vast machine, who may have
> deemed that they were going to be attacked, or
> wished to demonstrate to terrestrial military power
> with its antiaircraft batteries, the folly of any
> close approach. [35]

Remembering that Ruppelt later contacted Wright
Field in an unsuccessful effort to isolate any balloon
activity at Clinton Air Force Base on January 7, plus
the fact that the material alleged by Wilkins to have
been reported by observers at Clinton was never mentioned to Ruppelt, or if it was, not by him to the
public, Wilkins makes one other assertion that is
singularly interesting. According to him, very shortly
after the Mantell crash, at approximately five o'clock,
a sighting was made at the Lockbourne airport, near
Columbus, Ohio.

A glowing disk was seen hurtling across the sky

at an estimated speed of 550 miles an hour.
[Which seems slow enough today, but at the time
probably only one man, Major Charles E. Yeager,
who had accomplished the feat three months
earlier, on October 14, 1947, had yet penetrated
the supersonic barrier.] It was white and orange,
and emitted an exhaust some five times its own
length.[36]

Quotes from observers located, on that afternoon
at Clinton Air Force Base, follow:

" 'A flaming red cone trailing a gaseous green mist
tore through the sky at 7:55 P.M.' " [37] Then he has a
control tower sergeant and corporal seeing the " 'red
cone maneuvering for 35 minutes, when it seemed to
vanish over the horizon.' " [88] Wilkins concludes his
quotes from Clinton AFB with their addendum: " 'It
seemed to hang suspended in the air at intervals. Then
it came down. It then ascended at what looked like a
terrific speed. The intense brightness from this phenomenon in the sky pierced through a heavy cloud
layer which intermittently passed over the region.' " [39]

It is Wilkins' contention that "thousands of people
witnessed this phenomenon" [40] and that it is highly
likely that it was the UFO pursued by Mantell. Ruppelt
conjectured that Mantell died because of the remote
possibility that a balloon may have been released from
Clinton AFB, although no records exist to support the
suggestion, and that this hypothetical object conformed
to a complex series of guesses regarding the atmospheric conditions about which little is known, that a
well-trained professional aviator operating a superior
craft killed himself by not recognizing a balloon (which
scores of other persons did not identify as such), and
by hazardously ignoring absolutely minimum standards
of personal and aeronautical safety, plus other unfounded speculations. If one is willing even tentatively
to consider Ruppelt's imaginative solution, then one
can hardly arbitrarily dismiss the argument that, instead, Mantell was following a widely seen object the
characteristics and behavior of which are, to a considerably greater degree, consonant with the details of

the Maysville, Godman Air Force Base, and Owensboro UFO.

A fresh perspective was introduced to ufological writing, although it confined itself to the better-known United States sightings. It was contained in the English version of the noted Aimé Michel's book on the phenomena,[41] which appeared as a result of the efforts of a small, but worthy, New York organization titled Civilian Saucer Intelligence, which was based upon the unceasing efforts of Isabel Davis, Ted Bloecher, and the late Alexander Mebane. The French researcher opens his narrative on the Mantell case by noting that "the decree setting up the Project," [42] meaning Project Sign, which he chooses to call by its "colloquial" name "Saucer," was "signed on December 30, 1947." [43]

The actual date of the establishment of Project Sign is not of monumental importance, but the widespread uncertainty about the time is curious. Ruppelt was inclined to regard the inauguration to have taken place in September, presumably on the twenty-third, but technically his pragmatic approach must defer to Michel's calendar as the letter from Maj. General L. C. Craigie, director of Research and Development, Office of the Deputy Chief of Staff, to the commanding general, Air Materiel Command, Wright Field, was dated as cited by him. Yet, that substantive work *The UFO Evidence* [44] lists January 22, 1948, as the point at which Project Sign was initiated; Major Keyhoe places the commencement of its activities after Mantell's death,[45] as well. The United States Air Force specifically says, "The Technical Division of the Air Materiel Command issued Headquarters Air Materiel Command Instruction No. 2185, February 11, 1948, and the project was inaugurated with a code name of 'SIGN.' " [46]

Michel has the first and second in command at the field, Colonel Hix and Major Woods,* seeing the object approaching and being able to define it quite clearly as huge and apparently metallic. He specifies, without citing any source for his data, that "all had

---

* Elsewhere—e.g., Wilkins—"Lt. Col. Woods."

seen that: 1. the object was a sort of disc, with the top side shaped like an inverted cone. 2. It was of 'gigantic' size. 3. At the top was a red spot which glowed intermittently." [47] Obviously, his description is far more graphic than that attributed to the Godman personnel, or he is combining details from the military and the civilian sightings. Additionally, he errs in relating how Colonel Hix ordered three F-51 planes, under Mantell's command, to take off and pursue the UFO. As we know from Ruppelt and other sources, there were originally four fighter craft (one continued to his base because of low fuel supply), they were out of Standiford Field, to the north, and were requested by radio to investigate.

The account of the Mantell communication is more specific, dramatic, and lengthy than Ruppelt's later version, being almost exactly as Wilkins has it, suggesting the latter as his most likely source. At that point he introduces new material, origin unknown, reporting that Colonel Hix ordered the remaining wingmen to search for Mantell, with one of the pilots going up to "nearly 35,000 feet," [48] *twice as high* as Ruppelt, an experienced aviator himself and one familiar with the F-51, says *the hardiest of pilots could get* since the ships had *no supplemental oxygen supply*.

Michel then speaks of the Lockbourne sighting, once more in terms nearly identical to Wilkins'. He remarks quite correctly that it is relevant to the Mantell case only if satisfactory evidence can be adduced that it and the Maysville, Godman, and Owensboro unknown constituted a single object. He argues that Hynek's "investigations" * had determined that the Mantell UFO had been identical to that seen over Madisonville—which came later in the day, at the conclusion of the sighting "sequence." Further, he asserts that it was one of the two "balloon" sightings reported by in-

---

* At this point, Hynek has written, he had "joined my scientific colleagues in many a hearty guffaw at the 'psychological postwar craze' for flying saucers . . . and at the naïveté and gullibility . . . [of those] being taken in by such obvious 'nonsense.' " J. Allen Hynek, *The UFO Experience* (New York: Ballantine Books, 1972), p. 2.

dividuals purportedly employing telescopes. Accounts
from Elizabethtown and Lexington, Kentucky, are
credited to the same object. Neither is mentioned in
Ruppelt's book, but both follow the line of a shallow
arc southwestward. All of these contentions are
founded on the unknown being both large enough and
at a sufficiently great altitude to permit it to be seen
by the other communities in question, such as Godman
and Owensboro.

Michel finds one aspect thwarting, that the numerous
accounts fail to offer reliable estimates of the size of
the Mantell UFO, anonymously quoting "gigantic,"
"enormous," "huge," and "tremendous." [49] The last
of these descriptions is attributed not only to the flight
leader, but to his pair of wingmen as well, contrary to
any testimony offered by Ruppelt, early Keyhoe, and
others. Once more reflecting Wilkins, Michel concludes
that the object's "proportions must have been formid-
able." [50] While there definitely seems to have been a
consensus regarding the UFO being large, the fact that
it was also described as "a small white object," "one-
fourth the size of the full moon," and "a parachute" [51]
should be kept in mind and incorporated into any
analysis, even if regarded as variances deriving from
the distance between it and the spectator.

Continuing to tread a path similar to Wilkins', the
French author remarks that the object, presumably
the Mantell UFO, was visible, at the same time, from
geographical points up to 175 miles apart. Emphasizing the *single unknown* thesis, he incorporates the alleged speed at which Lockbourne observers are reputed to have seen the "flaming red cone" travel, i.e.,
about 500 miles an hour. Adding a few other unat-
tributed "facts," some confident conjecture, and a brief
exercise in fundamental geometry, he surmises that the
dimensions of the UFO were between 300 and 450
feet in diameter. He also satisfies himself that it was
"a good many miles high—25 to 30—in order to have
been seen clearly, almost simultaneously, from places
175 miles apart." [52] No concrete evidence is offered
for his proposition, from which he infers a conclusion

as easily accommodated by an acceptance of greater UFO velocity.

Michel spends a number of additional pages on an evaluation of the Godman-Lockbourne UFO, assuming the sightings involved a lone object. Much of his argument is clear and interesting, but one problem remains at the end of his estimate. He devotes a couple of pages to the chronology of the episode, beginning with a UFO at "Madisonville (Kentucky): 2:10 P.M. or a little later." [53] But virtually all other records have the Madisonville sighting as the penultimate or final viewing of the complex, placing its time as well after three o'clock. At about two thirty Michel has it over Godman, rather than at the generally accepted one forty-five—almost a half hour before Michel has it first being seen. At five, or shortly thereafter, the object has passed over Lockbourne—i.e., Columbus, Ohio—just as Wilkins had it also, but Wilkins did not confuse the issue by bothering with pre-Godman sightings to the north. Wilkins simply left it to his readers to connect the isolatedly described Mantell UFO and the thing seen in Ohio, if they wished. Michel specifically draws a continuous northward arc as the path of the unknown. Regrettably, this creates a major difficulty. His UFO is traveling in almost precisely the opposite direction of practically everyone else's UFO.

In his final paragraph on this case, Michel relegates the entire matter to the sea of unsolved sightings, asking: "What sort of object was it which was watched by hundreds of people from Madisonville [located in far western Kentucky, longitudinally almost a continuation of the Illinois-Indiana state line, about 50 miles north of Tennessee] to Lockbourne,[54] nearly three hundred miles to the northwest, near Columbus, Ohio?"

If it was anything like the one that thousands of spectators saw first at Maysville, Kentucky, in the eastern third of the state, adjacent to its Ohio border, no more than 100 miles from Columbus, and thereafter at Owensboro and Godman (and, if Michel's chronology meshed, Elizabethtown and Lexington might well drop into the possible continuum) as it swept a slightly curved path to the southwest, it must have been quite a spectacle. Should the UFO actually have been in all of the cited places at the specified times, not only did it fly in two directions simultaneously (which is even more interesting than being seen *from* several locations at a single moment, or, perhaps, even than being *in* two places at once), it flew in a number of directions, at considerable velocity, within a short span of time.

It may well be that is the essence of this matter. Regardless of origin and destination, setting aside how many unknowns were involved, to slightly paraphrase a line from the actual lore: what the hell was everyone looking at?

Curiously, later works on Unidentified Atmospheric Phenomena and Unexplained Aerial Objects tend to bypass the Mantell incident entirely—e.g., Saunders,[55] Fuller,[56] Hynek,[57], Sagan,[58] and others. But when the government decided to mummify and inter the entire subject of ufology in the archives over which the swiftly sifting sands of public memory piles, the first United States aviator to give his life in what may one day be noted as the initiation of extraterrestrial diplomacy— or war—was mentioned. He received about thirty lines in the so-called Condon Report. (Two and a half pages were devoted to one of the more fanciful contactees, but then the director was considerably more interested in the fabulous than the fact.) Leaving out numerous essential elements, the *Scientific Study of Unidentified Flying Objects* concludes that "what Capt. Mantell chased was probably one of the large 100 ft. 'skyhook' balloons that were being secretly flown in 1948 by the Navy. [This long-after and faraway judgment is based completely on Ruppelt's reinvestigation of the case which unearthed *two,* only two, references to any sort of balloons in the original inquiry, neither fitting the known character of the case.] Their existence was not known to most Air Force pilots." [59] This, obviously, does not establish that *all* aviators were ignorant of them—e.g., Capt. Mantell "chased the object for at least fifteen to twenty minutes," [60] during which time one is supposed to accept the contention that an experienced war and peacetime flier could not distinguish a balloon—even one he had not encountered before—from something else.

The Condon Report concludes its penetrating analysis of Ruppelt's reinvestigation of the original Air Force farce with a statement alluding to the ephemeral Skyhook balloons: "This explanation, though plausible, is not a certain identification." [61]

"Not a certain identification!" Ruppelt in his amended Air Force-approved brief for the government's conduct regarding UFO could bring himself to go no further than to suggest, in his own words: "It *could* * have been a balloon. *This is the answer I phoned back to the Pentagon.*" †

The only argument that has ever been made for the indecipherability of the proposed Skyhook balloon has been its size, i.e., "the large 100 ft. 'skyhook' balloon." Yet, one can hardly regard as immense a balloon of nearly identical size to that sent aloft by the brothers Joseph and Jacques Étienne Montgolfier nearly two centuries before, in 1783! In the same year another balloon went up carrying a man. Ruppelt *speculates* that such a device, could he have established one was there, which he in no wise could, *might* have reached "about 60,000 feet." Not a very impressive argument by those who contend that the Skyhook was inexplicable because of its great height. It need only be recalled that Auguste Piccard was soaring in a balloon at an altitude of 55,000 feet in 1932! An effort which his brother, Jean, topped two years afterward with a record of 58,000 feet. Yet it is to be assumed that Thomas F. Mantell never heard of big balloons and couldn't recognize one if he were chasing it into the upper troposphere, without oxygen, at the risk of his life. It is superfluous to comment on the argument, but not to remark that it is a gratuitously unworthy epitaph for a professional pilot, a duty-directed military officer, and a courageous man.

---

* Emphasis Captain Ruppelt's.
† Emphasis added.

Notes

1. Ruppelt, *Report on Unidentified Flying Objects*, p. 34.
2. Ibid.
3. Ibid., p. 35.
4. Ibid.
5. Ibid., p. 36.
6. Ibid., p. 37.
7. Ibid.
8. Ibid., p. 36.
9. Ibid.
10. Ibid., p. 37.
11. Ibid., p. 38.
12. Ibid.
13. Ibid.
14. Ibid.
15. Ibid., p. 39.
16. Ibid.
17. Ibid., p. 38.
18. Ibid., p. 39.
19. Ibid.
20. Donald E. Keyhoe, *The Flying Saucers Are Real* (New York: Fawcett, 1950).
21. Donald E. Keyhoe, *Flying Saucers from Outer Space* (New York: Henry Holt, 1953).
22. Ibid., p. vii.
23. Ruppelt, p. 35.
24. Keyhoe, *Outer Space*, pp. 37–38.
25. Ibid., p. 38.
26. Cf. Chapter 12. Also Ruppelt, p. 35.
27. Keyhoe, *Outer Space*, p. 39. Cf. with Menzel "explanation" later in this chapter.
28. Harold T. Wilkins, *Flying Saucers on the Attack* (New York: Ace, 1954), pp. 83–84.
29. Ibid.
30. Ibid., p. 84. This account endorsed by Arnold and Palmer, *Coming of the Saucers*, p. 88.
31. Ibid. This account endorsed by Arnold and Palmer.
32. Ibid.
33. Ibid., p. 85.
34. Ibid.
35. Ibid., pp. 85–86.

36. Ibid., p. 86.

37. Ibid.

38. Ibid., p. 87.

39. Ibid.

40. Ibid.

41. Aimé Michel, *The Truth About Flying Saucers* (New York: Pyramid, 1967; originally published by Criterion Books, New York, 1956).

42. Ibid., p. 38.

43. Ibid.

44. *UFO Evidence*, p. 106.

45. Keyhoe, *Outer Space*, pp. 33–42.

46. Letter and material to author from Department of the Air Force.

47. Michel, p. 39.

48. Ibid., p. 40.

49. Ibid., p. 42.

50. Ibid., p. 43.

51. Ruppelt, p. 36.

52. Michel, p. 43.

53. Ibid., p. 44.

54. Ibid., p. 51.

55. Saunders and Harkins, *UFOs? Yes!*

56. John G. Fuller, *Aliens in the Skies* (preponderantly a House of Representatives scientific committee reply to the Condon Report). A latecomer to the field, Fuller devoted his two earlier "flying saucer" works to somewhat "novelized" (à la Capote) versions of isolated alleged almost-contactee and contactee episodes.

57. J. Allen Hynek, *The UFO Experience*. Not only the sole researcher of this group who is an old hand in the field, Hynek ranks among the infinitesimal clique who are as close as one can come to being a genuine "expert" on the subject; therefore his omission, although explained to a great degree by the fact that he judiciously seldom comments upon cases he has not personally investigated, is a loss to the overall estimates of Mantell's still enigmatic death.

58. Carl Sagan and Thornton Page, eds., *UFO's: A Scientific Debate*. A series of, for the most part, prejudiced and ill-informed essays on the possibility that USE may be UFO, and that UFO may be "flying saucers," featuring many of the standard hypothetical "technical" hyperbolisms. Despite

its predisposition, the book is worth reading if only to
view the anti-UFO position through the eyes of competent
skeptics and escape the frequently contorted "explanations"
of most analysts supporting the Air Force posture.

59. Condon, *Scientific Study*, p. 505.
60. Ruppelt, p. 37.
61. Condon, *Scientific Study*, p. 505.

13

Things That Go By in the Sky

**I feel that the Air Force has not been giving out all the
available information on the Unidentified Flying Objects. You cannot disregard so many unimpeachable
sources.**

> —John W. McCormack, Speaker
> of the House of Representa-
> tives of the United States. *True*,
> January 1965

THIRTEEN MONTHS to the day—plus a few hours—
after the Arnold sighting, and a little more than six
months after Mantell's death, the second episode
designated a "classic" by Captain Ruppelt occurred.
Yet, let it be fully understood that the intervening
period had been filled with Unidentified Atmospheric
Phenomena (UAP) and Unexplained Aerial Objects
(UAO) accounts submitted to authorities in countless
countries.

A large percentage of them were good, coming
from people whose reliability couldn't be questioned. For example, three scientists reported that
for thirty seconds they had watched a round ob-

ject streak across the sky in a highly erratic flight
path near the army's secret White Sands Proving
Ground.[1]

In addition to the hundreds of reports tendered,
apart from newspaper coverage, several magazines
turned their attention to the unknowns. These publications were almost exclusively "news" or popularized
"science" types of publications. The pieces in them
ranged from poor reportage, through outright skepticism, to pontificating debunking and what was apparently meant to be regarded as humor. Major
periodicals responsible for such commentaries were,
in more or less chronological order of the appearance
of "flying saucer" articles, *Newsweek, Time, Life,
Science Illustrated,* and *Science Digest.*

Curiously, the reliable running compilation of the
subjects treated by virtually all of the major magazines
in the country, the periodical index, listed no material
printed on the subject from October 1947 to January
9, 1950, although *Time* [2] and the *Saturday Evening
Post* [3] did return to the puzzle at least once. It was as
if someone had ordered an anti-communications
switch thrown, severing any and all channels of information between whatever was happening, whatever
was being done about whatever was happening, and
the public—a suspension of current data which effectively lasted for more than two years. Considering
the number of reports continuing to flow into various
agencies, nearly all "official" ones, it is difficult for a
reasonable individual to understand traders in news
and fascination abandoning coverage of the incredible
mystery of their own volition. Was the silence suggested, or directed, by an element of our society, presumably governmental, intelligence, military, and/or
industrial, able to enforce its wishes?

The second "classic" sighting is most frequently
identified as the Chiles-Whitted case, and was prefaced
by an international overture. Ruppelt noted that on
July 21, 1948, "several persons reported seeing a UFO
through high broken clouds over The Hague [Holland].

The object was rocket-shaped, with two rows of windows along the side." [4]

The European investigator Jacques Vallee put the date a day earlier and recorded that "a 'cigar' with eight lights, having 'two decks and no wings' had been observed . . . from the ground, on four occasions." [5] He also commented on a very similar sighting from Clark Airfield, in the Philippines, on about August 1, depicting a torpedolike vessel with a double tier of lights. [6]

An Eastern Airlines DC-3, flown by Captain Charles S. Chiles and John B. Whitted,* left Houston, Texas, on the evening of July 24,† 1948, at 8:30 P.M., headed for Atlanta, Georgia. Passing twenty miles southwest of Montgomery, Alabama, at approximately 2:45 in the morning, [7] "Chiles saw a light dead ahead and closing fast. His first reaction . . . was that it was a jet, but in an instant he realized that even a jet couldn't close as fast." [8] As he called his co-pilot's attention to the object it was "almost on top of them." Chiles whipped the plane into a tight left bank and "as the UFO flashed by about 700 feet to the right, the DC-3 hit turbulent air. Whitted looked back just as the UFO pulled into a steep climb." [9]

Ruppelt freely granted that the two aviators had seen the unknown clearly and gave detailed descriptions to Air Technical Intelligence Center personnel. According to him, the account had the UFO about the size of and resembling a wingless B-29, with " 'two rows of windows from which bright lights glowed,' " [10] a deep underbelly, and " 'a 50-foot trail of orangered' " [11] exhaust.

Versions of the encounter have appeared in more than one of Keyhoe's works, sometimes varying in detail, although not in essence. The ufologist remarks

---

* According to Captain Eddie Rickenbacker two "utterly reliable men." *Reader's Digest,* July 1950, p. 15.

† The same question regarding the date arises in *The Truth About Flying Saucers* by Aimé Michel, P. 52. The "July 23," found on p. 87 of *Flying Saucers: Top Secret* by Donald E. Keyhoe, is a typographical error; it appears correctly in the noted ufologist's earlier *Flying Saucers from Outer Space.*

that the object was initially seen "in bright moon-light," [12] appeared as a "brilliant cigar-shaped craft" [13] or "a rocket-shaped craft, brilliantly lighted," [14] and came "hurtling toward the airliner." [15]

" 'It was heading southwest,' Captain Chiles said later, 'and it flashed toward us at terrific speed. We veered to the left. It veered sharply, too, and passed us about 700 feet to the right.[16] It was about one hundred feet long, cigar-shaped, and wingless. It was twice the diameter of a B-29.' " [17]

According to Keyhoe and most other reports, including Ruppelt's, both aviators clearly saw parallel rows of windows as if along upper and lower decks, and, in Keyhoe's words, there was "protruding from the nose . . . something like a radar pole." [18] " 'A glow like a blue fluorescent light shone from inside,' said Captain Chiles. Though he could see no occupants, he had no doubt the mystery ship was intelligently controlled. 'Just as it went by,' he reported, 'the pilot pulled up as if he had seen the DC-3 and wanted to avoid us. There was a tremendous burst of flame from the rear. It zoomed into the clouds, its jet wash rocking our DC-3.' " [19]

Chiles, a former wartime lieutenant colonel in the Air Transport Command, with 8,500 hours of piloting to his credit, and Whitted, also a military veteran, an expert in B-29s who was soon to become a passenger captain, agreed that the UFO was traveling at a speed of between 500 to 700 miles an hour and that the after-burning shot out a flame of from 30 to 50 feet long.

The incident occurred in the middle of the night and most of the people in the plane were asleep. However, Clarence L. McKelvie, a managing editor of the American Education Press, despite not noting specifics, also observed the UFO.

Ruppelt, Keyhoe, and other investigators determined that the crew chief at Robbins Air Force Base, situated at Macon, Georgia, "confirmed that a huge wingless craft matching the pilot's description had rushed across the base that same night." [20] In slightly less detailed terms, Ruppelt verified this supportive sighting, and

added one reported by a pilot crossing the Virginia-
North Carolina state line who had participated in a
similar episode [21] at almost the same time as the Eastern Airlines incident.

Dr. Menzel's *The World of Flying Saucers* [22] includes an analysis of the Chiles-Whitted case. Only
four words into his commentary one encounters an
apparent discrepancy. It is stated that the object in
question was "sighted on July 24, 1948." [23] According
to Ruppelt's official account, it was the very early
morning of the following day.[24] On the other hand,
perhaps the head of Blue Book was wrong, for Major
Keyhoe—specifically in one presentation [25] and by implication in another [26] and Coral Lorenzen [27] support
Menzel's dating.

The fact of the plane's departure time being on the
evening of one day and the sighting taking place two
hours and forty-five minutes past midnight into the
next seemingly confused everyone. Wilkins chronicles
the encounter as having occurred at the agreed-upon
time but *on July 22*,[28] which means the airliner left
Houston on the twenty-first. This backdates the entire
affair two days earlier than reported by Menzel, Keyhoe, Lorenzen, and others, and three before the schedule postulated by Ruppelt, Stanton, and others.

Another curious inconsistency in the timing of the
Eastern Airlines adventure is that the National Investigations Committee on Aerial Phenomena records
the event as having happened on *July 23*,[29] leaving one
with the choice of the twenty-second, -third, -fourth,
or -fifth of the month as the actual time of the encounter.

Whichever, it is unfortunate that Dr. Hynek, although said to have accepted the "fireball" explanation
twenty-three years earlier,[30] does not deal with it in
his book.[31] The alleged investigation narrated in the
Condon Report merely lifts quotes and conclusions
from Menzel, a most questionable source for a purportedly objective inquiry, the purpose of which is to
observe phenomena, collect data, and analyze the
results. As he can explain nearly everything in the
sky—to his satisfaction [32]—it is quite apparent that

he is hardly the man to consult about anything *unidentified.*

The difficulty in determining the details of any UAP, UAO, or UFO sighting is evident when the foremost debunker out of the field and the most reputable and reliable spokesman the Air Force has yet to present to the public disagree as to when a major early case occurred.

It may be reasonably argued that the Menzel exposition is more comprehensive than the Ruppelt version. For that reason, his date of record is more likely to be accurate—a discerning commentary on the official half-page summation. In essence, this is Menzel's belief.

The plane left Houston on the evening of July 23, and at two forty-five on the following morning was southwest of Montgomery, flying about a mile high. Visibility was good as the night was clear, under scattered clouds located some thousand feet above the DC-3, through which shone a bright moon only four days past its full stage. Chiles noted a

> dull red glow some distance ahead . . . the brilliant glowing unknown continued to approach with incredible swiftness . . . [the aviators agreed] it looked like a wingless aircraft with no . . . protruding surfaces, was cigar-shaped, about 100 feet long, and about twice the diameter of a B-29 superfortress. It seemed to have two rows of windows through which glowed a very bright light, brilliant as a magnesium flare. An intense dark-blue glow . . . [emanated from] the bottom along the entire length, and red-orange flames shot out from the rear . . . neither man heard any sound and neither saw any occupants.[33]

Menzel grants that Chiles recalled seeing "a lighted pilot compartment . . . with a 'snout' similar to a radar pole, and that a kind of nozzle projected from the rear from which flames fanned out to a width of twenty or thirty feet," [34] but writes that Whitted was conscious of the UFO for less than the ten seconds estimated by the captain. The astronomer remarks that Whitted saw none of the characteristics except the exhaust, which appeared not to be any broader than the object itself. Although unmentioned in Ruppelt's book, Menzel contends that the flight officer took exception to his superior's judgment of about seven hundred feet of passing space, suggesting "the distance to be more than ten times greater, about a mile and a half." [35] Menzel observes that "these disagreements are not remarkable," [36] considering how short the duration of the incident was.*

Overenthusiastic advocates and professional debunkers pick and choose what they wish to believe. Menzel is no exception. At one point in his analysis he dismisses the assertion by Chiles that his DC-3 was buffeted by the object, despite the fact that the description is included in both of the only two official arguments for the Air Force position on UFO—Ruppelt's work [37] and the later updating by Colonel L. J. Tacker a decade and a half afterward.[38] Menzel argues that "in their original report to ATIC" the pilots agreed that "no disturbance was felt from the air waves, nor was there any prop wash or mechanical disturbance when the object passed." [39] Not to put too fine a point on this aspect, one might ask, "What air waves?" There were some, otherwise it would be senseless to assure an inquirer that "no disturbance was felt" from them. It must be assumed, as the entire discussion was related to it, that they were caused by the UFO. Second, it is superfluous to comment that Chiles and Whitted noted no "prop wash" as they had made it clear the question of propellers never arose during the sighting. Finally, the clarification that there was no "mechanical disturbance" can hardly be regarded as synonymous with no "physical disturbance," which then, perhaps, and

---

* The ten seconds estimated by Chiles constitutes a far longer period of time than Menzel seems to realize—in terms of human activity and/or consciousness, as may be determined by asking a deep-sea worker who uses no equipment, a skydiver, a foot racer, a stage performer who has forgotten his lines, or a broadcast interviewer who receives monosyllabic answers from his guests.

certainly later was entered as part of the testimony. "Mechanical disturbance" would assuredly suggest a *malfunction of the machinery* of the DC-3 or, at the least, a variance in the normal pattern of behavior of the vessel's equipment or operation.

Menzel alludes to selected points in the "original report," although it does not support his reasoning or conclusion. Contrarily, on the same page he reverses himself so that he may make light of something "Chiles and Whitted reported [regarding] their frightening * experience" [40] during the "prompt investigation" made by the Air Force. The something Menzel is so prepared to disregard is that "Chiles explicitly stated belief that the UFO was under intelligent control." [41]

Conceding that a check of air traffic eliminated the possibility that the unknown could have been any conventional craft, Menzel fails to mention that his examination screened 225 military and civilian flight schedules. He also neglects to incorporate a contradictory addendum from the Air Force, defining the behavior of the UFO as within understood laws of aerodynamics, a specification that seemed without purpose—i.e., "Application of the Prandtl† theory of lift indicated that a fuselage of the dimensions reported by Chiles and Whitted could support a load comparable to the weight of an aircraft of this size and flying at speeds in the subsonic range." [42]

Subsequently, Menzel comments on "reliable witnesses . . . seeing unusually bright meteors" [43] in the area that night. This is not the same representation as that of Captain Ruppelt, who describes "an extremely bright light pass[ing] overhead, traveling at a high speed," [44] among numerous other sightings in the southeast section of the United States that night.

The astronomer then proceeds to dedicate the remainder of his argument, a portion constituting more than half of his analysis, to an attempt to persuade his

---

* It may be a little presumptuous to assign—if only by implication—fear during the encounter to two wartim> pilots.

† Ludwig Prandtl, German physicist (1875–1953).

readers that "the evidence is overwhelming that the
UFO *was* a fireball." [45] Should one accept his ped-
agogic voice on tenuous points, it is quite possible to
envision the unknown as his convenient meteor. The
major problem with his argument is that it is more
rational to doubt his convenient explanation, so patently devised to fit the circumstances. The technique he
employs, that of fragmenting the incident and offering
possible interpretations for many individual pieces,
could successfully determine that the phenomenon was
atmospheric, neural, or occult.

Menzel weakens his case with assertions such as
"there is no doubt that Chiles and Whitted misinterpreted the appearance of an unusually brilliant
meteor. . . ." [46]

Menzel may or may not be an aviator, but if not
there is little chance that he knows the immediate skies
as well as Chiles or Whitted, or as well as he knows
the distant heavens. It seems that the same unlikeli-
hood would obtain, where instantaneous evaluations
and decisions are demanded, for the chances that he
has put in more than eight and a half thousand hours
in the air, including military flying, are remote. His "scientific" attack evolves from pure conjecture: ". . . a
meteor *often* has a veined or fibrous structure that
could easily have *suggested* the 'lighted window' and
'cockpit.' " [47] * From this point onward, the assumption that he has established the reality of his fireball
depends on the thesis that there were a number in the
sky during that particular month. He speaks of "it"
being fifty miles away. Chiles and Whitted with their
estimated distances—even in Menzel's book—of seven
hundred feet and a mile and a half have now long
since been excised from the astronomer's revision of
the sighting. It has become Menzel's personal and
personally solved problem. His summation is not the
least ephemeral portion of his commentary. He concludes that "it probably burned and disintegrated before it reached the earth," [48] thus explaining how

---

* Emphases added.

Whitted saw it "pulling into the clouds" [49] some thousand feet above the DC-3, and vanishing.

The Air Force, even several years afterward, rejected the Menzel explanation of the Chiles-Whitted affair. Major Keyhoe submitted the question to officialdom directly:

"*Question:* 'Does the ATIC accept his [Menzel's] explanation [fireball/meteor] of the Eastern Airlines sighting, in 1948, near Montgomery, Alabama?' *Answer:* 'No.' " [50]

One tends to wish that the preoccupation of the stargazer led him to more attractive speculations, but, as with most of the extremists, at both ends of the spectrum, he is more dogmatic, even doctrinaire, than objective. Working with second- and third-hand sources, he decided flatly that Chiles and Whitted were visual incompetents, that what he pictured in his mind was more real than what they saw, and, for all practical purposes, only he knew *the truth*. But it went much further than that: In dismissing any conflicting opinion and denigrating the highly trained professional pilots, he also tossed into the refuse pile the following:

> There is no astronomical explanation, if we accept the report at face value. But the sheer improbability of the facts as stated, particularly in the absence of any known aircraft in the vicinity, makes it necessary to see whether any other explanation, even though far-fetched, can be considered.[51]

Eleven years later, when the incident had been wholly forgotten, even by most of the onetime unofficial ufologists, the Air Force scratched a line through the "Unknown" evaluation and scribbled in "meteor."

Still, concentrated study by Edward A. Ruppelt had a cumulative effect on his Air Force-approved book. He wrote: "In intelligence, if you have something to say about some vital problem you write a report that is known as an 'Estimate of the Situation.' . . . The situation was UFO's; *the estimate was that they were interplanetary!*" [52] * It went to the very top.

Speaking conservatively, the judgment was as extraordinary a one as had been made, by presumably intelligent and educated men, in the entire twentieth century, and it was followed and seemingly supported by countless additional incidents. Two will be considered in some detail. The first constitutes the initial publicized "combat" between a UFO and a plane, one of the most inexplicable air-to-air interplays on record. It is commonly evaluated as possibly "hostile" by many ufologists, despite the persistent protestations of skeptics that such behavior has never been reported.† It is known as the Gorman Case.

Examination of the foregoing "classics" began with Ruppelt's officially approved (and amended) versions. The same practice will be followed here.

The incident occurred at approximately nine o'clock in the evening of October 1, 1948, when a second lieutenant of the North Dakota Air National Guard, twenty-five-year-old George F. Gorman, manager of a construction company, engaged in what is generally described as combat maneuvers (when it is not being defined as a "duel of death" [53]) with a UFO. Piloting an F-51, the flier was approaching Fargo at eight thirty, after an extended flight. He decided to cruise the area for a half hour before descending. Michel records the opening of the episode differently from other ufologists, saying that Gorman was not alone in his flight and that "other members of the patrol had already landed at the airport at Fargo, North Dakota, when the control tower notified him that it was his turn, and he could [sic] land." [54] As he communicated with the control tower for instructions, he was informed that there was a Piper Cub nearby; looking about, he clearly spied it below him. Moments afterward he was distracted by another craft sweeping past his right wing and he contacted the tower to complain

---

* Emphasis added; exclamation point in the original.

† Actually, "hostility" characteristics have not merely been chronicled, they are not at all rare. See Lorenzen, Edwards, Wilkins, and others.

and request clarification.[55] Not all accounts completely match this one. Gorman later recorded that, having been cleared to land, he "noticed what seemed to be the tail light of another plane, about 1,000 yards away." [56] Querying the ground, he was told that there was nothing close to him other than a Piper Cub, which he quickly and distinctly identified flying below him, and "it was *not* the one," [57] i.e., the origin of the bright unknown he still could see. Moving in, Gorman determined that the light was about "eight inches in diameter, clear white, and completely round, with a sort of fuzz at the edges." [58] After closing the distance between the phenomenon and himself considerably it "suddenly became steady * and pulled into a sharp left bend!" [59] The aviator gained the impression that the UFO was "making a pass at the tower." [60] Wilkins quotes Gorman regarding the actual "duel":

> I dived after it and brought my manifold pressure up to sixty inches, but I couldn't catch up with the thing. It started gaining altitude and again made a left bank. I put my F.51 into a sharp turn and tried to cut off the light, in my turn. By then, we were at 7,000 feet. Suddenly, the thing made a sharp turn right, and we were headed straight for each other! Just when we were about to collide, I guess I got scared. I went into a dive and the light passed over my canopy at about 500 feet. Then the thing made a left circle about 1,000 feet above me, and I gave chase again.[61]

While the Ruppelt version is not so stimulating, the facts presented differ in no material way, except that his "official" report has Gorman escaping the onward rush of the UAP or UAO "with only a few feet to spare." [62]

Another purportedly verbatim version, while forsaking little of the excitement, has relevantly different

---

* Ruppelt has the light "blinking on and off," p. 42.

wording, and even content. Gorman abruptly banked in
an effort to intercept the brilliant disk.

> When I attempted to turn with the light I
> blacked out temporarily, owing to excessive
> speed. I am in fairly good physical condition, and
> I don't believe there are many, if any, pilots
> who could withstand the turn and speed effected
> by the light and remain conscious.[63]

At this juncture it is interesting to know what was
happening, and being observed, below the aerial adventure. According to some investigators, L. D. Jensen, the traffic controller on duty, responded to
Gorman's contention that there was something aloft
with him other than a mere Piper Cub by acknowledging his sighting of the light. "Look out," he is said
to have shouted. "You were right! There *is* something.
Don't come down. I'll see what it is." [64]

Examining the phenomenon through a pair of high-
powered binoculars, he handed the glasses to a friend,
Manuel E. Johnson, who duplicated his actions. An
air-to-air and two ground-to-air sightings did nothing
to clarify the mystery.

Gorman's report to officialdom did not diminish in
fascination as it continued:

> I cut sharply towards the light which once
> more was coming at me! When collision seemed
> imminent, the object shot straight up into the air.
> I climbed after it to a height of about 14,000
> feet, when my plane went into a power stall. The
> thing now turned in a northwest-north heading,
> and vanished.[65]

The velocities reached by Gorman's F-51 were
estimated, by him, to have approached 400 miles an
hour, and the light was always handily faster, increasing the distance between the plane and it "at will,"
and outmaneuvering the ship effortlessly. What may
have been the first Earthcraft-UFO aerial combat, or

some sort of aerobatic competition, lasted twenty-seven minutes.[66] *Twenty-seven minutes.*

Certain aspects of the encounter were regarded as explicitly factual by Gorman, and a number of evaluations and deductions deriving therefrom incontestable. A few remaining points were considered induction, but, even to him, there was no explanation.

"I am convinced there was thought behind the thing's maneuvers," Gorman reported. Ruppelt's quote reads: "I had the distinct impression that its maneuvers were controlled by thought or reason."[67] "I am also certain that it was governed by the laws of inertia, because its acceleration was rapid, not immediate, and although it was able to turn fairly tightly, at considerable speed, it still followed a natural curve."[68]

This last sentence is of particular interest. It is the considered opinion of an experienced aviator, describing an actual vis-à-vis confrontation with a UAP or UAO in the air. Here we have the behavior of the unknown conforming with accepted physical "laws," in contradistinction to the countless reports by equally reliable and experienced pilots, as well as by expert radar operators, of enormous increases in speed within fractions of a second, even apparent teleportation, in some cases, and accounts of 90-degree or sharper course changes, and frequent testimony of total and instantaneous reversals of direction.

"It could out-turn and outspeed my plane and was able to attain a much steeper climb, and maintain a constant rate of climb far in excess of an Air Force Fighter," continues the Gorman quote.[69]

In addition to the flier and the two men in the control tower, L. D. Jensen and Manuel E. Johnson,* there were other important observers of this extraordinary experience. The Piper Cub, previously mentioned, had remained on the scene. Two occupants, pilot Dr. A. D. Cannon, an occulist, and Einar Neilson,[70] had witnessed the amazing contest, although

---

* Ruppelt, p. 42, tends to dismiss the sighting, remarking that the two "saw a light move over the field once."

their account, understandably, was more general and less dramatic than that of the actual participant.

The Project Sign people, of the Air Force, went into action reasonably swiftly, dispatching investigators to Fargo almost immediately and ordering the plane in which Gorman had flown grounded and left undisturbed. The examination that followed indicated that the craft was more radioactive than other ships at the field.[71] Ruppelt wrote that he "found an old memo reporting the meeting that was held upon the ATIC team's return from Fargo [to Dayton, Ohio, where the UFO office, at Wright-Patterson Air Force Base, was located]. The memo concluded that some weird things were taking place." [72]

Yet the Blue Book chief was merely setting up a situation that was as susceptible as possible to his official explanation. He remarked on several other unusual encounters: an F-47 combat choreography over the Atomic Energy Commission's Oak Ridge, Tennessee, installation, on June 21, 1952, which was like the Gorman case;[73] a sighting over the Hanford, Washington, nuclear plant on December 10, by the crew of an F-94, as well as a ground-based radarman, of a great, white disk emanating a crimson glow from two "windows" [74] and a "dogfight" between a Navy TBM and an inexplicable light on September 24, as the plane was passing over Cuba.[75]

Ruppelt then proceeds to single out the last of these observations and offers the disquietingly irrelevant point that "in *this* incident the UFO *was* a balloon." [76] His sole argument is that a lighted balloon was dispatched on the night after the chase and the pilot was ordered to follow and "compare his experiences" and that, pursuant to instructions from his superiors, "duplicated his dogfight—illusions and all." [77] Ruppelt then extrapolates this alleged resolution of the encounter to clarify the preceding, and other, cases.

Introducing even a small element of logic into the analysis reveals a pattern of inconsistencies: (1) Ruppelt's version devotes nearly thirty lines to a direct quote of the flier's original account of his adventure, but not a single word to an explanation of it. His dismissal of the occurrence is based upon purported *duplication* of the aerodonetics of a specifically directed balloon and a serviceman following orders—one, not so incidentally, whose name is never mentioned; (2) obviously, it would verge on statistical impossibility to actually "duplicate" the activity of the first night, even if the balloon contention were true. Variance of atmospheric conditions, the balloon being a different one and therefore unlike in countless minor respects, would prohibit any such replication. The best one might achieve is a vague and *unverifiable* approximation; (3) even if the experiment resulted in a recognizable, or even a statistically unbelievable, approximation, nothing was proven. Imitation does not, by any distortion of logic, establish that other phenomena, previously or subsequently observed, are the same as a manufactured one, nor that the subject consisted of like composition or derived from a similar origin. Whether sought among the efforts of man alone, as with forgeries, or where man competes with nature, as with simulacra—e.g., imitation diamonds—or within the natural world alone, where insects cluster into a floral form, or one reshapes itself into a leaf, the true structure of which deceives many of its enemies and most men, *likeness is not sameness*. So the duplication technique of debunking is of little scientific value—especially in the investigation of USE, in general, and UAP or UAO, in particular.

Having constructed an untenable analysis of what the anonymous TBM pilot had seen, Ruppelt proceeds to carousel around grabbing the other brass rings. "We plotted the winds and calculated that a lighted balloon was at the right spot" [78] in an effort to establish that the perceptions of the crew of the F-47, and the radarman in the control tower, were inaccurate. Despite all of the points of analytical invalidity described, voiding any such arbitrary conclusion.

Regarding the "white object with two windows," [79] illuminated by a reddish light, it was nothing more than a new, friendly, neighborhood *Skyhook balloon*.

One need hardly be told that Gorman's twenty-seven-minute confrontation was now "explained."

Patently the intention of the attempt to discredit the paralleled sightings. He fought a "duel of death" with a balloon. It is very fortunate that Gorman was merely a highly experienced aviator, a former flying instructor, and a member of the Air National Guard. Otherwise, rather than the half hour he spent in aerial confusion, he might have been racing around the skies after a balloon all night long.

The Air Force had been assigned a job. Propaganda grist was being ground out by the pressures and the presses. A condensation of an *Air Force* [80] article was reprinted in *Science Digest* [81] and emphasized the efforts to condition the UFO responses of career-conscious professional—particularly service—fliers. The report never mentions the Piper Cub or its supportive sighters, merely noting that Gorman "saw a small light in the air below him . . . [and] dived on the light." [82] Although Menzel tends to support the actual position of the unknown at the time of the initial sighting.[83] What Gorman saw at a lower altitude, after having been apprised of it by the control tower, according to Ruppelt,[84] was the Piper Cub. The size, "six to eight inches in diameter," [85] is omitted entirely. *Science Digest* states that "the pilot 'chased' it" up to 14,000 feet; Michel, Menzel, and Wilkins concur, the latter two noting that Gorman's plane stalled at that point, while Ruppelt, Vallee, and the Condon Report do not specify altitude, or have the "combat" centered around seven thousand feet.

Science Digest, in 300 words of debunking, spends more than half the space posing irrelevant possibilities and displaying a common lack of knowledge of the encounter, and of UAP and UAO collectively. The unresearched or revised aspect of the tract is the assertion that ". . . it is impossible to infer from the pilot's report whether the light pursued by him was maneuvering or not." This is untrue, as revealed in Ruppelt's account, which describes the unknown and the F-51 sweeping all around the sky, these activities being observed by others, and concluding with the results of Gorman's vis-à-vis experience, deliberations, and evaluations: "I had the distinct impression that its *maneu-*

vers were controlled by thought or reason." * [86] Hardly consonant with the argument that a "lighted balloon could *easily* have accounted for all of the pilot's observations. . . ." * [87]

The piece remarks on Gorman's possibly having "blacked out" because of the "violent acrobatics" in which he was engaged with the UAO. Clearly a total contradiction of the immediately preceding nonmaneuvering thesis. Still, every attempt is made to tone down the natural fascination a professional aviator would have with enigmas in the sky and *preemptively* to ridicule and discredit any flier courageous enough to admit and describe a confrontation with an Unidentified Flying Object.

Notes

1. Ruppelt, *Report on Unidentified Flying Objects*, pp. 39–40.
2. *Time*, May 9, 1949.
3. Sidney Shallett, "What You Can Believe About Flying Saucers," *Saturday Evening Post*, April 30 and May 7, 1949.
4. Ruppelt, p. 40.
5. Jacques Vallee, *Anatomy of a Phenomenon* (Chicago: Henry Regnery, 1965), p. 54.
6. Ibid. Michel, *Truth About Flying Saucers*, pp. 56–57, places the Hague sighting on July 20, also.
7. Henry J. Taylor has put the time at an hour later. *Reader's Digest*, July 1950, p. 15.
8. Ruppelt, p. 40.
9. Ibid.
10. Ibid.
11. Ibid.
12. Donald E. Keyhoe, *Flying Saucers: Top Secret* (New York: G. P. Putnam's Sons, 1960), p. 87.
13. Keyhoe, *Outer Space*, p. 33.
14. Keyhoe, *Top Secret*, p. 87.
15. Keyhoe, *Outer Space*, p. 33.
16. Ibid. *Top Secret* omits first four words and replaces "we" with "I."

---

* Emphasis added.

17. Keyhoe, *Top Secret,* version contains only final two sentences.
18. Ibid., p. 88.
19. Ibid.
20. Ibid.
21. Ruppelt, p. 40.
22. Menzel and Boyd, *World of Flying Saucers,* pp. 108–114.
23. Ibid., p. 108; also date cited by Michel, p. 52.
24. Ruppelt, p. 40. Also L. Jerome Stanton, *Flying Saucers: Hoax or Reality* (New York: Belmont Books, 1966), p. 38.
25. Keyhoe, *Top Secret,* p. 87.
26. Keyhoe, *Outer Space,* p. 33.
27. Coral E. Lorenzen, *Flying Saucers: The Startling Evidence* (New York: New American Library/Signet, 1966), p. 24.
28. Wilkins, *Flying Saucers on the Attack,* p. 97.
29. *UFO Evidence,* p. 34.
30. "Dr. J. Allen Hynek . . . in his report of April 30, 1949, identified it as an undoubted meteor." Menzel and Boyd, p. 109.
31. Hynek, *UFO Experience.*
32. Dr. Menzel has written of sighting a *pair* of "flying saucers," in an allusion to UAP or UAO. Of course, having put them up in the sky he then attempts to shoot them down. *Look,* June 17, 1952, pp. 80–96. Also see *Reader's Digest,* September 1950, pp. 11–16.
33. Menzel and Boyd, p. 109.
34. Ibid., p. 110.
35. Ibid.
36. Ibid.
37. Ruppelt, p. 40.
38. L. J. Tacker, *Flying Saucers and the U. S. Air Force* (Princeton, N.J.: D. Van Nostrand, 1960), p. 21.
39. Menzel and Boyd, pp. 109–110.
40. Ibid., p. 110.
41. Ibid.
42. Air Force press release, April 27, 1949.
43. Menzel and Boyd, p. 110.
44. Ruppelt, p. 40.
45. Menzel and Boyd, p. 111.
46. Ibid.
47. Ibid., p. 112.
48. Ibid., p. 113.

49. Ibid.
50. Keyhoe, *Outer Space*, p. 14.
51. *Project Grudge Report*. Reprinted in Keyhoe, *Top Secret*, p. 89.
52. Ruppelt, p. 41.
53. Ibid. Presumably meaning a "duel to the death."
54. Michel, p. 70.
55. Ruppelt, pp. 41–42.
56. Wilkins, p. 99.
57. Ibid. Also *Time*, May 9, 1949, p. 98.
58. Wilkins, p. 99.
59. Ibid.
60. Ibid.
61. Ibid.
62. Ruppelt, p. 42.
63. Michel, p. 71.
64. Ibid.
65. Wilkins, pp. 99–100.
66. Michel, p. 72; Menzel, p. 80; *Time*, May 9, 1949, p. 98. Vallee, *Anatomy*, p. 54, says "twenty minutes."
67. Ruppelt, p. 42.
68. Wilkins, p. 100.
69. Ibid.
70. Ruppelt, p. 42; Michel has "Nelson," p. 72.
71. Ruppelt, p. 42.
72. Ibid.
73. Ruppelt, p. 43.
74. Ibid.
75. Ibid.
76. Ibid., p. 44.
77. Ibid.
78. Ibid
79. Ibid.
80. *Air Force*, The Official Journal of the Air Force Association, February 1950.
81. "Psychoanalyzing the Flying Saucers," *Science Digest*, May 1950, pp. 29–34; condensation of article in *Air Force*.
82. Ibid., p. 33.
83. Menzel and Boyd, p. 78.
84. Ruppelt, p. 41.
85. Ibid.
86. Ibid., p. 42.
87. "Psychoanalyzing the Flying Saucers," p. 34.

14

The Washington Wonderland

Based upon unreliable and unscientific surmises as data, the Air Force develops elaborate statistical findings which seem impressive to the uninitiated public unschooled in the fallacies of the statistical method. One must conclude that the highly publicized periodic Air Force pronouncements based upon unsound statistics serve merely to misrepresent the true character of UFO phenomena.

—*Yale Scientific Magazine* (Yale University), Volume XXXVII, Number 7, April 1963

HALLS ACCUSTOMED to the echoes of ignorance, misinformation, and ineptitude suddenly began to reverberate with the tentative whispers of fear and the ominous orders of confusion. The UAP, UAO, UFO, "flying saucers," or by any other name, had targeted in on Washington, D. C.*

The extraordinary drama was prologued, almost immediately before its inception, by the irony of a Washington Sunday *Star* article by Dr. Menzel. It detailed his opposition to the unknowns, being seriously and exhaustively studied. The piece was modestly titled "The Truth About Flying Saucers." [1]

The astronomer was to make a second profession from composing denials of the existence of anything in the skies with which he was not familiar. Less than

---

* Unidentified Atmospheric Phenomena, Unexplained Aerial Objects. Unidentified Flying Objects, and allegedly intelligently controlled craft.

a week earlier he had attacked the idea of UFO in a national weekly magazine.[2] A condensation, published in a popular science magazine in the autumn, opened with the unsupportable claim that "I suppose that I should be especially well qualified to write about flying saucers since I happen to be one of the few persons who has actually seen one." [3]

1. In truth, by the time the statement was made tens of thousands of persons had seen, or seen and testified to having observed, what Menzel and others mistakenly designate as "flying saucers." * 2. How could he or anyone else be "well qualified" to discuss an unknown pattern of phenomena? Only the apparent characteristics of the various phenomena could be weighed. It is curious that practically all debunkers and most supporters of various "flying saucer" theses arrive at their conclusions or explanations by squeezing all of the data presented about any given case into the rigid cast of their convictions, when it is clear that the problem can be approached solely by inductive reasoning. 3. How can the professor write about the existence, let alone the nature, of that which he repeatedly denies even is?

Later in the piece he defensively points out that "as a scientist, I am not bothered if I cannot give a complete, ironclad explanation for every phenomenon I meet." [4] However, he demands of UFO sighters countless precise details, most of which he discounts as not worthy of consideration because of inadequate points of reference, with which they might be compared— e.g., a tree, building, mountain, or conventional aircraft. A few weeks earlier another astronomer, C. C. Wylie, wrote that "NOT ONE 'saucer' has been reported as the result of astronomical observations." [5] While the gentleman may be adequately schooled in his own specialty, he pretends to scholarship to which he demonstrably has no claim, i.e., ufology. Rather than insert a lengthy list of astronomers, both in and out of the observatories with which they are associated,

---

* The proper nomenclature for this subject has been discussed earlier, and further clarification may be found in the Glossary.

who have reported such sightings, only two will be mentioned. First we have the much discussed sighting, at eight in the morning of August 12, 1883, by the astronomer Jose A. Y. Bonilla, of the Zacatecas Observatory, in Mexico, which was located more than two miles above sea level. Observed and photographed, according to record, were a series of flights composed of from a dozen to a score of disks and ovoids crossing the radiance of the sun. While tending to be dark at some points, they were described as luminous at others. In a brief period forty-eight of these unknowns were counted, although more than five times that many were observed.

Wilkins quotes from the original report where Bonilla alludes to the second flight that appeared:

> I had not recovered my surprise when the same phenomenon was repeated . . . in the space of two hours I counted up to 283 bodies . . . I photographed [on a film, or plate, used for recording sun spots and other celestial activity] most of these strange bodies in projection and profile. Some appear round and spherical . . . before crossing the solar disk, these bodies threw out brilliant trains of light, but in crossing the sun they seemed to become opaque and dark, against its brighter background. The negatives of the photographs show the body surrounded by nebulosity. . . .[6]

On the following day he sighted another 116 of the mysterious objects.

The second example, in contrast, is modern and outside the confines of a laboratory. That is an involuntary "field trip" sighting, by world-renowned astronomer Dr. Clyde Tombaugh, discoverer of the planet Pluto. Two sightings were recorded by him.[7]

The remainder of Dr. Wylie's comments reflect knowledge, or even inquiry into, ufology so insubstantial as to offer nothing with which to contend.

Less than a week before the most unnerving sighting in American history, it was reported that a "Navy

Plane Has Flown Twice the' Speed of Sound." [8]
Launched at 30,000 feet, from a B-29 which had
taken off from Moffet Field, California, test pilot
Bill Bridgeman took the experimental D588-II Skyrocket to an altitude of 79,000 feet and a velocity of
more than 1,300 miles an hour. That information was
regarded as confidential, and its release a "leak," but
it was nothing compared to what happened in the skies
above the capital right afterward.

FLYING OBJECTS NEAR WASHINGTON
SPOTTED BOTH PILOTS AND RADAR

Air Force Reveals Reports of Something,
Perhaps 'Saucers,' Traveling Slowly
But Jumping Up and Down

Washington, July (AP)—The Air Force disclosed tonight that it had received reports of an
eerie visitation by unidentified aerial objects—
perhaps a new type of "flying saucer"—over the
vicinity of the nation's capital.

For the first time, so far as has been reported,
the objects were picked up by radar*—indicating
actual substance rather than mere light. [9]

The newspaper asserted that the UFO moved at
speeds between 100 and 130 miles an hour,† and that

---

* Regrettably, this remark by some Air Force spokesman
only and sadly reemphasized the service's ignorance or deception regarding many aspects of ufology. Ground radar
of both the United States and the Royal Canadian air forces
tracked unknowns (at 9,000 mph) at Goose Bay, Labrador, in
the summer of 1948. Radar recurrences at this location are
chronicled for at least two other occasions before the Washington furor. Other instances, which include both ground and
air scope blips, sometimes both, a few with visual confrontation, were recorded earlier all across this country and
around the world from Japan to Germany. See Richard Hall,
ed., *The UFO Evidence*, pp. 76–77.

† Fuller data had the unknowns at speeds up to 7,000 miles
per hour.

they fluctuated in altitude. Occasionally they remained
static in midair.

The Air Force had dispatched no planes to intercept the objects, according to the press.* Operations
Skywatch, the round-the-clock ground-observer effort
then monitoring across the skies of the northern
United States, reported no sightings.

Capt. Pierman, flying normal cruising speed of
180 to 200 miles per hour, reported that three of
the objects, which had the appearance of bright
lights, were seen traveling with tremendous speed.
No special attention was paid to those, he reported to company officials, because these were
taken for falling stars.

Later bright lights were observed, he reported,
flying horizontally, and fast, at a tremendous
height. They were watched from three to five
seconds.

The pilot said he hadn't the slightest idea what
the things were.[10]

Inquiry into the aviator's encounter indicated that
the reportage was less than penetrating. Either a few
key lines had been extracted as rapidly as possible to
make the last deadline for the coming day's issue, or
the entire experience was markedly and intentionally
modified.

Early on in the story it was evident that event was
not an isolated one. Sightings were being logged as far
north along the Atlantic seaboard as Staten Island,
New York, Burlington, Vermont, and South Portland,
Maine.

The New York *Times* detailed to its readers that
"two persons on Staten Island reported seeing saucers
at about 10:15 P.M. (E.S.T.) Friday night. The objects, described as silvery in color tinged with red on
the rims, were reported flying in a 'V' formation of
five, Said [sic] Mrs. Josephine Hetzel.

* Subsequently contradicted by Ruppelt and other Air Force
sources.

" 'I almost fainted when I looked up at the sky and saw what looked like five large dinner plates flying through the sky.'

"Frank Gonder said he saw them, too, 'flying like geese.' 'They gave off a glow and didn't make a sound,' he said." [11]

Ruppelt fully recognized the impact of the appearance of unknowns in the heavens above the seat of government. "No flying saucer report in the history of the UFO ever won more world acclaim than the Washington National Sightings," he remarked.[12] Then he added that inquiries poured onto his desk from London, Ottawa, Mexico City—i.e., from around the world—as well as from the office of the President.

From his perspective, the fires of this particular bewilderment began to spark on July 10, when a National Airlines crew turned in an account of a luminosity "too bright to be a lighted balloon and too slow to be a big meteor," seen at about 2,000 feet above Quantico, Virginia.[13] Three days later another plane's personnel, cruising 60 miles southwest of the capital, monitored a light which rose from beneath their 11,000-foot altitude, paced them briefly and hurtled up into the higher troposphere.[14] Eight objects were reported over Newport News, Virginia, south of Washington, along the coast, by a Pan American crew on the next day.[15]

"A high-ranking civilian scientist from the National Advisory Committee for Aeronautics Laboratory at Langley AFB and another man . . . saw two amber-colored lights 'much too large to be aircraft lights' " [16] traveling soundlessly northward suddenly totally reverse their direction. During the maneuver the witnesses agreed that the unknowns appeared to " 'jockey for position in the formation.' And this time a third light came out of the west and joined the first two; then as the three UFO's climbed out of the area toward the south, several more lights joined the formation." [17] The pair had considerable time to observe these extraordinary happenings—about three minutes. This sighting occurred at about nine in the evening on July 16.

The head of Blue Book made a number of remarks emphasizing the undeciphered nature of the anomaly, but none more emphatic than his concluding one regarding this incident, i.e., "And last, but not least, the man from the National Advisory Committee for Aeronautics was a very famous aerodynamicist and of such professional stature that *if he said the lights weren't airplanes they weren't.*"[18] *

Despite the rapid accumulation of highly provoking sightings only flying moments away from the capital of the United States, the Air Force was unprepared for what was to come and was to be completely immobilized by the tandem of main events yet to be revealed. The first of these incidents began, "according to the CAA's [Civil Aeronautics Association, now CAB: Civil Aeronautics Board] logbook at the airport, at 11:40 P.M. on the night of July 19 when two radars at National Airport picked up eight † unidentified targets east and south of Andrews AFB. The targets weren't airplanes because they would loaf along at 100 to 130 miles an hour then suddenly accelerate to 'fantastically high speeds' "[19] as they departed. "During the night the crews of several airliners saw mysterious lights in the same locations that the radars showed the targets: tower operators also saw the lights. . . ."[20]

Wholly unprepared, in spite of a half decade of writing on the sky, the "in" people felt they had been thrust into a whirlwind of bewilderment. They had employed so much effort denying and caricaturing that with which they were unexpectedly canopied that the skeptical public, the newsmen, the military, and other agencies of government were wholly unequipped to deal with the enigmas. Abruptly, it seemed not to matter how physically near or astronomically far their origin might be, nor what their impact was intended to produce. The journalists tried to cover the story.

---

* Emphasis added.

† It is not without interest that this was the number of unknowns reported in the Pan American, July 14 case, and *may* have been the total number recorded by the aerodynamicist on July 16.

A. F. PONDERS CALLING SCIENTISTS
TO PROBE OBJECTS IN D. C. SKY

The country's greatest scientists may be called in to probe the identity of the mysterious objects reputedly seen in the sky around Washington over the week end.

Thoroughly flying saucer conscious, the Air Force is taking special cognizance of the report of veteran Capital Airlines' Pilot S. C. "Casey" Pierman that he saw at least seven unidentified objects in the sky between Washington and Martinsburg, W. Va. early Sunday morning.

His sightings jibed with those of another transport pilot and other persons in this area and so far away as River Edge, N.J., where Associated Press reporter Saul Pett saw a strange phenomenon in the skies soon afterwards.

An Air Force spokesman last night said a special investigator from the Air Technical Intelligence Center at Wright-Patterson Air Force Base, Dayton, Ohio, will interview Capt. Pierman, a veteran of more than 17 years service with Capital Airlines.

WILL TELL STORY

Capt. Pierman told *The Star* by telephone last night, from his home near Detroit, that he would be very glad to tell his story to the Air Force investigator. The pilot expects to be in Washington Thursday and Friday.

On the basis of what it will learn through interrogation of Capt. Pierman and others, and from press reports, the Air Force will complete a report in this latest of saucer incidents. This report will be submitted to intelligence men at Wright-Patterson for evaluation. Then, it is understood, it will be sent to leading American scientists, who are on call from the Air Force, for analysis.

The Air Force expert on flying saucers reports last night said the service is taking the current sightings "very seriously," as it has all recent reports of strange objects reported in the skies.

In the early Sunday morning incidents, radar tracked the unidentified aerial objects as they reportedly soared high over the Washington area. There was some difference of opinion in official circles as to whether it was the first time that radar had ever accomplished this.*

OTHER "BLIPS" REPORTED

One Air Force Officer said that was so. Another contended radar screens had several times shown mysterious "blips." Another authority contended the screen may have been defective or disturbed [sounding as if he were not analyzing the situation but psychoanalyzing it] and produced objects that shouldn't have been there. [Of course, it is understood that anything that disturbs or confuses the military by definition "shouldn't be there," but, in this instance, presumably the officer also meant that malfunction of the instrument— not a few gliding spots on the scope—was causing the equipment to respond to some electronic defect, although, whatever the origin of the "blips," such impulses *on the radar* screen could hardly be regarded as *objects,* even if they were actually registering the presence of objects elsewhere. But that would have been far too nice a distinction for a "flying saucer expert" in the Air Force.] It was all very confused. [One need not underline that "they" rather than "it," would have been a far more appropriate pronoun in this case.]

The Air Traffic Control Center at Washington National Airport said its radar operators spotted eight of the objects around midnight Saturday, all of them flying in the vicinity of Andrews Air Force Base, in nearby Maryland.

No planes were dispatched in an attempt to intercept the objects the Air Force said. "Operations skywatch" reported no sightings. This is the new around-the-clock ground observer operation now underway around the northern arc of the country.

* See footnote, p. 271.

The story of early Sunday started both with
Capt. Pierman and observers of Air Traffic Control at National. They could not see the reported
objects, however, reported the fact that Capt.
Pierman and another transport pilot saw the objects.

SEVEN EERIE OBJECTS

A Capital spokesman said Flight 807, westbound for Pittsburgh and Detroit, left National
Airport at 1:45 A.M. Washington time, Sunday,
and when between Washington and Martinsburg
the objects were sighted. This was between 2 A.M.
and 2:30 A.M.* Capt. Pierman reported seeing
as many as seven of the eerie things in the night
sky. They were described by him as looking like
"falling shooting stars without tails."

The airline official said National picked up
radar "blips" or contact with aerial objects. Capt.
Pierman, who was cruising at the normal 180 to
200 miles an hour at 6,000 feet, was directed to
keep an eye open for any unusual objects in the
sky. Then, the report said, the objects were seen,
very high in the sky and still in the atmosphere.
At least two of them were in a deep 25-degree
vertical flight, as in descent, it was said.

Two more of the objects were observed in this
attitude of flight, and three more in horizontal
flight, the Capital pilot reported.

OBSERVED FOR 12 MINUTES

Capt. Pierman told reporters he watched the
objects for about 12 minutes. Then, he said, they
disappeared within three to five seconds, thus
attesting to their remarkable speed. At the airport late last night, unofficial disclosures told of
the objects, as "blips," on the radar screen, disappearing and reappearing from the screen in
rapid succession, and in entirely new directions,
which would imply that they were capable of
tremendous speed potentials.

---

* New York *Times*, July 22, 1952, p. 27, cols. 6–7, put this
time at 3:15 A.M.

At his home, near Detroit, Capt. Pierman said last night:

"In all my years of flying I've seen a lot of falling or shooting stars—whatever you call them—but these were much faster than anything like that I've ever seen. They couldn't have been aircraft. They were moving too fast for that.

"They were about the same size as the brighter stars. And they were much higher than our 6,000-foot altitude.

"Please remember, I didn't speak of them as flying saucers [obviously they were UAP or UAO] —only very fast moving lights."

The airport traffic control center also reported another airliner, Capital-National Flight 610, pre-dawn trip reported seeing a light following it from Herndon, Va. to within four miles of National Airport.

Earlier in the day, the Air Force conceded the reports of strange aerial phenomena were increasing. Reports are being received this summer at a rate much higher than at any time since the sightings first flooded the Pentagon in 1947.[21]

If any doubts remain with respect to the tragedy of errors of which most official participation in UFO investigation was composed, Ruppelt's recollections—regarding this major of major cases, at least within the historical involvement of the American military—should destroy them forever. In spite of the air-to-air, radar, and ground observations, and the network [22] of private conversation among officers who either viewed the aerial mystery as their personal province or were intent on determining that whatever was actually going on should not be discerned, "nobody bothered to tell Air Force Intelligence about the sighting. When reporters began to call intelligence and ask about the big sighting behind the [already published] headlines, INTERCEPTORS CHASE FLYING SAUCERS OVER WASHINGTON," they were told that no one had ever heard of such a sighting.[23] Not surprisingly, "in the next edition the headlines were supplemented by, AIR FORCE WON'T TALK." [24]

The information Ruppelt was able to assemble led to the following account.

At 11:40 P.M., in the ARTC (Air Route Traffic Control) radar room of Washington National Airport, a monitor noticed a formation of seven "blips" on his scope, their position indicating that they were registering something slightly southeast of Andrews Air Force Base. Although eight men were on staff for that shift, he was the only scanner present at that precise moment. He thought the machine's response was to a leisurely group of planes, although none was charted for that time or area. Suddenly, as two of the "targets" shot forward and off the screen in an extraordinary acceleration, the radarman realized that he had not been watching any sort of aircraft. He shouted for his senior officer, in charge of the facility, who, glancing at the scope, summoned two other experts. Continuing to study the remaining "blips," the quartet concurred that, whatever the scope was registering, they were not planes.

The suggestion arose that the instrument might not be operating properly and a technician was called in to examine it. He pronounced that it was functioning perfectly.

Calling the control tower, which had its own equipment, the senior officer was informed that personnel there, too, were watching unknowns darting about on the radar screen. Additionally, they had received the report that their equivalents at Andrews Air Force Base were also pursuing similar observations. Each of the other installations had noted almost identical patterns of behavior, including the slow cruising flights and the explosive bursts of velocity. One "target" had been *clocked at 7,000 miles an hour * . . . moved into every sector of the scope[s] and had flown

---

* Emphasis added. Keyhoe credits Washington National Airport tower controllers Howard Cocklin and Joseph Zacko with calculating the UAP as traveling at a couple of hundred miles an hour faster—at two miles per second. Keyhoe, *Outer Space*, p. 65.

through the prohibited flying areas over the White House and the Capitol." [25]

Pierman, airborne just after midnight, was asked by the ARTC controller, at National, to watch for anything unusual. Very soon thereafter the pilot shouted "There's one—off to the right—and there it goes." [26] The "blip" which had been to the plane's right flashed off the edge of the screen. Six additional unknowns were sighted and reported to ARTC by the aviator within fewer than fifteen minutes.

Two hours afterward another excited airline pilot radioed National Airport that a light was following him. The control tower's radar confirmed the fact that something certainly was. Its screen was scanning a "target" behind the ship, and the equipment in the ARTC room was registering both. Four miles from touchdown the pilot said the unknown had soared out of sight; this was recorded by both ground stations.

Later the two separate scopes at National and the one at Andrews Air Force Base simultaneously and in triplication of patterns read a "blip" just north of the capital. Via the communication web, a trio of radar operators, at three different locations, "compared notes about the target" [27] for thirty seconds, before it vanished from the equipment of all of them at the same moment.

Yet, it was not until predawn that what Ruppelt called the clincher came. A new, or returning, "blip" was spotted by the scope at Air Route Traffic Control almost precisely above Andrews Air Force Base, which was immediately notified. The tower personnel there looked into the sky and saw "there was a 'huge fiery-orange sphere' hovering in the sky directly over their range station." [28]

Ruppelt verifies the inactivity of air defense that morning, in these words: "ARTC had called for Air Force interceptors . . . but they didn't show . . . ARTC called again—then again. Finally, just about daylight, an F-94 arrived, but by that time the targets were gone." [29]

It seems pertinent to mention one episode, related

by the director of Blue Book, before we examine his participation in the aftermath of this bizarre business.

A few days prior to the incident a scientist, from an agency that I can't name [intelligence branch certainly, Central Intelligence Agency probably, an even more secret sect quite possibly], and I were talking about the build-up of reports along the east coast of the United States. We talked for about two hours, and I was ready to leave when he said that he had one last comment to make—a prediction. From his study of the UFO reports that he was getting from Air Force [?] Headquarters, and from discussions with his colleagues, he said that he thought that we were sitting right on top of a big keg full of loaded flying saucers. "Within the next few days," he told me, and I remember that he punctuated his slow, deliberate remarks by hitting the desk with his fist, "they're going to blow up and you're going to have the granddaddy of all UFO sightings. The sightings will occur in Washington or New York," he predicted, "probably Washington." [30]

And there was.

The powers in control got around to notifying the *chief* of the Air Force UFO investigation division, Edward J. Ruppelt, midmorning on the following Monday, too long after the fact to have been an accidental delay, he intimates. The Blue Book director accompanied by Colonel Donald Bower, disembarked at Washington National Airport, shortly thereafter, and the top official ufologist telephoned the Pentagon, an effort which succeeded in putting him in contact with Major Dewey Fournet, who was supposed to be the "flying saucer" liaison man in the capital, but who knew little more about the incident than the Wright-Patterson expert.

Ruppelt settled into his room and, at about one in the afternoon, the major telephoned to say that some officer from Bolling Air Force Base (an installation located a short distance east of Washington National

Airport) was in possession of a "preliminary report on the sightings." [31]

The account began with a description of the geographical relationships among the facilities that had monitored the UAP (1) Washington National Airport, approximately two miles south of the city; it featured two radar systems, one designed for distance and situated at the Air Route Traffic Control, the second a limited-scope mechanism, covering a hundred-mile sweep, which, commonly called ARTC, handled all approaching and landing craft at the field. (2) Bolling Air Force Base, as mentioned, was to the east. (3) Farther to the east, on a nearly direct course, was Andrews Air Force Base, which was equipped with a shorter-range radar system, similar to that in the control tower at Washington National. These and other nearby facilities were interlocked with one another by a multiple intercommunications network.

Staffing the ARTC at National Airport were a senior traffic controller, Harry G. Barnes, and six experienced technicians.* There was little activity at twenty minutes to midnight as one of the men, controller Ed Nugent, was monitoring the scope before him. Unanticipated and according to no schedule, seven blips entered from the side of the screen, registering slightly southeast of Andrews Air Force Base. They appeared in patterned flight at a very slow airspeed of 100 to 130 miles an hour, until suddenly two of the unknowns flashed out of the frame at incredible velocity. The officer shouted for his superior as he realized that it was no flight of normal aircraft he was watching. A glance by the ranking officer caused him to summon two additional radar men, James Ritchey and James Copeland.† The consensus was immediate—these targets were no planes. And within minutes the possibility of mechanical malfunction was eliminated— the equipment was working flawlessly.

---

* Keyhoe has said seven. Keyhoe, *Outer Space*, p. 62.

† Keyhoe records that Ritchey and Copeland arrived first and then Nugent called his superior, Barnes. Ibid., p. 63.

The senior controller swiftly determined that the phenomena were being registered on the radar facilities at both the tower at National Airport, where controller Howard Cocklin was on duty, and at Andrews Air Force Base, including their slow pace, explosive speed —one being timed at 7,000 miles an hour. The blips were ranging around the screen, even crisscrossing the absolutely flight-restricted areas above 1600 Pennsylvania Avenue and the Capitol of the United States.

Soon after twelve o'clock Pierman's report came in, followed by his sighting of a half dozen additional UAP; at about two in the morning another commercial pilot reported a sighting; and, although not mentioned at the time, at least three more airline pilots made air-to-air observations of the phenomena registering on all three of the radars repeatedly, and in the location the ground scopes depicted them.

It was not long before dawn when Andrews Air Force Base received a notification from ARTC that it had a target moving fractionally south of the installation's tower, directly above the base's radio range station. Looking up, the personnel clearly saw a "huge fiery-orange sphere." [32] Then it swept out of sight.

Ruppelt has contradicted some Air Force spokesmen who seemed to have no idea of what was happening, or, if they did, were intent on reassuring their superiors that the press and the public never would understand. Perhaps the most important point is the matter of the ARTC request—made at least three times over a period of several hours—that Air Force interceptors be dispatched to investigate this fantastic invasion of national airspace—a petition that went unheeded twice, and resulted in an F-94 finally being sent up near sunrise, long after the UAO had vanished.

All of this data had been given to Ruppelt in a verbal briefing by the Bolling Air Force Base intelligence officer, who assured him—the top Air Force "UFO" investigator—that a written copy would be composed and forwarded to Air Technical Intelligence Center at Wright-Patterson.

Officialdom deluged the public with "possible" explanations ranging from various "false" targets to temperature inversions, but few were inclined to accept the thoughtless theorizing. The radarmen involved were skilled technicians who directed the activities of innumerable planes, and therefore thousands of lives, a day, as they approached and landed, as they taxied out for takeoffs and sailed into the sky. They had seen just about everything that could happen on a scope; the constant drama of "blips" that made their entrances and exits on it was the profession of these experts. The complement at Washington Airport radar facilities had said that what they had monitored "were caused by radar waves' bouncing off a hard, solid object. The Air Force radar operator at Andrews backed them up; so did two [actually more] veteran airline pilots who [air-to-air] saw lights right where the radar showed a UFO to be." [33] And this inexplicable extravaganza over the country's capital had occurred following a two-week concentration of most impressive sightings—by very reliable witnesses, many of them scientists, aviators, aircraft ground personnel, and others—yet chronicled.

Ruppelt made two decisions—to give the press nothing but a "No comment," and to pursue a more thorough inquiry into the Washington affair. He called Lieutenant Andy Flues, acting Blue Book head in his absence, only to find that reports were flooding Wright-Patterson, on an average of about thirty daily, and that many appeared as substantive as the great capital caper. Nonetheless, he declined to change his mind about returning; at least, for a day or two.

What ensued with respect to Ruppelt's attempts to assemble sufficient facts to construct a fully accurate picture of what had actually occurred was improbable in the extreme. First, he prepared his itinerary; he had to visit Washington National Airport, Andrews Air Force Base, two or three airline offices, the weather bureau, and a number of other locations throughout the city. Second, he contacted the Pentagon's transportation office to arrange for a staff automobile, only to be informed that they were for the exclusive use of "senior colonels and generals." Apparently Colonel Bower, who had arrived with him from Dayton, was not sufficiently "senior," as he fared no better in his efforts to procure military transportation for them. They were unable to reach either of the generals with whom they had made contact, and so another approach was obviously required. Forsaking "the hillbilly who was dispatching vehicles," [34] Ruppelt made his way to the finance department to arrange to rent an automobile and, as he was most certainly on official business, charge it to his traveling expenses. The idea of the Pentagon lending itself to such an irresponsible expenditure of the American public's taxes appalled the picayune personnel with their petty vouchers. Are there no buses? Ruppelt was asked. It did the director of UFO inquiries for the United States Air Force little good to explain that he hardly knew the city and even less its public transportation system, and, did he, it would hardly help as he had a dozen or more places to visit and such a mode of movement would stretch his odyssey into weeks. Let a cabbie do the driving, was offered as an alternative; it might be drawn from your per diem. How the officer was then going to be able to afford quarters and food was not explained.

In any event, none of the foregoing really mattered, Ruppelt was told by the strange female who seemed to be the final authority in the "finance department." His travel orders to town specified visiting the Pentagon only, and he should be on his return trip to Wright-Patterson by then, she remarked, concluding that if he didn't have his orders amended and correct his lax ways he would be AWOL, as well. He was then told that his time, and that of anyone else who happened to be around, was up. She was closing the office and going home. Ruppelt's summation of his sentiments regarding that interview is singularly understandable: "At five-one I decided that if saucers were buzzing Pennsylvania Avenue in formation, I couldn't care less." [35] The head of Blue Book was on the next flight back to Dayton, where he found reports descending upon the project with even greater frequency, more than forty every twenty-four hours.

Still, the capital press corps had converts of its

own. Some, including wire serviceman Saul Pett, had the courage to speak out.

A.P. MAN SIGHTS OBJECT IN SKY
NOW HE'S A SAUCER BELIEVER

River Edge, N.J., July 22—I saw a flying saucer myself Saturday night about the same time some unidentified objects were picked up on radar over Washington. From now on you can't convince me there is no such animal. And after 12 years as a newspaperman—almost six of them with the Associated Press in New York—I don't jump to conclusions.

It was like this:

I was sitting on my back porch alone. The night was clear and star-lit, unkissed by the wind.

Idly, I saw a tiny orange ball draw into view from the northwest. At first I thought it was a plane.

ONE CONSTANT LIGHT

Then, as it drew closer, so distant still that it appeared to be about the size of a quarter, I had two thoughts that hit me with an impact.

Planes have two lights that flicker on and off. This object had only one constant light.

Planes make noise. This object was as silent as death. Though my neighborhood—seven miles from New York—is very quiet, I couldn't hear a sound from above.

Later, when a plane did come by, I could see its lights distinctly . . . its engines were very audible.

The object flew to the southeast. I saw it for about a minute to a minute and a half. . . .

To me it looked like a sphere, so deeply orange colored that it appeared almost a shade of rust. It seemed to have depth.[36]

Pett, after dismissing a shooting star, meteor, search-light striking a cloud, balloons, etc., observed: "I wasn't frightened at all because the thing looked so peaceful and so serene. There wasn't any appearance of menace." [37]

The week that followed found Wright-Patterson getting some astonishing accounts of unknowns from sources that were difficult, if not impossible, to discount. For example, jet planes all around the country were pursuing UAP or UAO and losing them—as the unknowns swept into the brilliance of the sun, in locations as separated as Holyoke, Massachusetts, and Los Alamos, New Mexico. Elsewhere, during night confrontations, one also over the Bay State and another to the south in the skies of New Jersey, F-94 interceptors established air-to-air surveillance of indefinable lights called to the pilots' attention by the Ground Observer Corps. The intrinsic radar facilities, with which the craft were equipped, locked onto the targets, but a few moments later the phenomena executed extraordinary evasive maneuvers and were gone.

Within a few weeks the great conundrum had evolved into a matter of—what? The penultimate mass occult manifestation of modern times? The premiere scientific opportunity of recorded history? A threat to national security beyond the bounds of the most paranoid general's fondest nightmare? One could get no solution to the usurpation of the *American* heavens from the press, from the pilots, from the technicians, from the scientists, from the Air Force, from the government; not even the theologians, philosophers, or legitimate mystics had explanations. The only answers were coming from remote and previously unknown farmers and professional cultists who, on other occasions, had specified the exact date upon which the world would end. But did anyone actually have an understanding of what was taking place, all or part, then or later? Now that was, and remains, a question upon which one might speculate.

In any event, the new phase had begun.

Notes

1. Donald H. Menzel, "The Truth About Flying Saucers," Washington Sunday *Star,* July 20, 1952, p. A-34.
2. Donald H. Menzel, *Look,* July 17, 1952.
3. Donald H. Menzel, "A New Theory of the Flying Saucers," *Science Digest,* September 1952, pp. 11–16.
4. Ibid., p. 12.
5. C. C. Wylie, "Saucers Elude Astronomers," *Science News Letter,* June 14, 1952, p. 375.
6. Wilkins, *Flying Saucers on the Attack,* pp. 111–112. Also see Vallee, *Anatomy,* p. 13.
7. Flammonde, *Age of Flying Saucers,* pp. 18 and 27.
8. Washington *Evening Star,* July 15, 1952, p. A-2.
9. New York *Times,* July 22, 1952, p. 27, cols. 6–7.
10. Ibid.
11. Ibid.
12. Ruppelt, p. 156.
13. Ibid., p. 157.
14. Ibid.
15. Ibid.
16. Ibid.
17. Ibid.
18. Ibid., p. 158.
19. Ibid.
20. Ibid.
21. Washington *Evening Star,* July 22, 1952, p. A-15. Copyright 1952, The Washington *Star-News.* Reprinted by permission.
22. Ruppelt, p. 158. The UFO project director records that all of the installations playing any consequential role in this complex "were linked together by an intercom system."
23. Ibid.
24. Ibid.
25. Ibid., pp. 159–160.
26. Ibid., p. 160.
27. Ibid.
28. Ibid.
29. Ibid., p. 161.
30. Ibid., p. 159.
31. Ibid., p. 159.

32. Ibid., p. 160.
33. Ibid., p. 161.
34. Ibid., p. 162.
35. Ibid., p. 162.
36. Washington *Star-News*, July 22, 1952, p. A-15. Copyright 1952. Reprinted by permission.
37. Ibid.

BOOK III

Suspension of Disbelief

15

The New Phase

The only thing we know with tolerable certainty about the Ufos is that they possess a surface which can be seen by the eye and at the same time throws back a radar echo . . . we do not know whether they are manned machines or a species of living creature. . . .

> —Dr. Carl G. Jung, one of the major figures in the history of psychiatry, in his book *Flying Saucers* (New York: Harcourt, Brace, 1959, p. 149)

OFFICIALDOM WAS JOLTED from its easy chair of deficiency or deception by the introduction of a Washington whirligig that was to send Air Force fighters about the capital skies as if they had been caught up in a celestial carousel. The July 1952 carnival of confusion inaugurated phase two of the modern era.

Following the first great sighting of UAP or UAO above the seat of government, all sections of the country were studied with continuing and astonishing accounts. Then a week later—almost to the hour—the second act of the center ring performance of the aerial circus exploded. It was reviewed on the front page of the New York *Times*.[1]

'OBJECTS' OUTSTRIP JETS OVER CAPITAL
Spotted Second Time in Week by Radar.

Washington, July 27—The Air Force said today that jet fighter planes had made an effort to intercept unknown objects in the sky over Washington last night after the objects had been spotted by radar, but that no direct contact had been made.

It was the second time within a week that unidentified objects had been observed in the vicinity of the nation's capital, but no planes were sent up on the previous occasion, last Monday.*

The newspaper indicated that the Air Force had placed the reappearance of the unknowns on the scope of the Air Route Control Center, which functioned under the direction of the Civilian Aeronautics Administration, at 9:08 o'clock local (ESD) time. According to officials, from four to twelve "blips" began cavorting about the instrument's screen. The military was immediately informed of the situation by the civilian agency and a pair of jet fighter-interceptors were dispatched to investigate the nature of the new Washington overflight. These craft were not sent from the nearest Air Force base, but from one situated nearly a hundred miles away at New Castle, Delaware. It seems incredible that no air defense was available at any of the military flying fields nearer the heart of the United States government.

Air Force spokesmen explained that the fighters were clearly visible on the monitoring screen at 11:25 P.M. and were instrumentally directed to the whereabouts above the capital of the mystery "blips." *Two hours and seventeen minutes* were required to scramble a minimum investigative effort, after what were interpreted to be unknown craft transgressed forbidden (even to the planes of our own country) airspace— ten times as long a period as that between the warning and the arrival of, and annihilation by, atomic missiles in the event of a thermonuclear war. The Air Force had revealed either a terrifying incompetence or that it simply knew something that it never told the people. The latter possibility suggests the alternative that it was fully aware that the UAO offered no threat to

* As will be noted, this directly contradicts Ruppelt, who concedes that it took hours to get a ship airborne, but that one did finally attempt reconnaissance as dawn approached.

the security of the nation. It subsequently and repeatedly asserted this, although never clarifying why no danger was involved. Or it understood that an ultimately hazardous condition existed and was incapable of dealing with it.

The Air Force constantly insisted that UAO were not the experimental craft of this or any other country. Awareness of exploratory designs as represented by the Canadian AVRO project left doubt as to the reliability of such announcements by the American military. Therefore, regardless of which of the previously mentioned possibilities obtained—i.e., that it simply had no idea what was happening, that it knew and was positive that the phenomena offered no threat, or that it fully understood the situation and the danger implicit in it, but lacked the military capability to confront the UFO—it was incumbent upon the Air Force to reveal to the American public the truth as far as it was able to determine it. This it has not done to this day.

In an official press release, the Air Force acknowledged that "one of the jet pilots reported sighting four lights in front of him, approximately ten miles, and slightly above him, but he reported he had no apparent closing speed. They disappeared before he could overtake them." [2]

The press tended to agree that the monitoring of UAO by radar substantiated the contention that the unknowns were tangible, rather than merely light, notwithstanding the continual denials of this conclusion by Air Force spokesmen, especially those preceding and succeeding Ruppelt.

Until 11:49 P.M., radar efforts were made to home the jets in on the UFO, without any increased success. Then the aviator who had originally established visual perception of the mysterious lights radioed that he was observing "a steady white light." However, as in the previous instances, it was unapproachably swift.

Planes continued to patrol the skies above the capital until 2:20 A.M., but were not able to isolate any of the "unidentified objects" which were still slipping about various radar screens. Again, no one had bothered to notify the service's designated expert on the subject. Ruppelt's first knowledge of the encore came from a reporter who telephoned, almost immediately after the unknowns returned, seeking a comment regarding the official plans to deal with the persistent aerial intruders. Exasperated, Ruppelt replied: "I have no idea what the Air Force is doing; in all probability it's doing nothing," and rang off.[3]

The same could not be said of the media. The Washington *Star* carried prominent coverage.

UNIDENTIFIED OBJECTS SEEN AGAIN ON RADAR SCREEN AT AIRPORT

New sightings of unidentified objects occurred on the National Airport radar early today, but efforts to track them down proved fruitless.

The Civil Aeronautics Administration said that one of the 12 "blips" appeared on the Air Traffic Control Center screen off and on between 2:30 and 6:00 A.M.

They were fainter than the sightings of the last two Saturday nights, but they appeared in the same general area over Herndon, Va. and Andrews Air Force Base, and seemed to be traveling at from 90 to 120 miles per hour.

Unlike the other two instances of radar detection, it was impossible to get confirmation of anything unusual from airline pilots . . . [for which reason, it was alleged, no fighters were scrambled to investigate] . . . .

On Saturday night a National Airlines pilot reported seeing two lights which looked like a lighted cigar or cigarette and faded out when approached. A United Airlines pilot saw a reddish yellow light seven miles south of Herndon at about 1,200 feet. A CAA pilot spotted two blue lights northwest of Beltsville, and five white lights near Andrews.[4]

Alleged UFO experts at Wright-Patterson Air Force Base issued a statement on the evolving events.

"We don't know the answer positively and there's no use pretending we do," said a spokesman. "We are studying the reports of the sighting of unidentified objects which were spotted on radar screens at Washington National Airport over the week end.

"The only thing we can say is that these reports are being studied by the best technicians and that we are attempting to answer inquiries to the best of our ability."

Sightings over the week end brought about the dispatch of two fast jet interceptors to look for the objects. But actually the jets did not take off from their New Castle, (Del.) base until nearly two hours after the radar watcher at National Airport first saw the unexplained objects on his screen.* The delay was caused by the fact that the reports were sent to a flight center at Middletown, Pa., instead of through the command port at the Pentagon.

Capt. E. J. Ruppelt, from Air Technical Intelligence at Dayton and one of the experts on saucers, was expected to arrive here today for a conference with officials on the new reports.

Meanwhile, the Air Force maintained its stand that it still doesn't know whether any such thing as a saucer actually exists. For several years the experts at Dayton have studied and filed away thousands of saucer reports.

"Of the number, only a small per cent of those received from reliable sources remain unexplained," said an Air Force statement. "The remainder could be accounted for as misinterpretations of various conventional objects, a mild form of hysteria, meteorological phenomena, or hoaxes.

"Of the unexplained sightings it can be stated that they appear in a haphazard fashion and show

---

* Even by the spring of 1952 it was blatantly evident that both of these contentions were unsupportable in the face of expert testimony.

no pattern * which would indicate the objects are being controlled by a reasoning body." [5]

Notwithstanding the modified demurrers from spokesmen of the project, whose explanations were understood to reflect the opinion of the government of the United States, the Air Force was swift in recovering its momentary loss of authority. It took little time for the official policy to reemerge as information releases and to be dutifully promoted by the press. The New York *Times* was one of the earliest enthusiastic denigrators. It featured its dismissal of the subject in two front-page columns, topped by the boldface heading [6]

AIR FORCE DEBUNKS 'SAUCER' AS JUST 'NATURAL PHENOMENA'

Intelligence Chief Denies a Menace Exists—
Objects Believed to Be Reflections,
but 'Adequate' Guard Will Be Kept

The reportage began with an attempt at humor, swiftly proceeding to a "summary," offered by Major General James A. Samford, chief of intelligence. He was identified as the primary service expert on "saucers," ignoring the fact that Captain Ruppelt was the announced head of the small cadre assigned to maintain surveillance of, and analyze reports on, UFO.

General Samford, who soon and repeatedly left no doubt as to his lack of qualifications as an authority in the field, commenced by assuring his audience that the phenomena constituted absolutely no danger to the United States. A statement which, as allegedly nothing was known of those UAP or UAO, labeled "unidentified" even by the Air Force, lacked any reasonable basis.

He then preemptively disregarded tens of thousands

---

* The recurrent sense of déjà vu is a preoccupational hazard in the investigation, analysis, and speculation regarding USE, UAP, UAO, UFO, "flying saucers," and (perhaps) related subjects.

of accounts which had not been "checked by the Air Force, in the last six years," [7] by asserting that none of the several thousand "saucer" reports which purportedly had been examined could be regarded as indications of "the existence of any material object." [8]

How *six* years? The Air Force at no time had pretended that it was monitoring "flying saucers" before they were "invented" by the Kenneth Arnold experience on June 24, 1947, *five* years and five weeks earlier. Samford slip? Was something inexplicable in the skies being scrutinized before the observations of the Idaho flier? Or, perhaps, was what was going on in the heavens not such a mystery to some of the powers that were and be?

With respect to the tangibility of the phenomena, the chief of intelligence simply denied that there existed any evidence to support a positive thesis. This was in diametric conflict with the testimony of countless aviators, radar experts, and other observers who flatly argued that what they had perceived or monitored were "solid."

Samford then reiterated that the country's military equipment included nothing which could be mistaken for the phenomena called "flying saucers." At best, this was questionable. Among a number of possibilities which directly contradicted the statement was the fact that the Navy's Skyrocket D-588 was being tested at the time. On July 27, piloted by the noted aviator Bill Bridgeman, it was dropped from the belly of a B-29 mother-ship, at the altitude of 45,000 feet, and proceeded to hurtle along at 1,238 miles per hour and attain an apogee of more than 15 miles.

The intelligence officer then explained that "radar is capable of playing tricks for which it is not designed." [9] Still, he was no radarman, and it would have been foolish for anyone to succumb to the blandishments of a publicist and dismiss the studied evaluations of hundreds of authorities.

The newspaper reportage of the press conference continued with clichés about temperature inversions, fireballs, missiles, radar "mirages" or "ghosts." One journalist made it clear that he divined that the actual

witnesses were wholly out of their intellectual altitude
and presumed too much when they commented upon
phenomena they have actually seen.

"There are fashions in fantasies . . . in the Nineteen
Twenties there was the Loch Ness Monster in Scot-
land, which was 'seen' by hundreds.* In the Gay
Nineties, the newspapers were filled with reports about
a mysterious cigar-shaped 'airship' allegedly 'seen' over
many parts of the country," † wrote the newsman,
before stumbling among the deflated Skyhook balloon
discards of six months earlier.[10]

One week after the initial appearance of the UAO
above Washington a hardly noticed defense maneuver
was unobtrusively slipped into the press:

> Civilian and military air authorities have agreed
> on a plan to ground all non-military planes during
> any enemy attack.
> The main purpose is to keep civilian planes
> from interfering with radar or visual spotting or
> United States air and ground defense counter-
> action.[11]

As it appeared to have taken the Air Force a couple
of hours to begin to function, once being apprised of
the presence of unauthorized aircraft over the White
House and the Capitol, this arrangement put little
pressure on the private and commercial pilots of
America.

The day after the second sighting the Air Weather
Station of Andrews Air Force Base issued an evaluation which had been discarded by everyone, including

---

* During the last five years a constantly increasing acceptance of the probability of from one to possibly a score of
living creatures in the loch has been noted among both
scientific and nonscientific persons of reputation.

† There is a vast amount of material revealing the witnessing
of "the great airship of 1896 and 1897" by thousands, likely
tens of thousands, of people and absolutely no viable explanation for, let alone acceptable solution to, the mystery has
ever been presented. See Chapters 5 and 6.

most of the service "experts," nearly two years earlier, namely that "those flying things may prove to be only balloons." [12]

Meanwhile, Captain Ruppelt was attempting to find some avenue through an atmosphere of bureaucratic fog, so that he might approach his assigned task of dealing with UAO phenomena for the Air Force. Following the inquiry from his reporter friend about the renewed invasion of restricted Washington airspace, he telephoned the chief intelligence officer on duty in the Pentagon. No confusion there: the officer had never heard of any sighting over the capital. Ruppelt's next effort was to instruct the officer to contact Major Dewey Fournet, the liaison link between his Project Blue Book and the Pentagon, and ask that he race out to the airfield, only a few miles from his home, and check on the situation. The message reached Fournet who, accompanied by Lieutenant Holcomb, an electronics expert working with the Air Force Directorate of Intelligence, took the course recommended. At the ARTC radar room, at National Airport, they encountered the official UFO press representative Al Chop, who had already arrived. These three members of Air Force personnel assigned to deal with problems of this nature, two directly responsible for aspects of the official Blue Book investigation, stood there and watched the radarscopes populated with unknowns. They were privy to the plane-to-tower conversations of the jet pilots vainly pursuing the high-speed objects.

At dawn, Fournet called the Blue Book director, waiting impatiently in Dayton for a report, and told him what had occurred at Washington National Airport that night. For comparison with the previous accounts, this is Ruppelt's record of the event.

About 10:30 P.M. on July 26 the same radar operators who had seen the UFO's the week before picked up several of the same slow-moving targets. This time the mysterious craft, if that is what they were, were spread out in an arc around Washington from Herndon, Virginia to Andrews AFB. This time there was no hesitation in following the targets. The minute they appeared on the big 24-inch radarscope one of the controllers placed a plastic marker representing the unidentified target near each blip on the scope. When all the targets had been carefully marked, one of the controllers called the tower and radar stations at Andrews AFB—they also had unknown targets.

By 11:30 P.M. four or five of the targets were continually being tracked at all times, so once again a call went out for jet interceptors. Once again there was some delay, but by midnight two F-94's from New Castle County AFB were airborne and headed south. The reporters and photographers were asked to leave the radar room *on the pretext* * that classified radio frequencies and procedures were being used in vectoring the interceptors. All civilian air traffic was cleared out of the area and the jets moved in.[13]

The immediate Air Force bases were unable to accommodate the required defense maneuver and planes had to be summoned from much farther away. Despite the same kind of incident having occurred almost exactly a week earlier, the military took more than an hour to investigate.

Alleged security precautions, reflected in the clearing of the room, were dismissed as nonsense by Ruppelt.

When I later found out that the press had been dismissed on the grounds that the procedures used in an intercept were classified, I knew that this was absurd because any ham radio operator worth his salt could build equipment and listen in on any intercept. The real reason for the press dismissal, I learned, was that not a few people in the radar room were positive that this night would be the big night in UFO history—the night when

* Emphasis added.

a pilot would close in on and get a good look at a UFO and they didn't want the press in on it.[14]

When the fighters finally reached the general locale of the unknowns, all UFO immediately vanished from the screens. The pair of F-94s began returning to their base and, as will have been anticipated, the UFO were darting about the radarscopes once more.

Immediately, reports of revolving colored lights over Virginia began to come in, unknowns which were quickly observed on the radar equipment. Another call for jet planes was issued. One ship got into the sky promptly, raced toward the point indicated on the screens, and achieved an air-to-air sighting of the object. Swinging his craft directly toward the UFO and accelerating to maximum velocity only resulted in the unknown vanishing as if somebody was "turning off a light bulb." Nonetheless, the interceptor continued in the same flight path and was able to get a spotting with its own radar, but within moments the incredible speed of the target erased it from perception, physical or electronic. This pattern of found and lost was repeated several times, to no ultimate avail.

Almost instantly, the "blips" were back on the Washington scopes, with the Air Defense Command frantically calling for the fighter planes to hurtle northward again in an attempt to make contact with the UAO over the nation's capital. The results were no different from before. Two F-94s made visual and radar contact at the juncture to which they had been directed by the tower technicians, only to have their targets dissolve in an explosion of unbelievable speed.

Without warning, it seemed as if "our" side got lucky. One of the UFO continued to cruise about the sky over the city as the Air Route Traffic Control radar monitored its movements. A jet was raced to the location and the aviator made air-to-air visual contact with it. As this was *the* chance he shot after it as swiftly as he could, and even went to his afterburners. Again, the object left the military craft alone in the heavens within seconds. The pilot, Lieutenant William Patterson, reported:

I tried to make contact with the bogies below 1,000 feet, but they [the radar controllers] vectored us around. I saw several bright lights. I was at my maximum speed, but even then I had no closing speed. I ceased chasing them because I saw no chance of overtaking them. I was vectored into new objects. Later I chased a single bright light which I estimated about 10 miles away. I lost visual contact with it about 2 miles.[15]

Fournet told Ruppelt that all the specialists, as well as other military personnel, in the radar room during the period were "convinced that the targets were very probably caused by solid metallic objects," [16] and that "there had been weather targets on the scope" [17] simultaneously; this eliminated the argument—subsequently and persistently forced upon investigators and the public—that the UAO were the product of atmospheric conditions. Nonetheless, countless periodicals which invariably assume UFO stances in support of the scientific and/or military continued to promulgate these discredited arguments. A simple example of the maintenance of such positions was to be found in the popularly edited *Science News Letter* [18] five months later. It was asserted that "the Civilian Aeronautics Authority has now confirmed that the 'flying saucers' seen on radar scopes at National Airport near Washington last July were the results [sic] of temperature inversions bending the radar wave." The brief USAF press material went on to contend that "a temperature inversion almost always [exists] when such [UFO] targets appear on . . . radar," [19] a statement in direct contradiction to facts. Afterward, it cut away the ground upon which it had erected its thesis by conceding that "while the temperature inversion explanation for the radar echoes is quite reasonable, it would take quite terrific temperature inversions, which occur only rarely, to produce visual light reflections from the ground." [20]

Specifically, this particular phenomenon occurs extremely infrequently, but the radar screen viewing of unknowns, accompanied by ground-to-air and air-to-air visual sighting, had become an almost uninterrupted chain from long before the incident above the capital and has continued since.

Even as early as a couple of days after the Washington episode, as Ruppelt remarks, radarmen had collectively agreed that if physical sighting supported the radar surveillance they "would have a lot more to worry about." [21] Although it had occurred often earlier on, now these radar operators, the head of Blue Book, and the rest of the military knew "people were seeing the same targets that the radars were picking up, and not just in Washington." [22]

On the night of the second capital affair, all the way across the country, in California, an Air Defense command radarscope had locked onto an unknown and an F-94C had been sent up at once, swiftly converging with the UAO, and achieving its own, confirming radar contact. Racing to the sky point indicated, the pilot and the radarman saw a great amber-rust light directly ahead of them. Two sets of radar equipment and two highly skilled technical observers were monitoring the Unidentified Flying Object, all at the same time. The F-94 pursued the object tenaciously, but, along with the radar equipment below, its scope revealed that whenever it even approached its gunnery range the unknown—as if it was conscious of exactly how far the fighter's threat extended—suddenly accelerated at unbelievable velocities, only to let the plane come closer again before it repeated its amazing performance.

Ruppelt interviewed the aviator and the radarman, who told him that they felt they had been involved in some vast cat-and-mouse game, which they did not enjoy at all. "At any moment they thought the cat might have pounced." [23]

Then came General Samford's famous press conference, the lengthiest and most heavily attended for the Air Force since the Second World War, which had concluded seven years earlier. That debacle, which accomplished the AIR FORCE DEBUNKS SAUCERS AS JUST NATURAL PHENOMENA headlines, has already been examined.

In his summation of his investigation and analysis of the Washington furor, the director of Blue Book made every attempt to offer possible explanations, but there is little doubt that their fragility was evident, even to him. On the other side, employing his usual fairness, the supportive material with respect to the presence over the capital of something yet to be defined was singularly strengthening. Ruppelt conceded "that the UFO's frequently visited Washington." [24] Ruppelt continues:

On May 23 [approximately two months before the initial pair of appearances] fifty targets had been tracked from 8:00 P.M. to midnight. They were back on Wednesday night between the two famous Saturday-night sightings, the following Sunday night, and again the night of the press conference; then during August they were seen eight more times. On several occasions [notwithstanding protestations, such as the one previously mentioned which found its way into the *Science News Letter*] military and civilian pilots saw lights exactly where the radar showed the UFO's to be.

On each night that there was a sighting there was a temperature inversion but *it was never strong enough to affect the radar the way inversions normally do.** On each occasion I checked the strength of the inversion according to the methods used by the Air Defense Command Weather Forecast Center.[25]

Quite properly Ruppelt regarded as of particular consequence the fact that "hardly a night passed in June, July, and August in 1952 that there wasn't an inversion in Washington, yet the slow-moving, 'solid' radar targets appeared on only a few nights." [26]

The Air Force's UFO expert defended the perfected skills and intelligence of the much-maligned specialists manning the radar equipment, again calling attention

---

* Emphasis added.

to their responsibility for shepherding thousands of passengers and crews into Washington National Airport daily, and emphasizing the certainty that their perception was more than adequate to distinguish a material object, which they directed in and out of the field scores of times on each shift, from an atmospheric phenomenon plainly discernible in any of its usual forms and especially so in those rare instances when they assume uncommon attributes on the screens.

Blue Book had come, inquired, inspected, and weighed the equipment, testimony, and circumstances, and, finally, drawn a conclusion, which was, in Ruppelt's words, even in the modified version published four years afterward: "So the Washington National Airport Sightings are still unknowns." [27]

In conjunction with scientific policy, amplified through the press, the Air Force persisted in its more general denials that anything of consequence was happening, except in the most isolated instances. The month of July, during which two Saturday night mysteries were manifest above the government of the United States, featured other important sightings. There were—

The United States Air Force captain, plus a young couple, who saw two mercury-colored, elongated, ovoid-shaped UAO cross over Boston at about seven thirty in the morning on July 1, outracing a pair of pursuing F-94 fighters; [28]

The tracking of two objects on SCR 584 equipment by three radar instructors and a dozen apprentices at Fort Monmouth, New Jersey, followed closely afterward on the same day. The unknowns, moving around at about 50,000 feet, were visible on the screen for more than five minutes; [29]

And later in the day there occurred an eight-minute observation by at least a hundred people, including a physics professor from George Washington University, of a neutral-toned UFO moving about the sky. [30]

July 2 was the date that Warrant Officer D. C. Newhouse recorded UAO over Utah on motion-picture film. Details of that will be introduced shortly.

Sightings of lesser and greater import were coming

in daily. Ruppelt summed up the growing number of accounts later, saying "By July 1 we were completely snowed under with reports." [31]

Off the coast of North Korea, the complement of the *Crusader,* a Canadian destroyer, saw and tracked a pair of UAO operating at about two miles altitude. The date was July 10. Two days later a considerable number of people, among which was an Air Force weather officer holding the rank of captain, watched a large red object, ringed with small white lights, fly overhead, stop, and reverse its course, along the Lake Michigan beachfront in Chicago.[32]

Pan American Airways pilots monitored a flight of a half dozen UFO, which altered direction at aeronautically improbable angles, and were subsequently met by two additional unknowns, above Newport News, Virginia, on July 14. Forty-eight hours passed and an aeronautical research engineer observed four yellowish lights "rendezvous" above Hampton, Virginia.

This episode took place at nine o'clock in the evening, on July 16, 1952, and was witnessed by Paul R. Hill, an aeronautical research engineer, with a BS degree from the University of California and thirteen years of practical experience in his field of expertise. He said of the amber-colored lights which caught his attention:

> Two were seen first coming over Hampton Roads at about 500 mph from the south. These slowed down as they made a "U" turn at the southern edge of the Peninsula [formed by the confluence of the James River and the Chesapeake Bay]. They moved side by side until they revolved around each other at a high rate of speed in a tight circle 2 or 3 hundred feet in diameter. This appeared to be a rendezvous signal as a third UFO came racing up from the direction of Virginia Beach and "fell in" several hundred feet below the first two, forming a sort of "V" formation. A fourth UFO came in from the James

River and joined the group which headed on south at about 500 mph.[33]

This is the same sighting mentioned by Ruppelt in his study of the incident and mentioned earlier, but the subject's direct quote is pertinent and adds value to the Air Force expert's testimony. The head of Blue Book has flatly conceded that while some B-26 planes from Langley Air Force Base were aloft that evening "all of them had generally stayed well north of Norfolk [the sighting area] until about 10:30 P.M. [an hour and a half after the observation]" [34] Granting the nonaircraft thesis, he supports the UFO argument with a series of concessions, including the fact that the unknowns were absolutely silent, that neither military nor civilian ships feature one, or two, "amber" lights, and that the spacing of the illuminations was so great as to have required the vessel to have been huge. Finally, and perhaps of greatest importance, was Ruppelt's summation that "the man from the National Advisory Committee for Aeronautics [Mr. Hill] was a very famous aerodynamicist and of such professional stature that if he said the lights weren't airplanes they weren't." [35]

Earlier photographs from military personnel included one taken by a Coast Guard seaman, Shell Alpert, on the same July 16, as it traversed the skies of Salem, Massachusetts. It consisted of four brilliant elliptical white lights on black and white film. According to an official letter, of August 8, 1962, ten years later, a copy of which is in the files of the National Investigation Committee on Aerial Phenomena, ". . . it has never been determined what caused the phenomenal lights shown [in the photograph]." [36]

This was succeeded by a two-minute sighting, two days afterward, by an American Airlines pilot. Captain Paul Carpenter and crew members saw three UAO, which apparently made a 180-degree change in course in an instant. The incident occurred near Denver, Colorado.

Two officers, weather specialists, stationed at Patrick Air Force Base, in Florida, as well as other persons, watched four yellowish lights moving about the perimeter of the installation, on the same day.

The first Saturday-night amazement hit Washington then.

A couple of days following that, an F-94 flier spotted a blue-green UFO, which was also viewed from the ground, and was able to secure it on his radar equipment. He pursued the unknown at maximum speed, but was wholly unable to maintain its pace. It disappeared in the upper altitude.

Again and again, fact contradicted the persistent propaganda of the Air Force that "qualified" individuals were not among those who contributed observations of these spectacular phenomena.

The evolution continued to the incredible climax in Washington during the final third of July 1952, and for all of the years since. One can hardly contest that the government, usually in the form of the Air Force, has constantly denied that in any of these tens of thousands of cases a reality existed. Authority did protest too much.

Notes

1. Associated Press. From New York *Times*, July 28, 1952, front page, col. 2.
2. Ibid.
3. Ruppelt, *Report on Unidentified Flying Objects*, p. 163.
4. The Washington *Star-News*, July 29, 1952, p. A-3. Reprinted by permission.
5. Ibid.
6. New York *Times*, Austin Stevens story, July 30, 1952, front page, cols. 2–3, cont. p. 10.
7. Ibid.
8. Ibid.
9. Ibid.
10. New York *Times*, William A. Laurence story, July 30, 1952, p. 10.
11. Washington *Star*, July 28, 1952, p. B-1.
12. Ibid., front page.
13. Ruppelt, p. 164.
14. Ibid.

15. Ruppelt, pp. 165–166.
16. Ibid., p. 166.
17. Ibid.
18. *Science News Letter*, December 20, 1952, p. 388.
19. Ibid.
20. Ibid.
21. Ruppelt, p. 167.
22. Ibid.
23. Ibid., p. 168.
24. Ibid., p. 170.
25. Ibid.
26. Ibid.
27. Ibid.
28. Richard Hull, ed., *UFO Evidence*, p. 84.
29. Ibid. Also, p. 158.
30. Ibid.
31. Ruppelt, p. 151.
32. *UFO Evidence*, p. 132.
33. Ibid., p. 57.
34. Ruppelt, p. 158.
35. Ibid.
36. *UFO Evidence*, p. 88.

16

Era of Evidence

If the Intelligence of these [UFO] creatures were sufficiently superior to ours, they might choose to have
little, if any, contact with us.

—Brookings Institution (in a report on extraterrestrial life).
New York *Times*, December 15,
1960

THE PANORAMA of remarkable UAO sightings preceding and following the Washington affair constituted

one of the most amazing periods of American, even world, history. It is of secondary consequence whether one views the picture drawn as an intimation of interplanetary communication, or even travel; of new and, as yet, inexplicable astronomical activity; of serendipitous encounters with unknown variations on accepted physical laws or the initiation, for the earth, of unknown ones; of long-awaited messianic, or less specific religious, or general theological, metaphysical, or occult principles; of socio-psychological aberration or adjustment affecting the majority of mankind. The point of concern is that something globe-engulfing was under way. A collective phenomenon had been inaugurated for which the most respected scientific, philosophic, and artistic sages had no explanation, and which, for all practical purposes, was being totally ignored by them, their societies, and their governments alike. Only the public cared.

And the public be damned!

There are incidents that preceded the aerial assault on the capital's airspace which cannot be ignored in even the most general reflection on the modern age of UFO. This is not to say there were not numerous other cases preceding the Washington escapade deserving of recognition, only that limitations of space require the introduction of personal selectivity. The wisdom of the balance, in this exercise, between arbitrariness and critical acuity is a determination which must be left to the reader.

May 11, 1950. McMinnville, Oregon. Paul Trent, a citizen of a small town, with a reputation for integrity, took two photographs of round UAO, featuring a cabin, resulting in a pair of the most detailed such pictures in the chronology of the subject. Printed in a national magazine, with the editorial comment that "the negatives show no signs of having been tampered with," [1] they remain visual evidence of phenomena yet to be explained.

August 15, 1950. Great Falls, Montana. Simple still representations of UFO are most difficult to come by. Even the best, unless they contain undeniable points of reference, may be subject to attacks which

are difficult to totally dismiss, for, as the historical,
maritime, science and horror motion pictures have
made clearly evident, simulation is a highly developed
technique. The characteristic of spontaneity seems inherent in the rare examples of cinematically recorded
unknowns; therefore, a full and careful analysis must
be demanded in the case of such movie film. Among
the most extraordinary ever obtained were taken by
Nicholas Mariana, of Missoula, Montana. Accompanied by his secretary, he was checking out the local
sports park, when a pair of UAO were sighted high
overhead. Mariana, owner of the local radio station,
hurried to his nearby automobile for his 16mm camera
and raced back to preserve these "flying saucers" for
posterity. His equipment was a Revere turret-design
camera, which was filled with Daylight Kodachrome
film, 315 frames of which were exposed on the unknowns. To Mariana's naked eye, as he trained the
lens on one of the glistening objects, the UFO appeared to halt. Soon they continued drifting away
along their original flight path. The motion picture reproduced what they saw. Processed by the professional
Eastman Laboratory, it was shown to a number of
people, and then delivered to the Air Technical Intelligence Center, of the United States Air Force,
Wright-Patterson Air Force Base, for the purposes of
analysis. Despite the contention of the Pentagon,
through the voice of UFO spokesman Al Chop, the
consensus of the military was that nothing decisive
could be established from the film. Nevertheless, Ruppelt later completely dismissed the suggestion that
Mariana had been photographing balloons. While allegedly devoting time and expertise to a study of photographs, neither the Air Force nor the Navy ever
supplied the press or public with any official position
paper on this remarkable motion picture.

Subsequently, Robert M. L. Baker, Jr., for some
time with the Douglas Aircraft Corporation, and an
expert photogrametric analyst, studied the film. He
dismissed the suggestion that the UFO were jet aircraft as highly unlikely. The objects could not be
assumed to be any specific phenomenon. That is to

say, Baker's exhaustive analysis positively concluded that, like the Establishment, he had no idea what had flown, as a series of "bright circular points of light . . . confirming visual observation of discs with rotating rims," [2] over the baseball field in Montana two years before similar objects transgressed the privacy of the air above the center of American politics.

August 25, 1951. Lubbock, Texas. A report was delivered to Captain Edward J. Ruppelt, from the 34th Air Defense Command at Kirtland Air Force Base, located near Albuquerque, New Mexico. It informed him that an employee of the highly restricted Sandia Corporation, a subsidiary of the Atomic Energy Commission, and his wife had a startling visual experience. The incident occurred on the night of August 25, as the couple enjoyed the evening in their yard, in the outlying district of the town. Simultaneously, the pair perceived what appeared to be an enormous, swift, and noiseless airship passing over at an extremely low altitude, which they agreed to have been no more than a thousand feet. The witnesses described the object as having the shape of a fuselageless flying wing, constructed in a swept-back design so that it resembled the letter *V*. It was at least half again larger than a B-36, craft of which kind constantly passed above their home. While no color was apparent to them against the evening sky, they concurred that there appeared to be dark stripes running along the wing, and a half dozen or more bluish lights studding the afteredge of the vessel.

The head of Blue Book then received another report for the identical date, and for the same time, plus twenty minutes. This sighting must be ranked as among the best witnessed of the decade, if one measures in terms of the scientific expertise of the observers, which the professional demeaners usually contend never appear as the source of such reports. The company that watched a formation of from one to three dozen turquoisish lights sweep the sky, from north to south, consisted of Dr. W. I. Robinson, professor of geology; Dr. A. G. Oberg, professor of chemical engineering; Dr. George, professor of physics; and Professor W. L. Ducker, head of the department of petroleum engineering, of the Texas Technological College.

On the morning following the twin report, which Ruppelt felt was a "truly amazing" tandem, a nearby radar station, of the Air Defense Command network, reported two separate sets of equipment registering a target at 13,000 feet, and traveling 900 miles an hour. The UAO was locked on both scopes for six minutes before an F-86 scrambled after it, only to be left alone in the sky. Ruppelt makes a particular point of the report's emphasis that "the target was not caused by weather," adding, "the officer in charge of the radar station and several members of his crew had been operating radar for seven years and . . . this target was real." [3]

"This was by far the best combination of UFO reports I'd ever read and I'd read every one in the Air Force's files," [4] Ruppelt remarked.

The four Texas scientists were sitting on the rear lawn of Dr. Robinson's home discussing micrometeorites. When afforded the extraordinary opportunity they absorbed as much data as they could, individually and collectively. Nonetheless, they immediately agreed on how much they would like to have had a few moments longer to commit their observations to swift analysis and memory. Fortunately, it was a more remarkable night than they imagined. As a matter of fact, a most important period in their lives, at least from a scientific point of view. Within about an hour a *second* overflight occurred. Except that the regulated flight pattern had altered from a formal geometric design to what might be best described as a cluster, it was similar to the earlier episode. Yet, things did not end there.

The double sighting led the professors to anticipate the possibility of further such aerial exhibitions and they prepared themselves to monitor that area of the sky nightly and to get as much information as they could. Over a period of about a month, during the later phase of which two additional monitors were added to their group, twelve more sightings were ac-

complished. In a number of these cases quite explicit
particulars were reported, e.g., they "traveled through
90 degrees of sky in three seconds, or 30 degrees per
second. The lights usually appeared 45 degrees above
the northern horizon, and abruptly went out 45 degrees
above the southern horizon. They always traveled in
this north-to-south direction. Outside of the first flight,
in which the objects were in a roughly semicircular
formation, in none of the rest of the flights did they
note any regular pattern. Two or three flights were
often seen in one night." [5]

The Lubbock Lights story involves the testimony of
hundreds of people, mostly located within a few miles
of the community. Many of these observers saw the
lights repeatedly and in various numbers. On the night
of August 31 amateur photographer Carl Hart, Jr.,
got two photographs of the phenomenon with a Kodak
35 still camera set at f 3.5. The formation shown is a
definite echelon pattern and the photographs generally
seemed to be analytically acceptable to some experts
and questionable to others. After hearing and weighing
the opinions of various laboratories, Ruppelt issued
the official conclusion on the Hart pictures: " 'The
photos were never proven to be a hoax but neither
were they proven to be genuine.' There is no definite
answer." [6]

The summation of Ruppelt's sixteen-page review of
the Lubbock episode, fifteen and a half pages of which
had been reasonably objective, suddenly converted
into a three-paragraph piece of propaganda. He granted numerous points which were totally contradictory
to this final fillip, among which was his concession
that a group of "scientists—rocket experts, nuclear
physicists, and intelligence experts," [7] who "due to
their association with the government, had complete
access to our files," [8] found that the Lubbock business
"convinced them all the more that their ideas of how
a [extraterrestrial] spaceship might operate were correct," [9] and, perhaps, had been demonstrated.

In a penultimate passage amplifying the position of
this openminded clique within the inflexible scientific
and intelligence communities, and an admission that

a Canadian government project for a device similar to the "flying saucer" concept had been relinquished to an aerial development laboratory of the United States Air Force, Ruppelt resolves his treatment of the case in a fashion consonant with the general tenor of his examination and commentary:

> This is the complete story of the Lubbock Lights as it is carried in the Air Force files, one of the most interesting and most controversial collection of UFO sightings ever to be reported to Project Blue Book. *Officially all of the sightings,* except the UFO that was picked up on radar [a peripheral incident not discussed here], are unknows.[10] *

Ruppelt adds that he had thought the lights might have been reflections from birds, and immediately proceeds to say they weren't. Then, blatantly an afterthought reflecting hard-line officialism, comes the logically insufficient and reportorially inadequate addendum: "The lights that the professors saw—the backbone of the Lubbock Light series—have been positively identified as a very commonplace and easily explainable natural phenomenon. It is very unfortunate that I can't divulge exactly the way the answer was found," [11] or how "a scientist" discovered it, as "telling the story would lead to his identity and, in exchange for his story, I promised the man complete anonymity." [12] All of which is to say that Ruppelt was asking the public to dismiss what he regarded as "by far the best combination of UFO reports I'd ever read." They were nothing man-made, no animal, but a simple atmospheric condition, the nature of which he was not at liberty to tell, isolated by a famous scientist, the identity of whom this great man was too modest to have revealed. Fortunately for those who like a good tale, the people who tell of their travels in flying saucers tend to provide more convincing explanations —and virtually no one believes *them.*

---

* Emphasis added.

July 2, 1952. Tremonton, Utah. At less than an hour before noon, on a bright, clear morning, Warrant Officer Delbert C. Newhouse, accompanied by his wife and two children, was cruising casually along the open highway a half dozen miles from Tremonton, in northern Utah. Shortly thereafter he testified that

> . . . my wife noticed a group of objects in the sky that she could not identify. She asked me to stop the car and look. There was a group of about ten or twelve objects—that bore no relation to anything I had seen before—milling about in a rough formation and proceeding in a westerly direction. I opened the luggage compartment of the car and got my camera out of the suitcase. Loading it hurriedly, I exposed approximately thirty feet of film. There was no reference point in the sky and it was impossible for me to make any estimate of speed, size, altitude or distance. Toward the end one of the objects reversed course and proceeded away from the main group. I held the camera still and allowed the single one to cross the field of view, picking it up again and repeating for three or four passes. By this time all of the objects had disappeared.[13]

Delbert C. Newhouse, at the time of his sighting, had been graduated from the naval photographic school, and was a veteran with nineteen years' service as a warrant officer, logging more than a thousand hours on aerial photography missions, and twenty-two hundred as chief photographer.

The equipment Newhouse employed in the motion picture of the flight of UAO against the deep blue morning sky was a Bell and Howell Automaster 16mm camera on which he fortunately had time to pivot the turret mount to the three-inch f.1 telephoto lens. The film was Kodachrome Daylight type and the camera was hand-held during the f/8 and f/16 exposure times.

Subsequently, this motion picture was analyzed at the Wright-Patterson Air Force Base—i.e., Blue Book's laboratory—an examination duplicated by a second exhaustive evaluation by the photographic section of the Navy's Anacostia facilities. The former determined that the UFO were neither airplanes nor balloons, and most unlikely to be birds. The subsequent investigation of the other service concluded that the objects were none of the foregoing. In view of later official claims, it behooves one to remember that *neither* analysis remotely suggested that the objects photographed were birds of any type. To the contrary, there was almost a complete consensus that such a deduction was untenable. Ignoring these concurring summations, a decade later the Air Force thought public amnesia sufficiently advanced for it to issue an uncirculated press release, caustically titled: *"Ode D Classic—Seagulls."* It attempted to persuade the tiny handful of people who would ever see the material that Warrant Officer Newhouse—with more than a thousand hours in military aerial photography—had filmed a flight of birds, and not known it.

The witness, in a second deposition, a month later, recalled that he had heard no sounds, seen no exhaust or wake effects emanating from the objects. Neither before, during, nor after did planes, birds, balloons, or other recognizable phenomena appear in the UAO viewing area. He restated that the one unknown which took off on its own pursued a course opposite to its original one and to the flight path maintained by the remainder of the group. Newhouse was convinced that the light from the objects resulted from reflection and that they were as long as they were wide.

The Condon Report devotes nine pages to *not* proving that the Tremonton film shows birds. In fact, it pointed out that the reiteration of this discounted conclusion, as drawn by Menzel, was "phrased in a way inconsistent with the facts." [14] America's foremost private denigrater of ufology had written: "The pictures are of such poor quality and show so little that even the most enthusiastic home-movie fan today would hesitate to show them to his friends. Only a stimulated imagination could suggest that the moving objects are anything but very badly photographed birds." [15] The Colorado project emphasized that this description gave a "totally wrong impression that the objects are difficult to identify merely because of poor photography . . . the images are small and relatively sharp, and lack of a clear identification [attributable to less than desirable resolution because of distances involved] cannot be ascribed to poor photography." [16]

The U.S. Naval Photographic Interpretation Center found, in brief, that the unknowns give the impression of being "a light source rather than reflected light," [17] and that no species of bird could be responsible for the glow inherent in the objects. Added to these determinations they estimated the speed of the UAO "to be 3780 mph." [18]

The question of the Newhouse, as well as the Mariana, photography has been evaluated by numerous groups, the majority of which have eliminated all probability of misidentification of balloons, aircraft, birds, clouds, radar foil, ice particles, and just about anything else tangible found in the air. Not even Menzel has opted for temperature inversions or sundogs in this case. There are advantages to having captured your sighting on "celluloid." Nonetheless, most official groups continued to have demanded of them some sort of conclusion. The pressure resulted in various of them persisting in the suggestion that Newhouse, a professional observer if ever one could be found, didn't know what he was seeing. This he concedes, but, additionally, they strain the impression of disbelief to the extreme when they assert that he and his family didn't know what they *weren't* seeing.

July, 14, 1952. Norfolk, Virginia. Captain William B. Nash and co-pilot William H. Fortenberry had flown for more than ten years and were credited with many thousands of hours of air time, when, at nearly a quarter past nine, on July 14, 1952, they were cruising their Pan American DC-4 8,000 feet over Virginia, approaching Norfolk, and perceived a great crimson light directly in their path, but slightly below their altitude. The sky was unclouded, visibility unlimited, and the lights of Newport News could be seen off to their right.

Suddenly the enigmatic radiance became discernible

as a half dozen, separate, enormous disks, testified
Captain Nash. The conformation of the UFO

> was clearly outlined and evidently circular . . .
> [and the] edges were well-defined, not phosphores-
> cent or fuzzy in the least . . . we could observe
> that they were holding a narrow echelon formation
> —a stepped-up line tilted slightly to our right.
> With the leader at the lowest point and each
> following craft slightly higher.[19]

The foremost of the UAO reduced thrust and the
objects immediately behind it closed the intervening
distance rapidly. Nash and Fortenberry calculated
their uninvited companions to be flying a couple of
thousand feet below. Each unit was estimated to be
about 35 yards in diameter. The maneuvers of the
disks were often abrupt, in that they would instantane-
ously adjust their position by 90 degrees, only to alter
their angle moments later. All in unison. For example, ". . . they flipped on edge, the sides to the left of
us going up and the glowing surfaces facing right." [20]
The professional fliers established that the under-
surface of the vessels featured no illumination, at least
none was ever made visible to them. The rims, which
they gauged to be about five yards from top to bottom, also lacked lights. In terms of configuration, the
Pan American pilots found the analogy of "like coins"
acceptable.
The sighting progressed. During a period when the
UAO were tilted on their sides five of the craft slipped
out and ahead of the leader, causing, in effect, a complete inversion of the echelon. The previous lead ship
then was nearer to the DC-4 than any of the others,
as the remainder of the flight moved out to take their
positions in the reverse formation. If all this were not
sufficiently disconcerting to the veteran pilots, the situation was intensified with the arrival of a pair of new
unknowns which unerringly shot into position within
the flight. The complexity was then compounded as
all eight of the disks became lightless only to become
visible again a moment later, at which point they arced

northwest of the airliner and disappeared, by what seemed to be the process of extinguishing all light emanating from them, one by one. Yet even this was not accomplished in a foreseeable fashion. The UAO simply blinked out randomly, or at least, in no order that made any sense to the observers.

The Air Force descended on Nash and Fortenberry —by telephone, at seven the next morning—to arrange for an inquiry. When effected, officialdom consisted of one uniformed Air Force officer and four men in civilian clothing flashing about identifications indicating they were "Special Investigators" * for the service. The two distinguished commercial aviators were interrogated for nearly two hours separately, and for an additional thirty minutes together. They answered all possible questions, offered all possible observations applicable to areas overlooked by the inquisitors, made sketches, and roughed out charts, and the oral aspect of the interview, with each and with both, was recorded by a stenotypist. It was quite evident to the pilots that the Air Force men were fully informed on other aspects of the situation, pertinent and peripheral —e.g., the Pan American flight plan, an analysis of weather conditions, and additional observations of the same phenomena by more than half a dozen ground observers.

Needless to say, with so explicit and extraordinary a sighting there was great interest in the behavior characteristics of the UAO, many of which have been described. Still, nothing, except possibly maneuverability, so captures the imagination of the citizenry, the scientific community, and actual sighters as much as the incredible velocities displayed.

Employing known geographical locations, such as Newport News, their altitude, and other factors, the fliers were able to make supportable evaluations of the pace of the UFO. Having established a line from one known point to another, and incorporating these physical considerations, Nash testified:

---

* The general supposition is that these were agents of the Central Intelligence Agency (CIA).

We had seen them cross this line twice, so we knew they had travelled at least 50 miles. . . . To get a time, we, seven times, separately, using our own panel stopwatch clocks, pushed the button, mentally went through the time, even to saying to ourselves again. 'What the hell's that!' Each time we came up amazingly close to 12 seconds. To be conservative, we increased it to 15 seconds . . . 50 miles in 15 seconds equals 12,000 miles per hour.[21]

Interestingly, this is one of the very few cases on which Dr. Donald H. Menzel has expressed any uncertainty, even to the degree of granting that, along with the sighting of noted astronomer Clyde W. Tombaugh, it has "never been completely explained even though the witnesses were unusually competent, the incidents fully described, and the basic facts not in dispute."[22] His presentation is objective and informative, closely reflecting the original and amplified testimony of the participants, in relationship to which he stipulates that each was highly experienced, and that "Nash had flown more than 10,000 hours at altitudes of 7000 to 8000 feet and held the rank of captain for eight years."[23] Additionally, the astronomer most justly acknowledges the implied expertise, deriving from the described background, and in summation admits that ". . . no reasonable explanation of the disks was [ever] found."[24]

Nonetheless, temperament and talent drove Menzel to elaborate for five and a half pages on "A Possible Explanation of the Nash-Fortenberry Disks."[25] Even this effort, which focuses on a ground light source as the explanation for six UAO flying in formation, being joined by an additional pair of unknowns, all executing an almost instantaneous reversal of flight path, etc., concludes with the concession that the entire preceding argument has done no more than suggest one of countless possible explanations, and that specifically his "solution does not identify the particular beacon, searchlight, or other ground light that produced the Chesapeake Bay Disks."[26]

All of which is to say that despite his subsidiary efforts to extrude the facts regarding the sighted, sighting, and sighters, "no reasonable explanation of the disks was found." [27]

December 15, 1952. Goose Bay, Labrador. In terms of timespan, the episodes around the north Atlantic United States Air Force Base are exceptional, if not unique, in that they occurred and recurred, and with a fascinating frequency. The high-point plateau is generally regarded to be a period from 1948 to the midfifties. Major Edwin A. Jerome, after retiring from the Air Force, delivered testimony to the National Investigations Committee on Aerial Phenomena. The specific period to which he alluded was encompassed by the time he was a command pilot, air provost marshal, covering about eight years, and, subsequently, intelligence officer and CID investigator, at the installation.

His information included the summer of 1948, during which top brass visited to inspect the radar facilities for the base, which provided refueling, servicing, and other military and civilian aircraft needs, for air routes in that vicinity. The senior officers of Royal Canadian Air Force and United States Air Force officers, included a "General as I recall." The deputation was particularly interested in the critical Ground Control Approach equipment. Major Jerome reported that while the radar was being monitored by the visiting superiors

the operator noted a high-speed target on his scope going . . . about 9000 mph. This incident caused much consternation. . . . The poor airman technician was brought to task for his apparent miscalculation. Again the target appeared and this time the inspectors were actually shown the apparition on the radar screen.[28]

The high-ranking party then moved along to the Royal Canadian Air Force Ground Control Approach segment of the installation to monitor the radar equipment there, only to be told that they had just missed seeing a "most unbelievable target." From the limited data available, the inexpert thesis of the moment was that the two scopes had scanned a meteor maintaining a flat altitude path of 60,000 feet, with the hardly varying velocity heretofore mentioned.

Jerome recollects that the astonishing quality of the incident was substantiated and emphasized on the following day when both of the sophisticated radar sets locked on a UAO at about 45,000 feet. It was floating along at an intriguing 10 miles an hour. That is, nearly hovering.

Over the ensuing years Goose Bay was the location of continuous UAO activity. Almost concurrent with the Washington sightings, on the night of June 19, 1952, the American radar crew began tracking an object which, to field personnel who made visual contact outside appeared as a "strange, red-lighted machine." [29]

According to Donald E. Keyhoe: "The radar blip suddenly enlarged, as if the device had banked, exposing a larger surface to the radar beam . . . airmen saw the red light wobble . . . turn white and quickly" [30] disappear.

Six months later, on December 15, the complements of both a T-33 jet trainer and an F-94B interceptor observed a brilliant scarlet and white UFO at nearly three miles altitude. A pursuit followed for close to half an hour, with the jetcraft achieving speeds of 375 air knots without being able to close on the foreign object. So convoluted was the course of chase, the ships covered an area of only twenty square miles before the unknown vanished. The radar in the fighter got a lock on the target that, although at an azimuth reading coinciding with that of ground radar crews, was regarded as too brief to be acceptable by Air Force Intelligence, and so was dismissed as a mechanical malfunction—as far as the F-94B fighter's radarscope was concerned. Originality was not an aspect of the Air Force explanation. The planes were chasing, and presumably the radar was scanning, none other than our old friend the planet Venus. Popular among official and unofficial ufological units was the observation that without the planet it was becoming increasingly apparent the Air Force would be unable to explain anything.

On June 30, 1954, Captain James Howard, commanding a BOAC Stratocruiser transatlantic flight, added his experience to the Goose Bay chronicle. Having departed Idlewild in the late afternoon, he entered the Labrador area at shortly after 9:00 P.M., its time, where he sighted a large dark object, "something like an inverted pear suspended in the sky,"[31] surrounded by smaller UAO.

The attention of co-pilot Lee Boyd was called to the phenomena by Howard as it began to pace the plane, with three of the lesser companions in front and three aft, although "Sometimes five stretched out in a line ahead and only one behind." [32] The ground installation assured Howard that there were no conventional aircraft in the area and that a fighter ship would be scrambled to check out the unknowns. However, this assurance was less satisfying as the UAO suddenly seemed to go into a state of physical flux, reshaping itself ". . . into what looked like a flying arrow—an enormous delta-winged plane turning in to close with us." [33] The object abruptly began to chase again, growing larger, then reformed once more, maintaining distance. It continued altering, now to an elongated, less rounded appearance. All the time the smaller unknowns whirled in some sort of predetermined pattern about it. The witnesses were not confined to Howard and Boyd but included chief navigator George Allen, chief radio officer Douglas Cox, engineers Daniel Godfrey and William Stewart, and chief stewardess Daphne Webster, as well as a number of the passengers.

Shortly thereafter, according to Allen, the companion unknowns "looked to me as though they went inside the big one." [34] Moments later the primary UAO underwent a swift diminution of size as it hurtled away at incalculable speeds. Reducing to a pinpoint of light in the pitchiness of the upper atmosphere, it was gone.

The British commander emphasized that "it was a solid thing. I am sure of that. Maneuverable and controlled intelligently—a sort of base ship linked somehow with those smaller attendant satellites. . . . It must have been some weird form of space ship from another world," [35] concluding that it was "the strangest eighty-mile journey of my life." [36]

And Goose Bay had not heard the last of UFO.

January 27, 1953. Livermore, California. Seventeen years of flying simply must be regarded as impressive accreditation for a UAO observer. If it is not, then few concentrations of experience are. John B. Bean had such as his minimum qualifications on the afternoon of January 27, as he drove away from the Atomic Energy Commission Research Facilities and encountered his first Unidentified Flying Object. To procure some papers from his briefcase, on the rear seat of his automobile, he pulled onto the shoulder of the highway and prepared to exit on the driver's side. He saw a DC-6, at a couple of thousand feet, descending for a landing at the Oakland Municipal Airport, to the west. Moments afterward, as he paused to observe the airliner, his attention was attracted to a white unknown crossing the Atomic Energy Commission facility. Bean's first thought was that he was seeing some sort of desert plant material which had been caught in an updraft. This speculation withered as the aviator recollected that it was still the middle of winter, during which period, even in radiant, golden, sun-soaked California, such botanical gossamer was unlikely to be afloat. With this recognition came the determination that his vision was concentrating on a more substantial object, and a swiftly moving one, at that.

It began a shallow left turn and at that point I could see that it was perfectly round and had a metallic sheen somewhat similar to that of aluminum with a satin finish. I believe another term for this type of finish on aluminum is known as brushed aluminum. It did not have a sharp glint which one often sees when light is reflected from a conventional aluminum aircraft. The light was more diffused and whitish in color. . . . [37]

Bean was now fully concentrating on the UAO and its maneuvers, following it as it switched directions, to the south, followed by an abrupt, nearly 90-degree spin to the right, as it ascended with immeasurable speed. The witness remarked, in a later statement, that only days before he had watched two F-86 fighters circle, bank, and climb "almost vertically," but instantly realized that neither their velocity nor maneuverability was even remotely in a class with the unknown he was studying. Recalling that he began counting in three-syllable steps, i.e., one thousand, two thousand, etc., he found that the UAO was gone within a couple of seconds.

> At this moment, coming in from the East on a due westerly heading, at an altitude somewhat lower than that at which I had sighted the disc, was a jet . . . on a collision course with that of the disc prior to its rapid ascent. When I say collision course, I mean that directionally the two objects were on a collision course but that actually they were separated by several thousand feet . . . it occurred to me that the disc might have taken evasive action in order to avoid the jet.[38]

Of particular interest is that Bean "had three distinct types of aircraft within my sight range simultaneously so that it was possible to evaluate their relative speeds. There was no question that the disc-like object had far more power and far more rapid maneuverability than the other two [the DC-6 and the jet fighter]." [39]

Bean discerned no sound or contrail from the UFO, the overflight of which he put at 1:43 P.M. in a clear sky with unlimited visibility. The sighting was sustained for nine seconds or longer, but, according to the witness, it was positively not fewer. "Three of those seconds were counted time, three or four of them were observed time when I had my wits about me, and the other two to four were initial-reaction time," [40] testified the unusually precise monitor.

November 23, 1953. Kinross Air Force Base. The Air Defense Command radar equipment at the military installation near Soo Locks, Michigan, locked on a UAO flying over Lake Superior one autumn evening. A multipurpose jet fighter, an F-89C, was sent aloft to investigate or, if possible, observe. Directed from the ground, the interceptor was soon visible on the scope to controllers, who clearly saw the F-89 converge on the unknown. They did not anticipate the immediate disappearance of both blips, as if a collision had occurred and nothing remained of either craft. However, "No trace of the jet has ever been found." [41]

The vanished jet was recorded, from its last radar contact, at a location 160 miles northwest of Soo Locks, at an altitude of about 8,000 feet. Subsequently, the U.S. Air Force asserted that the unknown had been recognized by the F-89 as a Royal Canadian Air Force C-47 transport on its way "from Winnipeg, Manitoba to Sudbury, Ontario," [42] adding that, having so recognized it, the American aviator returned to base. Originally, the Public Information Office, at Truax Air Force Base, Wisconsin, simply indicated that the radar failed to continue monitoring the plane after it "collided" with the mysterious object over Lake Superior. There was no further mention of the jet, its course, or even its existence.

The National Investigations Committee on Aerial Phenomena, through the efforts of several of its members, pursued this case further. They sent inquiries directly to the Royal Canadian Air Force. One elicited a reply from Flight Lieutenant C. F. Page, responding for the chief of the Air Staff, specifying that its "records [have] revealed no report of an incident" [43] involving one of their planes in the designated area on the noted date. Afterward, in 1963, another letter received an even more detailed answer. Squadron Leader W. B. Totman wrote a NICAP member that "after extensive checking by this directorate we have been unable to come up with any information regarding any intercept of a RCAF C-47 by a USAF F-89 on November 23, 1953." [44] He suggested that further information might best be obtained from our own Air Force. Any humor here seemed involuntary and unconscious, but he also notes that presumably "they were the agency control-

ling their aircraft." [45] Squadron Leader Totman concluded by remarking that the alleged "C-47 was travel-
ling on a flight plan taking it over *Canadian territory,*
[which] alone would seem to make such an intercept
[as the previously described Kinross case indicates]
unlikely." [46]

The alternatives offered by the National Investigations Committee on Aerial Phenomena are limited to
two, and seem to cover the reasonable possibilities.
NICAP's pair of speculations is that our military
pursued a UAO, rammed it, causing a collision in
which both were destroyed, or that the F-89 was in
some wholly incomprehensible manner simply *absorbed*
by the mysterious object, which then hurtled away at a
speed beyond our radar power to monitor, or translated itself into a state or dimension about which we
know nothing. The option offered by the private inquiry group is that USAF screens picked up a temporarily unidentified Canadian aircraft and sent one
of its interceptors for the purposes of identification
(over Canadian territory?), after which the interceptor
crashed for unexplained or unknown reasons. Regarding the official denial, one may infer that the location
of the wreckage remains a mystery. In sum, this
analysis presumes that skilled radar technicians have
no idea what they are doing, and that our intelligence
community attributes to the Royal Canadian Air Force
a similar incompetence in terms of knowing which of
their planes are where at what time. This seems especially presumptuous when the territory in question is
solely the national airspace of our northern neighbor.
Another United States Air Force publicity sheet states:
"It is presumed by the officials at Norton AFB (Flying
Safety Division) that the pilot probably suffered from
vertigo and crashed into the lake." [47] This conjecture
bears little relationship to other Air Force explanations
of the incident. The disparity among the official positions taken on this and other enigmatic episodes leads
one to the suspicion that the Air Force hasn't the
faintest idea of what occurred a mile and a half above
the black, hacking waters of Lake Superior on the night
of November 23, 1953.

In fairness, the professional debunker's point of view is offered. Dr. Menzel, disregarding some of the Air Force's assertions, and piecing together others, has presented a scenario consisting of little more than a Canadian C-47 being spotted by American radar, being pursued *over its own territory* by an American fighter, which then identified its object and almost immediately proceeded to plummet into Lake Michigan, from which accident no trace, including minimal wreckage evidence, was ever located. The noted astronomer appears to have fully recognized the tenuousness of his conjecture, and concludes his one-page analysis with an attempt at irony by devoting the last 20 percent to suggestions that *serious* inquiries had suggested that "the saucer might have used the G-field to scoop the plane out of the air and take it aboard the spacecraft; the captured pilot might have been needed to teach the English language to his alien captors." [48]

June 11, 1954. Charleston, West Virginia/Atlanta, Georgia. The late Percy Wilkins was among the world's foremost astronomers and, quite possibly, its premier selenographer. These, among other, qualifications should satisfy even the most noted of his lower-ranking colleagues who have devoted their lesser efforts more to the prevention of full and scientific investigation of UAO than celestial inquiry.

The English scientist is the source of a remarkable account. During a plane journey along the eastern seaboard he glanced out of his window at about 10:45 A.M. toward a cluster of cumulus clouds a couple of miles away. Immediately above them, Dr. Wilkins sighted two radiant ovoids about which he remarked:

> They looked exactly like polished metal dinner plates reflecting the sunlight as they flipped and banked around beside the clouds. Presently a third object came slowly out of a huge cloud, remaining motionless in the shadow of the cloud and therefore darker than the others. Presently it zipped away and plunged into another cloud mass. After

about two minutes, the first two did the same maneuver and I did not see them again.[49]

Extrapolating from his estimate of the distance between the clouds and his plane and the seeming size (approximately the radius of the moon) of the objects, the lunar astronomer projected the actual diameter of the unknowns as nearly fifty feet.

The sightings and accounts of such preeminent astronomers as Dr. Clyde W. Tombaugh, Dr. Percy Wilkins, Professor Frank Halstead, and many others—whose stature in their discipline of the sky far exceeds that of most of the detractors of the argument for a serious study of unknown aerial phenomena—completely destroy the frequently heard argument that scientists never see or report on Unidentified Flying Objects. Not only are members of that demanding community found among the foremost observers, many are specifically from the elite clique, members of which have devoted their lives and considerable intellects to celestial studies.

Of course, within the profession, there are those who assert that pilots lack the scholarly expertise of astronomers and, therefore, may be deceived by clouds, atmospheric conditions, planets, or stars, which the former have probably identified thousands of times in their flying careers. With the same breath, such scientists complain that their colleagues, while possessed of vast theoretical knowledge, are wanting in the practical, applied experience of men who fly tens of thousands of people through the airplanes every year or whip supersonic military jets around the heavens at incalculable speeds. They simply cannot have it both ways.

Even now, one usually has to introduce the commercial debunker, identify him, and alert the reader to any qualifications justifying his having an opinion on the subject at all, before one can treat his obsolete ideas. Since about three-quarters of the American public accepts the likelihood of UFO being extraterrestrial, the remaining proponents of fading and vanished positions are rarely known to it.

There is a distinct possibility that there is no new world a-coming, or that, if there is, we will have to erect it ourselves. In either case, only the open-minded will perceive what is ahead, what must be recognized and confronted, and what can be identified and avoided, and when, where, and how such ends may be accomplished. Those who do not grasp that the flights to the lunar surface and the probes to the other planets are the results of what will eventually be categorized as tinker-toy technology simply haven't the least understanding of what has already happened. They are wholly blind as to the implications of socio-scientific evolution, both in space and on this rapidly deteriorating Earth.

Notes

1. *Life*, June 26, 1950, p. 40.
2. Richard Hall, ed., *UFO Evidence*, p. 88.
3. Ruppelt, *Report on Unidentified Flying Objects*, p. 98.
4. Ibid.
5. Ibid., p. 99.
6. Ibid., p. 107.
7. Ibid., p. 109.
8. Ibid.
9. Ibid., p. 110.
10. Ibid.
11. Ibid.
12. Ibid.
13. Edward U. Condon, ed., *Scientific Study*, p. 419.
14. Ibid., p. 422.
15. Menzel and Boyd, *World of Flying Saucers*, p. 131.
16. *Scientific Study*, p. 419.
17. Ibid., p. 423.
18. Ibid.
19. *UFO Evidence*, p. 38.
20. Ibid., p. 39.
21. Ibid. Also see *True*, October 1952.
22. Menzel and Boyd, p. 256.
23. Ibid., p. 259.
24. Ibid.

25. Ibid., pp. 260–265.
26. Ibid., p. 265.
27. Ibid., p. 259.
28. *UFO Evidence*, p. 83.
29. Keyhoe, *Outer Space*, p. 52.
30. Ibid.
31. *UFO Evidence*, p. 126.
32. Ibid.
33. Ibid.
34. Ibid.
35. Ibid.
36. Ibid.
37. Ibid., p. 40.
38. Ibid.
39. Ibid.
40. Ibid.
41. Ibid., p. 114.
42. Ibid., p. 115.
43. Ibid.
44. Ibid.
45. Ibid.
46. Ibid.
47. Ibid.
48. Menzel and Boyd, pp. 154–155.
49. Frank Edwards, *Flying Saucers—Serious Business* (New York: Lyle Stuart, 1966), p. 47.

17

Continuation of Accounts

Reliable reports indicate there are objects coming into our atmosphere at very high speeds and controlled by thinking intelligences.

—Admiral Delmar Fahrney, former head of United States Navy guided-missile program. Press conference, January 16, 1957

THE SECOND HALF of the decade saw no decline in the numbers of sightings reported, although they constituted only a small percentage of the unknowns observed. Actually, there proved to be an ever-increasing growth of accounts submitted to official and unofficial bodies and local authorities, such as police organizations, which had no idea of how to deal with the remarkable stories delivered to their personnel.

Fortunately, the general unpreparedness of the country to collect, record, and evaluate major sightings did not prevent some excellent examples from being catalogued. Among them may be counted many of the most fascinating in the ufology of the period. For example:

April 8, 1956. Schenectady, New York. Captain Raymond E. Ryan and First Officer William Neff, commanding American Airlines Flight 775, departed Albany, New York, on the night of April 8, with a course set for Syracuse. Except for a sparse overcast visibility was good. At two twenty, 6,000 feet above Schenectady, they observed "This very brilliant white light, like an approaching aircraft with its landing lights on." [1]

The team of the twin-engine Convair responded immediately. Ryan banked to widen the distance, only to see the UAO spin into a right-angle turn and hurtle past them. Neither airman had any delusions that he had encountered a conventional plane. The captain estimated the unknown had accelerated to "800 to 1000 miles an hour . . . much faster than a jet." [2] Neff agreed that the object was traveling "certainly much faster than another airplane would." [3]

The aviators saw the UFO decrease speed by two-thirds or three-quarters as its radiance swiftly faded. Having no idea where the unknown was, Ryan hit the landing lights switch, apprehensive of colliding with the craft in the dark. However, he was anticipated. As his beams shot forward into the pitchy sky, the UAO reappeared, glowing orange. Evidently it was monitoring the Convair from some distance ahead. In Ryan's words:

> It changed color after it got to the west of us, probably 8 to 10 miles . . . the light went out . . . momentarily, and we knew there was something up there, and now here we were with a load of passengers with something on our course up ahead, and what are we going to do, so we watched where this light went out and this orange object came on. [4]

Radioing Griffiss Air Force Base, near Rome, New York, Flight 775 reported the encounter, and the officers were told to extinguish the ship's landing lights.

"Now we can see an orange object near you," reported the field immediately after Ryan followed its request. "Our radar isn't on, but we're going to scramble two jets. Keep on watching the object and report what you see." [5]

When interviewed, the captain quoted Griffiss as confirming " 'We have a definite silhouette in sight south of the field.' "[6] Unexpected was the Air Force

Base's admission to the plane that its scanning equipment wasn't operating and, according to the chief pilot, it would have taken them a half hour to activate their radar.

By this point an additional witness, stewardess Phyllis Reynolds, who had entered the flight cabin, was watching the unknown aerial stranger. The condition persisted as Ryan continued to update the ground on the activities of the UAO. Both aviators were somewhat astonished when the Air Force Base usurped command of their nonmilitary American Airlines craft. Lacking any supporting Civil Aviation Authority provision for such action, it directed them to deviate from their approved course to pursue the unidentified object. Ryan decided the Air Force order took precedence, because of the sound of urgency conveyed from Griffiss, and conformed.

The passing of time without the appearance of the interceptors rapidly increased Ryan's discomfort and sense of indecision. He was miles off his flight path, in violation of fundamental safety rules, and his communication with the Air Force Base was swiftly diminishing. Ahead, along the shore of Lake Ontario, the unknown was accelerating, leaving the Convair with the option of maximum speed or a lost cause. Opting for the former gained nothing as the phenomenon sped away at ever-greater velocities toward Canada and nearly out of sight.

Ryan resolved that he could not jeopardize the lives of his passengers and swung his ship toward Syracuse. Later, he would say: "The object was heading northwest over the lake toward Canada. I knew I couldn't catch it or keep up with it." [7] After twenty-three years as a pilot, Ryan could only conclude: "This was absolutely real. I am convinced there was something fantastic up there." [8]

"The shift supervisor on duty in the tower at Griffis [sic] Air Force Base, alerted by Captain Ryan, was able to observe the unknown through binoculars," wrote Menzel. "He described it as apparently round, larger than any star, at an estimated altitude of 3000 or 4000 feet; when first sighted it looked white with

an orange tint but after about ten minutes changed
to orange with a red tint. During the *twenty-three* *
minutes he watched it, the unknown slowly descended
over the horizon. Interceptors from Griffis [sic] Air
Force Base were scrambled at 10:48 and 10:52, but
returned to base without finding anything." [9] However,
Ryan testified in a broadcast interview that he just
didn't "know where the jets were. Why didn't they get
the jets up?" [10]

Major Keyhoe, who conducted a personal and exhaustive investigation of this particular case, concluded
a number of things regarding the aftermath of the
sighting. His conviction was that intolerable pressure
had been put on Ryan to revise his account. In spite
of his printed and broadcast testimony to the contrary,
four and a half months later an official Civil Aviation
Authority release contained the flat denial of his previous comments by Ryan:

"I did not deviate from course at any time. I did
sight an object and it was witnessed." [11] Subsequently,
a Civil Aeronautics Board summation asserts:

"Captain Ryan stated most emphatically that he did
not deviate from his prescribed course, nor was he requested to do so." [12]

The question in the Ryan-Neff case is not what they
saw or what they did. The information is available
from permanent records of their own voices. As with
all other unexplained UFO sightings, what it was they
saw is the mystery. More intriguing, in this instance, is
what happened to the disintegrating testimony, the
completely contradictory official reports, and the carefully constructed cage of silence that was erected about
the entire episode and all of its major and peripheral
participants. Menzel airily dismissed the cacophony of
conflict and offered the true solution: the object was
the old and favorite character actress of celestial melo-
drama, "the planet Venus." [13]

It is difficult to be sufficiently emphatic about the
constancy and detail of sightings, hour by hour, day by
day, week by week, month by month, and, to this

---

* Emphasis added.

point, decade by decade. A proper chronology, with even minimal descriptions, would evolve into a catalogue of many volumes. A fragment of the problem, and the ensuing investigational inadequacy, may be indicated by the concentration of sightings, and the accompanying "flap," of November 1957. During this single month, the United States Air Force conceded the reception of 414 accounts of UFO—an extraordinarily high figure when one recalls that the best of their experts, Captain Edward J. Ruppelt, recognized that only the smallest proportion of reports of actual unknowns ever reached his desk. Drawing upon that number, officialdom classified 340 incidents "explained," 70 moot because of "insufficient data," and 4 "unknown." The National Investigations Committee on Aerial Phenomena concluded that 118 episodes were "not readily attributable to conventional objects or phenomena." [14] Which analyses one accepts makes little difference. Forty or fifty sightings, by competent observers, in the United States alone, within thirty days, justified demand for a full, even congressional, inquiry into this matter.

What happened in November 1957? Very briefly—

On the first day of the month, four men from an oil crew in Coleman, Texas, saw a crimson oblong object hover and sail away; a secretary in Sandia Mountains, New Mexico, viewed a UAO of similar shape, which ascended out of sight; and an executive of the Boy Scouts organization, near Campbellsville, Kentucky, watched an unknown of like configuration sweep overhead and away; on the second, a pilot made visual contact with an unidentified aerial enigma, while below, near Amarillo, Texas, automobile motors failed as something hurtled overhead; another motorist had his car stalled near Seminole, New Mexico, when a light dove at him and vanished in the distance; and a woman of Clemens, North Carolina, witnessed a brilliant yellow ovoid catapult into a bank of clouds. Such were the reports, literally hour by hour, during the month of November 1957. Even the most cursory description of all the events of this particular month is impossible. Therefore, attention will be focused on the complex generally designated as the Levelland, Texas, case. The first sighting to gain attention occurred at approximately 10:50 P.M. on November 2, and the intricate and inexplicable concentration concluded fewer than three hours afterward, probably about 1:30 the following morning.

On this quiet evening in early autumn, patrolman A. J. Fowler was the duty officer in Levelland, Texas, a community of some 10,000 people. The tranquility of the premidnight hours was broken by a staccato of similar, but disturbing, telephone reports and inquiries. Records seem to indicate that the first of these was received from Pedro Saucedo,* a farm worker. Accompanied by his friend Joe Salaz,† he encountered a blinding radiation on a collision course with his vehicle, on Route 116, four miles west of the town. Elsewhere the witness placed the illumination at a less aggressive point in a field running parallel to the highway. E.g., "We didn't think much about it, but then it rose out of the field and started toward us, picking up speed. When it got nearer, the lights of my truck went out and the motor died. I jumped out and hit the deck as the thing passed directly over the truck with a great sound and a rush of wind. It sounded like thunder, and my truck rocked from the blast. I felt a lot of heat." [15] The foregoing account is drawn from a compilation of evidence assembled by the noted astronomer Walter N. Webb. The following is a certified statement made by the same witness, regarding the same event:

> To whom it may concern: on the date of November 2, 1957 I was traveling north and west on route 116, driving my truck. At about four miles out of Levelland, I saw a big flame, to my right front . . . I thought it was lightning. But when this object had reached to my position it was different, because it put my truck motor out and lights. Then I stop, got out, and took a look, but it

---

* Occasionally found as Saucido.
† Also found as Salvos, Salav, Palav, Palaz, etc.

was so rapid and quite some heat that I had to hit the ground. It also had colors—yellow, white—and it looked like a torpedo, about 200 feet long, moving at about 600 to 800 miles an hour.[16]

Officer Fowler later freely admitted that he suspected the caller of being slightly inebriated and gave the report little credit. As a matter of fact, things hardly had started.

Jim Wheeler, approximately eight miles distant from the original report, four miles *east* of Levelland, but still on Route 116, had almost driven into a huge, brilliantly illuminated object, perhaps seventy yards long, and shaped like an egg, sitting in the middle of the road. He need not have feared running into it, as his headlights and engine simply stopped functioning before he got too close. Apparently a man of great personal courage, the subject exited his automobile, but almost immediately the unbelievable obstruction drifted into the sky, its glare swiftly decreasing, and vanished. Nearly concurrent with the diminution and extinguishing of its glow, the engine and lights of Wheeler's car revived.

Very shortly thereafter the telephone rang again, and Patrolman Fowler received a third report. This time from Jose Alvarez, who was calling from Whitharral,* slightly fewer than a dozen miles north of the community, on Route 51. His account, although a little less dramatically presented than his predecessor's, was almost identical in details.

Midnight came, followed minutes later by another incident. However, it was not until the next day, at the urging of his parents, that the witness reported it to the besieged officer in Levelland. The informant was Newell Wright, a freshman, of nearly twenty years, who attended Texas Tech. The episode had also taken place on Route 116, when the student found the lights

---

* Dr. Hynek alludes to "Mr. W." (Wheeler) of Whitharral, as well as "another Whitharral man" (Alvarez), meaning an individual *from* that town. Lest any reader, because of references to "four miles west" and "eleven miles north" be confused, they are different persons.

and motor of his vehicle fading to inoperation. Leaving the driver's seat, Wright proceeded to lift the hood to check the wiring and battery, but could not determine the cause of the difficulty. He slammed the hood down and turned. Before him, occupying the center of the highway, rested a hundred-foot vessel of luminous greenish-blue tone. Startled, the young man leapt back into his automobile and attempted to back it away, but the entire electrical system was unresponsive. Soon the UAO rose in the traditionally silent, vertical manner, and was gone. The car became functional again, and the youth drove home.

If the Levelland area was having more than its share of sightings that night, Whitharral was not being neglected. The station received another account at twelve fifteen from Frank Williams, who was speaking from a telephone booth nine miles away, near Whitharral. He, too, had come upon the huge UFO and discovered his vehicle had slowed to a standstill for no apparent cause. In this instance, the radiance was alternating, rising to intense brilliance and subsiding to comparative invisibility. Inexplicably, his headlights fluctuated in counter-rhythm to the pulsations of the unknowns. Williams remained in the car. Finally his patience was rewarded and the vast object rose, this time with a thunderous roar, leaving the witness to relax and the automobile to start.

Patrolman Fowler had reported the events to his superiors, and Sheriff Weir Clem and his deputy Pat McCulloch * were combing the highways in an effort to isolate and identify whatever was frightening their neighbors.

A half hour after the Williams encounter, another episode was in progress, not far from the site of the Saucedo sighting. Driving a medium-sized truck along Route 116, Ronald Martin witnessed not merely the presence, but the landing, of an extremely large, bright rust-colored object on the pavement on the road before him, blocking his passage. As with the earlier observers, the entire electrical system of his vehicle went

---

* Also found as McCullough.

dead. Having come to rest, the device became bluish-green, but when it began to take to the sky again it reverted to its original color.

Thirty minutes later, a new adventure was recorded when James Long encountered a vast ovoid on a secondary thoroughfare. The failure of the lights and engine was repeated, but somewhat more quickly, the unknown departed.

One thirty in the morning found the entire business coming to the law directly. Sheriff Clem and Deputy McCulloch were cruising along the Oklahoma Flat Road, approximately four miles from town, when they sighted an enormous egg of light "looking like a brilliant red sunset across the highway." [17] The object was about a thousand feet south of them. "It lit up the whole pavement in front of us for about two seconds," recalled the sheriff.[18] In this isolated instance the electrical function of the automobile did not seem to have been arrested.

A few miles to the rear was a patrol car occupied by Lee Hargrove and Floyd Gavin. The former recounted what he and his partner had seen. Their report tallied with the earlier ones. The same was true of the testimony of fire marshal Ray Jones, whose experience occurred around the same time. His car suffered disfunction, but not complete stoppage, as was the effect in most of the Levelland cases.

During the three hours throughout which the complex evolved, Patrolman Fowler received between fifteen and two dozen telephone calls attesting to similar events with a great UFO. Many of the adventures are most impressive individually, especially on the occasions where there was more than one witness. However, the localized series of sightings, or, as Hynek properly calls them, "close encounters," within so brief a period of time is astonishing. Additionally, the apparent electrical effect, found in all of the nearest approaches, presents a constant, quite apart from the visual, which cries for proper analysis. Or, certainly did at the time. It is now a little late, two decades after the fact, to accumulate the desirable testimony and the automobiles involved.

The Condon team took the later point as an excuse to omit the Levelland case from its project, but Menzel doubted and dismissed some things, and disarranged and interpreted others to fit his conviction that "The evidence, however, leads to an overwhelming probability: the fiery unknown at Levelland *was* * ball lightning." [19] Contrarily, according to the astronomer, it is a phenomenon so rare and "so little understood that some scientists have doubted its reality." [20]

Dr. J. Allen Hynek, the United States Air Force's scientific expert on all astronomical and atmospheric aspects of ufology for twenty years, has included a comment pertaining to this thesis in his later writings— those which belong to the period when his experience had finally weighed the scales of his perception into objective balance, possibly making him the ultimate authority on these matters, at this time.

> I am not proud today that I hastily concurred in Captain [G. T.] Gregory's evaluation as "ball lightning" [as a solution for the Levelland incidents] on the basis of information that an electrical storm had been in progress in the Levelland area at the time. That was shown not to be the case. Observers reported overcast and mist *but no lightning*.† Besides, had I given it any thought whatever, I would soon have recognized the absence of any evidence that ball lightning can stop cars and put out headlights.[21]

Hynek's book on his personal investigations and evaluations of numerous varieties of UFO sightings and aftereffects, in contradistinction to Menzel's ivory-observatory solutions, was published a decade later than his colleagues' commentaries. Therefore, in addition to his nearly unique expertise, the former advisor to officialdom had all of the supporting data and clarifications of earlier errors ten years can provide. The evidence leads to little possibility that fifteen or

---

* Emphasis by Menzel.
† Emphasis added.

twenty people, concentrated within a few miles area, in Texas, during three hours of a night on late November 2 to early November 3, saw ball lightning or anything remotely related to it.

February 24, 1959. Newark to Detroit. It was twenty minutes past eight as American Airlines Flight 713, recently out of Newark and headed for Detroit, became engaged in an extraordinary incident. The DC-6, piloted by a veteran of fifteen years, Capt. Peter W. Killian, was a dozen miles west of Williamsport, Pennsylvania, at 8,500 feet. Beside him, in the co-pilot's seat, was First Officer James Dee.* A few minutes later, the airliner cruised over the community of Bradford, at approximately 350 miles an hour. The sky was brilliantly clear around and above, although scattered clouds a few thousand feet below occasionally obscured the ground. Abruptly, the flier became aware of three iridescent objects proceeding in a direct line to the south of his path and at a higher altitude. Initially, the thought of the constellation Orion occurred to him but, as quickly, he realized that the lighted UAO, which he estimated to be about 15 degrees overhead, were not stars—certainly not those of Orion, which were clearly visible some distance away. The unknowns were larger and brighter, and their color, a concentrated amberish ivory, distinctly different. As Killian was aware of entering Erie, Pennsylvania, airspace, one of the flight snapped away from the formation, and seemed to direct its course toward the DC-6, but soon slowed, as if it had suddenly become conscious of the airliner. In Keyhoe's words: "Killian knew now it was a UFO—some unknown machine, under intelligent control. He could not be sure, but it seemed at least triple the size of [his] plane." [22] Apparently, the object then returned to its previous position.

Major Keyhoe's account, based upon National Investigation Committee on Aerial Phenomena interviews with Killian, records that the Captain apprised the passengers of the presence of the aerial escort,

---

* Keyhoe has this *John* Dee. *Top Secret*, p. 27.

soon after which stewardess Edna LeGate entered the cockpit with a fearful traveler whom the pilot attempted to reassure. Killian told him that there seemed to be no immediate threat, that the DC-6 was merely under surveillance and that if they were of the hostile type of UAO they would have demonstrated their antipathy by then. This relieved the passenger, who returned to the cabin. Flight Officer Dee then noted they were being approached again, even more closely this time. General relaxation ensued as the unknown whirled away again to realign itself with its fellows.

Either a little earlier or at about this time, Killian radioed other flights inquiring whether they had viewed the phenomena. One response, in Keyhoe's version, confirmed his hope. "We've been watching the formation for ten minutes," reported an American Airlines colleague. "I'll give you their bearing—you can figure their approximate speed." [23] Other pilots in the vicinity also attested to seeing the objects. The UAO paced and followed the DC-6B as it proceeded west until Killian began his descent for a landing at the Detroit airfield.

The sighting persisted for three-quarters of an hour, during which time the intensiy of the UFO brightness fluctuated greatly and the color ranged from a golden tone to a blue-white and back again. "I saw these objects in a clear sky," Keyhoe quotes Killian. "They were round and in precise formation. I've never seen anything like it." [24] The pilots concurred that "It could not be any clearer than it was that night above 5,000 feet." [25]

In addition to Killian's testimony, confirmation was obtained that three United Airlines crews also monitored the objects. Among the personnel involved in supportive sightings was Captain A. D. Yates and Flight Engineer L. F. Baney. Simply put, a considerable number of flying and nonflying commercial airlines officers watched the activities of a trio of unknown, lighted objects. Their combined airtime experience ran to tens of thousands of hours.

Captain Killian was interviewed by various periodicals and on numerous radio shows, including one produced by the author and upon which he frequently appeared as panelist in charge of devil's advocacy. Meanwhile, the Air Technical Intelligence Center at Wright-Patterson Air Force Base, deferred to public demands that some explanation be offered and suggested that the phenomena sighted might have been the constellation of Orion, which the pilot had already dismissed for valid astronomical reasons. The press release granted its speculation was tentative. To the New York *Herald Tribune* Killian remarked: "I am sure there are people on other planets and that they have solved the problem of space travel . . . I sincerely believe that their vehicles are coming close to earth." [26]

Ultimately, relinquishing the untenable Orion argument, the Air Force opted for the KC-97 tankers refueling three E-47 bombers explanation, a conjecture with which Menzel heartily allied himself.

Major General W. P. Fisher, Air Force director of Legislative Liaison, wrote to Senator Harry Flood Byrd, on May 6, 1959, asserting that

> The investigation of this incident revealed that an Air Force refueling mission, involving a KC-97 and three B-47 aircraft, was flown in the vicinity of Bradford, Pennsylvania at the time of the sighting by Captain Killian. The refueling operation was conducted at 17,000 feet altitude at approximately 230 knots true air speed about 265 mph) for a period of approximately one hour. [27]

Superficially, this explanation seems consonant with the conditions obtaining during the sighting, presupposing, of course, that Killian, his crew, some United Airlines and other American airlines aviators and complements were too visually incapacitated to discern what was happening in the atmosphere in which they made their living and spent a good deal of their lives.

The contention is that the refueling process occurred over Bradford, Pennsylvania, on the border with New York State. Confirmation of the Air Force argument would have placed it considerably to the south where Pittsburgh or Johnstown would have been more logical points of reference. To really make the official explanation work is to displace the UAO, or the alleged refueling location, by three-quarters the width of the entire state. Captain Killian saw the unknowns to his south, not almost directly north as General Fisher's explanation would demand. Even farther in that direction was the flight path of Captain Yates, who saw the lights at a less latitudinal position, as he headed toward Akron, Ohio. Various checks, made immediately afterward, indicated there were no three aircraft in the vicinity and one investigation determined that that specifically included "jet tankers."

> If the Air Force wants to believe that [the refueling story], it can. But I know what a B-47 looks like and I know what a KC-97 tanker looks like, and I know what they look like in operation at night. And that's not what I saw.[28]

Despite prolonged arguments through the years by mostly anonymous Air Force debunkers, it seems inconceivable that the official solution to this case bears any resemblance to accuracy. As this was a multiple sighting, the witnesses to which was a group of professional men of extraordinarily high UAO-viewing credentials, it remains one of the most amply observed and seemingly irresolvable puzzles in the annals of air-to-air ufology.

August 13, 1960. Red Bluff, California. Sightings, especially multiple sightings of the same UAO, intrigue in direct relationship to the character and behavior of the unknown, the duration of the episode, the reliability of the witnesses, and many other considerations, but concentrations—i.e., a number of sightings over a brief period of time, in a relatively limited geographical area—have a special fascination. There are many of these, a couple of which have been detailed, but one of the most impressive followed after the Killian case. Beginning during the evening of August 13, 1960, the northern California complex continued for five days. In total, scores of witnesses, among which were more than a dozen police officers, gave detailed accounts of disks, ellipses, and elongated ovoids, many highly maneuverable, a number featuring red lights, that overflew numerous communities.

At ten thirty a red object hovered over and departed the skies of Hollywood; at eleven a similar UAO appeared, cruised, and vanished from Willow Creek; from just before midnight to after two in the morning a sighting of what, by description, appeared to be the same phenomenon persisted over Red Bluff. As this particular observation continued the unknown was joined by a similar companion, before they both were engulfed by the black heavens.

Corning was afforded the spectacle of two long ovoids, with red and white illuminations, at eight thirty in the evening on August 16, and an hour later a half dozen or more lights of like color, operating in formation, excited the citizenry of Eureka. Twenty minutes later, a seemingly boomerang-shaped unknown swept above Corning. Countless observers, including several Tehama County law enforcers, monitored six UAO above Mineral. These iridescent effects hovered, dove, climbed, at incalculable speeds. A circular object, with fluctuating red and blue lamps, performed only slightly modified exercises above Concord and Pleasant Hill from a quarter to twelve until fifteen minutes into the new day, which was to find a flattened dull and bright red sphere stalling and moving slowly over Healdsburg and Santa Rosa.

On the evening of August 17 a police captain and sergeant, with a number of companions, watched two bright oblong UFO sport above Roseville for about an hour, and later an apparent vessel, emitting a whining noise and featuring two white lights to the front and crimson ones at the tail, sailed around Folsom. Minutes after midnight a similar shape of crimson hue, featuring a smaller amber light, came near the ground of Dunsmuir and rushed away with a high-pitched sound. Redlands was treated to a domed, egg-shaped unknown, with its ring of red lights, shortly before two o'clock in the morning.

The postmaster of Honeydew saw a sharply defined delta-winged object as ten o'clock approached on the evening of August 18. The sighting of the enigmatic shape, glowing red to the fore, with its interior allegedly illuminated, persisted for a couple of minutes.

This is merely an extremely abbreviated list of the primary episodes which occurred during the five-day span noted. Of particular interest is that collectively one or the other of these incidents is supported by the testimony of police witnesses, often more than one to a case, among whom were State Highway Patrolmen Stanley Scott and Charles A. Carson; Tehama County Sheriff's Deputies Clarence Fry, Bill Gonzalez, Officer Montgomery, and Chief Criminal Investigator A. D. Perry; Sonoma County Sheriff's Deputies William Baker and Lou Doolittle; Plumas County Sheriff's Deputy Robert Smith; Roseville Police Captain Hugh McGuigan and Sergeant James Hall; and Mount Shasta Police Officers Pete Chinka, Jack Brown, and George Kerr.[29]

Space limitations prohibit zeroing in on each of these singular episodes; therefore, an example of one police officer's official report, also signed by his partner, is presented verbatim. An explanation for what is described is yet to be found.

Officer Scott and I were E/B on Hong Road, east of Corning, looking for a speeding motorcycle when we saw what at first appeared to be a huge airliner dropping from the sky. The object was very low and directly in front of us. We stopped and leaped from the patrol vehicle in order to get a position on what we were sure was going to be an airplane crash. From our position outside the car, the first thing we noticed was an absolute silence. Still assuming it to be an aircraft with power off, we continued to watch until the object was probably within 100 feet to 200 feet off the ground, when it suddenly reversed completely, at high speed, and gained approximately 500 feet altitude. There the object stopped. At this time it was clearly visible to both of us. It was surrounded by a glow making the round or oblong object visible. At each end, or each side of the object, there were definite red lights. At times about five white lights were visible between the red lights. As we watched the object moved again and performed aerial feats that were actually unbelievable.

At this time we radioed Tehama County Sheriff's Office requesting they contact local radar base. The radar base confirmed the UFO—completely unidentified.

Officer Scott and myself, after our verification, continued to watch the object. On two occasions the object came directly towards the patrol vehicle; each time it approached, the object turned, swept the area with a huge red light. Officer Scott turned the red light on the patrol vehicle towards the object, and it immediately went away from us. We observed the object use the red beam approximately 6 or 7 times, sweeping the sky and ground areas. The object began moving slowly in an easterly direction and we followed. We proceeded to the Vina Plains Fire Station where it was approached by a similar object from the south. It moved near the first object and both stopped, remaining in that position for some time, occasionally emitting the red beam. Finally, both objects disappeared below the eastern horizon. We returned to the Tehama County Sheriff's office and met Deputy Fry and Deputy Montgomery, who had gone to Los Molinos after contacting the rader base. Both had seen the UFO clearly, and described to us what we saw. The night jailer also was able to see the object for a short time; each described the object at 2350 hours and observed it for approximately two hours and 15 minutes. Each time the object neared us we experienced radio interference.

We submit this report in confidence for your information. We were calm after our initial shock, and decided to observe and record all we could of the object.

Stanley Scott 1851
Charles A. Carson 2358.

Notes

1. *UFO Evidence*, Richard Hall, ed., p. 41. Reprinted from an interview, "Meet the Millers," broadcast on WBEN-TV, Buffalo, New York, April 16, 1956.
2. Ibid.
3. Ibid.
4. Ibid.
5. Keyhoe, *Top Secret*, p. 168.
6. *UFO Evidence*, p. 41.
7. Keyhoe, *Top Secret*, p. 170.
8. Ibid.
9. Menzel and Boyd, *World of Flying Saucers*, p. 68.
10. *UFO Evidence*, p. 42.
11. Keyhoe, *Top Secret*, p. 172.
12. Ibid., p. 174.
13. Menzel and Boyd, p. 69.
14. *UFO Evidence*, p. 163.
15. Ibid., p. 168.
16. J. Allen Hynek, *UFO Experience*, p. 142.
17. Ibid., p. 145.
18. Ibid.
19. Menzel and Boyd, p. 176.
20. Ibid., p. 177.
21. Hynek, p. 146–147.
22. Keyhoe, *Top Secret*, p. 28.
23. Ibid., p. 29.
24. Ibid.
25. *UFO Evidence*, p. 43.
26. Menzel and Boyd, p. 54.
27. *UFO Evidence*, p. 116.
28. Ibid.
29. Ibid., p. 170.

Dissembling in the Sixties

The New York World-Telegram has confirmed this reporter's exclusive report of several weeks before . . .
Air Force people are convinced the flying disk is real.
The clincher came when the Air Force got a picture
of three disks flying in formation. . . .

—Walter Winchell, New York
Daily Mirror, June 5, 1949

SERIOUS UFOLOGICAL INQUIRY by private agencies from
the late 1950s and through the 1960s was considerably
distorted by the introduction of strange, self-cast
characters who presented and promulgated fantastic
tales of their personal liaisons with extraplanetary personalities and, even, trips to outer space and beyond.

During the phase of the "contactees" it was fashionable and useful for officialdom to include all persons
advocating a serious and comprehensive investigation
of UFO in the same category as such "kooks," as
they were defamatorily called. The intention was to
discredit the sightings, evaluations, and/or suggestions
of men of extraordinary professional expertise, unquestioned reliability, and indisputable sincerity, let
alone countless numbers of individuals whose reports
were comparably inexplicable but whose "qualifications" did not satisfy the demands of the infinitesimal
staff allotted to the subject by the government.

Still, the techniques of ridicule and of censorship
seemed inadequate and a canopy of silence descended
over the media to such a degree as to convince the
American public that there had been not simply a

diminution of UAO sightings, but a virtual cessation. The truth of the matter is that the reports continued in equal, and frequently greater, numbers than ever before.

After 1961 or 1962, the fun characters who had gone to Venus faded into their personal oblivion, and the general citizenry tended to lose interest in lights in the sky, and often near or on the ground, which performed unbelievable aeronautical maneuvers and defied climatic and astronomical explanation. Those who were still interested had to subscribe to outré little newsletters or the publications of the Aerial Phenomena Research Organization (APRO) or the National Investigations Committee on Aerial Phenomena (NICAP) just to keep vaguely au courant. As far as the newspapers and the television network news facilities were concerned, at a certain point in the early 1960s UFO simply ceased to exist.

Inference or implication, the conclusion was false.

Lonnie Zamora, of the town of Socorro, was the primary participant in one of the major sightings of 1964, or, in the words of J. Allen Hynek, "one of the classics of UFO literature." [1] At approximately a quarter to six in the afternoon on April 24, New Mexico Highway Patrol Officer Lonnie Zamora, a veteran of several years, was in pursuit of a speeding automobile. As he passed an area of low rolling hills to the south of Socorro, on United States Route 85, his attention was diverted from the motorist to a descending machine, exhausting blue and orange flames and periodically hovering. Swinging onto a secondary road, he attempted to climb a precipitous incline. Following repeated efforts he mounted the rise and observed what appeared to be a craft approximately five hundred feet away, in a gully. Zamora's original description was odd. He thought it looked like "a car turned upside down." [2] Immediately, he radioed the sheriff's office and reported the situation. Then, as he watched, two figures in white uniforms seemed to appear. Whether from inside the craft or behind it he was unable to determine. To continue his approach, he followed the road as it dipped, at which time he momentarily lost sight of the object. Reaching the top of another small hill, he found he could see it again. It was

> an egg-shaped metallic craft resting on legs extended from the craft. Loud sounds from the interior of the craft caused Zamora to seek shelter as rapidly as he could. Glancing back over his shoulder at the craft, he saw it rise vertically and take off horizontally, disappearing shortly thereafter in the direction of "Six Mile Canyon." [3]

Accounts of the patrolman's experience were sought by innumerable official, semi-official, unofficial, reportorial, and other investigators. Among some of his comments were included ones that indicated "it was a shiny-type object . . . like aluminum . . . whitish against a moss background, but no chrome. Seemed like a football shape . . . I saw two pair [all subsequent testimony seems to indicate that here he meant "a pair of persons in"] of overalls." [4]

Zamora's summons to the police station did not go unrewarded. Soon Sergeant Chavez arrived. According to one version of his testimony:

> When I arrived I went to where [Zamora said] the object had been. I noticed the brush was burning in several places. I could see the tracks on the ground. I noticed smoldering bushes, but they felt cold to the touch. I knew Lonnie had seen something . . . he had made a sketch of an insignia he saw on the side of the object. I secured the area and called the local military authorities. [5]

By the time they arrived at least one agent of the Federal Bureau of Investigation was there, as were many spectators, cameramen, and reporters. In a quote credited to Quintanilla, then chief project officer for Unidentified Flying Objects in the Air Force: "I directed Dr. Hynek to Socorro to get additional information." [6]

The astronomer arrived and observed the alleged

landing marks and the indisputable seared vegetation. He spoke with Zamora and Chavez at length, determining "that the diagonals of the quadrilateral formed by the four landing marks intersected almost exactly at right angles." [7]

"One theorem in geometry states that if the diagonals of a quadrilateral intersect at right angles, the midpoints of the sides of the quadrilateral lie on the circumference of a circle, and it is thus of considerable interest that the center of the circle so formed virtually coincided with the principal burn mark on the ground," wrote Hynek later. "Under certain conditions the center of gravity of the craft would have been directly over the center of the circle, hence making the presence of the burn mark more significant." [8]

Dr. Hynek conducted an extensive investigation into the physical details available for observation and measurement, and as thoroughly verified Zamora's credibility, reputation for integrity, and general professional reliability.

A number of considerations suggest strongly, if they do not support definitely, that at least one additional witness saw the craft. Regrettably, in view of the general mockery of officialdom regarding such sightings, the unknown never stepped to the fore, although within fewer than a hundred hours a number of identified witnesses—Opal Grinder, Orlando Gallegos, Nick Naranjo, George Mitropolis, and others of the area— saw striking UAO. Yet, it was always the simultaneous sighting by the anonymous look-and-run driver who stopped for gasoline immediately north of Socorro, commenting on the extraordinary vessel which had swept over his head and of the police car in the distance, that was regarded as the greatest loss.

I tried my best at the time to induce the air force to make an intelligence problem of finding the missing witness, but they evinced no interest whatsoever. At the time I thought that, had this been a federal case involving narcotics or counterfeiting, the FBI would certainly have located the missing witness. Because it was merely a UFO case, the usual pattern of doing nothing was followed.[9]

It had taken Air Force authority Hynek a decade to assume a Ruppeltian perception; the ensuing one would clear his mind entirely, producing perhaps, the most technically proficient, certainly generally respected and objective crusader for an honest, precise, and effective investigation of UAO.

The nature of sightings varies enormously, as has become evident, but another inconsistent and unpredictable aspect is the public's response to a given sighting, or sighting series. For no apparent reason some considerably lesser incidents attracted a great deal of attention and received broad coverage by a press which normally went to great lengths to avoid the subject. Fortunately, from time to time, the focus of the media centered on cases which were both objectively interesting and flavorful in that fashion which heightened the curiosity of those who heard or read about it.

On Sunday, March 18, 1966, according to countless witnesses, at least two score identified, and including a dozen minions of the law, a most unusual "quilted"-surface UAO, with blue and white lights fore and aft, as well as a larger beacon midship, antennae, and a small cabin, was sighted in marshlands near Ann Arbor, Michigan. Further, the peculiar apparition was being escorted by an entourage of four smaller craft. Among the people to view the unknown from the nearest position were forty-seven-year-old farmer Frank Mannor and his nineteen-year-old son, Ronald, who reported that the device—at least during the period of their observation—never actually settled upon the sedge, but "sat on a base of fog." [10] The two claimed they had raced to within fifteen hundred feet of the football-shaped device and determined that it was approximately the length of an automobile, had a grayish-yellow, cockled surface, and exuded a pulsating radiance.

The elder Mannor also managed to execute a sketch of the primary vessel, as viewed from the side. It gave the distinct impression of an eye with the center light as the iris, or of a plump tugboat viewed from an airplane.

Robert Hunawill, a patrolman in the area, said that he and a number of other local citizens watched such a craft during the early-morning hours of the following Monday and Wednesday. These witnesses also agreed that the UAO hovered rather than landed, and moved constrictedly about.

Sheriff's Deputies Stanley McFadden and David Fitzpatrick, of Washtenaw County, verified the overflight of the unknown at approximately the same time the Mannor men specified it had become airborne.

State Police Commissioner Fredrick E. Davids, who functioned as head of the state's civilian defense corps, immediately instituted an investigation, with the comment: "I used to discount these reports too but now I'm not so sure." [11]

Suddenly, from Washington, flashed the news that the Air Force was completely ignorant of the whole affair. Not to be outdone, its Michigan headquarters, in Battle Creek, issued a detailed statement that it had no comment.

Yet, as comprehensive as the initial sighting was, it could hardly compare with what followed at Hillsdale, Michigan, on the following evening. At that time, there occurred one of the most correlated sightings of the period, when a civilian defense director, an assistant dean, and eighty-seven women students witnessed the erratic flight of a glowing UAO, the configuration of which was brilliantly outlined by light during its lengthy visit over and past the dormitory of Hillsdale College, before it vanished several hours afterward into the adjacent marshes.

Two students, twenty-one-year-old Barbara Kohn, from New Castle, Pennsylvania, and Cynthia Poffenberger, of Cleveland, Ohio, three years her junior, were the first observers of the phenomenon. Their descriptions, as well as those of all the subsequent witnesses, seemed to conform almost completely with those offered by the people who monitored the quintet of UAO in the Ann Arbor swamp area forty-five miles to the northeast on the previous evening.

William Van Horn, forty-one-year-old civil defense authority; Kelly Hearn, seven years a journalist before becoming dean of women at the institution; and the nearly one hundred women students recounted how the luminosity of the object diminished when the summoned police arrived in their automobiles, but returned to normal upon the departure of the lawmen. A number of its other activities were also described, including a sweep around an airport beacon, a pass by dormitory windows, and other demonstrations of high maneuverability. "It was definitely some kind of vehicle . . . it was either round or oblong," [12] recounted Van Horn, who had employed binoculars to view the craft.

The story of the Michigan sightings swept across the country, and the Air Force decided it should dispatch an investigator to go and see what was happening. It made the best possible choice in the person of its regular scientific advisor to Project Blue Book, Dr. J. Allen Hynek, who was then also director of the Dearborn Observatory of Northwestern University. The astronomer established his field office at Selfridge Air Force Base, Mount Clemens, Michigan, located in the area of the most recent sightings. Typically refusing to comment before he had begun his inquiry, Hynek, fitted out in rough clothes and hip boots, personally checked out various of marshland reports, including one near Dexter, Michigan, where a farmhand had announced the landing of a "ghost ship."

Mostly alone, and consulting little with local officialdom, the scientist went from place to place and from person to person, checking on the possibility of physical evidence and accumulating testimony. Finally, to gratify the impatient press, he made his first comment, essentially an unofficial, somewhat off-the-cuff observation:

It's like reports from people who saw a fire. You get as many different facts as you get people who saw the fire. So far, all I've been able to come up with is reports of a variety of lights. These reports are more consistent than most of the other sightings I've investigated.[13]

Regrettably, in later years, Hynek was disinclined to pursue the possible interpretations of the incident. Yet, his reticence was understandable as his name had become inseparably intertwined with the phrase "marsh gas," a possible explanation he had offered for the phenomena which had been grasped by the press collectively and announced as his expert evaluation of the various seemingly related cases in Michigan. This was then compounded by the insistence of Project Blue Book, which, in the voice of Major Hector Quintanilla, presented it as the official position.

However, for once, the service was not able to funnel the facts into the abyss of oblivion. A member of Congress with a Michigan constituency received enough mail and found the media material sufficiently pervasive to write an official letter to another member of the House of Representatives, on March 28. The message was directed to L. Mendel Rivers, chairman of the Armed Services Committee. In part, and in essence, it read as follows:

Dear Chairman Rivers:
No doubt you have noted the recent flurry of newspaper stories about unidentified flying objects (UFO's). I have taken special interest in these accounts because many of the latest reported sightings have been in my home State of Michigan.
The Air Force sent a consultant, Astrophysicist Dr. J. Allen Hynek of Northwestern University, to Michigan to investigate the various reports; and he dismissed all of them as the product of college pranks or swamp gas or of an impression created by the rising crescent moon and the planet Venus.* I do not agree that all of

---

* It was singularly unfortunate and unfair to Hynek that the press and others engulfed him in his casual, but injudicious speculations, for such caused him to seriously review the

these reports can be or should be so easily explained away.

Because I think there may be substance in some of these reports and because I believe the American people are entitled to a more thorough explanation than has been given them by the Air Force to date, I am proposing that either the Science or Astronautics Committee or the Armed Services Committee of the House schedule hearings on the subject of UFO's and invited testimony from both the executive branch of the Government and some of the persons who claim to have seen UFO's.[14]

The letter then continues by calling attention to, and liberally quoting from, a column by Roscoe Drummond,[15] which strongly urges a full and open investigation of the matter. Further, a series of six essentially anti-Air Force columns by Bulkley Griffin, along with quotes from telegrams and letters sent by Air Force personnel, scientists, aeronautical engineers and a large number of other individuals are included. It concludes:

In the firm belief that the American public deserves a better explanation than that thus far given by the Air Force, I strongly recommend that there be a committee investigation of the UFO phenomena.

I think we owe it to the people to establish credibility regarding UFO's and to produce the greatest possible enlightenment on this subject.

Kindest personal regards.

     Sincerely,

     Gerald R. Ford, Member of Congress [16]

---

value of continuing his advisory function for the Air Force, and may quite possibly have been among the major reasons for his subsequent resignation from the post. In any event, he did disassociate himself from the service soon afterward; a great boon to the serious investigation of ufology, as he now ranks as one of the two or three most important centers of data and sources of intelligent analysis and speculation functioning in the United States.

Additionally, Rep. Weston E. Vivian from the Second Congressional District in Michigan was also demanding an inquiry by the Defense Department, as well as the Air Force, of the disturbing aerial phenomena.

In a style typical of the chairmanship of Representative Rivers, the House Armed Services Committee conducted an "open" hearing. Despite the fact that hundreds of personal witnesses could easily have been summoned, and that many could have been individuals with extraordinarily suitable backgrounds for this kind of inquiry—e.g., astronomers, pilots, radar crews, and others—*only a trio of Air Force representatives* was invited to testify. None had ever laid claim to seeing anything remotely resembling a UFO, and only one, the nonmilitary consultant, knew anything of field investigation.

In addition, the latter was the sole member of the group with any acceptable qualifications for scientific inquiry into and evaluation of the field of these unknowns.

This group, which was to explain UFO to one of the most powerful committees in the Congress, consisted of Secretary of the Air Force Harold Brown, then Project Blue Book Director Lieutenant Colonel Hector Quintanilla, and Dr. J. Allen Hynek.

Brown unilaterally thwarted even the slightest chance for the overwhelmingly necessary comprehensive congressional investigation of UAO. The House Space Committee, controlled by similar types of Representatives, anticipated the Rivers group and delivered an even swifter rejection of Ford's suggestion.

Representative Vivian's demands elicited a more interesting result; an interdepartmental Air Force message regarding his efforts. The message was coded in bureaucratese:

FROM: FTD, Wright-Patterson AFB, Ohio
TO: AFSC, Andrews AFB, Md
Unclass FM TDEW/UFO 14644 March 1966.
For SAFOI-CC, for SCFA (Major Gregory).
Confirming telecon between Maj Gregory

(SCFA and Maj Quintanilla (TDEW). Congressman Vivian (Michigan) called Maj. Quintanilla on 24 March 1966 at 1120 hours and requested. . . .[17]

The report on the Congressman's activities which followed included a request that he be apprised of UFO press conferences, advised of a telephone number, etc., until it reached a most pertinent point:

Congressman Vivian then asked if Maj Quintanilla had a degree and if so in what field. Maj Quintanilla replied that he had a BS in physics. Congressman Vivian then asked how long Maj Quintanilla had been in charge of Project Blue Book. The Maj replied that he had been in charge for 32 months. Congressman Vivian then asked to whom Maj Quintanilla reported and he replied that he reported to Col Eric T. De Jonckheere. Congressman then asked to whom Col De Jonckheere reported and Maj Quintanilla replied that he reported to B/G Cruikshank. Congressman Vivian asked who assisted Maj Quintanilla in investigations. Major replied that Sgt. Moody assists and has a degree in psychology with 24 hours post-graduate work. . . .

(Signed) Major H. Quintanilla, Jr.
29 Mar 66[18]

The Ann Arbor case, or the Dexter case, or the Hillsdale case, or merely the Michigan sightings of 1966, however one wishes to designate the complex of that March, remains among the more intriguing chronicles for a year rife with improbable, but widely witnessed, aerial phenomena.

Praise of Dr. J. Allen Hynek, especially during his later years with the Air Force and following his disassociation from it, is commonplace. Among a considerable number of lesser known, although, perhaps, equally competent, scientists, one name in particular rose to receive rarely paralleled respect in the field of ufology—Dr. James E. McDonald, professor of meteorology at the University of Arizona and senior physicist at the Institute of Atmospheric Physics in Tucson, Arizona. McDonald rarely spoke on the subject without being interesting and introducing exciting new speculations, or refocusing one's perception of chronic characteristics of the problem in general. He spent a great many years interviewing persons who had had sightings, evaluating such observations, and analyzing the collective considerations deriving from his efforts. In late 1966, he concluded that two decades of "official explanations"—e.g., ones based upon astronomical geophysical, technological, psychological, and atmospheric suppositions—produced the overwhelming majority of arguments against the suggestion that UAO might be extraterrestrial in origin. He felt that the old and new theses resolved into eight major classifications:

1. Hoaxes, fabrications, and frauds;
2. Hallucinations, mass hysteria, rumor phenomena;
3. Lay misinterpretations of common physical phenomena (meteorological, astronomical, optical, etc.);
4. Advanced technologies (test vehicles, satellites, re-entry effects);
5. Poorly understood physical phenomena (rare atmospheric-electrical effects, cloud phenomena, plasmas of natural or technological origin, etc.);
6. Poorly understood psychological phenomena;
7. Extraterrestrial probes;
8. Messengers of salvation and occult truth.[19]

Dr. McDonald concurred with the many investigators who held that the preceding twenty years had offered a great deal of evidence to support the contention that the initial four categories supplied answers for a substantial percentage of the sightings recorded. Quite properly, he regarded numbers 5 and 6 as types of accounts extremely difficult to isolate and examine in a systematic and rational way. Although realizing that there was sufficient evidence and there were some techniques by which further serious insight might be gained within the framework of these propositions, it was his conviction that "poorly understood psychological phenomena" was the only consequential alternative to category 7.

The only element of rigidity apparent in McDonald's evaluation was his summary dismissal of group 8. Without any actual examination he rejected the possibility that this category may well offer dimensions never imagined by the unknowledgeable and uninitiated.

> My own study of this problem has led me to the conclusion that Category 7 [extraterrestrial probes] now constitutes the *least unsatisfactory hypothesis* for accounting for the intriguing array of credibly reported UFO phenomena that are on record and that do not appear to fit acceptably into the first six categories.[20]

With respect to the Establishment's investigations preceding his remarks, Dr. McDonald had decided that—

> My study of past official Air Force investigations (Project Bluebook [sic]) leads me to describe them as *completely superficial*. They have, for at least the past dozen years, been carried out at a *very low level of scientific competence* as a very low-priority task (one of about 200 within the Foreign Technology Division, Wright-Patterson AFB). Officially released "explanations" of important UFO sightings have often been almost absurdly erroneous. In only a few instances has there been any on-the-spot field investigation by Bluebook personnel, and much of that has been quite superficial. On the other hand, official press releases, statements to Congress, etc., have conveyed an impression of expertise and investigative thoroughness that has led both the public and the scientific community at large to accept the conclusion that no significant scientific problem exists with respect to UFOs. . . . Much more effort seems warranted, and agencies such as NASA and NSF

should participate actively in the task of rapid clarification of the long-standing confusion over the UFO problem. The work of independent organizations such as the National Investigation Committee on Aerial Phenomena (whose efforts impress me as much more thorough and open-minded than those of Project Bluebook) should be exploited and incorporated into all future studies.

A part of the background to the manner in which Bluebook has handled the UFO problem in the past dozen years is to be found in the complete report of the 1953 Robertson Panel. That scientific panel concluded that there was no strong evidence of any hostile UFO action. The Central Intelligence Agency, represented at the policy-drafting sessions closing the activities of the Robertson Panel, requested that the Air Force adopt a policy of systematic "debunking of flying saucers" to decrease public attention to UFOs. The reasons for this request were associated with the 1952 wave of UFO Reports, the largest wave ever recorded in the United States (possibly exceeded in *intensity* by the French wave of the fall of 1954). So many UFO reports were flooding into air bases throughout the country and other parts of the world in the summer of 1952 that the CIA regarded them as creating a national security problem: In event of enemy attack on the country, the clogging of military intelligence channels with large numbers of reports of the evidently non-hostile UFOs was regarded as an accepted hazard. This CIA request, made in January 1953, was followed by the promulgation, in August, 1953, of Air Force Regulation 200-2, which produced a sharp drop-off in public reporting of Air Force UFO sightings, by forbidding release, at air-base level, of any information on sightings of unidentified aerial phenomena. All sighting reports were to be funneled through Project Bluebook, where they have been largely categorized as conventional objects with little attention to scientific considerations. The strictures implicit in AFR 200-2 were made binding with promulgation of JANAP-146, *which made any such public release of UFO information at air-base or local-command level (by any of the military services and, under certain circumstances, commercial airlines) a crime punishable with fines up to $10,000 and imprisonment up to 10 years.* [*] These regulations have not only cut off almost all useful reports from military pilots, tower operators, and ground crews, but even more serious from a scientific viewpoint has been their drastic effect on non-availability of military radar data on UFOs. Prior to 1953, many significant UFO radar sightings were disclosed. Since then, military radar sightings have been scientifically compromised by confusing denials and allusions to "weather inversions" or "electronic malfunctions" whenever word of radar observations accidentally leaked out in the midst of a UFO episode. Air Force Regulation 200-2 contained the specific admonishment that "Air Force activities must reduce the percentage of unidentifieds to the minimum." This has been achieved.[21]

Notes

1. Hynek, *UFO Experience*, p. 165.
2. Robert Emenegger, *UFO's Past, Present and Future* (New York: Ballantine Books, 1974), p. 63.
3. Hynek, pp. 165–166.
4. Emenegger, p. 64.
5. Ibid., p. 65.
6. Ibid.
7. Hynek, p. 166.
8. Ibid.
9. Ibid., p. 167.
10. New York *Times* (United Press International), March 22, 1966.

* Emphasis added.

11. Ibid.
12. Ibid., March 23, 1966.
13. Ibid., March 24, 1966.
14. This letter written by Gerald R. Ford is public record; it also appears in Emenegger, pp. 73–74.
15. Roscoe Drummond, "Hello, Out There," New York *Herald Tribune,* March 27, 1966.
16. Cf. footnote 14.
17. Emenegger, p. 81.
18. Ibid., p. 22.
19. James E. McDonald, "The Problem of the Unidentified Flying Objects." Summary of an address given before the District of Columbia Chapter of the American Meteorological Society, October 19, 1966.
20. Ibid.
21. Ibid.

19

The Sightings and the Silence

I believe the flying saucers come from outer space, piloted by beings of superior intelligence.

—William Lear, president of Lear, Inc., designers and manufacturers of aircraft and electronic equipment

The disks use a means of propulsion different from ours. There is no other possible explanation. Flying saucers come from another world.

—Louis Breguet, French designer and manufacturer of aircraft.
(From *The Flying Saucer Story* by Brinsley Le Poer Trench. London, Neville Spearman, Ltd., 1966)

IT IS DIFFICULT to determine at what point the Air Force began its program of suppression with respect to reports, evaluations, and interpretations of Unexplained Aerial Objects, but there is no way to dispute that the inauguration of such procedures antedated the great Washington concentration of 1952. Even more unresolved is the date at which the Central Intelligence Agency (CIA) began manipulating the service's handling of the subject and, by extension, was happening throughout the skies of America. Nonetheless, as suggested by Dr. McDonald, somewhere along the way the deception was introduced and by the mid-sixties it was achieved.

Within a decade after Arnold's sighting, the public's fascination was caught up in more theatrical approaches to ufology. One was so imaginative that for a while it dominated the entire field. It was called saucerology, and further complicated the problem of definition, for it was precisely what Captain Ruppelt was attempting to avoid when he coined the expression Unidentified Flying Objects.

As it was explained earlier, saucerology is a term that included practically everything observed in the heavens, near the ground, or landed, from which occupants exited, or aliens established communication with privileged, if inexplicably chosen, Earthians. In contradistinction, Ruppelt's specification Unidentified Flying Objects (UFO) was intended to bypass the phantasmal. It was meant to indicate explicitly what it said: aerial phenomena, the nature of which was unknown.

The late 1950s and the very early 1960s saw the press and entertainment outlets attach themselves to the more exaggerated theories concerning ufological conjecture. The public, so long deprived of science fiction pulp magazines and, subsequently, comic books, was hypnotically enthralled by the new expression of extraterrestrialism.

Then came the space age, providing another set of possible explanations of the Unexplained Aerial Objects (UAO).

Despite the carefully channeled announcement by the Air Force that a scholarly investigation was to be conducted toward the end of establishing the nature and origin of UFO, several academic institutions declined to undertake the project. Eventually, the reluctant acceptance by the University of Colorado to form a team for such an effort, under the administrative head of Dr. Edward U. Condon, led to the creation of the program the Air Force envisioned.

Yet the official plan for disenchantment was uneffected, and the effort to convince the citizenry that the age of "flying saucers" had finally come to an end continued. The contention was without foundation, and, considering that three-quarters of the public believed in the actuality of UFO, the propagandistic diversion directly impinged upon the people's constitutional "right to know." In any event, if all of the extravagance of saucerology had been mitigated, it no way altered the fact that the phenomenon of UAO had not diminished.

Skimming through the enormous intensification of accounts recorded during the months before this work was undertaken, one finds pieces of an answer to the query: "What ever happened to UFO?"

They kept coming in greater and greater numbers.

October 9, 1972. Smithtown/Coram, Long Island, New York. The NICAP publication *UFO Investigator* attributed to Ted Bloecher and Sylvia Meagher a report on a couple from Smithtown, on their way to Coram, some twenty miles away, who observed "a bright, white light, similar to the bright landing light on an airplane, low in the sky to the east and just slightly to the left. . . . It's brightness considerably exceeded that of a star . . . so much brighter, so much bigger." [1]

As they proceeded on their journey they passed through Seldon, Long Island, where the object which they had continued to see was temporarily lost to view but reappeared shortly thereafter. The UAO took the form of a pressing iron with a rectangular shield at the flat end, according to the sketch the witnesses provided, although their verbal description was minimally different. In the latter they recollected the unknown as a lengthy ellipse, dotted by five or six lights "of a highly geometric shape . . . they appeared like elongated rectangles." [2]

January/February 1973. Cherokee County, South Carolina. Commencing fairly early in the year, a continual flow of sightings emerged from various communities in a South Carolina area. These included Asbury-Rehoboth, Beaverdam, Cashion Crossroads, Corinth, Macedonia, White Plains, as well as other locales, but nowhere were they reported in such numbers as Draytonville. Among the various observations offered during the first two months of this concentration were a quartet of red and yellow UFO sailing in a pattern; a disklike or spherical apparition that gave the impression of spinning on its own axis; a large ovoid, accompanied by three cylindrical scouts; a star-white, luminescent triangular shape; and a radiant object with windows and antennae. Before spring hundreds of individuals had observed some kind of UAO, among which were a number of lawmen, and frequently groups of several persons who agreed on what they had seen.

February 1973. Piedmont, Missouri. A similar rash of reports emanated from an area of the "show me" state from persons who had sighted phenomena. An example of the incidents is amply represented by the case of Reggie Bone, athletic director for the local high school, who at eight thirty in the evening on February 21, 1973, was driving home from an out-of-town game with five of his basketball players. Four pulsating and revolving white, amber, blue, and red lights were sighted by the coach and team. They continued to monitor the luminosities for nearly a quarter of an hour, during which time the UFO remained almost stationary and silent. The witnesses were unable to ascertain whether they were independent objects or features of some single dark or natural-colored unknown of much greater dimensions, the totality of which was obscured by the brilliance of what they did see. Eventually the lights rose at an increasing speed, seemed to halt momentarily, and then swept off down the sky. As in the South Carolina complex, there were a great many additional reports submitted to various agencies.

March 1, 1973. Saylors Lake, Pennsylvania. Over a period of approximately three hours, a minimum of a dozen witnesses testified to the persisting presence of from thirty-nine to forty-two unknown white objects, a number featuring red or blue lights. The area, and some of the observers, were visited by UAO of like description on one or more occasions during the following month.

April 1–8, 1973. Los Angeles, California. The multiple-sighting syndrome soon appeared to be spread throughout the country. April Fool's Day started briskly on the West Coast when shortly after dawn an inhabitant of Hollywood had his attention caught by a radiant globe spinning over his head toward the International Airport. Describing the unknown as disklike, the witness flatly stated that whatever he saw was sharply defined against the barely lightened sky. Of special interest to the ufological historian was his depiction that, while the flight path was direct, the object undulated in the manner of "a cork bobbing on an ocean." Needless to say, this was highly reminiscent of accounts recorded of the "great airship" that had confounded Californians seventy-seven years earlier.

June 28, 1973. New York City. Approximately a dozen persons asserted they witnessed a pair of lights, near clouds, pulsating in what appeared to be deliberate communication. Seen to be red and moving in a circular pattern, the objects were said to have been observed during the middle of the evening for more than an hour.

. .*July 25, 1973. Marble Falls, Texas.* An aeronautical engineer, accompanied by two adult friends, reported watching a UAO being maneuvered along various courses, including circling, for three-quarters of an hour.

August 14, 1973. Douglas Island, Alaska. A location classified by the local press as "historically a favorite resting place for unidentified flying objects" maintained its reputation. No fewer than a half dozen inhabitants of a small, offshore island reported a motionless "small glowing object" overhead, before it disappeared at about eleven at night. The sighting lasted twenty minutes. It was examined by two residents through a telescope which permitted each to note it more carefully.

"I looked . . . and it looked like a bright boiled egg yolk with a needle stuck through it. The points on each side were giving off a glow which would get brighter, then duller," [3] recounted Wayne Smallwood, Jr.

August 22, 1973. Hollywood, Florida. Mr. and Mrs. Frank Burke reported the presence of what appeared to be a rocket, with "flames at the bottom," [4] during the middle of the evening, as they sat relaxing in their

backyard. The unknown disappeared into the Ever-
glades area about twenty-five miles away. Investigation indicated the phenomenon had been sighted by a
number of pilots, in addition to which Kennedy Space
Center confirmed there had been no launchings during
the period in question, thus eliminating a reentry explanation.

August 30, 1973. Albany, Georgia. The year-long
plethora of aerial puzzles swept a large area of southern Georgia as dispatches about unknowns were received by police in the towns of Adel, Albany, Ash-
burn, Camilla, Cordele, Dawson, Doe Run, Dougherty
County, Leesburg, Macon, Moultrie, Pelham, Vienna,
Waycross and elsewhere. Even Robins * Air Force
Base in Macon, Eglin Air Force Base in Florida, and
the Naval Air Station in Albany, Georgia, were put on
special alert. The period of activity ran from midnight
to dawn as intermittently visible yellow, blue, and green
objects were reported.

Among the Georgia sightings were many which included police as witnesses. For example, State trooper
A. L. Cahill, and Sergeant Jerry Crawley and Officer
John Harris, of the Americus Police Department, along
with several additional lawmen, saw mysterious objects in the sky passing over Dawson toward Albany.
"It was a real bright white light traveling in the sky
. . . rather large," [5] recalled Cahill.

A patrolman in Leesburg said that "the object is
round, with orange, red, green, and blue lights." [6]
Camilla was treated to a three-and-a-half-hour display,
seen by at least six or seven people. "It looks like a
white light with blinking green and red lights. It has
moved in a zigzag pattern and then moved slowly to the
west." [7]

The Georgia concentration grew rapidly, for the
most part spreading northward until much of the center of the state had contributed reports. In addition to
towns previously mentioned, Sandersville and Tifton
were added to the list. In the former, announcer Ray

---

* Variously spelled "Dobins," "Dobbins" and "Robbins,"
as well.

Smith of WSNT accounted for a dozen different colored lights after having been alerted by listeners calling his program, while in the latter police stared at UAO overhead for nearly an hour.

"We've seen about 10 or 12 of these things. They're generally blue in color but change into red and sometimes green. They're smaller than stars and change colors, kind of like a kid's top," [8] said Smith.

Robins Air Force Base, in the area, received a considerable number of calls over a period of forty-eight hours; however, the base officials explained, in the words of a journalist, that "they did not record the calls because the Air Force does not admit the existence of UFOs." [9]

The problem was also causing turbulence in the Air Force's Washington home as Major James A. Durham, speaking for Assistant Secretary of Defense for Public Affairs, clarified his service's positions with the announcement that "The department of Defense does not have a statement to make," [10] to which he added refusals to reply to a number of other queries. Asked why he declined to offer any information, he declined to offer any explanation: "I can't answer that question." [11] This exchange continued for a while and then the press went home.

Other Pentagon officials who joined the chorus of people who were unable to provide any explanation included Colonel Jack Powell, and a Lieutenant Colonel Williams. The latter made more of rejecting requests for his name than anything else, an attitude that elicited a response from Powell, who declared that such was his subordinate's business and "I don't know his first name myself." [12] Everyone seemed to be suggesting that the source sought by the press was in reality one O. G. Wiloughby, a name no one appeared to be able to spell. Finally, the gentleman, described as the "chief of the defense news branch in the Pentagon," [13] was reached on the telephone. Unfortunately, Wiloughby waits for no man: "It's time for me to go off duty, and I cannot talk to you," [14] he announced.

On the fourth straight day of sightings in southern and central Georgia, two Manchester state troopers, using binoculars, perceived a craft that had a "blue and white light on either side and something hanging underneath." [15] Chester A. Tatum, publisher of the Sowega *Free Press,* in Camilla, claimed he photographed one of the blinking, multicolored lights, saying it had a "ribbed type design with some sort of center down the middle," [16] adding that it also displayed a luminous exhaust.

The Establishment expressed its indifference editorially as the public was told that "Despite an unprecedented flurry of unidentified flying object reports by Georgia residents, military and civilian authorities yesterday indicated they planned no investigation of the sightings." [17] This attitude was confirmed elsewhere. "The Air Force used to have a program to check up on this type of thing but they dropped it. I seriously doubt there will be any investigation," [18] said Lieutenant Colonel Richard Davies of Warner-Robins Air Force Base.

Sightings were as plentiful throughout the rest of the country. In Ohio a number of Harrison County people called police agencies to report a UAO,[19] while in Sandersville, Georgia the local activity continued. Meanwhile, in Macon, Officer Dennis Brown reacted to the suggestion that all the hundreds of sightings were merely satellite and like debris. "I'll go against any man who says these things are a planet or scrap metal falling from space," [20] he remarked, after viewing four UAO through a ten-power rifle scope. "I believe the yellow or white lights are from the propulsion system. There is something inside. I believe the American government is experimenting with something and don't want us to know about it." [21]

An incidental quote found its way into the discussion when Pete Conrad, the astronaut crew chief on Skylab I, said in Tallahassee that if an alien "showed up it wouldn't surprise me." [22]

A coastal sighting stimulated considerable interest when a UFO was reported to have plummeted into the ocean off Tybee Island. The United States Coast Guard station located there evinced so little interest that no search craft was directed to investigate the incident. Among the witnesses were the usual contingent of law enforcement personnel plus Savannah Beach Mayor Allen Hendrix.[23]

Even more impressive was the account of police corporal John Kitchell, who responded to a call that some people had observed "a large circular craft something like a flying saucer." [24] Kitchell elaborated on the description, noting that it had "a large spot-light which changed color from red to green," [25] as well as referring to blinking blue lamps of smaller size. Military policemen, Specialists 4 Bart J. Burns and Randy Shade, turned in a description of an encounter with an unknown which "came in at tree-top level and made a dive," [26] diverting their vehicle into a roadside gully. A number of other reports were recorded the same evening, the third consecutive one during which UAO had been over Chatham County. Of particular interest was the announcement that a WAGA-TV cameraman had captured ninety seconds of film of one of the objects as it hovered and rapidly fluctuated in color near Manchester.[27]

Sightings continued to canopy the South as law enforcers in Auburn, Carrville, Lanett, Notasulga, Tuskegee, and other communities of Alabama registered their observations. Simultaneously, more military installations, e.g., Maxwell Air Force Base, in Montgomery, reaffirmed they had no explanation for the sightings, and weather and space officials admitted that none of their activities could explain the enormous number of accounts.

As had been the case in Georgia and other states, Alabama seemed to be suddenly flooded with Unidentified Flying Objects.[28]

The Georgia concentration seemed to intensify and it became extremely difficult to keep track of the hundreds, perhaps thousands, of incidents. The observations included every classic shape, maneuver, color, variance of illumination and other characteristics chronicled throughout the history of the subject. Among the scores of particularly puzzling cases was the claim of Rast Clayton,* from a small community near Griffin, Georgia, in which he asserted he saw a brilliant, gold device. It spun in a cloud of smokelike atmosphere, landed about a hundred feet from his home, and soon afterward sailed out of sight. Clayton communicated with a local radio station to report the episode and also describe a residual ring of scorched grass.

Dr. O. E. Anderson of the Agricultural Station at the University of Georgia investigated the seared circle within a couple of hours after the local broadcaster had gotten the farmer's call. He remarked that "The soil was unusually hot for just grass to be burning. It was hot down to a depth of at least a half an inch and [down to] as much as an inch the soil was very, very hot." [29] While these were only initial observations it seemed obvious to Anderson that if he had been attracted to a hoax it was not an obvious one, and further examination and analysis were justified. Subsequently, he conjectured that the phenomenon might have been "something in the nature of a small meteorite or a piece of space hardware." [30]

Day by day the list of sightings in various southern states, especially Alabama and Georgia, lengthened. It is unlikely that anything remotely resembling a full picture of this incredible concentration will ever be known, since the federal and lesser military, and nonmilitary, agencies had long since abandoned their responsibilities regarding UFO.

Yet, if authorities failed to confront the problem of the enigmatic phenomena, this did not deter major figures from acknowledging their own experiences. Returning home, with a group of friends, on a September evening in 1973 Georgia Governor Jimmy Carter,† later a contender for the presidential nomination revealed that he had seen one of the curiosities. "I don't laugh at people any more when they say they've seen UFOs, because I've seen one myself." [31]

---

* Elsewhere identified as Ress Clanton.
† The successful Democratic candidate for the presidency of the United States in 1976.

The frequency with which Unknown Aerial Phenomena are seen, especially within the context of particularly high concentration such as occurred throughout 1973, is inestimable. So that some small portion of the current ufological environment might be understood, in terms of quantity, if not fully with respect to quality, a few random citations follow. It is hoped that they will serve to illustrate the geographical sweep and chronological consistency of Unidentified Flying Objects.

October 1, 1973. Mrs. Pearl Keene, of Rogers, Arkansas, saw something resembling four flying headlights; [32] Debbie Adams, of radio station WGIG in Brunswick, Florida, and a number of other observers watched an unknown described as "red at the top, green in the bottom, and white in the middle," [33] performing unlikely aerial gyrations; Mrs. H. W. Steffen, of Jacksonville, Florida, was attracted by "amber lights and then brighter lights" [34] hovering northwest of her home.

October 3, 1973. Highway Patrolmen J. D. Green, Charles Loving, and Charles Hinds reported an unidentified object blinking yellow, red, and green, at an altitude of about two thousand feet, in the area of Ashland-Holly Springs, Mississippi. [35]

October 4, 1973. Bobby Laney, in Oxford, and M. E. Burke, in Pine Flat, both in Mississippi, had sightings; [36] inhabitants of Little Rock, Colliersville, Benton, West Helena, and other Arkansas communities accounted for reports; [37] the sheriff's office recorded the story of "a very bright light moving up and down with a tail similar to a comet," near Shady Grove, in the same state; [38] and Grenada, Mississippi, had a widespread "flap" of its own as the Reverend Clint Holley, Deputy Sheriff Charles Whitfield, radio station sales manager Arlin Mohundro, and photographer Fletcher W. Ross, the first two of that town, the others from Corinth, Mississippi, and Greenville, North Carolina, respectively, all had impressive sightings. [39] Thomas E. Westmoreland, a National Park Service ranger, gave an account of a UAO the size of a house barely moving in the sky as it pulsated red, green, and yellow. A resident of Tupelo, Mississippi, he stated: "I've been dealing with the public for years and I know people exaggerate and see what they want to see, but I know I saw this." [40] Summoned by the Ollie Berry family, near Hell Creek Bottom, Mississippi, Sheriff's Deputy Irwin Carroll confirmed their observation, saying the unknown was "like a quarter moon but five times as big." [41] Mrs. Berry's daughter, who had a longer opportunity to view the phenomenon, gave a particularly detailed depiction, relating that it was "first like a star, but longer. Then like a half moon. Then like a kite with a lot of red lights on its tail. Then it got round. Then it divided into three pieces," [42] a pattern of physical change consonant with some of the most remarkable and mystifying "classic" sightings by highly qualified monitors.

By October 5 virtually the entire Deep South had been saturated by the startling occurrences. Arkansas, North and South Carolina, Tennessee, Mississippi, Alabama, Georgia, and Florida had all reported hundreds of cases, and while this extraordinary deluge of accounts attracted the primary attention of the public, hundreds of other sightings were finding their way into the files of the investigators throughout other regions of the nation. What was happening north of the Mason-Dixon line was exemplified by Dayton, Ohio's multiple spectacle of October 10, when fifteen objects, radiating red, blue, and green lights, buzzed the housetops in the southwestern part of the state, around mid-evening. A policeman, who asked his superiors to permit him to remain anonymous, delivered a report to Michael Sullivan, sheriff's deputy of Montgomery County, who said:

> The officer said it was oblong and covered with lights. It appeared stationary in the sky about tree top level for several minutes until he tried to shine his spot on it. It then zoomed toward him and then shot straight up in the air—after he turned out his light—and disappeared. [43]

October 12, 1973. Suddenly, Ohio was becoming the

focus of UFO attention, as accounts came in from
scores of towns, including St. Marys, Moulton, Greenville, Shawnee, Lima, Cridersville, Piqua, Wapakoneta,
and Buckland, Ross, Millville, New Lebanon, Dayton,
and north to Bellefontaine. Many observations were
made in rural areas of Montgomery, Butler, Clark,
Greene, Logan, and other counties.[44]

On October 11, two residents of Pascagoula, Mississippi, were allegedly confronted by a spacecraft which
landed and temporarily were abducted by its occupants,
presumably for "examination." This account began to
break in the local newspapers five days afterward.
Soon the tale was ballooned into a national feature
story by the press and television networks.

The month entered its second half, and a notable
rise in activity in Louisiana occurred,[45] as was the
case in California, where reports increased rapidly, as
well. San Francisco, Madera, San Luis Obispo, and
desert regions were overflown.[46]

Elsewhere—

Army Reserve helicopter pilot Captain Lawrence J.
Coyne, a flier for ten years, in and out of the military,
was serving as commander of the 316th Medical De-
tachment, helicopter ambulance service, attached to the
Cleveland, Ohio, Hopkins airport on the night of
October 18, 1973. Having left Columbus forty minutes
earlier with a crew of three, he was cruising at 2,500
feet when Staff Sergeant Robert Yanacsek * advised
him of a red light on the eastern horizon which appeared to be pacing the helicopter on a parallel path.
Unexpectedly, the object altered course and raced
directly at Coyne's craft. Immediately the officer adjusted his controls for a shallow 20-degree dive as
the sergeant shouted, "That tower is closing in fast," [47]
alluding to the converging unknown. The evasive action
appeared to Coyne to have failed. "The light was
traveling in excess of 600 knots. It came from the
horizon to our aircraft in about 10 seconds. We were
on a collision course." [48]

---

* "Janacsek" in *The A.P.R.O. Bulletin*, September–October
1973.

The helicopter was now at 2,000 feet and descending.

"I had made no attempt to pull up," said Coyne. "There was no noise or turbulence either." [49]

"At 1700 feet I braced myself for the impact with the other craft. It was coming from our right side. I was scared. There had been so little time to respond. The thing was terrifically fast." [50]

However, to the crew's astonishment, there was no crash, and as they looked out the UAO was clearly visible some 500 feet overhead. It had reduced its speed to 100 miles an hour and was hovering above and apparently inspecting the helicopter.

It had a big, gray, metallic-looking hull about 60 feet long. It was shaped like an airfoil, or a streamlined fat cigar. There was a red light on the front. The leading edge glowed red a short distance back from the nose. There was a center dome. A green light at the rear reflected on the hull. This light swiveled like a spotlight. It was shining brightly through the bubble canopy of our helicopter, completely flooding out our red instrument lights and turning everything inside green. [51]

It occurred to Coyne that he might have seen a jet, and he attempted to contact Mansfield Air Force Base —some reports have this during the instants the unknown was hurtling at his ship, [52] others do not specify the time. [53] In any event, the report is that while the radio seemed to be technically functioning, it would not transmit or receive. "I couldn't get the keying sound and there was no reflection," [54] recalled the pilot. One account has him making momentary contact with the Mansfield tower, only to have his radio go dead almost immediately. [55]

Whatever the actuality of this point, it was established that none of the Air Force base's F-100 Super Saber Jets were aloft at the time. [56]

Yet, if the entire preceding episode had seemed astonishing, at least it made some physical sense. The discovery which followed defies even good theorizing.

Coyne, in attempting to avoid the imminent danger of collision, had swooped down to a mere 1,500 feet and was still on a descending path when the object overhead suddenly swept away. But when he looked back at his altimeter, he was amazed.

> I could hardly believe it was reading 3500 feet, climbing to 3800. I had made no attempt to pull up. All controls were set for a 20-degree dive. Yet we had climbed from 1700 to 3500 feet with no power in a couple of seconds with no G-forces or other noticeable strain. There was no noise or turbulence either.[57]

A few minutes after the UFO vanished, the radio renewed its normal function.

There seems no reasonable solution for this riddle, but the *A.P.R.O. Bulletin* has very tentatively offered an answer which does have the value of allowing for the facts if not explaining the how and why of the incident, i.e., "that the air surrounding the copter moved along [rose] with it." [58]

After having an opportunity to confer with whomever one consults in the Air Force or CIA these days when he experiences a singular detailed and incomprehensible encounter with a UAO, Captain Coyne seemed to attempt to modify the texture of his original account, although he altered none of his statements relative to fact. It was merely that he added: "I'm a military commander. I don't believe in UFO's, little green spacemen and all that stuff. But I had to file an official report in detail to the Army on this thing." [59]

What thing, Captain Coyne? What thing?

Notes

1. *UFO Investigator*, February 1973, p. 2.
2. Ibid.
3. Juneau (Alaska) *Empire*, August 15, 1973.

4. Hollywood (Florida) *Sun-Tattler*, August 22, 1973.
5. Americus (Georgia) *Times-Recorder*, August 31, 1973.
6. Ibid.
7. Ibid.
8. Jacksonville (Florida) *Journal*, September 1, 1973.
9. Marietta (Georgia) *Journal*, September 2, 1973.
10. Albany (Georgia) *Sunday Herald*, September 2, 1973.
11. Ibid.
12. Ibid.
13. Ibid.
14. Ibid.
15. Los Angeles *Herald Examiner*, September 3, 1973.
16. Boston *Herald American*, September 4, 1973.
17. Seattle *Post-Intelligencer*, September 4, 1973.
18. Denver *Rocky Mountain News*, September 4, 1973.
19. New Philadelphia (Ohio) *Times-Reporter*, September 4, 1973.
20. Macon (Georgia) *Telegraph and News*, September 6, 1973.
21. Ibid.
22. Little Rock (Arkansas) *Gazette*, September 7, 1973.
23. Savannah *Morning News*, September 7, 1973.
24. Seattle *Post-Intelligencer*, September 9, 1973.
25. Ibid.
26. Ibid.
27. Winston-Salem *Journal*, September 10, 1973.
28. See Seattle *Post-Intelligencer*, Los Angeles *Times*, Montgomery (Alabama) *Journal*, Fort Walton Beach (Florida) *Playground News*, all of September 10, 1973. Montgomery (Alabama) *Advertiser*, September 11, 1973.
29. Atlanta *Constitution*, September 11, 1973.
30. Little Rock (Arkansas) *Gazette*, September 15, 1973.
31. Wichita *Beacon*, September 14, 1973.
32. Rogers (Arkansas) *Daily News*, October 1, 1973.
33. Jacksonville (Florida) *Journal*, October 1, 1973.
34. Ibid.
35. Tupelo (Mississippi) *Daily Journal*, October 3, 1973.
36. Oxford (Mississippi) *Eagle*, October 4, 1973.
37. West Helena (Arkansas) *Twin City Tribune*, October 4, 1973.
38. Mountain Home (Arkansas) *Baxter Bulletin*, October 4, 1973.
39. Grenada (Mississippi) *Sentinel Star*, October 4, 1973.

40. Ibid.
41. New Albany (Mississippi) *Gazette*, October 4, 1973.
42. Ibid.
43. Cleveland *Press*, October 11, 1973.
44. St. Marys (Ohio) *Evening Leader*, Cincinnati *Post* and *Times Star*, Springfield (Ohio) *Sun*, all of October 12, 1973.
45. Anita (Louisiana) *Tangi Talk*, Hammond (Louisiana) *Daily Star*, both October 17, 1973. Alexandria (Louisiana) *Town Talk*, Lafayette (Louisiana), *Advertiser*, both October 18, 1973.
46. Madera (California) *Tribune*, San Diego *Evening Tribune*, both October 17, 1973. San Francisco *Chronicle*, San Luis Obispo *Telegram-Tribune*, both October 18, 1973. San Mateo *Times*, October 20, 1973. Van Nuys *Valley News* and *Green Sheet*, October 21, 1973.
47. *A.P.R.O. Bulletin*, September–October 1973.
48. United Press International, November 3, 1973.
49. Ibid.
50. *UFO Investigator*, November 1973. *A.P.R.O. Bulletin*, September–October 1973. United Press International, November 3, 1973.
51. Ibid. (all).
52. *A.P.R.O. Bulletin*, September–October, 1973.
53. *UFO Investigator*, November 1973. United Press International, November 3, 1973.
54. *UFO Investigator*, November 1973.
55. *A.P.R.O. Bulletin*, September–October, 1973.
56. United Press International, November 3, 1973.
57. *UFO Investigator*, November 1973.
58. *A.P.R.O. Bulletin*, September–October, 1973.
59. United Press International, November 3, 1973.

20

The History of the United States Air Force and Unidentified Flying Objects

British scientists and airmen, after examining the wreckage of one mysterious flying ship, are convinced that these strange aerial objects are not optical illusions or Soviet inventions, but are actually flying saucers which originate on another planet. My source of information is a British official of cabinet officer rank, who prefers to remain unidentified. "We believe on the basis of our inquiries thus far that the saucers were staffed by small men—probably under four feet tall," my informant told me. "It's frightening but there is no denying the flying saucers come from another planet."

> —Dorothy Kilgallen, noted investigative reporter and columnist.
> May 22, 1955

THE ULTIMATE MYSTERY regarding Unidentified Flying Objects is the puzzle of their nature and origin. This is obvious. Immediately following is the question of the Establishment's treatment of the problem. Generally it has been the property of the Air Force and the Central Intelligence Agency, and the latter has always remained as far in the background as possible. Yet, to understand the approach taken by the government, as publicly represented by the service, one must be aware of the actions of the Air Force with respect to UAO. A large volume could be devoted to this subject, but the following is a necessarily concise, but complete, chronicle of its revealed program.

September 23, 1947. Lieutenant General Nathan F. Twining, Chief of Staff of the United States Army, sent an official letter to Brigadier General George Schulgen, Commanding General of the United States Army Air Force. It states that it was the opinion of the highest military level of government that "the phenomenon [sic] reported is something real and not visionary or fictitious," that "there are objects probably approximating the shape of a disc," and are of sizes comparable to conventional aircraft, that natural atmospheric occurrences might have accounted for "some of the incidents," and that "reported operating characteristics . . . and action must be considered evasive when sighted or contacted . . . [lending] belief to the possibility that some of the objects are controlled either manually, automatically or remotely."

The communication from the head of the United States Army to the head of the (then subordinate) United States Air Force proceeds to review the "apparent common description of the objects," and their likely origin, emphasizing, in reverse order, a foreign government, the lack of physical evidence which might lead to some, even tentative, determination, and "the possibility that these are of domestic origin—the product of some high security project not known to" even the Chief of Staff of the United States Army or the Commanding General of the United States Air Force.*

---

* "We adopted the term 'conspiracy hypothesis' for the view that *some agency of the Government either within the Air Force, the Central Intelligence Agency, or elsewhere knows all about UFOs and is keeping the knowledge secret. Without denying the possibility that this could be true,* we decided very early in the study, that we were not likely to succeed in carrying out a form of counterespionage against our own Government, in hope of settling this question. *We therefore decided not to pay any special attention to it,* but instead to keep alert to any indications that might lead to any evidence that not all of the essential facts known to the Government were being given to us. [Emphasis added.]

"Although we found no such evidence, it must be conceded that there may be a secret government UFO laboratory hidden away somewhere of whose [sic] existence we are not aware.

The conclusion of the directive stated General Twining's recommendations, which were that the Headquarters of the United States Air Force issued an order for the establishment of a section specifically devoted to the investigation and analysis of unknown aerial activity, give it priority and security classification and a code name, and keep him, and various other official and semi-official agencies, advised via progress reports, with a preliminary evaluation to be dispatched as quickly as feasible.

December 30, 1947. Major General L. C. Craigie, United States Air Force, Director of Research and Development office, Deputy Chief of Staff, Material (sic), wrote to the Commanding General, Wright-Patterson Air Force Base, affirming that "it is Air Force policy not to ignore reports of sightings and phenomena in the atmosphere, but to recognize that part of its mission is to collect, collate, evaluate and act on information of this nature."

The instructions were then given to form a project to "implement this policy," suggesting that reports should be prepared for quarterly issuance, with supplementary dispatches disseminated with the frequency events demanded. Further, the order specified that the project should be "assigned priority 2-A" (the second highest possible), a security designation of "restricted," and the code name "SIGN," which was soon inappropriately translated into "Saucer" by the press. The military memorandum added that where required even more rarefied security classifications might be applied to data accumulated.

December 13, 1948. Brigadier General Donald Putt,

But I doubt it. I do not believe it, but, of course, I cannot prove its non-existence!" (Condon Report, pp. 522–523.)

Despite spending nearly a thousand pages in an effort to prove the "non-existence" of UFO, Condon and his apologia lunge into the dusty disproving-the-negative refuge on this vital—conceivably the most ominous of all—considerations, with the old "if you can't trust your Government, whom can you trust?"

Obviously, as some of us have been attempting to convey for years, that, indeed, is the question.

director of Research and Development, Office of the Deputy Chief of Staff, Air Material Command Headquarters, received a commentary from Dr. James E. Lipp, Rand Corporation consultant in missiles to the United States Air Force, speculating on the likelihood of extraterrestrial investigations of Earth and the theses of life elsewhere in the known universe.[1] Mars and Venus are the only planets in this system regarded as being worth any such consideration. Lipp observed that knowledge of evolution is minimal, that "we do not know the origin of life, even on Earth," and that "it is not too unreasonable . . . [to hypothesize that either Mars or Venus might be] a possible home for intelligent life." Despite the detailed inhospitality of the atmosphere of both neighbors, the concession was granted that:

> living organisms might develop in chemical environments that are strange to us: the vegetable kingdom, for example, operates on a fundamentally different energy cycle from Man. Bodies might be constructed and operated with different chemicals and other physical principles than any of the creatures we know. One thing is evident: fishes, insects, and mammals all manufacture within their own bodies complex chemical compounds that do not exist as minerals. To this extent, life is self sufficient and might well adapt itself to any environment within limits of temperature (and size of the creature).

In light of these admissions, virtually any additional conjectures are justified, including those beyond the size and temperature limitations suggested. Dr. Lipp's approach was traditionally channeled so that he presupposed that "long-time practice of space travel implies advanced engineering and science, weapons and ways of thinking." Apparently he is oblivious to the fact that the last of these points may well obviate the foregoing ones, for truly "advanced . . . ways of thinking" certainly allow for different, quite likely radically different, mental processes. Beyond that is the possibility of a highly sophisticated, seemingly primal, undecipherable, nature capable of establishing and controlling symbiotic functions. The results of such motivations or forces might be incomprehensible to our way of "thinking."

Dr. Lipp revealed a second characteristic of scientists attempting to operate in fields about which their education and experience has taught them little or nothing. Near the end of his memorandum he wrote that

> As far as this writer knows, all incidents [of UFO-type phenomena] have occurred in the United States, whereas visiting spacemen could be expected to scatter their visits more or less uniformly over the globe. The small area covered indicates strongly that the flying objects are of Earthly origin, whether physical or psychological.

It is evident the theorist is unaware of thousands of years of activity by aerial incomprehensibles, as well as the many incidents recorded in the decade immediately preceding his analysis. In each case, events were chronicled throughout the world.

Dr. Lipp concludes that "although visits from outer space [he confines his ideas to aeronautical ones] are believed to be possible, they are believed to be very improbable."

February 1949. Professor George E. Valley of the Massachusetts Institute of Technology, consulting member of the Scientific Advisory Board, Office of the Chief of Staff, United States Air Force,[2] delivered an analysis of UFO activity. It is presented in three sections, *summary, possibilities, and recommendations,* and divided the objects into essentially physical descriptions—disks, lights, rockets (including cigar-shaped), probable known balloons, and those "in which little credence can be placed," a category apparently reserved for anything not consonant with the scholar's "reality." Employing somewhat simplistic mechanics, the professor offers the conclusion that the

size of the unknowns is not determinable.* Relegating
to the ashcan of absurdity all speculations on pro-
pulsions other than those which appear to have
fascinated writers of interplanetary fiction, Dr. Valley
decides that "the tentative proposed assumption . . .
[is] that the objects are supported and propelled by
some normal means, or else they are not solids." His
review of the "possible causes for the reports" includes
ball lightning; a phyla to species of animals—especially
fireflies, hallucinations, and foreign aircraft; or extraterrestrial phenomena, among which are listed meteors,
animals not of this earth, and spaceships. Of vehicles
from elsewhere Valley observes that

> if there is an extraterrestrial civilization which
> can make such objects as are reported then it is
> most probable that its development is far in ad-
> vance of ours. This argument can be supposed
> on probability alone without recourse to astro-
> nomical hypotheses.
>
> Such a civilization might observe that on earth
> we now have atomic bombs and are fast develop-
> ing rockets. In view of the past history of man-
> kind, they would be alarmed. We should, there-
> fore, expect at this time above all to behold such
> visitations.

The final recommendations of the evaluation are
that the project should be continued; meteorological,
aerodynamic, and mass-psychological studies relating
to cited problems should be conducted; official inter-
viewers should be better trained and equipped; and
optical and atmospheric investigations should be directed toward clarification of certain consistencies and
inconsistencies common to the reports.

Hardly a demand for a comprehensive and penetrating survey, even twenty-five years ago.

August 1949. The Project Grudge [sole] Report
No. 102-AC 49/15-100, classified "Secret," was issued
to proper authorities.[3]

---

* Obviously, not necessarily true in every instance.

It states that nothing indicated that the objects were the product of a foreign government with a superior technology, or were of any danger to the security of this country, and, therefore, that "the investigation and study of reports of unidentified flying objects be reduced in scope," adding that "it is apparent that further study *along present lines* * would only confirm the findings presented herein." The memorandum further suggests that "permanent [UFO sighting] collection directives be revised to reflect the contemplated change of policy." Yet, nothing so revealed the attempt to diminish and destroy inquiry into the subject as the Project statements that—

All evidence and analysis indicate that reports of unidentified flying objects are the result of:
1. Misinterpretation of various conventional objects.
2. A mild form of mass-hysteria and war nerves.
3. Individuals who fabricate such reports to perpetuate a hoax or to seek publicity.
4. Psychopathological persons.

This particular effort to dissuade the Establishment from pursuing an investigation of the phenomena capriciously dismisses virtually the entire catalogue of scientific entries relating to UFO. For that, and other, reasons it ranks as among the less imaginative and more inept commentaries on the subject channeled through the public relations office of the Air Force.

The report concluded with the recommendation that parentalistic press releases should be devised and dispatched to the public to "aid in dispelling public apprehension" as "there are indications that the planned release of sufficient unusual aerial objects coupled with the release of related psychological propaganda would cause a form of mass-hysteria. Employment of these methods by or against an enemy would yield similar results."

Most of this report was prepared by Ohio State

* Emphasis added.

University, the Air Weather Service, the United States
Weather Bureau, the Rand Corporation, Dr. J. Allen
Hynek, Dr. Paul Fitts, and Dr. Valley.

September 1949. The Air Force Cambridge Research Laboratory, after more than six months' discussion regarding the mystery of green fireballs over
the American Southwest, inaugurated Project Twinkle
to study the scientifically confounding phenomena. Dr.
Lincoln La Paz, internationally noted astronomical
authority and head of the University of New Mexico
Institute of Meteorics, was named to direct the effort.
Its primary goal was the photographing of the strange
objects, which its principal expert did not believe were
examples of the celestial wonders in which he specialized.

December 27, 1949. The United States Air Force
issued press release No. 629-49 announcing the liquida-
tion of Project Grudge. It conveyed the impression
that the service was abandoning all further examination of sighting accounts and the UFO mystery. In
actuality, a cursory sort of survey was maintained by
the Air Technical Intelligence Center, the product of
which was routinely handled by intelligence operations.

October 27, 1951. Major General C. P. Cabell,
director of Air Force Intelligence, ordered the re-
activation of Project Grudge, allegedly because of a
miscalculation of a radar operator at Fort Monmouth,
New Jersey, which indicated that a UFO target on his
scope was traveling at inexplicable velocities. The New
Project Grudge was inconsequentially "expanded," but
was no more equipped to deal with so complex a
problem than were its predecessors.

November 1951. The first of one dozen Status Reports, which commenced with the reinstitution of
Project Grudge and continued, until the late 1950s,
with Project Blue Book, was issued (actually dated
December 28, 1951), containing, among other data,
an exposition of the Fort Monmouth radar incident
before expurgation.

December 11 1951 (c.) Major General John A.
Samford, having replaced Major General Cabell as
director of intelligence, was given a full briefing of the

service's UFO program by Captain Edward J. Ruppelt
and Colonel Frank Dunn, chief of the Air Technical
Intelligence Center. Brigadier General W. M. Garland,
Samford's assistant for production, was assigned the
task of monitoring the activity for his superior. It was
clarified that, within the government, the Air Force
was wholly responsible for UFO inquiries and analysis,
and that the Air Technical Intelligence Center was the
agency specifically answerable for the surveillance.
Project Grudge was the first-line group directly ac-
countable for the effort.

Ruppelt and Dunn were assured unequivocally that
the United States had absolutely *no* secret aircraft, or
other device, which were being reported as UFO.

December 27, 1951. The final report of Project
Twinkle was issued, revealing that the program to capture green fireballs on film had achieved no success.

December 28, 1951. Special Report No. 1 (see
Status Reports mentioned above) from Project Grudge.

March 1952. The New Project Grudge was designated the Aerial Phenomena Group, apparently a
purely nominal change of little more than a few
months' duration, after which it was permanently renamed Project Blue Book. The Condon Report carries
a sole reference to the Aerial Phenomena Group (p.
781), citing March 1952 as the date upon which
Project Blue Book was established (p. 511).

April 3, 1952. The Air Force issued a press release
confirming that the investigation and evaluation of
Unidentified Flying Object sightings had not been discontinued, as previously it had been announced. If
"news" to the public, it was merely the admission of
what was common knowledge to all serious unofficial
investigators and much of the press.

April 29, 1952. The Air Force Regulation No.
200-5 indicated an intensified interest by higher authorities in the phenomena, and appeared to promise
improved communications between local military inter-
viewers of persons reporting a sighting and the upper
levels of responsibility. However, it resulted in little,
if any, implementation of the Project staff or its facilities.

May 8, 1952. Secretary of the Air, Thomas K. Finletter, after a briefing from Captain Edward J. Ruppelt, then head of the service's UFO group, and Lieutenant Colonel R. J. Taylor, of Colonel Frank Dunn's staff at Air Technical Intelligence Center, issued a press release stating that the Air Force would continue investigating selected sighting accounts.

June 15, 1952 (c.) Captain Edward J. Ruppelt gave an updating briefing to Brigadier General W. M. Garland and an unnamed general from the Research and Development Board, who usually took such periodical reports and distilled them into a summary for Major General John A. Samford, Director of Intelligence. Unlike previous meetings, the audience included Samford himself, a number of officers from his staff, two anonymous Navy captains from the Office of Naval Intelligence, and a few other nameless individuals, from unspecified origins—at least in Ruppelt's and other "official" writings. The latter were almost certainly from the Central Intelligence Agency. Ruppelt recorded that there was, as had been the case since the inception of study of the subject by the Air Force, a strong UFO-are-interplanetary faction at this conference.

July 29, 1952 (A.M.) President Harry Truman's air aide, Brigadier General Landry, called Air Force Intelligence, at the Commander in Chief's request, to—in Ruppelt's words—"find out what was going on."

July 29, 1952 (P.M.) Major General John A. Samford, director of Air Force Intelligence, conducted a press conference in an attempt to explain the collective mystery of UFO and the specific pair of "classic" Washington overflights (7/19-7/20, 1952 and 7/26-7/27, 1952), in particular. It was the largest and longest such Air Force activity since World War II. Samford, lacking answers to most of the questions, and having to deal with the results of widespread incompetence and conflict of opinion and interest, appeared to spend most of his time being wholly unresponsive. His hope that some semi-technical jargon from Captain Roy James, a radar expert from the Air Technical Intelligence Center, would achieve a more convincing denegation was unfounded. The absence of Major

Dewey J. Fournet, Jr., liaison officer between Project Blue Book and the Pentagon: Al Chop, official public relations man for the Air Force on Unidentified Flying Objects; and Lieutenant Holcomb, a Navy electronics expert assigned to the Air Force Directorate of Intelligence, all of whom had actually been in the Air Route Traffic Control radar room at Washington National Airport on the night of the second incident, had watched the radar blips and listened to the radio conversations with the pursuing F-94 jet interceptor pilots, and were all commonly known to doubt seriously that the phenomena had anything to do with weather effects on the equipment—the arguments being presented— was intentional and apparent.

August 1, 1952. Project Grudge Technical Report 102-AC 49/15-100, a survey of 244 cases, with the astronomical evaluations of Dr. J. Allen Hynek prevailing, and originally classified as "Secret," was officially declassified. Approximately 32 percent are regarded as having astronomical origins, 12 percent are catalogued as observations of some sort of balloons, 33 percent are dismissed as hoaxes or as of too inadequate an amount of data from which to draw even tentative inferences, and the remaining *23 percent* were conceded to be "Unknowns."

June–August, 1952 (c.) Captain Edward J. Ruppelt, Major Dewey J. Fournet, Jr., and two of his superiors, Colonel Weldon Smith and Colonel W. A. Adams, had a semi-official conference about a proposal to institute a study of Unidentified Flying Objects in terms of their motion—random or pattern—to determine if intelligent control reasonably might be inferred. As Project Blue Book's limited staff and facilities were being strained to capacity, Major Fournet assumed responsibility for the implementation of the idea.

September 1952. Captain Edward J. Ruppelt, Major Verne Sadowski, the Air Defense Command Intelligence's liaison officer with Project Blue Book, and several other officers engaged in an informal exchange, emphasizing the former organization's uncertainty as to whether the latter was supplying it with the full Unidentified Flying Object story. Sadowski was reassured, and there was a general conflict of opinion regarding the possibility that the unknowns were extra-terrestrial.

Autumn 1952 (c.) Brigadier General W. M. Garland, having replaced Colonel Frank Dunn as chief of the Air Technical Intelligence Center, inaugurated a program for the development of a tracking system to maintain a coordinated surveillance of Unidentified Flying Objects. Essentially it would rely upon photography, careful geometrical calculations, and swift communication. It was budgeted at an amazingly inexpensive initial $250,000 with an annual maintenance cost of about $25,000.

November 1952. A panel of four scientists was convened in a three-day seminar, by the Air Technical Intelligence Center, for procedural recommendations regarding the study of Unidentified Flying Objects. It unanimously agreed that a larger panel of specialized authorities should be presented with the problem and suggested six top practical and theoretical scientists, who were understood to have formed no definite opinion with respect to the unknowns, for the task. The projected date for the effort was December 1952 or January 1953.

December 1952. The Air Technical Intelligence Center approved General Garland's new monitoring approach, but it could not be effectuated until several higher levels of authority ratified the positive decision.

January 14–18, 1953.* The Central Intelligence Agency introduced its full force into the situation—although its influence had permeated the official operation of ufological "research" from a considerably earlier time—with the establishment of the Scientific Advisory Panel on Unidentified Flying Objects, usually referred to as the "Robertson Panel," after the name of its chairman.

---

* *The UFO Evidence* (Hall, ed.), p. 107, cites January 12, 1953, as the opening day of the conference. *The Report on Unidentified Flying Objects* (Ruppelt), p. 210, concurs. The dates indicated above are those appearing on the group's final report, itself dated February 16, 1953.

According to Captain Edward J. Ruppelt, the initial business of the day was the reading of its instructions. Three conclusions would be regarded as acceptable, clearly meaning that it was specifically ordered not to reach any conviction which fell outside the prescribed limitations, regardless of whether it might be true or not. Presumably, should such a circumstance arise, the scientists would be expected to select the least vulnerable of the untruths. In any event, the options presented were:

1. All UFO reports are explainable as known objects or natural phenomena; therefore the investigation should be permanently discontinued.
2. The UFO reports do not contain enough data upon which to base a final conclusion. Project Blue Book should be continued in hopes of obtaining better data.
3. The UFO's are interplanetary spacecraft.[4]

The Robertson Panel included men of considerable eminence in their own fields, although, individually and collectively, their skills were best designed to determine what UFO were *not*, rather than what they were. Additionally, despite the separate prestigious specializations brought to the conference table, only a small percentage of the immediately available potential theories regarding the nature, habits, and origin of the phenomena was subject to the gentlemen's peculiar talents.

Professor H. P. Robertson, of the California Institute of Technology, who had done work in cosmology, the theory of relativity, mathematics, and weapons systems evaluation, functioned as chairman. The other participants were Professor Samuel A. Goudsmit, who had done work in theoretical physics and intelligence with respect to enemy weaponry; Professor Luis Alvarez, of the University of California, who had done work in the radar subcategory of microwave instrumentation for aircraft blind landing and on physical problems while on the staff of Dr. J. Robert

Oppenheimer, at Los Alamos; physicist **Dr. Lloyd Berkner**, who had been an administrator in the Navy's aeronautical radar program when the war commenced, had conceived the idea of the International Geophysical Year, and had been affiliated with the Navy for most of his life, acquiring the rank of rear admiral; and Professor Thornton Page, astronomer at Wesleyan University, in Middletown, Connecticut, concentrating on the atomic spectra of planetary nebulae, and, earlier, on naval weaponry.

Among the specializations represented were highly particularized aspects of mathematics, physics, cosmology, blind landing radar, nebular astronomy, weaponry, and administration, with the greatest focus of expertise or, at least, experience, in subcategories of physics, astronomy, weaponry, and administration. The committee contributed approximately four (or two normal "working") days to its "study" of the Air Force's "best reports" [5] and two films, although why the Tremonton and Missoula exhibits were included is difficult to determine since none of the identified consultants had any stipulated knowledge of photography, especially motion pictures. Climatologists, meteorologists, planetologists, aerodynamicists, plasmologists, and countless other immediately relevant sciences seem to have been unrepresented, to say nothing of the disciplines any properly directed demand for knowledge would include, such as authorities from several branches of zoology (entomology, ornithology, etc.), botany, chemistry, electronics, psychology, philosophy, and, if it would not have been regarded as too esoteric, an experienced aviator. Testimony was submitted from, and by, Air Force personnel and advisors who presented its policy-of-denial.

The initial meeting began with the Central Intelligence Agency position being made perfectly clear and the only acceptable alternatives being emphasized. This was followed by briefings on a few earlier reviews, an exchange about national security, and extracts from some commentaries on cases, selected by the Air Force for the committee's perusal. A few relating to radar and visual sightings were set aside for examination.

The two very short Tremonton and Missoula films were shown, and the meeting adjourned, after approximately two hours, at noon. The Condon Report cites the attendance of only Robertson, Page, Goudsmit, and one unidentified member, specifically noting the absence of Berkner.

The meeting, which was taking place on a Wednesday, reconvened at two in the afternoon and adjourned three hours later. During this session a pair of Navy witnesses presented the official interpretations of the motion pictures shown previously and Captain Ruppelt testified for Project Blue Book for nearly three-quarters of an hour, as the Central Intelligence Agency men monitored the remarks and exchanges.

On the following morning the same panel members, and the CIA observers, heard further comments from Ruppelt, watched a film of some seagulls, and conversed, breaking at twelve o'clock. Upon their return, Project Twinkle, a study of still unexplained phenomena, which was admittedly a total failure, was given nearly an hour and the problems of establishing a nationwide, twenty-four-hour surveillance of the skies was explained. At about seven, the meeting adjourned.

Friday, at nine o'clock, a portion of the panel, and the Central Intelligence Agency, began the fifth session. It seems to have consisted mostly of an unnamed witness (Dewey Fournet, or possibly Captain Robert R. Sneider who served as director of the Air Force study of UFO from about November 1948 to March 1951, from the capital, not Blue Book, in Ohio) speaking "on his fifteen months' experience in Washington as Project Officer for U.F.O.'s and his personal conclusions." [6] In addition to this evidence, some Air Force analyses of cases were introduced. Noon signaled the departure of everyone for the midday break.

Dr. Berkner brought some changes to the five-hour afternoon meeting with his first appearance at the inquiry. Robertson devoted some time to reviewing what had occurred during the preceding two and a half days and "tentative conclusions reached" [7]—in fewer than fifteen hours, or in less time than is consumed by

two normal working days. A discussion of recommendations to be made ensued and it was agreed that
the chairman would draft a final report for review by
the panel and the Central Intelligence Agency pro-
grammers on the next day.

Two hours on Saturday morning were given over to
an examination, discussion, and various revisions of
the paper presented, and at eleven o'clock a courier
"reported that he had shown and discussed a copy of
the initial rough draft to the Director of Intelligence,
USAF [Samford, or his successor], whose reaction was
favorable." [8]

The panel's efforts were concluded that afternoon
and the report ordered prepared for delivery to the
proper recipients. Then the Scientific Advisory Panel
on Unidentified Flying Objects was dissolved.

During its approximately two days of listening to
briefings and examining exhibits, as distinguished from
the remaining time, which was spent in refining conclusions already generally accepted by it for the final
version of its report, it weighed the following data:

1. Seventy-five case histories, most particularly the
   Missoula, Montana (August 15, 1950), and film;
   Tremonton, Utah (July 2, 1952), and film; the
   Washington, D.C. area (July 19–20, 1952); the
   Port Huron, Michigan (July 29, 1952); the Belle-
   fontaine, Ohio (August 1, 1952); the Haneda Air
   Force Base, Japan (August 5, 1952); the Yaak,
   Montana (September 1, 1952); and the Presque
   Isle, Maine (October 10, 1952) sightings. All cases
   were selected by the Air Technical Intelligence
   Center, probably with the approval of the Central
   Intelligence Agency.
2. Testimony and reviews from the Air Technical
   Intelligence Center, chosen from material collected
   by Project Grudge, the New Project Grudge, the
   Aerial Phenomena Group, and Project Blue Book.
3. Reviews of the activities of New Mexico's "green
   fireballs" and Project Twinkle, which was created
   to investigate them, and Project Stork, and the
   proposed, but never implemented, Project Pounce.

4. Summaries of eighty-nine accounts of various alleged Unidentified Flying Object activities, i.e., maneuvering in echelons flashing lights, remaining motionless in the sky, etc., culled from the official files by the Air Technical Intelligence Center.

5. An outline of a proposed regulations book on the proper method to prepare and submit a "flying object" report, as drafted by the Air Technical Intelligence Center—or the Central Intelligence Agency.

6. Charts depicting geographical locations of UFO concentrations in 1952, balloon launching areas in this country, actual balloon courses and reported observations of them, sighting frequency patterns from 1948 to 1952, and primary explanations of UFO sightings, as designed by the Air Technical Intelligence Center.

7. Photographic transparencies of balloons chosen for their demonstration of high reflectivity of sunlight, and films of seagulls selected for the abnormally high amount of sunlight being reflected from them.

8. Intelligence reports relating to Soviet Union interest in sightings of UFO in the United States.

9. Examples of official United States Air Force forms to be filled out and filed by any of its personnel wishing to submit an account of such personal experiences, with additional regulations operative in the United States Army, Navy, and Air Force relating to Unidentified Flying Objects; and a manual (JANP 101) explaining exceptional performances a radarman might encounter while using his equipment.

10. Incidental correspondence, intelligence reports, newspaper and magazine cuttings, and books about Unidentified Flying Objects and peripheral subjects, and a sample polyethylene balloon fifty-four inches square.

How thoroughly could a panel of some half dozen men, even eminent scientists, peruse, let alone assimilate, analyze, correlate, evaluate, and resolve, 169 second-, third-, and fourth-hand accounts of Undefined Sensory Experience (USE). Particularly ones chosen by an explicitly biased organization, the United States Air Force, and approved by an even more predisposed operation, the Central Intelligence Agency.

After having so delved into the subject of Unidentified Atmospheric Phenomena, Unexplained Aerial Objects, and similarly inexplicable happenings, the board decided that "Reasonable explanations could be suggested for most sightings," a judgment based upon accounts consisting of a fraction of one percent of those carefully selected by the Air Technical Intelligence Center, as prepared by Project Blue Book. The latter's most respected director, Captain Edward J. Ruppelt, wrote of the commission in his subsequent book. Regarding the year preceding the deliberations of the advisory committee, he stated that "it would be safe to say that Blue Book only heard about 10 per cent of the UFO's that were seen in the United States." [9] This means that the technologists convened by the Central Intelligence Agency considered reports of what was probably less than a thousandth of the UFO sightings occurring in the nation during the two-year period "analyzed," and that even in those instances they were dealing with company-worn, reviewed, interpreted, and stylized data. The results were extrapolations too remote and physical for respectable thinkers to regard as bases for the most tentative speculations, and inconceivable as foundations for any serious theorizing.

The overall conclusions and recommendations of the Scientific Advisory Panel were—

—that no concrete evidence had been adduced that the unknowns were any threat to national security;

—that at least a portion of the Air Force's concern relating to Unidentified Flying Objects derived from public interest, but that it had an effective operation "for receiving reports of nearly anything anyone sees in the sky and fails to understand," [10] which was patently untrue;

—that the data gathered was "of low-grade reports

which tend to overload channels of communication
with material quite irrelevant to hostile objects (e.g.,
terrestrial enemy missiles) that might some day appear," [11] which certainly was partially the case;

—that, while not having the least idea what the remaining "unidentifieds" were, the enigmatic phenomena were different, in kind, from the V-1 and
V-2 hardware the Germans produced in World War
II but, perhaps, not wholly unrelated to the so-called
foo-fighters of that period (generally catalogued
as electrostatic or electromagnetic effects, or, possibly, refracting ice crystals) in any event, phenomena which have never been explained;

—that although the panel did not completely dismiss
the possibility of Earthly visits from extraplanetary
aeronauts, and despite the testimony of the unnamed officer who had headed "Project Bluebook
for 15 months" [12] (probably Ruppelt, possibly Captain Robert R. Sneider) to the effect that during his
service in such capacity "he had eliminated each of
the known and probable causes of sightings leaving
him 'extra-terrestrial' as the only one remaining in
many cases," [13] the material reviewed failed to suggest the arrivals of space travelers;

—that the Tremonton and Missoula films could be
simulated and that some explanations satisfied various of the characteristics of the objects photographed, but the first point proved nothing and the
second was insufficient, thus leaving the committee
with no answer for either motion picture;

—that in the absence of any argument in favor of the
unknowns being potential actual threats to the nation, they might constitute psychological or incidental dangers, e.g., misidentification of a real
attack from a mundane alien enemy, cloggings of
lines of communication during a practical emergency, and the stimulation of mass hysteria and
potent psychological warfare;

—that it could deduce nothing from the geographical
dispersal of the phenomena;

—that a hundred inexpensive 35 mm cameras be distributed to control tower personnel throughout the

country for the purpose of attempting to get some good photographs of the UAO, primarily because the effect would reassure the public, since it was not expected to produce any success pictorially;

—that no government-sponsored comprehensive surveillance of the skies was worth the effort, but that general support from the professional and amateur astronomical community might be encouraged;

—that there was little justification to equip radar with special devices so that tracking of extremely high-speed blips might be verified, and none regarding the possibility of cosmic rays having some relationship with the aerial puzzle;

—that a concentrated program should be instituted to *train* the public and *debunk* all accounts of Unidentified Atmospheric Phenomena and Unexplained Aerial Objects; or simply put, the inauguration of a brainwashing project;

—that the ufological group, within the service, should be somewhat enlarged in staff, although in no way to a degree as to create an efficient or even cursorily productive program—not with a staff of from one to two dozen persons;

—that independent investigative UFO organizations should be monitored, as if foreign spy cells;

—and that periodic increases in sightings should be anticipated.

As most of the conclusions contained large elements of predisposition and, additionally, were based upon little data regarded with undue haste, the only results that could be of any importance were the panel's "recommendations." Of these, the suggestion of an increased Project Blue Book staff was by far the most important, although the conditioning of the American public was the most disturbing. The former was never implemented; the second was, but via different techniques from those indicated by the committee, at least, different in emphasis. The Air Force and the Central Intelligence Agency, with occasional assistance from Naval Intelligence, and internal security organizations pursued their plans. The citizenry's degree and nature of UFO information was directed as they wished, or to the degree they were in a position to control it. Certainly a small clique was telling the government how this mystery was to be handled. Was anyone exercising a similar authority over their decisions?

August 23, 1953. The Secretary of the Air Force issued Regulation No. 200–2, classifying it under "Intelligence Activities," which updated, essentially by simplifying procedures, the official approach to Unidentified Flying Objects. It was a modification of the April 29, 1952, position established in Air Force Regulation No. 200-5 of that date.

November 2, 1953. The Air Force issued Regulation No. 200-2A, constituting a continuation of the contemporizing policy of the service, as it adjusted August 23, 1953 Regulation No. 200-2 toward that end. It directed certain minor changes, as did subsequent incidental amendations until the foregoing instructions were fully displaced by Air Force Regulation 80-17, which appeared on September 19, 1966.

March 17, 1954. The Project Blue Book Special Report No. 14, which concluded that it was highly improbable that available data on Unidentified Flying Objects indicated the perception of any level of technology not encompassed by contemporary scientific accomplishment or theory, was completed and distributed to authorized departments and individuals.

October 25, 1955. The Air Force released a summary of Project Blue Book Special Report No. 14 to the press, accompanied by a release implying that the service would soon have its own disklike craft, presumably after the configuration of the Canadian AVRO device, which was an almost total failure.

October 4, 1956. A special briefing on Project Blue Book progress was conducted by General Lewis. It was basically an exercise in standard public relations.

September 16, 1957. The Defense Science Board Briefing, similar to the foregoing, but with a slightly more technological orientation, was held.

Circa 1955–1960. "Fact Sheets" were issued by public relations officers handling the UFO subject for the Air Force. They usually consisted of a few (occasionally mathematically impossible) statistics and reaffirmations that the small percentage of undetermined unknowns were of absolutely no danger to the United States.

August 8, 1958. The (John) McCormack Sub-Committee, of the House of Representatives of the United States, received a briefing on Unexplained Flying Objects.

January 31, 1959. The (John) McClellan Sub-Committee, of the Senate of the United States, received a briefing on Unidentified Flying Objects.

February 1959. Air Force policy meetings to review the situation and the service's approach to it were conducted.

December 24, 1959. The Air Force Inspector General issued an order to the Operation and Training Command headed "UFO'S SERIOUS BUSINESS." It opens with the directive that "Unidentified flying objects— sometimes treated lightly by the press and referred to as *'flying saucers'—must be rapidly and accurately identified as serious USAF business* * in the ZI [Interior Zone]. The phenomena or actual objects comprising UFO's will tend to increase with the public more aware with goings on in space. . . . Technical and defense considerations will continue to exist in this era." [14]

August 15, 1960. The Office of the Secretary of the Air Force issued policy statement Vol. XIV, No. 12, to all Air Force base commanders, headed "AF Keeping Watchful Eye on Aerospace," in which the following concession was prominent: "There is a relationship between the Air Force's interest in space surveillance and its continuous surveillance of the atmosphere near Earth for unidentified flying objects—'UFOs'."

September 9, 1960. The Project Grudge and the Project Blue Book "Status Reports," numbered from 1 to 12, were declassified, although copies remained hard to procure. Nine of the reports had been catalogued "Confidential"; the final three "Secret."

July 11–15, 1961. A congressional subcommittee

---

* Emphasis added.

hearing on the topic of Unidentified Flying Objects was conducted. For the most part the legislators merely heard the Air Force position reiterated.

Circa 1960–1961. Colonel Lawrence J. Tacker, spokesman on UFO for the Air Force and nominal author of its policy as presented in the commercial hardcover book *Flying Saucers and the U.S. Air Force,*[15] toured the country lecturing and appearing on radio and television promoting the position presented by the volume. In the spring of 1961, Colonel Tacker was reassigned to Europe.

February 6, 1962. The last of the "Fact Sheets," No. 179–62, was issued, and this informational procedure was abandoned.

Circa 1962–1965. Public relations packages were issued from time to time by the Air Force, replacing the earlier "Fact Sheets." These usually offered re-evaluations of various statistics and outlines of a few examples of Project Blue Book explanations of apparently inexplicable phenomena. By this time, the classification of "Unknown," which heretofore had indicated instances of cases careful investigation and analysis could not catalogue, had been broadened to include many examples of raw data, poor accounts, inadequately investigated sightings, and generally useless material. This practice tended to depreciate the functional designation to one of no consequence.

September 28, 1965. Major General E. B. LeBailly, director of information for the United States Air Force, issued a Memorandum for Military Directors, Scientific Advisory Board,* informing same that of the 9,267 reports investigated by the service from 1948 to June 30, 1965, 663 "cannot be explained." It continues, noting that the Assistant Deputy Chief of Staff/Plans and Operations regarded the inquiry as of sufficient value as to be supported by all agencies and commands, and that the responsible Project Blue Book should continue its activities at its Wright-Patterson Air Force Base facilities.

The memorandum remarks that, while hostility does

---

* Condon Report, p. 816–817.

not seem a factor in considering the unknowns, they cannot be ignored because of the indisputable qualifications of many observers and because of the extremely small percentage of accounts actually finding their way to a Project Blue Book officer.

In light of the foregoing, LeBailly recommended that a new committee of both physical and social scientists, including Dr. Hynek, who had agreed to participate, be convened to review the Air Force approach and policy with respect to Unidentified Atmospheric Phenomena, Unexplained Aerial Objects, and related mysteries, for the purpose of advising fresh perspectives and actions to the Air Force.

February 3, 1966. The United States Air Force Scientific Advisory Board Ad Hoc Committee to Review Project "Blue Book," consisting of Dr. Brian O'Brien, who chaired the meeting, Dr. Launor F. Carter, Jessee Orlansky, Dr. Richard Porter, Dr. Carl Sagan, and Dr. Willis H. Ware, with Lieutenant Colonel Harold A. Steiner, Assistant Secretary, the United States Air Force Scientific Advisory Board, attending, met. Following opening remarks by O'Brien, Lt. Colonel Spaulding explained the difficulties Unidentified Flying Objects presented to the Air Force and Major Hector Quintanilla offered a briefing on Project Blue Book and its activities up to that time. The morning concluded with a review of the work of previous panels and some case histories. Reconvening after lunch, the group discussed the material collected during the earlier session and prepared its recommendations. It need hardly be observed that the breadth and depth of this conference made the "Robertson Panel," which devoted almost two full working days to its efforts, although a complete complement was never present at one time, appear like a modern Council of Trent.

The committee's Special Report alluded to a fractionally longer time frame than LeBailly's, i.e., through the year 1947 to the end of 1965. This, of course, produced slightly different sighting and "Unidentified" figures: 10,147 in the former instance and 646 in the latter. This leads one to assume that, since the grand total was larger and the subcategory smaller, than the general's, a few of the older cases had been relabeled. Yet, six percent still remained unresolved. The group tended to slough off these "unidentifieds" as cases of insufficient data.

Some point was made of "not a single unidentified object" ever having been represented on astronomical photographic plates deriving from the efforts of specific institutions. The argument failed to recognize that the particular observatories were not looking for such exceptions, in fact were specifically tuned for other effects. Or that, were there intelligently operated phenomena occasionally entering our atmosphere, they might merely avoid such areas. Or that the few thousand hours encompassed by the work to which the scientists referred constituted but a parsec in the time/place continuum available to such animals, minerals, machines, etc.

While reassuring the reader as to the lack of menace to be inferred from whatever they were discussing, the panel's report refers to *the nineteen years* "since the first UFO was sighted"—hardly indicating an awareness of the centuries, or millennia, such phenomena have been recorded.

Not surprisingly, the Ad Hoc Committee commended the Air Force's ufological procedures and programs during the preceding two decades, despite recognizing that the ten thousand plus sightings purportedly investigated had been processed by a standard staff of an officer, a sergeant, and a secretary. On average, the entire effort of the United States Air Force to determine the activity, nature, and origin of Unexplained Aerial Objects, and similar unknowns had devolved to a working team of three members.

The final suggestions of the panel were that a few universities, suitably distributed geographically, provide teams, consisting of at least one physical scientist and one psychologist, to function in tandem with an Air Force officer, specifically assigned to such liaison, at the most propinquitous base; that one "private" institution or organization be induced to coordinate these efforts; that approximately one hundred sightings a year be closely studied, with, perhaps, an average of ten working days devoted to each case; and that both the full report of such inquiries and abstracts be made available to the press and public.

The Ad Hoc Committee's proposals were as disregarded as those offered by the advisory groups previously convened.

March, 1966. The United States Air Force Scientific Advisory Board Ad Hoc Committee submitted its report and recommendations on Unidentified Flying Objects.

April 5, 1966. The House of Representatives' Committee on Armed Services, chaired by L. Mendel Rivers, conducted a brief hearing of the subject of Unidentified Flying Objects.

August 31, 1966. Colonel Ivan C. Atkinson, deputy executive director of the Air Force Office of Scientific Research, after several other such institutions had declined participation and/or full responsibility for such a project, approached the University of Colorado with the request—presumably pursuant to one aspect of the recommendations made by the Air Force Scientific Advisory Board Ad Hoc Committee on Unidentified Flying Objects—that it conduct a comprehensive examination of the subject in question. This program was allegedly to be independent and beyond the authority of the service—but that did not include, and meant nothing to, the Central Intelligence Agency. Additionally, it was extremely difficult to visualize an operation of this kind being wholly financed by the Air Force, but completely exterior to its influence. It is *conceivable* that this might have been possible had the funds been appropriated by Congress, an effort independent investigators had attempted to put in motion for nearly twenty years, an effort always thwarted by the Air Force, other military agencies, and the entire intelligence community.

September 19, 1966. The Air Force issued Regulation No. 80–17, which totally superseded Air Force Regulation No. 200-2 and its numerous amendments, transferring full responsibility for investigating and analyzing reports of Unidentified Flying Objects from

Air Force Intelligence to Air Force Research and Development.

October 7, 1966. The Air Force announced the engagement of the University of Colorado for the investigation and evaluation of Unidentified Flying Objects by the Air Force Office of Science Research, Office of Aerospace Research, under contract F 44620-67-C-0035. The initial phase, for which the service was providing $313,000, was to run from November 15, 1966, to January 1968. The project was to be placed under the direction of Dr. Edward U. Condon; Robert J. Low was appointed project coordinator. The first gained immediate notice in the field by referring to Unidentified Flying Objects by their acronym, UFO, but to the amusement of some with any knowledge of the field mispronounced it, actually and in the final report, "OOFO," rather than the proper "YOU-FOE." The second attracted considerable attention to himself when it was revealed that he was the author of a memorandum, written before the project was actually inaugurated, stating that "The trick would be, I think, to describe the subject so that, to the public, it would appear a wholly objective study but, to the scientific community, would present the image of a group of non-believers trying their best to be objective, but having an almost zero expectation of finding a saucer." [16]

Condon demonstrated that he was not to be outdone in predisposition when he was quoted by the Elmira, New York *Star-Gazette* as having remarked that unidentified objects "are not the business of the Air Force. . . . It is my inclination right now to recommend that the Government get out of this business. My attitude right now is that there's nothing to it . . . but I'm not supposed to reach a conclusion for another year. . . ." [17]

November 1, 1966. The Scientific Study of Unidentified Flying Objects, under the direction of Dr. Edward U. Condon and the coordination of Robert J. Low, began at the University of Colorado.

November 8, 1966. The Air Force issued Regulation No. 80-17A, updating Air Force Regulation No. 80-17.

October 26, 1967. The Air Force issued Regulation

No. 80-17 (Cl), updating Air Force Regulation No. 80-17A.

January 31, 1968. The originally proposed date for the conclusion of the Scientific Study of Unidentified Flying Objects, at the University of Colorado.

July 29, 1968. The Committee on Science and Aeronautics of the House of Representatives of the United States convened for a symposium of the subject of Unidentified Flying Objects and the investigation of the phenomena by the government. While Representative George P. Miller, of California, was the chairman of the committee, acting chairman Representative J. Edward Roush directed most of the ensuing proceedings. Among the persons invited to offer testimony were Dr. J. Allen Hynek, the head of the department of astronomy at Northwestern University, and twenty years the sole continuing scientific consultant to the United States Air Force on the subject of Unidentified Flying Objects; Dr. James E. McDonald, senior physicist in the Institute of Atmospheric Physics at the University of Arizona; Dr. Carl Sagan, of the department of astronomy and Center for Radiophysics and Space Research at Cornell University; Dr. James A. Harder, associate professor of civil engineering at the University of California, in Berkeley; Dr. Robert L. Hall, head of the department of sociology at the University of Illinois, in Chicago; and Dr. Robert M. L. Baker, Jr., of the Computer Sciences Corporation and the department of engineering at the University of California, in Los Angeles.

Dr. Donald Menzel complained that, as he had not been invited to testify, the witnesses presented a pro-Ufo view. If this is true, it was unique in the history of official inquiries into the mystery of Unidentified Flying Objects, which boasted no record of even an unbiased governmental hearing on the subject. In any event, Dr. Menzel was invited to submit a paper of his opinions to the committee, and did.*

---

* The full coverage of this session may be found in John G. Fuller's excellent *Aliens in the Skies,* which is recommended to the serious student.

September 30, 1968. The Air Force issued Regulation No. 80-1 (C2), updating Air Force Regulation No. 80-17 (C1).

October 31, 1968. The Scientific Study of Unidentified Flying Objects, at the University of Colorado, under the direction of Dr. Edward U. Condon, submitted its final report.

November 15, 1968. The Scientific Study of Unidentified Flying Objects final report was submitted by the University of Colorado to the National Academy of Sciences for its rubber stamp of approval, and it was so applied.

January 8, 1969. The Scientific Study of Unidentified Flying Objects final report was released to the press and public.

December 17, 1969. The United States Air Force, through the Office of the Assistant Secretary of Defense (Public Affairs), issued press release No. 1077-69 allegedly totally and completely dissolving all official investigation of Unidentified Flying Objects, disbanding all groups employed in such tasks, and reassigning any personnel so engaged. The text that purportedly concluded the service's twenty-two-and-a-half-year interest in the subject read:

AIR FORCE TO TERMINATE PROJECT "BLUE BOOK"

Secretary of the Air Force Robert C. Seamans, Jr., announced today the termination of Project Blue Book, the Air Force program for the investigation of unidentified flying objects (UFOs).

In a memorandum to Air Force Chief of Staff General John D. Ryan, Secretary Seamans stated that "the continuation of Project Blue Book cannot be justified either on the ground of national security or in the interest of science," and concluded that the project did not merit further expenditures of resources.

The decision to discontinue UFO investigations was based on an evaluation of a report prepared by the University of Colorado entitled *Scientific Study of Unidentified Flying Objects,* a

review of the University of Colorado's report by
the National Academy of Sciences, past UFO
studies, and Air Force experience investigating
UFO reports during the past two decades.

Under the direction of Dr. Edward U. Condon,
the University of Colorado completed an 18-
month contracted study of UFOs, and its report
was released to the public in January, 1969. The
report concluded that little if anything had come
from the study of UFOs in the past twenty-one
years that had added to scientific knowledge, and
that further extensive study of UFO sightings was
not justified in the expectation that science would
be advanced.

A panel of the National Academy of Sciences
made an independent assessment of the scope,
methodology, and findings of the University of
Colorado study. The panel concurred in the University of Colorado's recommendation that "no
high priority in UFO investigations is warranted
by data of the past two decades." If concluded
by stating that "on the basis of present knowledge,
the least likely explanation of UFOs in the hypothesis of extraterrestrial visitations by intelligent
beings."

Past UFO studies include one conducted by a
Scientific Advisory Panel on UFOs in January,
1953 (Robertson Panel), and a review of Project
Blue Book by the Air Force Scientific Advisory
Board Ad Hoc Committee, February-March,
1966 (Dr. Brian O'Brien, chairman). These
studies concluded that no evidence had been found
to show that any of the UFO reports reflect a
threat to our national security.

As a result of investigating UFO reports since
1948, the conclusions of Project Blue Book are:
(1) No UFO reported, investigated, and evaluated
by the Air Force has ever given any indication of
being a threat to our national security; * (2)

* As the Air Force has frequently admitted it does not
know what many UFO are, the foundation for this conclusion

there has been no evidence submitted or discovered by the Air Force that sightings categorized as "unidentified" represent technological developments or principles beyond the range of present-day scientific knowledge; † and (3) there has been no evidence that sightings categorized as "unidentified" are of extraterrestrial vehicles.**

Project Blue Book records will be retired to the USAF Archives, Maxwell Air Force Base, Alabama.†† Requests for information will continue to be handled by the Secretary of the Air Force, Office of Information (SAFOI), Washington, D.C. 20330.***

Notes

1. Project Sign, Report No. F-TR-2274-IA. For full text, see Condon, ed., *Scientific Study,* pp. 844–852.
2. Ibid., pp. 898–904.
3. For full text, see *Scientific Study,* pp. 509–510.
4. Ruppelt, *Report on Unidentified Flying Objects,* p. 210.
5. Ibid.
6. "Report of Meetings of Scientific Advisory Panel on Unidentified Flying Objects." See *Scientific Study,* p. 908.
7. Ibid.

---

seems shaky; also, the assumption clearly dismisses the often described "hostility" of such phenomena as a purely personal hazard unrelated to the common welfare or danger.

† Again, as the Air Force concedes that it does not know the nature of many of the unknowns, how can it make this assertion, especially as countless "unidentifieds" defy all aerodynamic characteristics of which we have any knowledge.

** It is not a matter of whether some UFO *are* extraterrestrial, but whether they *may* be, which can never be determined until they have been "identified." Further, extraterrestriality is not the only alternative to advanced technology by a foreign government or our own.

†† All Project Blue Book records have been consigned to the Modern Military Branch, Military Archives Division, National Archives, Washington, D.C.

*** Or directly by the National Archives office cited in the preceding footnote.

8. Ibid.
9. Ruppelt, p. 149.
10. Scientific Advisory Panel. See *Scientific Study*, p. 910.
11. Ibid.
12. Ibid., p. 911.
13. Ibid.
14. A further portion of this order may be found in Frank
    Edwards, *Flying Saucers—Serious Business*, p. 97.
15. Tacker, *Flying Saucers and the U.S. Air Force* (Princeton,
    N.J.: Van Nostrand, 1960).
16. John Fuller, *Look*, May 14, 1968, p. 58.
17. Ibid.

21

Over the Shoulder
and Down the Sky

**I am completely convinced that they [UFO] have an
out-of-world basis.**

> —Dr. Walter Riedel, one of the
> "fathers" of modern rocketry
> and space travel. *Life*, April 7,
> 1952, p. 96

**. . . while it may be that some operators of UFO are
normally the parapsychical denizens of a planet other
than Earth, there is no logical need for this to be
so. For, if the materiality of UFO is paraphysical . . .
UFO could more plausibly be creations of an invisible world coincident with the space of our physical
Earth planet. . . .**

> —Royal Air Force Air Marshal Sir
> Victor Goddard. May 3, 1969

THERE IS NO way to know when it all began. Analytically speaking, perhaps it doesn't matter. Yet, being it

did, whenever, wherever, however, *and it is with us until this very moment*. A great many things happen in this world, even to the most ordinary people, for which no explanation is available—not at the door of the village crone, the town doctor, the city lawyer, the national statesman, or the world philosopher. We live much less in the dimensions of material "reality" than we conceive; we exist much more on endlessly and mysteriously vacillating planes than we ever dream.

It is not necessary for us immediately to conjure concepts of extradimensionality and forces beyond our awareness when one is faced with a problem of such socio-psychological and technical complexity as that which constitutes not the delightfully mythical "flying saucers," but the interminable intricacies of UAP, UAO, or UFO. The initial choice one must make is whether he has confronted something outside the framework of "natural laws," or another of the complex creations of Man; perhaps products of his intellect of which he has lost command. There may be entities and energies beyond the normal understanding of the human world, capable of activities and effects over which we have no influence. Certainly, Man himself long ago created physical, organizational, and conceptual mechanisms which have freed themselves from his direction and control.

Television, computers, and genetic engineering are simply the latest of Man's monsters.

What commonly are referred to as Unidentified Flying Objects are more accurately divided between the categories of Unidentified Atmospheric Phenomena and Unexplained Aerial Objects. An effort should be made to treat the allegedly "real" and allegedly "unreal" interpretations separately. This work has concentrated on what may seem a rather particularized point, namely whether there exist and function above the United States, and occasionally on its surface, phenomena for which no offered explanation suffices. It has not attempted to establish the specific nature of such, if they, in fact, exist. First, the long and broad argument for the existence of UFO has been demonstrated. Second, careful, conservative, comprehensively researched inquiries into certain fundamental cases of the modern age have been presented. Third, the geographically widespread and chronologically unbroken testimony on such phenomena, contrary to the contentions of the scientific, military, intelligence, and political communities, has been made apparent. And fourth, evidence has been assembled to clarify that this continuum persisted, often even intensified to extreme degrees, long after Establishmentarians pronounced it dead, and a dead *myth* at that. Finally, there is a last consideration. It is that the American public, in general, and the ever diminishing number of serious investigators, in particular, have lived through nearly three decades of lies and frauds, or amateurism and irresponsibility, with respect to the UFO—and probably both.

No treatment has been offered regarding allegations of aliens exiting craft from other spheres, galactic cruisers, temporary abductions of Earthians by extraterrestrials for purposes of anatomical examinations, or the flights of humans in vehicles from remote planets, at the invitations of their crews, and occasionally tall, statuesque blond astral commanders looking like Arthurian concepts of Viking Amazons.

It will also be apparent that few allusions have been made to foreign sightings, even ones so propinquitous as those reported from Canada, Mexico, and the Caribbean, let alone Australia, New Zealand, England, France, Italy, Spain, all of Scandinavia, most of Africa, the Middle East, and almost every other area of the world. Foreign experiences would include even the Union of Soviet Socialist Republics, from which, in recent years, an increasing amount of ufological data and interest have emerged. Nearly the only regions from which UFO material is difficult to obtain are the People's Republic of China, Cuba, Albania, and North Vietnam.

The substantive nature of this book should dispel any suggestion that an attempt was being made to simplify the task at hand. Hundreds of heavily annotated, persuasive sightings emanating from sources of countries around the world provide a catalogue of evidence regretfully excluded. Nonetheless, so incontrovertible is our home-flown experience that using only material recorded in the United States seemed effectively to emphasize the need for an open, thorough, unbiased, apolitical study and analysis of UAO—a program somehow kept free and far from the fingers of people who pull the national and international secret intelligence strings.

Therefore, as an initial premise, this work, excluding the historical necessities of Book I, has devoted its attention to aerial phenomena for which we have no reasonable explanation, observed and chronicled by our own citizens.

Simply stated, this book has been a study of the origin of UFO, and the history of their major aspects, as they relate to the United States, most particularly in recent times, with a final focus on the fact of the mystery's continuation up to the moment you read this.

However, there remains the inescapable question. Not what are they. Nor from where do they come. These clearly may be unanswerable. More important —is Man confronted by a problem with a solution, *or* a riddle the extenuations of which range far beyond his intelligence? Yet, the primary consideration is not the answer to either of these puzzles, *but whether either of them is the answer* or, more accurately, the true query.

If Man is faced with extraterrestrial, but comprehensible, intelligences, the probability is high that this may be determined, providing the proper effort and financing are invested. Even were the "visitors" to be enormously superior intellectually, there is every reason to believe that they ultimately could be identified as thinking creatures. If the mental capabilities of such astro-voyagers are immensely beyond those of man, let us say approximating the ratio of snail to human, it seems that even the most optimistic would accept that no degree of reciprocal communication would ever be achieved.

If the phenomena represent something even more remote from us than that, it would indicate that an impassable barrier *of kind* existed, for we would be speaking of active abstract principles, or, if one prefers, gods, and we certainly are in no intellectual or spiritual condition to execute exchanges with such rarefied elements or entities.

Considering other options, one is swiftly led to the speculation that some of the phenomena may be organisms, the intelligence of which could be comparable to, or greater or less than, Man's. This is not a wholly new concept, but it has become no easier to contemplate. Regardless of the mental capacity of a totally unknown plasmic animal, vegetable, or inorganic material, the likelihood of establishing intercommunication verges on *nil*. Even if lightning has an intelligence quotient dwarfing Einstein's to relative idiocy, it and Man are never going to effect a really symbiotic relationship.

The late Ivan T. Sanderson suggested that the enigmas may be, on occasion, a more developed stage of life, of which Man is a low form. The possibility of contact in such a circumstance seems improbable in the extreme.

Yet these avenues of inquiry describe only the most obvious pattern of radial shafts that shoot out from the axle of ufology. A number of religious and "occult" theses have spoked forth from the hub of extranormal explanations. The former tend to be theologically traditional, if usually somewhat miraculous. The latter interpretations are far more various and, unlike the general consistency of orthodoxy, often trail off into the fog of deep mysticism. For the most part, "occult" analyses of UAO are essentially contemporary versions of classical demonological lore, or rather technological reformations of the old religion—the *old* religion of invisible races or inconceivable entities who ruled the Earth before Man, before the dinosaur, before the tiny creatures of the sea. To many, there is reason enough to believe that long before the emergence of any of these something other than sub- or pre-human influences directed the destiny of the third planet from the sun.

The second course of consideration with respect to

the origin and nature of UFO leads one to the terminus of terrestriality. If UAO derive from neither the mystical nor the spacial (and we are not concerning ourselves with inner-earth, cults in the Himalayas, or laboratories in the Brazilian jungle theories here), then the remaining probability is that either the United States, some other country, the United States and some other country or countries, or an alliance of other countries, is experimenting with extraordinary craft or other kinds of phenomena. We are fully aware that the United States, Canada, England, France, and the USSR have all investigated the possibility of devices, the prototype of which in test flight might well give the appearance described by persons who claim to have seen Unidentified Flying Objects or even actual spacecraft. On the other hand, it is common knowledge that such attempts, as exemplified by Canada's AVRO circular disk, proved stylistically intriguing and aeronautically useless. It was subsequently bequeathed to the United States Air Force, which could do nothing with it either, and ultimately deposited it in the service's museum at Fort Eustis, Virginia. The foregoing, and other tenable reasons, present extremely convincing arguments that, while undoubtedly many things seen in the sky are conventional and, occasionally, experimental military craft, the UAO with which the serious investigator is concerned—that is, the objects that do not conform to known possibilities with respect to design, maneuverability, speed, ascent capability, and other characteristics—are not of this category. The remaining alternatives within the compass of terrestriality are that, despite the aforementioned indications, some government, or governments, has produced a vehicle, or vehicles, able to function beyond the understood laws of aerodynamics; or that it has been done by some private, although possibly official, clique, such as the Central Intelligence Agency (which certainly operated its own mini air force in Southeast Asia for a decade) or its equivalent elsewhere, or a similar but unknown organization secreted within the vast bureaucracy of our own government, if the operation is here and almost certainly so if it is elsewhere.

Since the modern age of UAO began, twenty-eight years ago, attempts have been made on the lives of three American Presidents, with the attackers of the two survivors being caught, and the murderers of the victim free to this day. An almost inevitable future President has been assassinated and an influential candidate crippled for life, and in both instances there are grave doubts that the official dispositions of the cases approached any sort of complete solution.* We have been engaged in a war by proxy, and the longest conflict in our history without the consent of the Congress of the United States, which solely has power to commit the country to such peril. We have had the foremost declaimer of the absolute necessity for law-and-order and the return to the old principles of honesty, integrity, and service to one's country revealed as the most corrupt resident of the White House, at least in any moral or ethical sense, in its history, as well as the criminal conviction of the overwhelming majority of the most powerful figures closest to him in the administration of the affairs of the United States.

The list could go on interminably without departing the level of *enormous influence and incalculable economic strength.*

It requires, therefore, little imagination to conceive that the creation of a modest, private air force by a nongovernmental cabal, or the sequestering of some amazing advance in flying technology by the military, or even the arrival of one, or many, extraplanetary vessels, could be achieved with virtually no effort. The public would respond with an aroused curiosity about lights in the sky. It would be told that it was seeing conventional craft, ball lightning, and Venus.

The experience of what has happened to succeeding administrations in Washington and to the entire psycho-philosophic manner of modern America makes such things appear insignificant by comparison. However, although the actual phenomena may rank more

---

* Governor George C. Wallace has publicly stated that he strongly suspects a conspiracy was behind the attempt on his life.

as curiosities than as threats, their purpose may be a greater danger than we can conceive.

Something unthinkable. Something which could not possibly happen here, or anywhere, for that matter. Something like the assassination of a radiant young President at high noon, in the brilliant sunlight of one of America's great cities.

There are no Watergates.

Is it inconceivable that somewhere people who know something you should know about what has been happening in the skies across our land for a quarter of a century are—only obeying orders?

There are Unidentified Flying Objects, there are Unexplained Aerial Objects, there are Unidentified Atmospheric Phenomena. Something is happening up there.

It is about time you knew what.

Appendix I

A Brief Chronology of Unidentified Flying Objects

THE FOLLOWING is a selected chronology of Unidentified Flying Objects and other relevant observations. It attempts to present the variety, the historical development, the concentrations, and the major events, interspersed with a number of "good" sightings, in such a way as to provide a full, if highly condensed, catalogue of the phenomena, as well as a guide to further data on the cases listed through date, nature of the unknown, principal witness, or location. Only a few modern non-American entries will be found because this work has focused on the mystery as manifested in, and over, this country, and because of the ever-present space limitations. Names (only last) associated with primary sightings are usually included in parentheses, before the location, at the conclusion of a notation. For brevity, a number of abbreviations are used in this appendix; both common and coined ones are defined below.

"Flying saucer" incidents, "contactees," "abductions," and similar reports, however "classic," are not dealt with in this book and, therefore, are not incorporated in this selected chronology. For further information regarding them, consult Flammonde, *The Age of Flying Saucers,* especially its Bibliography.

Abbreviations
AA—air-to-air (sighting)
AFB—Air Force Base
ARA—air radar-to-air (monitoring)
ATIC—Air Technical Intelligence Center

BOAC—British Overseas Airways Corporation
CBC—Canadian Broadcasting Corporation
com.—commercial
CP—commercial pilot
(directions)—NW, SE, etc.
doz.—dozen(s)
ext.—extremely
form.—formation
GA—ground-to-air (sighting)
GG—ground-to-ground (sighting)
GH—ground-to-hovering (sighting)
GOC—Ground Observer Corps (Air Defense Command)
GRA—ground radar-to-air (monitoring)
HMS—His (Her) Majesty's Ship
Hq.—headquarters
MP—military pilot
mph—miles per hour
NAS—National Academy of Sciences
obj.—object(s)
obs.—observation(s)
OS—outer space
pers.—personnel
photo.—photograph(s)
photog.—photographer(s)
PP—private pilot
prof.—professional
rect.—rectangle (-ular)
ref.—reference(s)
rpt.—report(s)
SA—sea-to-air (sighting)
sec.—second(s)
sight.—sighting(s)
SRA—ship radar-to-air (monitoring)
U.S.—United States
USAF—United States Air Force
USAFB—United States Air Force Base
USMC—United States Marine Corps
USN—United States Navy
USSR—Union of Soviet Socialist Republics
wit.—witness(es)
WP-AFB—Wright-Patterson Air Force Base

Prehistoric—alleged ref. on Brahman tablets, Egyptian, Lemurian, Atlantean, Hindu, Pali, Inca, Aztec, and other unrecovered records.

Ancient—allusions, interpreted by some to be ref. to UFO, found in early Egyptian, Indian, Chinese, Japanese, Greek, Roman, South American, and other religious and historical papyri, wall carvings, paintings, etc.

12th century—Wolpite's (in *Historia Rerum Anglicarum;* Wulpates in *Chronicon Anglicanum;* and other spellings) case. Speculation re aliens, with ref. to UFO. Ampleforth Abbey case. Records regarded as probable recent hoax by some investigators.

14th-18th centuries—Many volumes written on the existence, or possible existence, of intelligent life elsewhere in the solar system.

18th century—Emanuel Swedenborg, philosopher and theologian, asserted positive knowledge of inhabitants of other planets.

1717—Astronomer Halley watched unknown obj. two hours. GA. (Eng.)

1762—Astronomers DeRostan and Croste saw obj. before sun. GA. (Swtz.)

1777—Astronomer Charles Messier obs. unknown disk. GA. (France)

19th century—Sight. throughout Europe and U.S.

1820—Physicist Francis Arago obs. objs. in form. GA. (France)

1824—Astronomer Gruythuisen obs. moving lights on moon. GA.

1831—Astronomer Wartmann obs. bright objs. nightly for months. GA. (Swtz.)

1845—Malta sight. SA. (Mediterranean)

1850 (c.)—Astronomer E. W. Maunder sight. (Greenwich Observatory, Eng.)

1859—Astronomer Richard Carrington obs. two non-meteoric disks. GA. (Redhill Observatory, Surrey, Eng.)

1866—Ernest Turner sight. GA. (east coast, U.S.)

1868—Several astronomers obs. bright obj. alter course. GA. (Radcliff Observatory, Oxon., Eng.)

1873—Bonham, Tex./Fort Scott, Kan. sights. GA. (U.S.)

1877—Schiaparelli obs. "canali" on Mars. GA. (Italy)

1880—Kattenau, Germany, sight.

1880—Persian Gulf (Brit. India Co. SS *Patna*) sight. SA.

1883—Zacatecas Observatory sights. GA. (Mexico)

1883—Astronomer Camille Flammarion obs. stationary aerial obj. GA. (France)

1890—China Sea (HMS *Caroline*) sight. SA.

1893—Astronomer Raymond Coulon obs. bright ellipse. GA. (Val de La Haye Observatory, France)

1896—Beginning (Nov. 1) of "the great airship" mystery, GA. (Calif., U.S.)

1897—Conclusion (April 30) of "the great airship" mystery. GA. (N.Y., U.S.)

1904—Large ovoid (6>suns) w/two satellite disks, paced and climbed. Ship crew wits. SA. (USS *Supply,* off Calif.)

1908—"Tunguska," Siberia. UFO collision with, and explosion on, the earth.

1909—Worcester, Mass., the northern east coast airship sight.

1910—Chattanooga, Tenn., airship sight.

1913—East coast sight. (Canada to Caribbean)

1914-18—Aerial "ghost" ships seen by fighter pilots of World War I. (Europe)

1921—Marconi, and subsequently other radio operators, believed signals from beyond the Earth had been monitored.

1926—Silver ovoid. Prof. explorers and associates. GA. (Himalayas, Tibet)

1928—"Inverted soup plate," emitting rays of light. GA. (Milton, N.D.)

1932—Silver disk, with amber "portholes." GA. (Durham, N.Y.)

1935—African sights. GA. (Ethiopia)

1938—Small globe, seemingly pure electricity ("ball lightning"; Menzel) shot into a BOAC cockpit, bouncing into cabin to explode. (Iraq)

1941—Initiation by military of designs for "saucer type" crafts. (Germany)

1942 (Aug. 29)—Two red disks hover over USAFB. GA. (Columbus, Miss.)

1943—Formation of unknowns sighted by police officer. GA. (Washington, D.C.)

1943-45—"Foo-fighters" seen by many combat pilots. AA. (widely in western Europe; occasionally in Pacific theater)

1944 (summer)—Pulsating red fireball hovered for 15 mins. Four USA officers, and newsmen. (Normandy, France)

1944-45—Various unknown disks, occasionally rects., red or amber. GA, AA. (Austria, France, Germany, Holland, and elsewhere in Europe)

1945 (March)—Dark spheres rise from sea into air, circle ship, and depart. Fourteen U.S.A.T. pers. wit. USS *Delarof*). SS, SA. (Aleutian Islands, Pacific)

1945—Terrestrial "flying disk" first tested. (Germany)

1945—Scandinavian sights. (Sweden)

1945—Five TBM Avenger bombers, and a huge Martin air-sea rescue flying boat, total crews of twenty-seven, vanished in flight, w/o any trace, on clear afternoon in "Bermuda Triangle." (off Florida)

1946—Scandinavian "ghost rockets" continue. (Sweden and elsewhere)

1947

June 14—Over thirty 12″ disks sailing in form. AA. (Rankin. Bakersfield, Calif.)

June 21—Six metallic inner-tube shapes. Several wit. in boat. SA. (Puget Sound and Maury Island, off Tacoma, Wash.)

June 23—Ten silver, undulating disks. GA. (Cedar Rapids, Iowa)

June 24—Nine silver, undulating disks. AA. (Arnold. Mt. Rainier, Wash.)

June 28—Five, or more, bright disks in form. USAF F-51 pilot. AA. (Armstrong. Lake Meade, Nev.)

July 4—Two groups flat disks, probably nine total. CP, and others. AA. (Smith. Boise, Idaho)

July 4—Single obj., and groups. Police, and other wit. GA. (Portland, Ore.)

July 8—Short concentration. Two spheres, joined by third; white metallic ovoid against wind, thin undulating disk, "light reflecting" obj. passed F-51. Other wit. were MP, and air technicians. GA, AA. (Muroc AFB and Rogers Dry Lake, Calif.)

July 9—Flat black, intricately maneuvering, disk. AA. (Johnson. Boise, Idaho)

July 10—Bright, light ellipse. Astronomer & family. GA. (Port Sumner, N.M.)

July—"By the end of July the UFO security lid was down tight." (Ruppelt)

August 1—Capt. William Davidson and Lt. Frank M. Brown, USOF intelligence, became first officers recorded killed during a UFO investigation. (Kelso, Wash.)

September 23—USAF preliminary UFO study determined "the reported phenomena were real." Plans for *Project Sign* initiated.

October 14—The first known supersonic flight in a terrestrial craft. (Yeager)

1948

January 7—Capt. Thomas F. Mantell first pilot reported killed while pursuing a UFO (Fort Knox, Ky.)

January 22—*Project Sign* formally established, according to NICAP. (Wright-Patterson AFB, Ohio)

January-February—Concentration of "ghost rockets" and fireballs. Air attaché offices throughout northern Europe. (Denmark, Germany, Holland, Norway, Sweden)

February 11—*Project Sign* formally established according to USAF. (Wright-Patterson AFB, Ohio)

April 5—Silver disk, one-fifth moon, erratic maneuvers. Three USAF scientists. GA. (White Sands, N.M.)

Summer—Radar tracking of unknown at 9,000 mph. (Goose Bay, Labrador)

July 23—Cigar-shaped, B-29 sized, deep blue, w/

two horizontal tiers of lights. CP & other wit. GA, AA. (Chiles-Whitted. Montgomery, Ala.) NICAP date.

July 25—Above encounter, Ruppelt date.

August 1—"Estimate of Situation" by USAF: "They were interplanetary." (Ruppelt) Report sent to USAF Chief of Staff, Gen. Hoyt S. Vandenberg. Months later all official copies destroyed.

October 1—Flat disk "dogfights" MP. Other aerial obs. GA, AA. (Gorman. Fargo, N.D.)

October 15—"Rifle-bullet" shape outmaneuvers F-61. GRA, AA. (USAF, Japan)

November 1—Radar tracking of unknown at 6,000 mph. (Goose Bay, Labrador)

December—Concentration of green fireballs. GA. (Southwest, U.S.)

December 16—*Project Grudge* replaces *Project Sign.*

1949

February 11—*Project Grudge* replaces *Project Sign.* (Ruppelt, 1955)

June 10—Two white disks maneuver near missile. Naval captain & other wit. GA. (McLaughlin. White Sands, N.M.)

August 20—Six to eight rects., w/second sight. Noted astronomer & family. GA. (Tombaugh. Las Cruces, N.M.)

August—*Project Twinkle* established. (Los Alamos, N.M.)

Autumn—Top USAF officers tracked 5 UFO on radar over key atomic installations. (Location suppressed)

December 27—*Project Grudge* dissolved; report issued claiming all UFO product of misunderstanding, delusions, madness, or hoaxes.

1950

January—First "flying saucer" article in general national magazine. (Keyhoe. *True*)

March 8—Brilliant disk. Aerial pursuit obscured by clouds. GRA, AA. (WP-AFB, Dayton, Ohio)

May 11—Among earliest seriously regarded photos (2). GA. (Trent. McMinnville, Ore.)

August 11—Large cigar-shaped blue-green fireball, divided. 100+ wit. GA. (Far NW U.S.)

August 19—Among earliest seriously regarded motion pictures. Two unknowns, horizontal flight. GA. (Mariana. Great Falls, Mont.)

September 20—Great fireballs through West. 100+ wit. GA. (Idaho to N.M.)

November 27—Six ovoids, loose echelon, 500 mph. CP. GA. (Blair. Evansville, Wisc.)

1951

January 16—Two dull disks, near a Skyhook. Two balloon specialists, and other wit. GA. (Artesia, N.M.)

January 20—Dark cigar shape, w/red & white lights. CP, & other wit. AA. (Vinther, Sioux City, Iowa)

February 19—Large cigar shape. Photographed. Airliner crew wit. AA. (Kenya, Africa)

March—Ruppelt becomes head officer re ATIC UFO activity. (Ruppelt, 1955; USAF, 1968)

May 29—Thirty silent, glowing disks, w/90° turns, 1,700 mph. Three science writers & other wit. GA. (Downey, Calif.)

August 25—Bright lights, often in form.; several consecutive evenings. GA. (Lubbock, Tex.)

August 25—"Flying wing." Sandia Corp. employee & family. GA. (Lubbock, Tex.)

August 31—Carl Hart, Jr., photos, unknowns in form. (Lubbock, Tex.)

September 16—Ruppelt becomes head officer re ATIC UFO activity. (NICAP, 1964; Condon Report, January 8, 1969)

October 27—*New Project Grudge* established, Ruppelt in charge. (USAF, 1968)

November 2—Missile, ejecting flames. CP & crew. AA. (Tex.)

November 7—Elongated orange obj., w/6 "portholes." Steamship captain & crew. SA. (Lake Superior)

November 9 to November 20—Green fireball concentration, 7 of 11 evenings. Astronomers & others. GA. (La Paz. Inst. of Meteorics, N.M.)

December 27—Project Twinkle dissolved. (Los Alamos, N.M.)

1952

January 20—Spherical blue-wite obj., 1,400 mph. Two Master Sgts, USAF intelligence wit. GA. (Fairchild AFB, Wash.)

January 21—White-domed disk, pursued by, and outmaneuvering, Navy TBM pilot. AA. (Mitchell AFB, L.I., N.Y.)

January 22—Blips on GA radar and two AA radar. Outpaced military planes. (USAFB, Alaska)

January 29—Huge silent blue-green disk. 500+ wit. GA. (Maine to Virginia)

February 20—Three bright silver spheres in form. Minister & other wit. GA. (Baller. Greenfield, Mass.)

April 7—Article, cleared by USAF Com. Gen., implied UFO interplanetary. ("We Have Visitors from Space," *Life*)

June 15—Silver or gold sphere, 50,000'. GA, AA. (across Va.)

June 21—Very high blinking light. F-47 unable to intercept during 18 min. pursuit. GA, AA. (Oak Ridge, Tenn.)

July—Concentration nationwide throughout month.

July 2—Dozen shining disks, irregular pattern. Prof. Navy photog. & family. Motion pictures. USAF concluded not of definable phenomena. GA. (Newhouse. Tremonton, Utah)

July 7-18—Heavy concentration throughout western, and northwestern U.S. Last few days coincided with beginning of annual meteor stream (△Aquarids: 7/14–18/19)

July 14—Great crimson 100' disk. AA. (Nash-Fortenberry. Norfolk, Va.)

July 16—Four brilliant ovoids. Coast Guard photog. Two photos. GA. (Alpert. Salem, Mass.)

July 19-20—First great Washington, D.C., concentration. GA, AA, GRA, ARA.

July 24—Three silver delta-wings, 1,000 mph. Two USAF cols. AA. (Carson Sink, Nev.)

July 26-27—Second great Washington, D.C., concentration. GA, AA, GRA, ARA.

July 27—Vertical form. of disks, redeploying into echelons. Pilot & 6 other wit. GA. (Manhattan Beach, Calif.)

July 29—Large brilliant polycolored obj., 180° turns, 300 to 1,400 mph. F-94 unable to intercept during 30 min. pursuit. GRA, ARA, AA. (Port Huron, Mich.)

August 24—Two silver 6' disks, altering color & shape, disappeared, reappeared, USAF col. in F-84-G wit. AA. (Hermana, N.M.; El Paso, Tex.)

December 10—Large white obj., pink "windows," 180° turns, great speed. F-94 pilot wit. AA, ARA. (Odessa, Wash.)

December 15—Red-white obj. T-33 trainer & F-94-B interceptor wits. GA, AA, GRA, ARA. (Goose Bay, Labrador)

December 29—Bright obj., moving red, green & white lights. USAF F-84-G pilot. AA. (USAFB. Honshu, Japan)

December-January, 1953—Concentration from Honshu, main island of Japan, spreading outward to Korea and northern Pacific area. Mostly AA, ARA.

1953

January 27—Brilliant metallic disk. GA, AA. (Livermore, Calif.)

August 5—Brilliant large blue-white obj. F-84 unable to intercept during 120 min. pursuit. GA, AA, GRA, AA. (Black Hawk, NW of Rapid City, S.D.)

Autumn—Concentration across northwest Europe.

November 12—Canadian government establishes UFO observatory, *Project Magnet*. (near Ottawa)

November 23—Blips cause USAF jet to be scrambled. It and target converged over Canadian territory, both vanishing, leaving no trace. GRA, AA. (Kinross AFB, Mich.)

November 28—Large blue-white to vermilion on disk. 100+ wit. GA. (NE U.S.)

1954

Winter—Concentration in northwest Europe continues.

January 6—Reporters seeking data banned from USAF UFO Hq. (WP-AFB, Dayton, Ohio)

May 14—Sixteen unknowns in form. pursued by USMC pilots. AA. (near Dallas, Tex.)

June 1—Large, white disk traveling against wind. Trans-World Airways pilot & two crew. AA. (near Boston)

June 11—"Polished metal dinner plates." World-famous astronomer during flight. AA. (Wilkins, W. Va. to Ga.)

June 30—Inverted pear shape. USAF pilot. GA, AA. (Goose Bay, Labrador)

September 18—Enormous green fireball. GA, AA. (Calif. to Mexico)

Autumn—Major concentration in Europe, especially France.

Autumn—Concentration in Eastern Europe. (Rumania, Hungary)

1955

February 11—Two red-green obj., high speed. CP & other wits. AA. (King. Maine to NYC flight)

April 23—World-famous astronomer & meteorologist: ". . . they aren't ordinary meteorite falls. [After 40 years of studying the skies] I've never seen any meteoric fireballs like them." (La Paz. Albuquerque, N.M.)

August 23—Three brilliant spheres. F-84s scrambled, pursued at max. speed, objs. outdistanced them. GOC & MP. GA, AA, GRA. (Cincinnati, Ohio)

Summer-Winter—Concentration in Cincinnati continues. Scrambles all fail.

November 1—Cigar shape, followed by domed disk. Astronomer wit. GA. (Halstead. Mojave Desert, Calif.)

November 25—Very large white globe, instantaneous reversal of course. USAF flying instructor & physician. AA. (Miller-Ward. Near Bannings, Calif.)

1956

January 22—Large elongated obj., yellow exhaust, passes aircraft. Flight engineer wit. AA. (Gulf of Mexico)

April 8—Large brilliant orange-to-red obj., 250-1,000 mph. USAF scramble, no contact. AA. (Ryan-Neff. N.Y.)

July 19—Brilliant teardrop. Police, USAF pers., et al. wits. GA, AA, GRA. (Hutchinson, Kan.)

Summer—Flaming vermilion ball smashed into transport propeller, electrically destroying radio and compass. (USSR)

August 8-19—Concentration of oblongs, ovoids, disks. Scores of wits. GA. (Conn.)

November 8—Radar monitors obj. at 4,000 mph. Six Pan. Amer. experts wits. GRA. (Miami, Fla.)

1957

March 9—Glowing pale green disk. Six, or more. Com. flights wits. AA. (Jacksonville, Fla.)

March 23—CAA radar tracks four objs. Visual crimson obj. w/white lights. GOC, Oxnard AFB pers. & other wits. ARA, GA. (Los Angeles, Calif.)

June 18—Haloéd obj. w/three "portholes." Physicist w/telescope wit. GA. (Carlock. Jackson, Miss.)

November—Concentration for first two weeks. Midwest, South, Southwest U.S. USAF concedes 400+ reports during period.

November 2—Specific several-day concentration w/ many electromagnetic disturbances. (Levelland, Tex.)

November 3—Brilliant vermilion 20′ to 300′ ovoid. Police & other wits. GA. (White Sands, N.M.)

November 5—Brilliant obj., very swift, over sea. Many naval wits. SA, SRA. (Coast Guard cutter *Sebago*. Gulf of Mexico)

November 7—Brilliant obj., increasing in size & halving, separate segments landing in distance. Wit. departed scene hurriedly. GA, GH. (Moore. Montville, Ohio)

1958

>   *January 16*—Saturn-like disk, over sea. Many wits. Photos. SA. (Trindade Island, off Brazil)
>
>   *April 9*—Nine yellow disks in echelon, divide into two groups. Several wits. GA. (Cleveland, Ohio)
>
>   *April 14*—Twelve to eighteen gold disks, V-form., w/irregular positioned satellites. USAF pers. wit. GA. (Dean. Albuquerque, N.M.)
>
>   *July 26*—Silver spheres, tremendous speed. GOC supervisor wit. GA. (Highland. Durango, Colo.)
>
>   *September 8*—Cigar shape, w/satellites. USAF major & other officers wits. (Duich. Offutt AFB, Omaha, Neb.)
>
>   *October 7*—Gray ovoid, hovered, ascended. Ship's crew wits. SA. (*SS Nantucket*. Off Nantucket, Mass.)
>
>   *October 26*—Three bright objs., near moon. Chemist w/telescope wit. GA. (Schafer. Lafayette, Ind.)

1959

>   *January 8*—Brilliant 200′ blue-green teardrop. Two USAF pilots wits. AA. (Phillipsburg to Brookville, Pa.)
>
>   *February 24*—Three yellow-to-orange, varying intensity, disks. Com. flight & passengers. AA. (Killian-Dee. Bradford, Pa.)
>
>   *March-April*—Sequence of lights descend to mountaintop. Numerous wits. GA. (Sheep Rock Mt., Va.)
>
>   *June 20*—Four flaming blue-white globes, 15,000 mph., over sea. Two com. flights wits. AA. (Pacific Ocean)
>
>   *July 11*—Huge brilliant obj., w/four satellites, tremendous speed, over sea. Five, or more, com. flights wits. AA. (Pacific Ocean)
>
>   *September 24*—Brilliant white-to-vermilion globe hovered at 200′, departed at tremendous speed. FAA, police, & other wits. GA, GRA. (Redwood, Ore.)

1960

>   *February*—Special space advisor to President supported idea of Martian moons being artificial satellites. (S.F. Singer. *Astronautics*)

May 5—Triangle ¼-moon size, spinning on axis while flying. Astronomical observatory staff wits. GA. (Majorca, Mediterranean)

August 13—Brilliant apparent craft, complex maneuvers, two hrs., later joined by second obj. Dozs. wits. GA. (Red Bluff, Calif.)

August 13-20—Concentration w/hundreds wits. Many communities. GA. (northern Calif.)

August 16—Two long red ovoids, followed by boomerang shape. Pilots & many other wits. GA. Corning, Calif.)

August 25—Mystery satellite, viewed on several days. Many wits. Photographed. (Grumman Aircraft Corp.)

October 3—Six disks, w/"mother ship," Anglican priest & other wits. GA, GH. (CBC report. Off Tasmania)

1961

February 5-7—Concentration of fireballs, various colors. Many wits. GA, AA. (Maine)

March 23-29—Concentration of brilliant, often red, objs. Pilots & many other wits. GA, AA. (Florida)

May—Twenty-one scientists call for full, open investigation. (Statement released through NICAP)

June 19—Large brilliant obj. hovered, tracked by radar. GH, GA, GRA. (Exeter, England)

July 4-5—Glowing obj. dives at plane; tracked by radar. USAF pilot wit. AA, GRA. (Stadvec. Akron, Ohio)

October 2—Brilliant silver metallic obj., thousands mph. GA, AA. (Salt Lake City, Utah)

1962

April 18—Fireball, general electrical disturbances. GA. (Eureka, Ohio)

April 24-25—Small concentration, one sight. of domed disk, w/lights. Many wits. GA. (Philadelphia, Pa.)

April 30—X-15 photographed "5 or 6 discs . . . or cylinders," w/o AA visual contact. USAF plane. AA. (Walker)

May 26—Bright red ovoid, w/sparks. USAF lists unidentified. GA. (Westfield, Mass.)

June 30—Red disk, 10 mins., climbed & banked. USAF lists unidentified. GA. (Richmond, Va.)

July 30—Red diamond and/or disk hovered & darted. USAF lists unidentified. GA. (Ocean Springs, Miss.)

September 15-28—Concentration, many reports. Seven, or more, counties. Numerous police & other wits. GA. (NE N.J.)

1963

January 5—NAS urges search for alien life be "top priority." (Pub. No. 1079)

January 24—Large disk E-W and delta-wing N-S intersect paths, then fly on. GA. (Lexington, Ky.)

June 18—Various colored obj. zigzagged & hovered. GH, GA. (Niagara Falls, N.Y.)

July 18—Disk hovers, vanishes when jets approach. Tech. writer & pilots wits. GA, AA. (Sunnydale, Calif.)

August 1—Triangle hovers long time. RAF pilot & instructor, & tower pers. wits. GA, AA. (Garston, Herts., England)

August 4-18—Concentration, various descriptions. Several counties. GA. (Illinois)

October 23—Silver disk, "loud pulsating sound." USAF lists unidentified. (Meridian, Idaho)

November—Large, low obj., "windows," hovers & flashes light on squad car. Police & other wits. GH, GA. (Port Huron, Mich.)

1964

April 11—Glistening obj. sailed & hovered, 45 mins. Former MP & other wits. GA. (Homer, N.Y.)

April 24—Landed ovoid craft, reported crew, close viewing Police officer wit. GG. (Zamora. Socorro, N.M.)

Christmastime—Floating obj. Doz. wits. GA. (Warminster, England)

1965

May 5—Three large obj., then four on radar, to 3,000 mph. GA, GRA. (Source: Hynek. Location not cited)

June—Silver cylindrical obj., w/"arms" or "antenna." Astronauts. Gemini IV. OS. (McDivitt)

August 1—Large multicolored disk. USAF pers. wits. GA. (Cheyenne, Wyo.)

August 1—Five objs. & two objs. USAF pers. wits. GA. (Cheyenne, Wyo.)

August 1—Nine objs. USAF pers. wits. GA. (Sydney, Neb.)

August 1—Large white ovoid, flashing red light. USAF pers. wits. GA. (west of Cheyenne, Wyo.)

September 3—Brilliant 90' ob., w/pulsating red lights. Police and many other wits. GA. (Exeter, N.H.)

September 3—Violent 200' x 50' obj. blinking blue light. Close encounter. Police wits. GH, GA. (McCoy-Goode. Angleton, Tex.)

1966

March 18—Shining blue-white "quilted" metallic ovoid, w/cabin, & 4 satellites. Police & many wits. GA. (Manor. Ann Arbor, Mich.)

March 19—Brilliant ovoid, similar to previous entry. 100+ wits. GA. (Hillsdale College, Mich.)

March 28—Future Pres. Gerald R. Ford, then Congressman, wrote House Armed Services Committee urging full, open inquiry. As appointed Vice President and unelected President he took no action in the field.

1967

January 9—"Hamburger" shape photographed. Hynek: hoax unlikely. GA. (Jaroslaw. Mount Clemens, Mich.)

March—Concentration from Montana to Maryland. Hundreds wits. scores communities. (Minn., Mich., Ark., Mo., Okla., Kan., etc.)

April 17—Five large ovoids, in form., high velocity. USAF intelligence officers wits. GA. (Saigon, Vietnam)

June 22—Large brilliant obj. circled by RAF plane. MP, coast guard pers., & other wits. GA, AA. (Brixham, England)

August 23—flashing white light; in area two days. GA, AA, GRA. Com. flight wits. (Halifax to Boston)

September 7—Gutted horse called victim of UFO, "15 exhaust marks" on earth, etc. (Snippy. Alamosa County, Colo.)

October—Large obj., 50' x 12', photographed. GA. (Smith. Calgary, Alberta, Canada)

1968

January 15—"Stunted dill pickle," fluorescent, low-flying. GA. (Three Hills, Alberta, Canada)

March 3-4—Concentration large luminous globes, 2 hours. Thousands wits. in twenty states. GA. (eastern U.S.)

November 20—Multicolored objs. in form. Military pers. wits. GA. (across Great Britain)

November 26—Two bright objs. interplay 5 to 7 mins. Eight airport tower pers. wits. GA. (Bismark, N.D.)

December—Dis. Att. Jim Garrison summoned Fred L. Crisman (see Maury Island) to testify before "assassination" grand jury in New Orleans.

1969

January—Irregular concentration, often glowing globes. Generally Midwest, Southeast, and Far Northwest. GA. (Minn., Iowa, Mich., Mo., Ohio, Ill., S.C., Fla., Ore., Wash.)

1970

January 22—Brilliant white 25' dome, w/jet exhaust. GA. (Willard, Ohio)

Spring—USAF Academy suspends use of textbook —*Introduction to Space Sciences*. Vol. II—warning of UFO. (Colorado Springs, Colo.)

October 26—Orange sphere w/trail of flame. MP & other wits. GA. (Banbury, Oxon., England)

1971

February—Concentration re brilliant objs. w/occupants. (throughout U.S.)

July 13—Reflecting disk CP. AA. (Kent, England)

November 2—Multicolored 10' obj. GH, GA. (Johnson. Delphos, Kan.)

1972

June 24—Twenty-fifth anniversary of the "age of flying saucers."

October 9—Bright elongated ellipse, w/rect. lights. GH, GA. (Smithtown & Corona, L.I., N.Y.)

October 9—Silver "blimp." Many wits. GA. (Vincennes, Ind.)

November 19—Seven yellow lights. College prof. & other wits. GA. (Albuquerque, N.M.)

November 29—Gallup Poll: 11% (double since 1966) of public had viewed UFO; 51% accept them as real. Concentration through second half of year continued. (Calif., Ill., Pa., Kan., Iowa, Mich., La., N.Y.)

1973

January-February—*Concentration.* Red-yellow disks, ovoids, cylinders & triangles. Hundreds wits. GA. (Cherokee, S.C.)

February—Concentration of pulsating amber-blue-red-white objs. GA. (Pennsylvania southward)

March 1—Forty white, objs. w/blue-red lights, over water. Police & doz. wits. GA. (Saylors Lake, Pa.)

April 1-8—Concentration, radiant globe, undulating path. Many wits. GA. (Los Angeles, Calif.)

June 28—Two red objs., in tandem, for hour plus. GA. (NYC)

July 28—Undetermined form crisscrossed over for 45 mins. Engineer & other wits. GA. (Marble Falls, Tex.)

August 14—"Small glowing object," 20 mins. Six wits., w/telescope. GA. (Douglas Island, Alaska)

August 22—Obj. w/"flames." Pilot & other wits. GA, AA. (Hollywood, Calif.)

August 30—Concentration, many blue-green objs. Hundreds wits., scores of communities. (Ga., Ohio, Ind., Ala.)

October 1-20—Concentration across entire eastern third of U.S.

October 1—Four brilliant disks. GA. (Rogers, Ark.)

October 1—Red-green obj., w/white band. Doz. wits. GA. (Brunswick, Fla.)

October 1—Amber & other color objs., acrobatic. GA. (Jacksonville, Fla.)

October 3—Blinking yellow-red-green obj. Police & other wits. GA. (Ashland, Miss.)

October 4—Brilliant light, w/tail, & others. Hundreds wits., scores of communities. (Ark., Miss., to N.C.)

October 5—Sweeping sight., entire south from Miss. to Fla.

October 12—Concentration expands northward to Ohio & Mich.

October 15—Concentration increases in La., also Calif. & SW desert.

October 17—Amber vertical obj., 30 mins. Governor & family. (Gilligan. Lima, Ohio)

October 18—Red obj. "attacking plane," tremendous speed. AA. (Coyne, Cleveland, Ohio)

1974

January 6—Large, bright w/fin. GH, GA. (Pellegrini-Logan. Orange County, Fla.)

January 26—Ten or more, bright objs. in form. CP, crew & other wits. AA. (Bergland, Boeing 727, Mallorca to Sweden)

February 6—Obj. three times size jumbo jet, w/ many lights. USA pers. wits. GA. (Bobay-Cope. Denver, Colo.)

May—Former Republican presidential nominee Sen. Barry Goldwater joins NICAP board of governors.

July 9—Silent 35' oblate obj. w/altern. red-green lights gliding & hovering at 200'. Two PO & other wit. GH, GA. (Wallace-Ramsell. Kingston, N.Y.)

July 30—"Large, red, dome-shaped" obj. w/eng. prop. blades & windows, "bobbing and fluttering" at 90', emitting white, blue, yellow sparks. Four+ wit. GH, GA. (Stevens-Mispilkin. South Hampston, N.H.)

August 5/7—Silent pink-orange 25' oblate obj. varying in size "like breathing" at 50'. Doz. wit. GH, GA. (Dugal-Voertman. Farmington, Mo.)

August 11—Ext. fast obj. w/blue, yellow, green, white flashing lights, + three other "saucer shapes." Doz. wit. Two PO. Six accomp. sight.

in area. GA. (Alder Payne. Tilton, Laconia, Gilford, etc., N.H.)

September 11—Five 11′ metallic disks hovered 15 mins, 1′ from earth, leaving depressions. GG. (Fuhr. Langenburg, Sask., Canada)

September 15/16—Swift metallic red-blue sphere overflew & hovered 2 hours. PO & other wit. GA. (Berry-Cockerman. Vale, Ore.)

October 12—Low-flying orange oblate obj. at 50′ scattering sparks on earth and auto. (Fifteen similar sight. w/1 week in Allegheny, Butler, Beaver, Fayette & Westmoreland Counties.) GA. (Loyal. Connellsville, Pa.)

October 20—"Ball, orange and green and spinning" obj. hovered. Auto eng. died. (Num. sight 1966 —or earlier—to date.) GH, GA. (Elkhart, Ind.)

November 1—Very bright "big white cigar," wingless, size of 747, obj. In view 15 mins. Doz. wit. GA. (McKoane-Burke. Bakers Lake, near Barrington, Ill.)

December 2—Craft w/curved transparent front. Figure obs. w/fur or fur garment, large eyes, inside. Sev. mins GG (Bosak. Frederic, Wis.)

1975

January 1—Yellow-orange obj., 360′ x 50′, landed, five mins. GG (Williams. Bond County, Ill.)

January 1—"Big yellow . . . bunch of moons" clustered, paced auto. GA. (Jannett-Kleine. Carlyle, Ill.)

January 1—"Large orange ball," size of 5 moons, obs. GA. (Caldwell. Kankakee, Ill.)

January 19—Sphere, circled w/white lights, paced auto. Nearby pair of unknowns spotted. GA. (Willingham. Vinita, Okla.)

February 10—Silent 20′ orange oblate obj. slowly diminished in size and vanished. Charred ground, snapped-off trees evident next day. GA, GH. (Sutter-Killian. Staten Island, N.Y.)

March 13—Numerous swift red, white, blue globes, straight and zigzag flight. PO in six counties rept. & many other wit. GA. (Armeson-Baker. Across N. Michigan & N. Wisconsin)

March 18—Huge, brilliant, rotating green-blue sphere. Many wit. GA. (Parsley-Nalley-Radke-Buchanan-Mills. Yakima, Wash.)

April 3—Silent "V"-shaped craft w/red lights along one arm, green on other, about 200 mph. Its searchlight swept communities. PO & other wit. various areas. GA. (POs Atkinson-Haggins-McCormick-McPasson-Driver. Five counties in North Carolina)

April 4/6—Concentration in Robeson & 5 counties in North Carolina.

—Wednesday: Many rpts. of unknown lights. PO, PP, CP, GA, AA.

—Thursday: Sixty-five rpts. boomerang w/white lights. PO & other wit. GA.

—Friday: Ten bright lights obs, along 400 miles of road, during 7 hrs. PO & other wit. GA. (Thompson: "We are *in pursuit* of UFO heading north." Moore: "V"-shaped craft w/3' portholes. Hammond: "V"-shaped or triangular obj. w/red-green-white lights. Floyd: boomerang shape w/ intense red-orange lights, four of seven nights. Strickland: five pink disks at 50 mph., some hovered, some landed.)

April 4—Blue "flashes" passing in few sec., 100' alt. Various wit. GA. (Gilbertson-Arneson. La Crosse, Wis.)

April 6/8—Swiftly moving, very large, orange, cigar-shaped obj. flashing blue light; also hovered. Many rpts. (W.-central Wisconsin into Minnesota)

—"A huge flaming object about the size of a football field . . . almost paralyzed [me] with fear," rpt. PO. Est. alt. 2000', 15,000 to 18,000 mph. Many rpts. GA. (Wheeler-Koehler. Elmwood. Wis.)

—four glowing obj., one large, three small. Sev. wit. & PO. GA. (Theis. Ellsworth. Wis.)

May 3—Two disks paced plane at 15,000', 140 mph, for 10 mins., terrifying PP to tears as his controls failed to respond. Two radarmen (Interian-Estanol) also tracked obj. GA, GRA, AA. (Montiel. Tequesquitengo/Tlalpan, Mexico)

May 5—"Tremendous . . . humming" white obj. like "searchlight," overflew 30 mins. Sev. nights. GA. (Beardsley. Sedona, Ariz.)

June 6—Huge silver (steel-colored, metallic) twin-domed obj., w/two brilliant lights, hovered. Dep. very fast. GA. (Sisneros. Carson City, Calif.)

June 6—Pearl-colored 50' disk flew & hovered sev. mins., landed, & dep., leaving ground marks. GA, GH. (Greensboro, N.C.)

July 4—Ovoid 30' diam., unearthly color, w/green band, obs. 20 mins. GA, AA. (Tiger-Cahill-Jahn. Parsippany, N.J.)

July 4—Dazzling, low-flying metallic funnel paced auto, nearly blinding two women. GA. (Bos-berger-Black. Russell, Kan.)

July 6—Shining 30' diam., domed obj. landed, de-positing blue-green oily substance. GA. (Borda. Mt. Pleasant, Ont., Canada)

July 11—Bright pink sphere overflew & hovered. GA. (Cray. Live Oak, Fla.)

July 15/16—High alt. UAP, varying white-green-red. Photo. by two PO. Also many wit. (Maracle-Fox, Koehler-Billyard. Dunnville, Ont., Canada)

July 22—Ext. fast 20' diam. red obj. split in two & filled air w/sulfur odor. GA. (Live Oak, Fla. Cf. July 11)

August 10—Humming, hazy blue, 40' diam., metal-lic ovoid w/substructure & tripod landing gear, hovered. GA. (Lugo. Gilroy, Calif.)

August 12—Large bright sphere w/red center skimmed treetops for 15 mins. GA. (Bluemmer. Gilroy, Calif.)

August 13—Large bright shapes low or on hilltop. PP & other wit. GA. (Cosio. Gilroy, Calif.)

August 13—Silent "triangular shape . . . (w/) two bright lights." Sev. wit. GA. (Dover. Gilroy, Calif.)

August 13—"Orange sphere" obs. 1 min. & van-ished. Sev. wit. GA. (Bambino. Los Gatos, Calif.)

Appendix II

United States Air Force UFO Personnel

Agency Responsible for UFO Project
1. Technical Intelligence Division, Air Materiel Command: 1947–1951.
2. Air Technical Intelligence Center (ATIC): 1951–1959.
3. Aerospace Technical Intelligence Center: 1959–7/1/61.
4. Foreign Technology Division: 7/1/61–12/17/69.

Designation of UFO Project
1. Project Sign: 2/11/48–12/16/48. (NICAP: 1/22/48; Condon: 12/30/47.)
2. Project Grudge: 12/16/48–12/27/49. (NICAP: 2/11/49; Condon: 12/11/49.)
3. Project Twinkle (Los Alamos, New Mexico, meteor study): 8/49–12/27/51.
4. New Project Grudge: 10/27/51–3/52.
5. Aerial Phenomena Group: summer 1952.
6. Project Blue Book: summer 1952–12/17/69.

Chief Officer of UFO Project
1. Captain Robert R. Sneider: 11/48–3/51.
2. Lieutenant Jerry Cummings: 3/51–9/16/51 (NICAP).
3. Captain Edward J. Ruppelt: 3/51–9/53 (USAF to author); 9/16/51–9/53 (Condon Report, p. 511).
4. Lieutenant Robert M. Olsson: 9/53–3/54. Note: Lieutenant Olsson was acting Chief Officer during

Captain Ruppelt's two-month tour of duty in the summer of 1953.
5. Captain Charles A. Hardin: 3/54–4/56.
6. Captain George T. Gregory: 4/56–10/58.
7. Major Robert J. Friend: 10/58–8/63.
8. Lieutenant Colonel Hector Quintanilla: 8/63–12/17/69.

Spokesmen for UFO Project
1. Al Chop: 4/52–3/53.
2. Various officers: 3/53–1954.
3. Captain Robert White: circa 1955.
4. Major Robert F. Spence: circa 1957.
5. Lieutenant Colonel Lawrence J. Tacker: 1958–3/61.
6. Major William T. Coleman: 4/61–1/62.
7. Major Carl R. Hart: 2/62–summer 1963.
8. Major Maston Jacks: summer 1963–12/17/69.

NOTE: Secretary of the Air Force Robert C. Seamans, Jr., issued press release number 1077–69, dated December 17, 1969, announcing the termination of Project Blue Book, and the total discontinuation of any publicly acknowledged United States Air Force inquiry of any kind regarding the subject of Unidentified Flying Objects, or any related phenomena.

Appendix III

A History of UFO Organizations and Periodicals

A hundred or more organizations devoted to the mystery of inexplicable things in the sky were established from the 1940s onward. The majority were "flying saucer" groups; a few assumed a reasonably agnostic, or UFO attitude. Most issued newsletters, and there were several independent "magazines" published. The majority were parochial and short-lived, some lasted a decade or longer. Of the early Unidentified Flying Object-oriented societies only two of the major ones survive to this day. With them, one of later date, and two founded fairly recently, constitute centers of unofficial UFO investigation, research, and dissemination of information. While strictly "flying saucer" groups have been omitted, these are listed below.

In addition, a comprehensive list of foreign bodies is included.

The cited data is as accurate as possible, but the transience of an overwhelming percentage of such projects makes complete contemporaneity impossible.

1. *Center for UFO Studies* (CUFOS). P. O. Box 11, Northfield, Ill. 60093. Founded January 1, 1974, by Dr. J. Allen Hynek, director. Dr. Hynek is professor of astronomy, Northwestern University, where, for fifteen years he was chairman of the Department of Astronomy and director of the Dearborn Observatory. For twenty-two years (until

1969) he served as chief scientific consultant on Unidentified Flying Objects to the United States Air Force. The center is primarily a "laboratory" of scientists and technologists who investigate reports submitted by responsible groups and individuals. Participation by invitation.

2. *Aerial Phenomena Research Organization* (APRO). 3910 East Kleindale Rd., Tucson, Ariz. 85712. Founded in January 1952 by its present directors Mr. and Mrs. L. J. (Jim and Coral) Lorenzen, the oldest UFO group in this country was still functioning in January 1976. Cooperates with *Center for UFO Studies*. Accepts extraterrestrial origin of UFO, and is receptive to claims of interplanetarian contacts. Has representatives in many countries. Open membership. Publication: *The A.P.R.O. Bulletin.*

3. *National Investigations Committee on Aerial Phenomena* (NICAP). 3535 University Boulevard West, Kensington, Md. 20795. Founded in 1956 by Townsend Brown and shortly thereafter reorganized by Major Donald E. Keyhoe, who served as its director until 1969. He was succeeded by Richard Hall, and others, until administration of NICAP was assumed by John L. Acuff in May 1970. Cooperates with the *Center for UFO Studies*. Accepts extraterrestrial origin of UFO, but for years completely rejected claims of interplanetary contacts. This attitude has modified somewhat. Organization's investigations have been international in scope. Open membership, although occasionally selective. Publication: *UFO Investigator.*

4. *Society for the Investigation of the Unexplained* (SITU). Columbia, N.J. 07832. Founded in July 1965 by Ivan T. Sanderson. Director: Robert C. Warth. Group treats UFO as a minor portion of its major program of recording a broad spectrum of anomalies in nature; but the breadth of its primary objectives makes it of great value to those interested in other than extraterrestrial explanations for aerial phenomena. Openminded on most "customarily discounted" questions. Open membership. Participa-

tion varies. Publication: *Pursuit* (established June 1968; preceded by an organization newsletter).

5. *Mutual UFO Network* (MUFON). 103 Oldtowne Rd., Seguin, Texas 78155. Founded on May 31, 1969. Director: Walter H. Andrus. A fairly new parochial group now attempting to become national in its operation, to a considerable extent through cooperation with the *Center for UFO Studies* (deriving from its former geographical proximity, in Quincy, Ill., to Dr. Hynek's organization). Accepts probability of extraterrestrial origin of UFO. Membership arbitrary and based upon officers' predisposition. Source of contemporary data, sometimes unfamiliar with much historical data and with earlier key figures in field. Publication: *Skylook,* 26 Edgewood Dr., Quincy, Ill. 62301 (established in 1967, allied with MUFON in 1969).

Foreign

Australia

Unidentified Flying Objects Investigation Centre
19 Hurlstone Avenue
Sydney, N.S.W., Australia   W. E. Moser, dir.

Queensland Flying Saucer Research Bureau
P.O. Box 111
North Quay, Brisbane, Queensland, Australia
                                  C. Lehman, dir.

Perth Unidentified Flying Object Research
40 Wendouree Road,
Wilson, Western Australia

The Australian Flying Saucer Research Society
Box 1457 G.P.O. Adelaide, South Australia, or
P.O. Box 32, Toorack, Melbourne, Victoria,
Australia

Warragul Space Phenomena Study Group
69 Latrobe Street
Warragul, Victoria, Australia

Ballarat Astronomical Society UFO Group
c/o Mr. H. Sloane
Mt. Clear, Victoria, Australia

CAPIO
P.O. Box 180
Moorabbin Victoria, Australia

Victorian Flying Saucer Research Society
P.O. Box 43
Moorabbin, Victoria, Australia

Tasmanian UFO Investigation
P.O. Box 162
Moonah, Tasmania, Australia

Austria

Informationen der Gesellshaft fur Interplanetarik
19 Pyrkerg,
Wien 21, Austria

Belgium

Belgishe Interplanetaire Studiege—Meenschap
Maasfortbaan 187, Lier (pr. Antwerp)
Belgium

Societé Belge d'Étude des Phénomènes Spatiaux
Boulevard Aristide Briand, 26,
1070 Bruxelles, Belgium
Pub.: *Inforespace*

Brazil

Sociedade Brasileira de Estudos Sobre Discos
Voadores
Rua Sen. Pedro Velho
50 ap. 201 (Cosme Velho)
Rio de Janeiro, Brazil

Canada

Canadian Aerial Phenomena Investigations
Committee
P.O. Box 98, P.
Station A, Scarborough,
Ontario, Canada

UFO Québec Recherches et Informations
(Publications)
P.O. Box 53 Dollard-des-Ormeaux, P.Q.,
H9G 2H5 Canada

Chile

Centro de Investigaciones en Coheteria y
Astronomia
(Division de Investigaciones de Objectos Volantes
no Identificados)
Alameda No. 264,
Santiago de Chile, S.A.

UFO Chile (publication)
Casilla 13202,
Santiago de Chile, S.A.

Denmark

Scandinavian UFO Information
Praestetgardsvej 40
Vojens, Denmark

England

British Flying Saucer Society
(see British U.F.O. Research Association)

British U.F.O. Research Association (BUFORA)
Newchapel Observatory
New Chapel, Stoke-on-Trent,
Staffs, England
Pub.: *BUFORA Journal*
P.O. Box 25,
Barnet,
Herts, En5 2NR
England

Flying Saucer Review (publication)
Charles Bowen ,ed., Eileen Buckle, asst. ed.
FSR Publications, Ltd.
London UFO Research Organization Bulletin
(LUFORA Bulletin)
12 Dorset Road, Cheam, Sutton
Surrey, England

Contact (formerly International Sky Scouts)
43 Walton Bridge Road, Shepperton,
Middlesex, England
Space Review
2 Station Road, Frimley-near-Aldershot,
Hampshire, England

France

Commission International d'Enquêtes Scientifiques
51 Rue des Alps
Valence, France
Pub.: *Ouranos*

Groupment d'Étude de Phénomènes Ariens
(GEPA)
69 Rue de la Tomb-Issoire,
Paris 14e, France

Lumières dans la Nuit (publication)
"Les Pins"
43 Le Chambon-sur-Ligon,
Haute Loire, France

Germany

UFO Nachrichten
62 Wiesbaden-Schierstein,
Milanstr. 5 (fr. wörhster), Germany

Italy

Clypeus (publication suspended?)
Casella Postale 604
Torino-Centro, Italy

Japan

Cosmic Brotherhood Association
Naka, P.O. Box 12
Yokohama, Japan

New Zealand

New Zealand Space Research
P.O. Box 21–007
Henderson, New Zealand

Civilian Saucer Investigation
P.O. Box 72
Onehunga, S.E. 5,
Auckland, New Zealand

Spain
Centro de Estudios Interplanetarios de Barcelona
Stendekcei, Apartado 282
Barcelona, Spain
Pub.: *Stendek*

Venezuela
Sociedad Venezuelana Investigadora del Ovni
Apartado Del Este 4067,
Caracas, Venezuela

Glossary

aerobatics—skilled maneuvering of aircraft

aerodonetics—art or study of glided or floated flight

aerolite—a mass of material, not meteorite iron, falling to earth; a meteorite

aeroplane—see *aircraft*

"age of flying saucers"—usually regarded as the aerological period from the Kenneth Arnold sighting to the early 1960s

aircraft—an airplane, aeroplane; generally a heavier-than-air, manned machine

airship—originally, and usually, a lighter-than-air vessel in contradistinction to an airplane, but occasionally meaning any manned vessel intended for controlled flight; a zeppelin or other air- or gas-supported device

alien—in ufology an extraterrestrial being, an occupant of a UFO, a saucerian; not of this planet

angel's hair—strange gossamer or ephemeral substance said to float to earth from the sky or UFO. It generally dissolves or disappears on contact with earth or on being touched.

anomalies—inconsistencies or discrepancies, especially in nature. Term often used by Ivan T. Sanderson and John Keel for UFO

anti-UFO—rejection of the reality of UFO, more specifically opposition to any objective, comprehensive study of UFO

astrology (-er, -ist, -ical)—divination by astral calculations

astronautics—technology of constructing and operating spacecraft

astronauts—operators of semi-space and spacecraft

astrophysics—branch of astronomy dealing with the physical and chemical nature of celestial bodies

Atlantis—see Chapter 9

auras—radiations, usually alleged to be visible only to "sensitives" or by the employment of special equipment, said to surround all organic and, by some, inorganic material

"blips"—registrations on a radar screen

CAA—Civil Aviation Authority
CAB—Civil Aeronautics Board
canopy—cockpit cover
canopy reflection—light mirrored by such a shield
chronocentric—preoccupation with one's own time, unable to relate to the past or the future
cigar-shaped—elongated UFO, designed like a zeppelin, perhaps more slender
cipher (cypher)—a code, a zero
clairaudient (-ience)—one who allegedly can hear beyond the normal range of aural perception with no artificial aid; occasionally, one who hears the voices of the dead or other spirits; (rare) a contactee who communicates with "space people" by telepathy
clairvoyant—one who allegedly can see beyond the normal range of visual perception with no artificial aid; occasionally, one who functions as a medium; (rare) a contactee who communicates with "space people" by telepathy
"classic(s)"—a historically notable sighting or confrontation
classified—government material restricted to specific personnel
cloak-and-dagger—espionage personnel or activity
concentration—exceeding normal frequency or congestion of UFO during a limited time or within a particular locality
contactees—individuals who claim to have established voluntary or involuntary relationships with occupants of a "flying saucer," or with "space people" by other means
contactology—the study of contactees and alleged Earthian/alien communication
conventional aircraft—any flying device, specifically

airplanes, of standard, recognizable design and construction, usually in contradistinction to UFO

cosmic consciousness—alleged mental and/or "spiritual" integration with universal harmonies and mystically heightened awareness deriving from same

cosmonauts—astronauts of Union of Soviet Socialist Republics (USSR)

craft—any vehicle, in ufology specifically a UFO with a determinable structure

cryptography (-ographic, -ographer)—writing in, or deciphering, code

cults—sects, secret societies

cusp—curves, technically a point at which two related lines of an arc meet, and stop, with a common tangent. Not used in the astrological sense (the beginning of a "house") in this work

debunk (-er, -ing)—attempt to discredit

delta-winged—see *flying wing*

demonism (-iac)—a more formal development of Satanism, with more complicated rituals, a broader deital hierarchy, in our millennium; earlier, any of the "old religions"; only obliquely, sometimes not at all, related to Christianity

demonology—a study of demons and demonism

disks—a UFO shape approximating two convex circles rim-to-rim; indiscriminately employed to indicate almost any unknown not cigar-shaped

dogfight—combat between, or among, fighter planes, or a conventional aircraft and a UFO

Earthian—indigene of the third planet from the sun

echelon—an aerial formation consisting of horizontal or vertical "steps," or symmetrically staggered aircraft

extrasensory perception (ESP)—the ability to sense beyond the range of presumably "normal" faculties

fireball—a globular UFO, a "shooting star," a meteor; occasionally used to describe "ball lightning"

fireball, green—unusual virescent UFO, most frequently

recorded in the southwest United States; subject of unsuccessful Project Twinkle; a light emerald meteor

flak—agitation, uproar, hyperactive media response; from expression used during World War II for antiaircraft fire

flap—exceeding normal media coverage of UFO during a limited time or within a restricted area; any sudden or concentrated reaction

flying saucer—a UFO; an allegedly intelligently operated, extraterrestrial vehicle

flying wing—an aircraft designed as an equilateral boomerang, or a triangle, with no fuselage

foo-fighter—any of various kinds of usually smallish UFO frequently observed by fighter pilots over Europe, and occasionally in the Pacific theater of combat, toward the conclusion of World War II

formation—disposition or pattern of two, or more, objects, either approximately symmetrically, or distinctively asymmetrically, spaced

fuselage—the body of an aircraft, as distinguished from the wings, rudder, etc.

galaxy (-actic)—and uncountable cluster of stars, as exemplified by the Milky Way, in which our own solar system is located

ghost rockets—European, especially Scandinavian, phrase for UFO; usage most common during the 1940s

"hard" evidence—physical, photographic, etc., proof as distinguished from that of circumstantial or testimonial nature

"hard" sighting—observation, under desirable conditions, by an unusually qualified witness, or a number of reliable reporters simultaneously

hex—a mild curse or bewitchment

hex sign—a design, usually painted, which allegedly protects against a hex, or serves to attract good fortune; "magical" attribution may well have evolved after the introduction of such motifs

hoax—a fraud, a deception

hostile—in ufology, unfriendly or threatening UFO

interplanetarians—space travelers, not necessarily exceeding the boundaries of our solar system; extraterrestrials

Jovian—indigene of Jupiter, largest planet in our solar system
Jupiterian—see *Jovian*

Lemuria—see Chapter 9
lunar—of the moon
Lunarian—indigene of the moon

magnetic (-ism)—a natural characteristic of attraction present in certain material and created by specific conditions; an alleged mystical or supernormal quality, either inexplicable or subject to the control of an adept, permitting the effecting of phenomenal results; concept popularized by Franz Anton Mesmer (1734–1815)
Martian—indigene of Mars, fourth planet from the sun
medium—an individual who claims the ability to communicate with the spirits of dead humans, other semiterrestrial entities, or space people by transmental means
Mercurian—indigene of Mercury, smallest planet in our solar system and closest to the sun
meteor—a small elemental mass flying through space which disintegrates upon entering the atmosphere of Earth; a "shooting star"
meteorite—a small elemental mass flying through space, some fragment of which reaches the Earth intact
meteoroid—a small elemental mass in space, considered only in terms of its physicality
moon—a smaller body circling a planet; a satellite
mother ship (mother-type ship)—allegedly an enormous interplanetary or interstellar craft, which rarely approaches near the Earth, commonly acting as a home port for smaller "flying saucers" able to function more efficiently in our atmosphere.

Usually zeppelin-, or cigar-, shaped, they are known almost exclusively to contactees

Neptunian—indigene of Neptune, third largest of the planets in our solar system

Objects Seen Floating—a term coined by Charles Fort for inexplicable aerial phenomena

occult—secret, hidden; the knowledge of alchemy, sorcery, and certain types of rarer magic; the natural and extranatural religion. Not to be confused with witchcraft, Satanism, or the majority of so-called magic

OSF—see *Object Seen Floating*

Ouranian—indigene of the sky, or of space

overflight—passage of airship above a specified area

parachute canopy—the "umbrella" of a parachute

plasma, plasm (-al, -ic)—a state of matter between liquid and solid; a form of electrical force with seeming physical tangibility. Various sciences use the term for many different conditions, substances, etc.

Plutonian—indigene of Pluto, the farthest planet from the sun in our solar system

prehistory—before written records were initiated, or an ancient period from which no contemporary chronicles remain

project—a special United States Air Force (or any military or governmental) program; generally, any undertaking or enterprise

protoplasm—a near fluid organism

prototype—an original or experimental design of model

psychic (-al)—an extra sense, or a developed sense latent in the average individual, or a supernormal sensitivity of one of the recognized perceptive faculties, or a subject possessing any of these attributes

Rosetta Stone—a "trilingual" piece of tablet unearthed in Egypt which provided information permitting the deciphering of ancient hieroglyphics; any key to a mystery

Sabbat, Sabbath—a holy day of ritual and/or rest; a convocation of witches

Saturnian—indigene of Saturn, the second largest planet in our solar system

saucerian—an occupant or operator of a flying saucer; an alien

saucerism—enthusiasm for the subject of flying saucers

saucerite—enthusiast of the subject of flying saucers

saucerological—of flying saucers, or the study of them

saucerology (-ist)—the study of flying saucers

"scramble"—order, or response to an order, to get aircraft into flight as swiftly as possible

spiritualism, spiritism—the belief that the living can establish, or reestablish, communication with the dead

subculture (-al)—a recognizable segment of society, or a division of another larger element of human activity

suborbit (-al)—a space flight path that does not circumscribe the Earth, or project extraterrestrial landing

sundog—a bright, colored spot of light sometimes seen on the ring of a solar halo (parhelion), *Webster's New World Dictionary* 2d ed. World Publishing Company, 1970. *Sundog*—tiny ice crystals floating in a layer of quiet air and reflecting a bright sun. Menzel and Boyd, p. 244

supersonic—transonic, faster than the speed of sound at sea level (738 mph), or slightly less at higher altitudes

symbiotic—reciprocal

"target"—see *"blips"*

telepath (-ic)—one capable of telepathy

telepathic contactee—an individual who claims to have established *mental* communication with operators of a flying saucer, or other space people

telepathy—thought transference and reception; unaided mental communication *teleportation*—the instantaneous projection of physical matter, including the human body, from one point to another, without regard for distance or intervening matter

theodolite—an instrument, equipped with a telescope, designed to determine horizontal, and usually vertical, angles

thought disk—a phenomenon allegedly sighted or brought into communication with contactees or remotely (sometimes telepathically) controlled UFO; in any case, almost invariably small, ranging from a few inches to a couple of feet in diameter

topography—the recording or mapping of the physical features, surface conformation, or general description, of an area of land

topology—the study of surfaces

transonic—see *supersonic*

UAO—see *Unexplained Aerial Object*

UAP—see *Unidentified Atmospheric Phenomena*

UFO—see *Unidentified Flying Object*

ufoism, ufologism—preoccupation with, or acceptance of, the reality of UFO

ufological—of UFO

ufologist—student or scholar of UFO

ufology—the study of UFO

ufonauts—operators of UFO; space travelers; aliens

Undefined Sensory Experience—a perception for which no natural or logical explanation can be determined

Underwater Unidentified Object—a term coined by *Flying Saucers* magazine for submarine and amphibious UFO

Unexplained Aerial Objects—a term preferred by Ivan T. Sanderson, and others, for seemingly substantial UFO

Unidentified Atmospheric Phenomena—a term preferred by Ivan T. Sanderson, and others, for seemingly insubstantial UFO

Unidentified Flying Object—a term coined by Captain

Edward J. Ruppelt, USAF, to replace the fanciful, inaccurate, and ridiculed "flying saucer"

unknown—a term for UFO

Uranian—indigene of Uranus

USE—see *Undefined Sensory Experience*

UUO—see *Underwater Unidentified Object*

velocity—relating to speed

Venusian—indigene of Venus

witchcraft—a semireligious movement deriving from anti-Christianity, or more specifically from hostility toward the Roman Church, in the fourteenth and fifteenth centuries, usually taking Satan as its deity; not to be confused with magic, sorcery, the occult.

Selected Bibliography

The brief list below is devoted exclusively to those books dealing with Unidentified Atmospheric Phenomena, Unexplained Aerial Objects, and so on, in contradistinction to works on "flying saucers," i.e., any of the variety of volumes devoted to accounts of specifically recognizable spaceships in flight or landed, observation of, or communication with, extraterrestrials, temporary or permanent abductions of humans for whatever reason, or tours by Earthians in alien craft. Approximately one hundred additional books, on *all* aspects of this subject, including UFO, may be found in the Bibliography of the author's earlier volume: *The Age of Flying Saucers.*

Emphasis should be made that this is a *selected* bibliography, consisting of efforts the author regards as among the better in the field. An asterisk (*) indicates that a work is of greater than usual interest, and a double asterisk (**) designates a book the reading of which is essential for anyone seriously interested in the subject.

ARNOLD, KENNETH, and RAY PALMER. *The Coming of the Saucers.* Amherst, Wis.: privately published, 1952 (paperback).**

Bloecher, Ted. *Report on UFO Wave of 1947.* New York: 1967 (paperback).*

CATOE, LYNNE. *UFOs and Related Subjects: An Annotated Bibliography.* Washington, D.C.: United States Government Printing Office, 1969.

CONDON, EDWARD U., ed. *Scientific Study of Unidentified Flying Objects* (Condon Report). New York: Bantam Books, 1969 (paperback).**

DAVIDSON, LEON. *Flying Saucers: An Analysis of the Air Force Project Blue Book Special Report*

No. 14. White Plains, N.Y.: privately published, 1956 (paperback).*

EDWARDS, FRANK. *Flying Saucers: Serious Business.* New York: Lyle Stuart, 1966.*

————. *Flying Saucers: Here and Now.* New York: Lyle Stuart, 1967.

EMENEGGER, ROBERT. *UFO's: Past, Present and Future.* New York: Ballantine Books, 1974 (paperback).

FLAMMONDE, PARIS. *The Age of Flying Saucers.* New York: Hawthorn Books, 1971.**

FORT, CHARLES. *The Books of Charles Fort.* New York: Henry Holt and Company, 1941.*

FULLER, JOHN. *Incident at Exeter.* New York: G. P. Putnam's Sons, 1966.

————. *Aliens in the Sky.* New York: G. P. Putnam's Sons, 1969.*

HALL, RICHARD, ed. *The UFO Evidence.* Washington, D.C.: NICAP, 1964 (paperback).**

HERVEY, MICHAEL. *UFOS Over the Southern Hemisphere.* Introduction by William E. Moser. Sydney, Australia: Howitz Publications, 1969 (paperback).*

HYNEK, J. ALLEN. *The UFO Experience.* New York: Ballantine Books, 1972 (paperback).**

JESSUP, MORRIS K. *The Case for the UFO.* New York: Citadel Press, 1955;* paperback, New York: Ballantine Books, 1955.*

JUNG, CARL G. *Flying Saucers: A Modern Myth of Things Seen in the Sky.* New York: Harcourt, Brace & World, 1959.

KEEL, JOHN A. *UFO: Operation Trojan Horse.* New York: G. P. Putnam's Sons, 1970.*

KEYHOLE, DONALD E. *The Flying Saucers are Real.* New York: Fawcett Publications, 1950.*

————. *Flying Saucers from Outer Space.* New York: Henry Holt and Co., 1953.

————. *The Flying Saucer Conspiracy.* New York: Henry Holt and Co., 1955.

————. *Flying Saucers: Top Secret.* New York: G. P. Putnam's Sons, 1960.*

————. *Aliens from Space*. Garden City, N.Y.: Doubleday & Company, 1974.

KLASS, PHILIP. *UFOs—Identified*. New York: Random House, 1968.

————. *UFOs Explained*. New York: Random House, 1975.

LE POER TRENCH, BRINSLEY. *The Flying Saucer Review's World Roundup of UFO Sightings*. New York: Citatel Press, 1958.

————. *The Flying Saucer Story*. New York: Ace Books, Inc., 1966.

LORENZEN, CORAL E. *The Great Flying Saucer Hoax* (later *Flying Saucers: The Startling Evidence of the Invasion from Outer Space*). New York: New American Library, 1962 (paperback).*

LORENZEN, JIM and CORAL. *UFOs Over America*. New York: New American Library, 1959 (paperback).**

LUSAR, RUDOLPH. *German Weapons and Secret Weapons of World War II and Their Development*. New York: Philosophical Library, 1959.*

MENZEL, DONALD H. and LYLE G. BOYD. *The World of Flying Saucers*. Garden City, N.Y.: Doubleday & Company, 1963.*

MICHEL, AIMÉ. *Lueurs sur les soucoupes volantes*. Paris: Mame, 1954; *The Truth about Flying Saucers*. New York: Criterion Books, 1956;* paperback, New York: Pyramid Books, 1974.*

————. *Mysterieux Objects célestes*. Paris: Arthaud, 1958; *Flying Saucers and the Straight Line Mystery*. New York: Criterion Books, 1958 (translated from the French by the Civilian Saucer Intelligence of New York).

Project Blue Book Special Report No. 14. Project No. 10073. Wright-Patterson Air Force Base, Ohio: Air Technical Intelligence Center, 1955.*

RUPPELT, EDWARD J. *The Report on Unidentified Flying Objects*. Garden City, N.Y.: Doubleday & Co., 1956;** paperback, New York: Ace Books, undated.**

SAGAN, CARL, and THORNTON PA7E, eds. *UFO's: A*

  Scientific Debate. Ithaca, N.Y.: Cornell University Press, 1972.*

SANDERSON, IVAN T. *Uninvited Visitors.* New York: Cowles Education Corp., 1967.**

SAUNDERS, DAVID R., *and* R. ROGER HARKINS. *UFOs? Yes!* New York: New American Library, 1968 (paperback).*

STANTON, L. JEROME. *Flying Saucers: Hoax or Reality?* New York: Belmont Books, 1966 (paperback).

TACKER, LAWRENCE J. *Flying Saucers and the U. S. Air Force.* Princeton, N.J.: D. Van Nostrand Company, 1960.

VALLEE, JACQUES. *Anatomy of a Phenomenon.* Chicago: Henry Regnery Company, 1965;* paperback, New York: Ace Books, 1966.*

————, and JANINE VALLEE. *Challenge to Science.* Chicago: Henry Regnery Company, 1966;* paperback, New York: Ace Books, undated.*

WILKINS, HAROLD T. *Flying Saucers on the Attack.* New York: Citadel Press, 1959.

Index